LISTS OF NOTE

LISTS OF NOTE

An Eclectic Collection Deserving of a Wider Audience

COMPILED BY SHAUN USHER

CHRONICLE BOOKS
SAN FRANCISCO

This book is dedicated to my three favorite people:

1. Karina
2. Billy
3. Danny

First published In the United States of America In 2015 by Chronicle Books, LLC

First published in Great Britain in 2014 by Canongate Books Ltd in conjunction with Unbound

Library of Congress Cataloging-in-Publication Data available.

ISBN: 978-1-4521-4457-3

Manufactured in China

MIX
Paper from responsible sources
FSC™ C008047

Book design by Here Design
Cover design by Amanda Sim
Typesetting for US edition by Liam Flanagan

10 9 8 7 6 5 4 3 2 1

Chronicle Books, LLC
680 Second Street
San Francisco, California 94107
www.chroniclebooks.com

CONTENTS

INTRODUCTION

Since we first began walking the earth, human beings have been creating lists of one kind or another, calmly content in the knowledge that all things are constantly being assigned, prioritized, ranked, and streamlined to within an inch of their lives. It doesn't bear thinking about, but to live in a world without them would, I reluctantly imagine, be an inchoate existence: not a single to-do list, shopping list, wish list, dictionary, list of favorites, rulebook, list of predictions, list of resolutions, address book, list of advice, list of contents—just a world full of things, muddled and overflowing, without a sense of purpose for collective identity.

To further explain our reliance on lists, it seems only right to list the reasons:

1. Life is chaotic—often unbearably so. The ability to divide some of that chaos into lists, to make the onslaught manageable, can bring much-needed relief.
2. Human beings are fearful of the unknown and so have a real need to label and group things, to assign them into comfortable lists.
3. Lists can make us more productive and can eradicate procrastination. Nothing on earth, resignation aside, cuts through the thick fog of a daunting workload as effectively as a to-do list.
4. Everyone is a critic. Ranking things—best to worst, biggest to smallest, fastest to slowest—can be strangely addictive, no doubt because it makes us feel knowledgeable.
5. Time is precious. Distilling huge swathes of monotonous information into easily digestible lists ensures that we have more time to enjoy ourselves make more lists.

The depth of mankind's obsession with lists became starkly apparent to me five years ago, at which point I was delving into various archives, museums, and libraries around the world to research my first book, *Letters of Note*, a collection of notable correspondence from throughout the ages, written by all manner of people. At almost every juncture of that journey, I was also discovering intriguing lists written by those same characters—lists of varying lengths, some handwritten, others typed, most of which captivated me for differing reasons.

Five years on and you now hold a gorgeous book that contains 125 of the most compelling lists I have been able to find. A list of lists. They span thousands of years: the oldest is an eye-opening list of workmen's absences written in Ancient Egypt; the most recent are merely a few years old. In between we have:

- a list of murder suspects scribbled by the long-serving secretary to John F. Kennedy just hours after the president's assassination;

- French novelist George Perec's magnificent *Attempt at an Inventory of the Liquid and Solid Foodstuffs Ingurgitated by Me in the Course of the Year Nineteen Hundred and Seventy-Four;*
- a shopping list written by Galileo that mentions the pieces of equipment he needed to produce his groundbreaking telescope;
- a list of dream interpretations written around 1220 BC;
- a backup list of alternatives to the famous line, "Frankly, my dear, I don't give a damn," written shortly after Hollywood censors deemed the word *damn* to be offensive;
- . . . and over one hundred more.

Many of the lists offer advice that you will take to your grave. Some offer a snapshot of history previously unknown. Others are simply a joy to read. Each and every one, however, is certainly a list of note.

THE LISTS

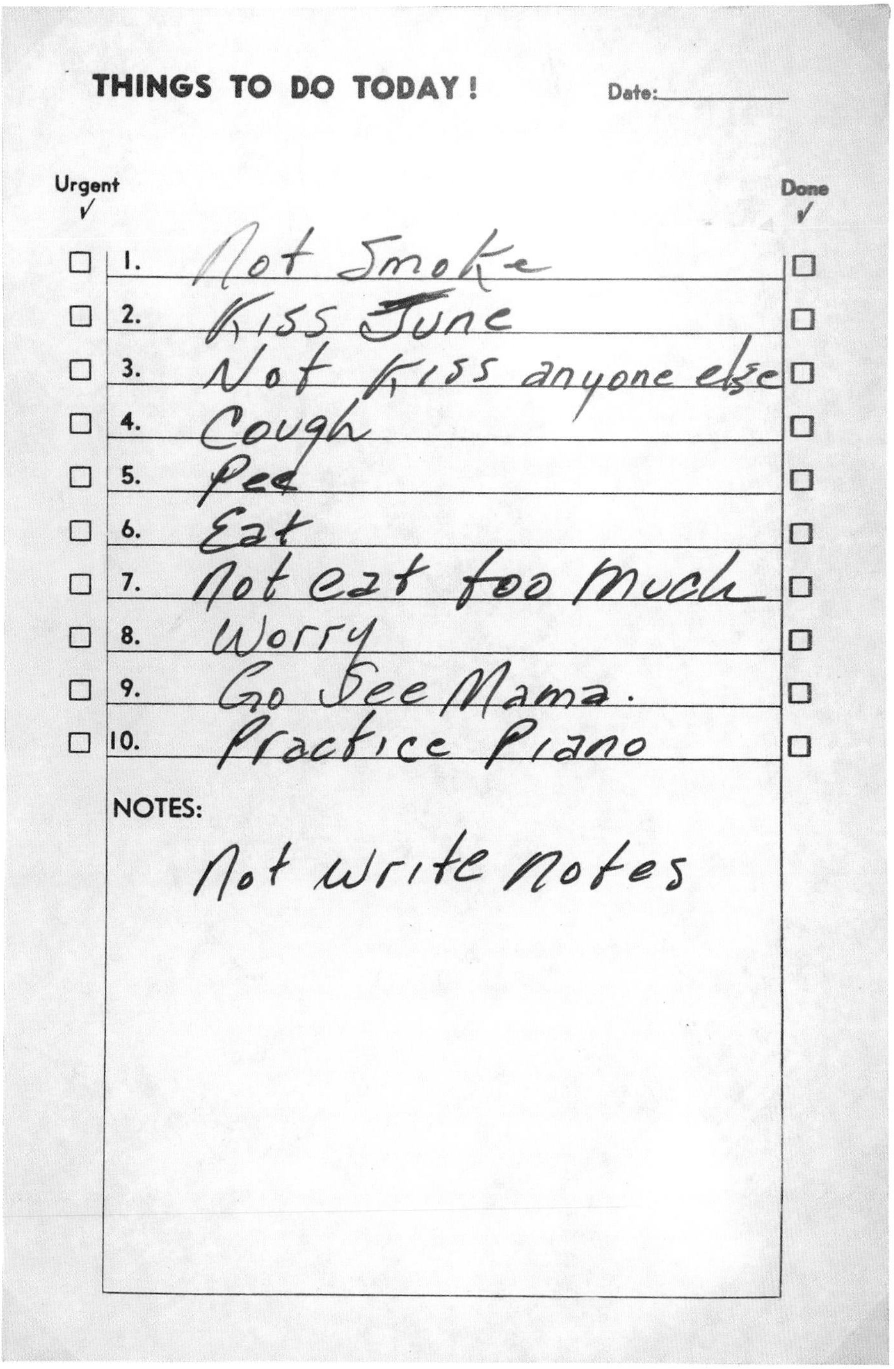
THINGS TO DO TODAY!
Date:
Urgent
Done
1. Not Smoke
2. Kiss June
3. Not Kiss anyone else
4. Cough
5. Pee
6. Eat
7. Not eat too much
8. Worry
9. Go See Mama.
10. Practice Piano
NOTES:
Not write notes

KISS JUNE

JOHNNY CASH
Date Unknown

Legendary singer-songwriter Johnny Cash proposed to the love of his life, fellow country star June Carter, on stage in 1968, thirteen years after first meeting her. Their relationship stood the test of time, and they remained together until her death, thirty-five years later. Cash was a romantic man and wrote countless handwritten love notes for his wife during their marriage; even his to-do lists, such as the one seen here, were brimming with affection.

List No. 002

TERMES OF A KERVER

WYNKYN DE WORDE
1508

The carving of meat was considered a fine art in the late Middle Ages, at least in the affluent homes where such foods could be afforded. Whole animals were routinely and precisely sliced for all to see, on the dining table, by household staff armed with specialist knowledge. In 1508, these rules of carving and general preparation of meat were collated by influential publisher Wynkyn de Worde, who had worked with William Caxton at England's first printing press. His guide, *The Boke of Kervynge (The Book of Carving)*, began with a list of appropriate verbs to be used when carving various victuals. (I have added a few explanations to the original translation.)

Termes of a kerver.	Terms of a carver.
breke that dere	break that deer
lesche yt brawne	leach that brawn
rere that goose	rear that goose
lyfte that swanne	lift that swan
sauce that capon	sauce that capon
spoyle that henne	spoil that hen
fruche that chekyn	frust that chicken [frust means fragment]
vnbrace that malarde	unbrace that mallard
vnlace that conye	unlace that coney
dysmembre that heron	dismember that heron
dysplaye that crane	display that crane
dysfygure that pecocke	disfigure that peacock
vnioynt that bytture	unjoint that bittern [a wading bird]
vntache that curlewe	untack that curlew
alaye that fesande	allay that pheasant
wynge that partryche	wing that partridge
wynge that quayle	wing that quail
mynce that plouer	mince that plover
thye that pegyon	thigh that pigeon
border that pasty	border that pasty
thye that woodcocke	thigh that woodcock
thye all maner of small byrdes	thigh all manner of small birds
tymbre that fyre	timber that fire
tyere that egge	tear that egg
chynne that samon	chine that salmon
strynge that lampraye	string that lamprey [a jawless fish]

splatte that pyke	splat that pike
sauce that place	sauce that plaice
sauce that tenche	sauce that tench [a freshwater fish]
splaye that breme	splay that bream
syde that haddocke	side that haddock
tuske that barbell	tusk that barbell [a freshwater fish]
culpon that troute	culpon that trout [culpon means slice]
fyne that cheuen	fin that chevin [a freshwater fish]
transsene that ele	transon that eel
traunche that sturgyon	tranch that sturgeon
vndertraunche that purpos	undertranch that porpoise
tayme that crabbe	tame that crab
barbe that lopster	barb that lobster

Here endeth the goodly termes.

¶ Here begynneth the boke of keruynge and sewynge / and all the feestes in the yere for the seruyce of a prynce or ony other estate as ye shall fynde eche offyce the seruyce accordynge in this boke folowynge

¶ Termes of a keruer.

Breke that dere
lesche ye brawne
rere that goose
lyste that swanne
sauce that capon
spoyle that henne
fruche that chekyn
vnbrace that malarde
vnlace that conye
dysmembre that heron
dysplaye that crane
dysfygure that pecocke
vnioynt that bytture
vntache that curlewe
alaye that fesande
wynge that partryche
wynge that quayle
mynce that plouer
thye that pygyon
border that pasty
thye that woodcocke
thye all maner small byrdes
tymbre that fyre
tyere that egge
chynne that samon
strynge that lamprraye
splatte that pyke
sauce that place
sauce that tenche
splaye that breme
syde that haddocke
tuske that berbell
culpon that troute
fyne that cheuen
trassene that ele
traunche that sturgyon
vndertraunche that purpos
tayme that crabbe
barbe that lopster

¶ Here endeth the goodly termes.

¶ Here begynneth Butteler and Panter.

Thou shalte be butteler and panter all the fyrst yere / and ye muste haue thre pantry knyues / one knyfe to square trenchoure loues / an other to be a

ATTEMPT AT AN INVENTORY

GEORGES PEREC
1974

French novelist Georges Perec (1936–1982) was an experimental writer whose affection for the trusty list is rivaled by very few. In 1974 he attempted to keep a record of every single thing he ate and drank for the duration of the year and then presented the results in a list which, having been translated to English by John Sturrock, is strangely compelling. It is titled, unambiguously, *Attempt at an Inventory of the Liquid and Solid Foodstuffs Ingurgitated by Me in the Course of the Year Nineteen Hundred and Seventy-Four.*

Nine beef broths, one iced cucumber soup, one mussel soup. Two *Guéméné andouilles*, one jellied *andouillette*, one Italian *charcuterie*, one saveloy, four mixed *charcuteries*, one *coppa*, three pork platters, one *figatelli*, one foie gras, one *fromage de tête*, one boar's head, five Parma hams, eight pâtés, one duck pâté, one liver pâté with truffles, one pâté *en croûte*, one pâté *grandmère*, one thrush pâté, six Landes pâtés, four brawns, one foie-gras mousse, one pig's trotters, seven *rillettes*, one salami, two *saucissons*, one hot *saucisson*, one duck terrine, one chicken-liver terrine.

One blini, one *empanada*, one dried beef. Three snails.

One Belon oysters, three scallops, one shrimps, one shrimp *croustade*, one *friture*, two baby eel *fritures*, one herring, two oysters, one mussels, one stuffed mussels, one sea urchins, two *quenelles au gratin*, three sardines in oil, five smoked salmons, one taramasalata, one eel terrine, six tunas, one anchovy toast, one crab.

Two haddock, one sea bass, one skate, one sole, one tuna.

Four artichokes, one asparagus, one aubergine, one mushroom salad, fourteen cucumber salads, four cucumbers à la crème, fourteen celery *rémoulades*, two Chinese cabbages, one palm hearts, eleven crudités, two green-bean salads, thirteen melons, two *salades niçoises*, two dandelion salads with bacon, fourteen radishes with butter, three black radishes, five rice salads, one Russian salad, seven tomato salads, one onion tart.

One Roquefort croquette, five *croque-monsieurs*, three quiche Lorraines, one *tarte aux maroilles*, one yogurt with cucumber and grapes, one Romanian yogurt.

One *torti* salad with crab and Roquefort.

One eggs with anchovy, two boiled eggs, two eggs *en meurette*, one ham and eggs, one bacon and eggs, one eggs *en cocotte* with spinach, two eggs in aspic, two scrambled eggs, four omelettes, one sort-of omelette, one bean-sprout omelette, one horn-of-plenty omelette, one duck-skin omelette, one *confit d'oie* omelette, one herb omelette, one Parmentier omelette.

One sirloin, three sirloins with shallots, ten steaks, two steak *au poivres*, three *complets*, one rump steak with mustard, five roast beefs, two ribs of beef, two top rump steaks, three beef *grillades*, two chateaubriands, one steak tartare, one *rosbif*, three cold *rosbifs*, fourteen entrecôtes, three entrecôtes à la *moelle*, one fillet of beef, three hamburgers, nine skirts of beef, one flank of beef.

Four *pot-au-feus*, one daube, one jellied daube, one braised beef, one beef mode, one beef *gros sel*, one beef in a thin baguette.

One braised veal with noodles, one sauté of veal, one veal chop, one veal chop with pasta shells, one "veal entrecôte," six escalopes, six escalopes *milanaise*, three escalopes à la crème, one escalope with morels, four *blanquettes de veau*.

Five *andouillettes*, three black puddings, one black pudding with apples, one pork cutlet, two sauerkrauts, one Nancy sauerkraut, one pork chop, eleven pairs of frankfurters, two port *grillades*, seven pigs' trotters, one cold pork, three roast porks, one roast pork with pineapple and bananas, one pork sausage with haricots.

One milk-fed lamb, three lamb cutlets, two curried lambs, twelve *gigots*, one saddle of lamb.

One mutton cutlet, one shoulder of mutton.

Five chickens, one chicken kebab, one lemon chicken, one chicken *en cocotte*, two chicken *basquaises*, three cold chickens, one stuffed chicken, one chicken with

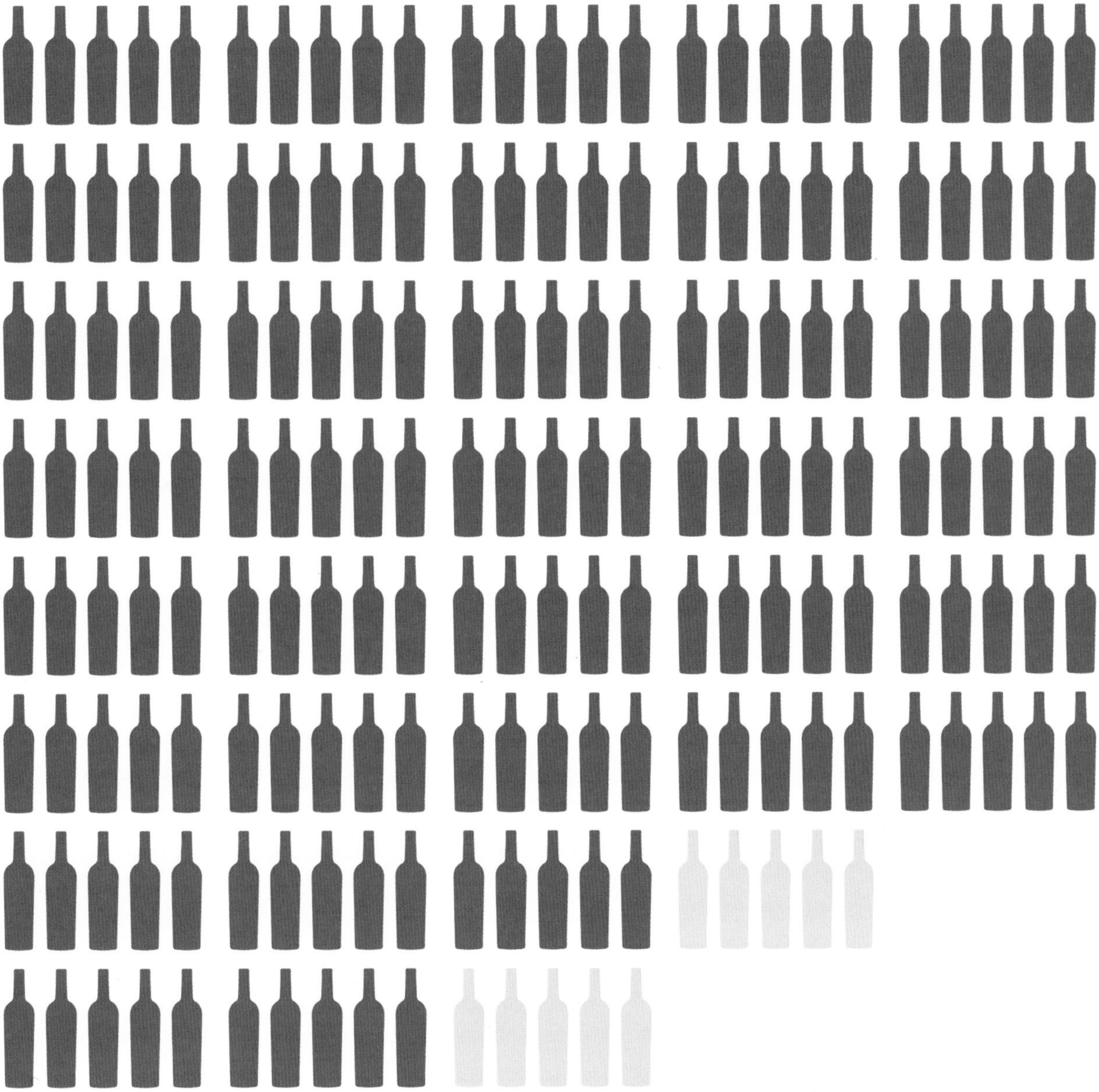

chestnuts, one chick with herbs, two jellied chickens.

Seven *poules au riz*, one *poule au pot*.

One pullet *au riz*.

One *coq au Riesling*, three *coq au vins*, one *coq au vinaigre*.

One duck with olives, one duck breast.

One guinea fowl casserole.

One guinea fowl with cabbage, one guinea fowl with noodles.

Five rabbits, two rabbits *en gibelotte*, one rabbit with noodles, one rabbit à la crème, three rabbits with mustard, one rabbit *chasseur*, one rabbit with tarragon, one rabbit *à la tourangelle*, three rabbits with plums.

Two young wild rabbits with plums.

One civet of hare *à l'alsacienne*, one daube of hare, one hare stew, one saddle of hare.

One wild-pigeon casserole.

One kidney kebab, three kebabs, one mixed grill, one kidneys with mustard, one calves' kidneys, three *têtes de veau*, eleven calves' livers, one calves' tongue, one calves' sweetbread with *pommes sarladaises*, one terrine of calves' sweetbreads, one lambs' brains, two fresh goose livers with grapes, one *confit* of goose gizzards, two chicken livers.

Twelve assorted cold meats, two *assiettes anglaises*, *n* cold cuts, two couscous, three "Chinese," one *moulakhia*, one pizza, one *pan bagnat*, one *tajine*, six sandwiches, one ham sandwich, one *rillettes* sandwich, three cantal sandwiches.

One ceps, one kidney beans, seven green beans, one sweetcorn, one puréed cauliflower, one puréed spinach, one puréed fennel, two stuffed peppers, two *pommes frites*, nine *gratins dauphinois*, four mashed potatoes, one *pommes dauphines*, one *pommes boulangères*, one *pommes soufflées*, one roast potatoes, one sauté potatoes, four rice, one wild rice.

Four pasta, three noodles, one fettucine with cream, one macaroni cheese, one macaroni, fifteen fresh noodles, three *rigatoni*, two ravioli, four spaghetti, one tortellini, five tagliatelle *verde*.

Thirty-five green salads, one *mesclun* salad, one Treviso salad à la crème, two chicory salads.

Seventy-five cheese, one ewe's cheese, two Italian cheeses, one Auvergne cheese, one Boursin, two Brillat-Savarins, eleven Bries, one Cabécou, four goats' cheeses, two *crottins*, eight Camemberts, fifteen cantals, one Sicilian cheeses, one Sardinian cheeses, one Epoisses, one Murols, three fromages blancs, one goat's-milk fromage blanc, nine Fontainebleaus, five mozzarellas, five Munsters, one Reblochon, one Swiss raclette, one Stilton, one Saint-Marcellin, one Saint-Nectaire, one yogurt.

One fresh fruit, two strawberries, one gooseberries, one orange, three "*mendiants*" [a mixture of almonds, dried figs, hazelnuts and raisins].

One stuffed dates, one pears in syrup, three pears in wine, two peaches in wine, one vineyard peach in syrup, one peaches in Sancerre, one apples *normande*, one bananas *flambées*.

Four stewed fruit, two stewed apples, two stewed rhubarb and *quetsch*.

Five *clafoutis*, four pear *clafoutis*.

One figs in syrup.

Six fruit salads, one tropical fruit salad, two orange salads, two strawberry, raspberry and gooseberry salads.

One apple pie, four tarts, one hot tart, ten tart Tatins, seven pear tarts, one pear tart Tatin, one lemon tart, one apple and nut tart, two apple tarts, one apple tart with meringue, one strawberry tart.

Two crêpes.

Two charlottes, three chocolate charlottes.

Three babas.

One *crème renversée*.

One *galette des rois*.

Nine chocolate mousses.

Two *îles flotantes*.

One bilberry *Kugelhupf*.

Four chocolate gateaux, one cheesecake, two orange gateaux, one Italian gateau, one Viennese gateau, one Breton gateau, one gateau with fromage blanc, one *vatrushka*.

Three ice creams, one lime sorbet, two guava sorbets, two pear sorbets, one chocolate profiteroles, one raspberry melba, one pear *belle Hélène*.

Thirteen Beaujolais, four Beaujolais Nouveaux, three Brouillys, seven Chiroubles, four Chenas, two Fleuries, one Juliénas, three Saint-Amours.

Nine Côtes-du-Rhônes, nine Châteauneuf-du-Papes, one Châteauneuf-du-Pape '67, three Vacqueyras.

Nine Bordeaux, one Bordeaux Clairet, one Lamarzelle '64, three Saint-Emilions, one Saint-Emilion '61, seven Château-la Pelleterie '70s, one Château-Canon '62, five Château-Négrits, one Lalande-de-Pomerol, one Lalande-de-Pomerol '67, one Médoc '64, six Margaux '62s, one Margaux '68, one Margaux '69, one Saint-Estèphe '61, one Saint-Julien '59.

Seven Savigny-lès-Beaunes, three Aloxe-Cortons, one Aloxe-Corton '66, one Beaune '61, one white Chasagne-Montrachet '66, two Mercureys, one Pommard, one Pommard '66, two Santenay '62s, one Volnay '59.

One Chambolle-Musigny '70, one Chambolle-Musigny Les Amoureuses '70, one Chambertin '62, one Romanée-Conti, one Romanée-Conti '64.

One Bergerac, two red Bouzys, four Bourgueils, one Chalosse, one champagne, one Chablis, one red Côtes-de-Provence, twenty-six Cahors, one Chanteperdrix, four Gamays, two Madirans, one Madiran '70, one Pinot Noir, one Passetoutgrain, one Pécharmant, one Samumur, ten Tursans, one Traminer, one Sardinian wine, *n* sundry wines.

Nine beers, two Tuborgs, four Guinnesses.

Fifty-six Armagnacs, one bourbon, eight Calvadoses, one cherries in brandy, six Green Chartreuses, one Chivas, four cognacs, one Delamain cognac, two Grand Marniers, one pink gin, one Irish coffee, one Jack Daniel's, four marcs, three Bugey marcs, one marc de Provence, one plum liqueur, nine Souillac plums, one plums in brandy, two pear eaux-de-vie, one port, one slivovitz, one Suze, thiry-six vodkas, four whiskies.

N coffees, one tisane, three Vichy waters.

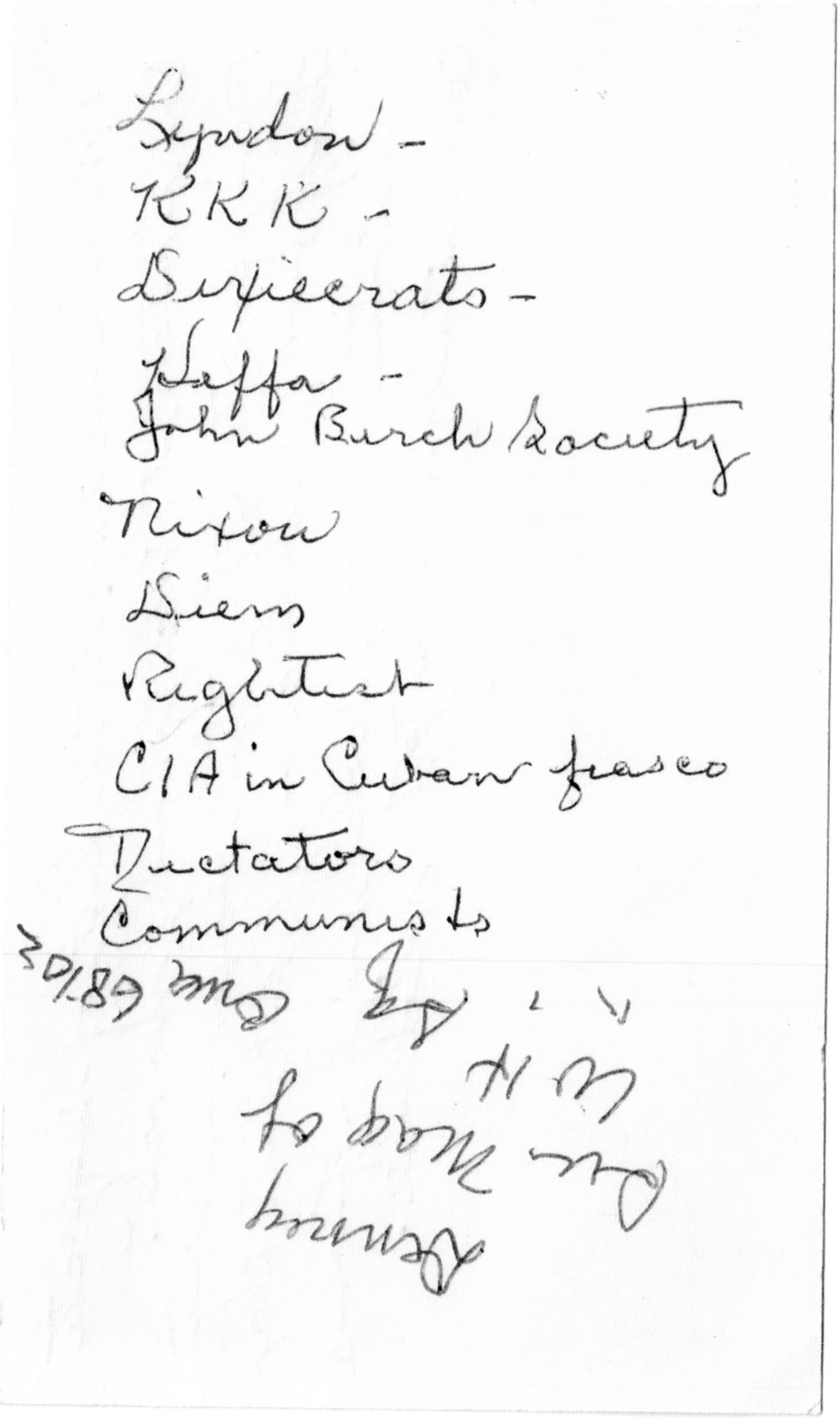
Lyndon -
KKK -
Dixiecrats -
Hoffa -
John Birch Society
Nixon
Diem
Rightist
CIA in Cuban fiasco
Dictators
Communists

List No. 004

WHO KILLED JFK?

EVELYN LINCOLN

November 22, 1963

On November 22, 1963, US President John F. Kennedy was shot and killed as he traveled in an open-top car through Dealey Plaza in Dallas, Texas, in one of history's most discussed murders. Also in the motorcade that fateful afternoon was his secretary of ten years, Evelyn Lincoln. Just hours after the assassination, as she flew back to Washington, DC, on Air Force One, along with the president's body, Mrs. Kennedy, and Lyndon B. Johnson, the vice president newly sworn in as president, Evelyn penned this list of suspects in the murder of her late boss, including the short-lived segregationist party the Dixiecrats, Teamsters union president Jimmy Hoffa, and those associated with the assassination of South Vietnamese leader Ngo Dinh Diem. Some years later, Evelyn added the note on the list's reverse shown here.

Lyndon —
KKK —
Dixiecrats —
Hoffa —
John Birch Society
Nixon
Diem
Rightist
CIA in Cuban fiasco
Dictators
Communists

There is no end to the list of suspected conspirators to Pres. Kennedy murder. Many factions had their reasons for wanting the young President dead. That fact alone illustrates how the world suffers from a congenital proclivity to violence.

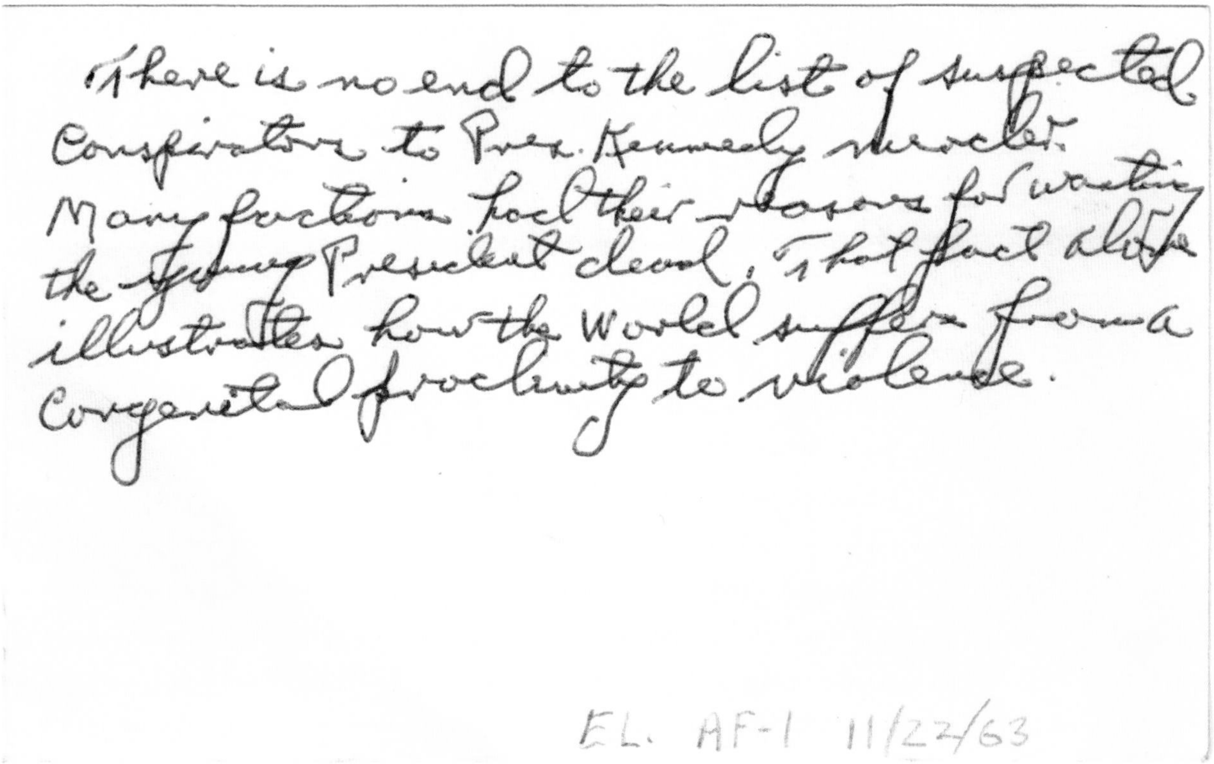
There is no end to the list of suspected Conspirators to Pres. Kennedy murder. Many factions had their reasons for wanting the young President dead. That fact alone illustrates how the world suffers from a congenital proclivity to violence.

EL. AF-1 11/22/63

List No. 005

THE ARMORY SHOW

PABLO PICASSO
1912

The 1913 International Exhibition of Modern Art, better known as the Armory Show after its venue in New York City, was a momentous occasion. It was the first modern art exhibition of any scale in the United States and introduced the avant-garde to a flummoxed and delighted public who had seen nothing like it. Organizing the show was American painter Walt Kuhn, who was unsure which European artists to invite. So he turned to Pablo Picasso for advice. Picasso responded with this handwritten list of recommendations. For the sake of clarity, I have appended the artists' full names.

Juan Gris
13 rue Ravignan

Metzinger *[Jean Metzinger]*

Gleizes *[Albert Gleizes]*

Leger *[Fernand Léger]*

Ducham *[Marcel Duchamp]*

Delauney *[Robert Delauney]*

Le Fauconnier *[Henri Le Fauconnier]*

Marie Laurencin

DeLa Fresnay *[Roger de La Fresnaye]*

Braque *[Georges Braque—added by Walt Kuhn]*

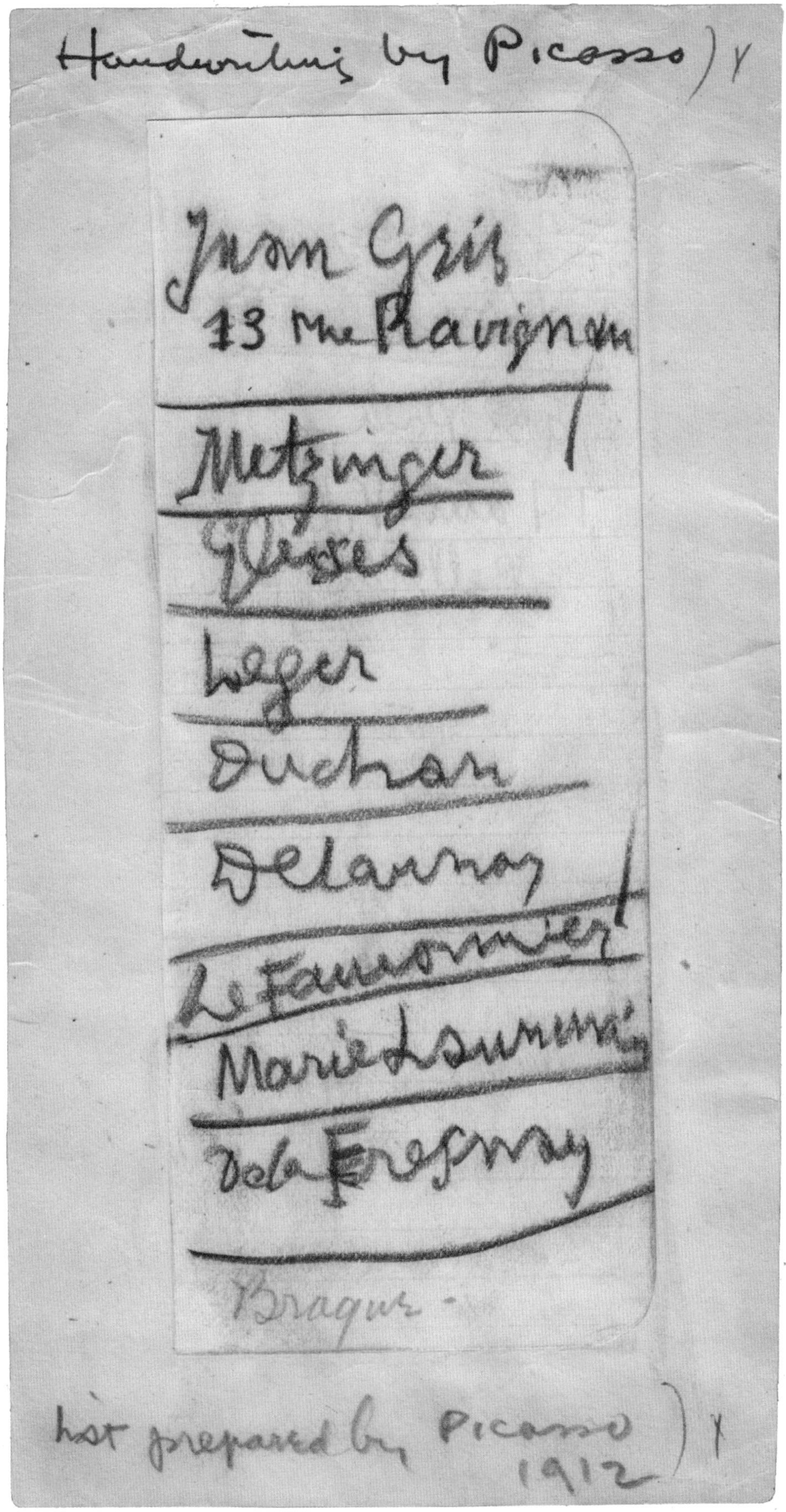
Handwriting by Picasso) X

Juan Gris
13 rue Ravignan

Metzinger

Gleizes

Leger

Duchan

Delaunay

Le Fauconnier

Marie Laurencin

de la Fresnay

Braque -

List prepared by Picasso
1912) X

List No. 006

ANTI-FLIRT CLUB

ALICE REIGHLY
1923

In the early 1920s, having been subjected to an unending stream of harassment from members of the opposite sex, a group of women in Washington, DC, decided to form the Anti-Flirt Club, an organization "composed of young women and girls who have been embarrassed by men in automobiles and on street corners," its aim being to protect such ladies from any further discomfort. As with all good clubs, a list of rules was issued to its members. It read as follows.

1. Don't flirt: those who flirt in haste oft repent in leisure.
2. Don't accept rides from flirting motorists—they don't all invite you in to save you a walk.
3. Don't use your eyes for ogling—they were made for worthier purposes.
4. Don't go out with men you don't know—they may be married, and you may be in for a hair-pulling match.
5. Don't wink—a flutter of one eye may cause a tear in the other.
6. Don't smile at flirtatious strangers—save them for people you know.
7. Don't annex all the men you can get—by flirting with many you may lose out on the one.
8. Don't fall for the slick, dandified cake eater—the unpolished gold of a real man is worth more than the gloss of a lounge lizard.
9. Don't let elderly men with an eye to a flirtation pat you on the shoulder and take a fatherly interest in you. Those are usually the kind who want to forget they are fathers.
10. Don't ignore the man you are sure of while you flirt with another. When you return to the first one you may find him gone.

DON'T SMILE

at FLIRTATIOUS

strangers

SAVE THEM FOR *people*

YOU KNOW

List No. 007

BOYLE'S WISH LIST

ROBERT BOYLE
1662

In 1662 a man often called the "Father of Modern Chemistry," Robert Boyle (1627–1691), wrote a remarkable and prophetic list of things that he hoped would one day be achieved by science—an eclectic selection of as-then unsolved problems he deemed the most pressing. The list was discovered shortly after his death, and in the three-hundred-plus years since he penned it, many of these advances—GPS, lightbulbs, organ transplants, cosmetic surgery—have been accomplished.

The Prolongation of Life.
The Recovery of Youth, or at least some of the Marks of it, as new Teeth, new Hair colour'd as in youth.
The Art of Flying.
The Art of Continuing long under water, and exercising functions freely there.
The Cure of Wounds at a Distance.
The Cure of Diseases at a distance or at least by Transplantation.
The Attaining Gigantick Dimensions.
The Emulating of Fish without Engines by Custome & Education only.
The Acceleration of the Production of things out of Seed.
The Transmutation of Metalls.
The makeing of Glass Malleable.
The Transmutation of Species in Mineralls, Animals, and Vegetables.
The Liquid Alkaest and Other dissolving Menstruums.
The making of Parabolicall and Hyperbolicall Glasses.
The making Armor light and extremely hard.
The practicable and certain way of finding Longitudes.
The use of Pendulums at Sea and in Journeys, and the Application of it to watches.
Potent Druggs to alter or Exalt Imagination, Waking, Memory, and other functions, and appease pain, procure innocent sleep, harmless dreams, etc.
A Ship to saile with All Winds, and A Ship not to be Sunk.
Freedom from Necessity of much Sleeping exemplify'd by the Operations of Tea and what happens in Mad-Men.
Pleasing Dreams and physicall Exercises exemplify'd by the Egyptian Electuary and by the Fungus mentioned by the French Author.
Great Strength and Agility of Body exemplify'd by that of Frantick Epileptick and Hystericall persons.
A perpetuall Light.
Varnishes perfumable by Rubbing.

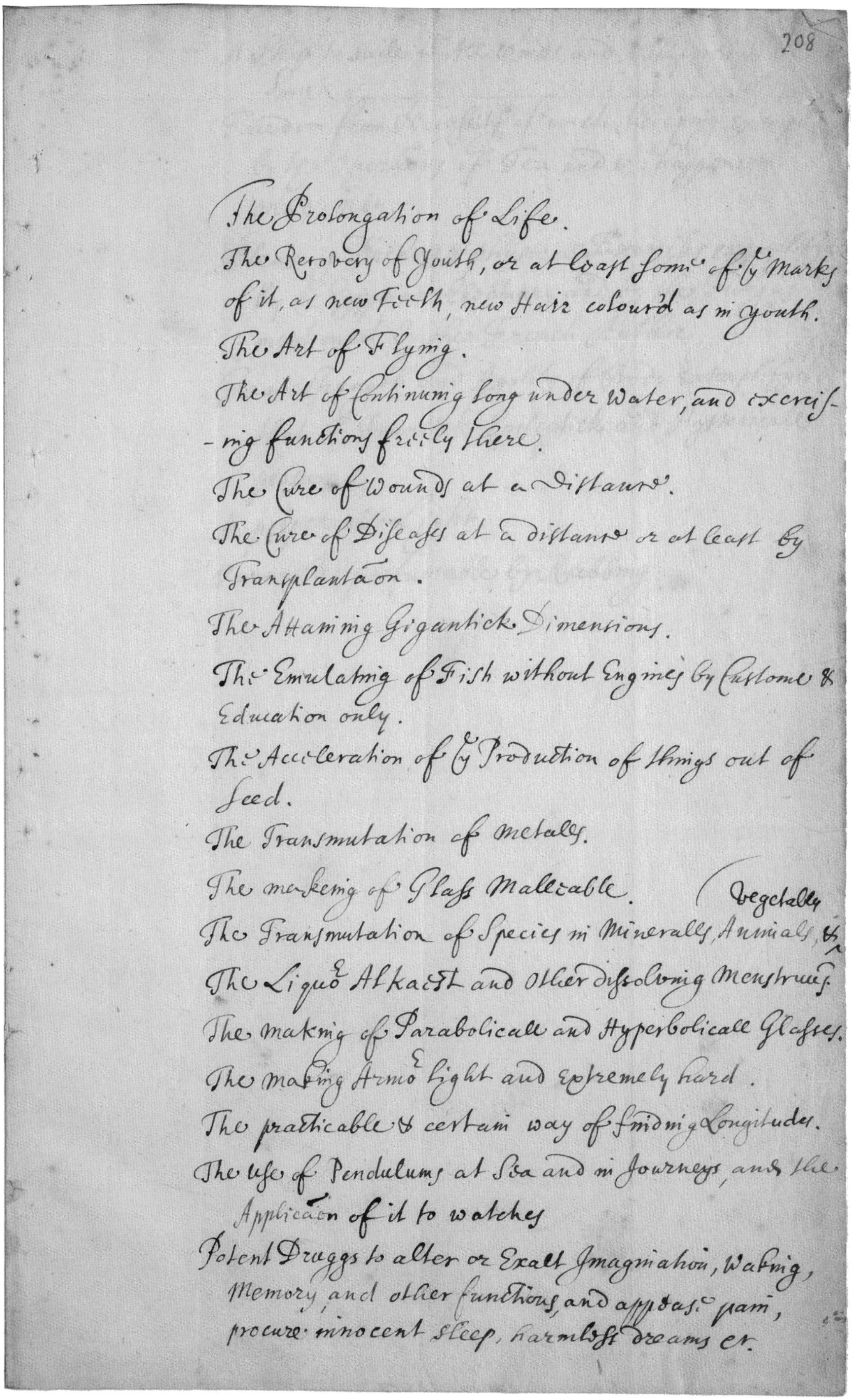
208

The Prolongation of Life.

The Recovery of Youth, or at least some of ye Marks of it, as new Teeth, new Hair colour'd as in youth.

The Art of Flying.

The Art of Continuing long under Water, and exercising functions freely there.

The Cure of Wounds at a Distance.

The Cure of Diseases at a distance or at least by Transplantation.

The Attaining Gigantick Dimensions.

The Emulating of Fish without Engines by Custome & Education only.

The Acceleration of the Production of things out of Seed.

The Transmutation of Metalls.

The makeing of Glass Malleable.

The Transmutation of Species in Mineralls, Animals, & Vegetables.

The Liquor Alkaest and Other dissolving Menstruums.

The making of Parabolicall and Hyperbolicall Glasses.

The making Armour light and extremely hard.

The practicable & certain way of finding Longitudes.

The use of Pendulums at Sea and in Journeys, and the Application of it to watches

Potent Druggs to alter or Exalt Imagination, Waking, Memory, and other functions, and appease pain, procure innocent sleep, harmless dreams etc.

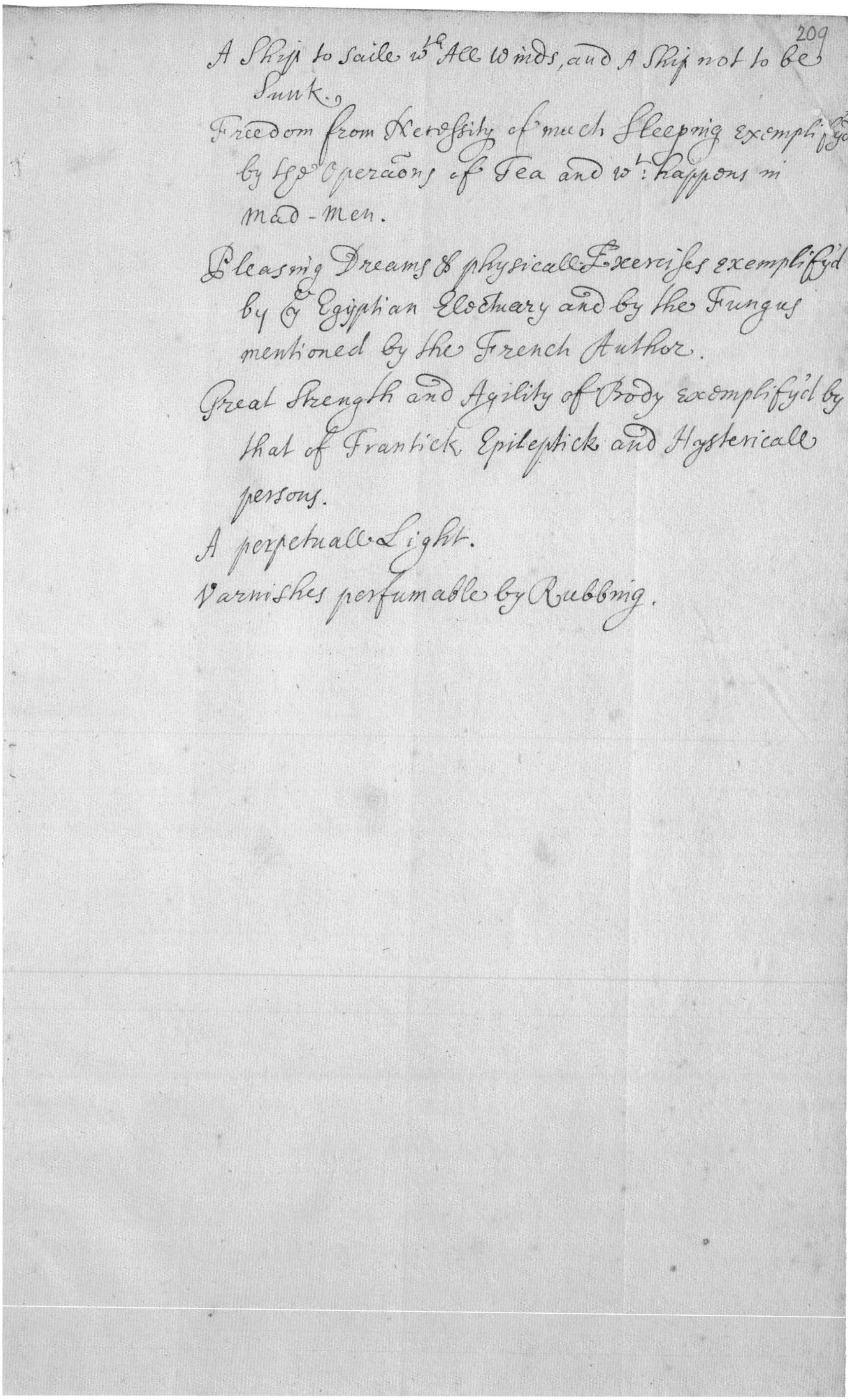

209

A Ship to saile wth All Winds, and A Ship not to be Sunk.

Freedom from Necessity of much Sleeping exemplifyd by the Operations of Tea and wt happens in Mad-Men.

Pleasing Dreams & physicall Exercises exemplifyd by the Egyptian Electuary and by the Fungus mentioned by the French Author.

Great Strength and Agility of Body exemplifyd by that of Frantick Epileptick and Hystericall persons.

A perpetuall Light.

Varnishes perfumable by Rubbing.

SHOPPING TRIP TO DUNHUANG

RATNAVṚKṢA AND PRAKETU
Tenth Century

One morning in tenth-century China, two Tibetan monks named Ratnavṛkṣa and Praketu set off on a shopping trip to the ancient town of Dunhuang, a major stop on the Silk Road trade route, to buy a plethora of goods—mainly fabrics in the form of blankets and cloths—for their monastery. This shopping list is the record they kept of their numerous purchases. Written in Khotanese and signed by witnesses, it is held at the British Library.

makala salya cvāvaja māśtä bistämye haḍai ṣa' khalavī cu ratanavaraikṣä āśī' u
prrakaittu būrä ṣacu vāṣṭä bauḍä va herä nauda. gaḍā-hvasta thauracaihä bera śā
u śaca prraiysge bira śā u kabalīja baysgyi hvāhyä ką̄madä śe u hūḍaigä
ysīḍai attaravāysä śau u hūḍaiga ysīḍai lahäpī śau u ką̄ra kagä khauṣa thą̄racaihä pabanā śa u khaucīja khauśka śā u īјīnai hī-
rāsä hvattarakīnai ūra-bada śau u gaḍā-hvastä śīyi haysänā-
līkä thauracaihä dva u mījī jūna baysgyi kabala dvī u haija maistä kabala u pe u śīyi maistä kabala śā u aysūra-gūna da-
jūna baimya kamaiśkä śā u nämāya śau baraka u ya.ma. hainai gaḍā hvastä
baysgi thauracaihä śau u haysnālīka gaḍā hvastä thauracaihä
dva u paha drau vī haysnālīkä śacī śau u haija baysgyi kabala
dvī u hainai thauna śacī u haysnālīkä thauna śaca dräya u śīya
baysgyi kabala tcaure u paima-vīstā kabalīnai draijsai śau u gahai śau u
eysnaṃśā maista u dairśvā khaucvā drauhye bitcä dairsa u tcaurrvā starrvā ñū-
ṣṭyelīka u śau barä khaucä pajsāsä sera u paima-vīstāva thauna śacä ha-
darā śa u gaḍā hvastä thauracaihä jsa dā-gū baysgye paima jsa bira śā
u kagīja ṣkaumaka vīlaka śā hatca ttrraba jsa u dą̄rmīnai ṣką̄ma dale śau u
habastā gahā śa : gahai va maistä śau u valaka gahai śau u hatca hasą̄ña jsa
aiysna śā u nauṣṭara śau u kabalījä bịrga kagyä karastä śe u kabalīnai rūśkagä thūḍa-pa śau u kaimeja ysīḍā-mejanya kamaiśka śā u haija baysgyä kabala pajse u hainā thauna : ną̄ u ysīra gū śacī śau u pai-
mīnā thauna tcaura u phrramaina kabala śā u ką̄ra-kagä khauṣa śa hatca
āvasakāṃ jsa u mījī jūna śadā kaimejä īśīma śa u {ysīcä spī-
yi drai gūna mnan pa kamaiśka śā} u painajä śī nama śau u thauna śacī nūvarä {-e}
parekṣi śau u chava nū kāṃhä parakṣa śau u hainā śadā damarāśī'nai maista kaimejä śau u śe' āṣana śadā damarāśī'nai maistä kaimejä śau u dai-
dä āṣana śadā śagīnai maistä kaimejä śau u paha drauvī sya-
dai hvaradai thauracaihä śau u haysnālīka hūḍaigä śau baysgi u hadā
naṣkūmāya namavīña thavalakañä khauca haudūsä sera pyaṣṭalīka
u hūḍaiga yą̄ma-bakä śau u thauracaihä śūkyainä dva u hų̄naugyä
jsaiṇyāṃ hīrāṃ jsa habaḍa pyaṣṭalīkya khadīrakya śe u pūstyą̄ na tcairma
tha valaka śā u mījījunä thauracaihä birä śā u maistä pū-
stye śau u ejsīnai vasīyikä śau u nūvarä barä u vatsāvīśī'-
nai hamauka śau pajūka śau u būśaunāṃ barakä śau habaḍa u ūla-ka-
gä baraka śau u nvadāvaunä auramūṣa pajsa u gahā śa maistä gahai
śau u valakä śau u thūra-ma śau u pūstyą̄nä : namavīja thavalakä śā
pūstyāṃ jsa habaḍa u badana dräya u ṣką̄mye herä nāsākä ranavarai-
kṣä āśī' akṣärä 井 u prrakai akṣä'rä byaunä kvāṃṣī-
thau āśī' akṣärä [signed] byauna būyunä śau-śū śvauñakä akṣärä [signed]

[Translation follows; the ellipses here denote words that are either illegible or missing.—S.U.]

In the Year of the Monkey, the month of Cvātaja, the twentieth day.

This is a record because the reverend Ratnavṛkṣa and Praketu rode to Shazhou and obtained things:

one . . . coat; one . . . coat of . . . silk; one pair of trousers of thick and wide blanket cloth; one undergarment of yellow . . . ; one . . . of yellow cloth; one pair of shoes of . . . leather with laces of . . . ; and one . . . ; one leather belt of black . . . ; two white . . . ; two blankets . . . ; a red large blanket; one . . . and white large blanket; and one asura-colored flaming . . . ; one thick . . . of beaten red . . .; two . . . of beaten . . . for washing; one silk cloth for washing with . . . ; two thick red blankets; three silk red cloths and wash cloths; four thick white cloths; one . . . ; one large . . . ; one wool- . . . for blankets; thirty . . . in thirty . . . ; . . . in four . . . ; one . . . of 15 ounces; one wool . . . silk . . . ; one smoke-colored coat of thick wool with . . . of beaten . . . ; one small . . . of leather; . . . one large . . . and one small . . . ; . . . one skin of wolf hide for blankets; one sheep-skin fur for blankets; . . . five thick red blankets; nine red cloths; one gold-colored silk; four woollen cloths; one silver-gilt blanket; one shoe of . . . -leather; one yellow-white three-color . . . ; one white . . . felt; one new . . . of cloth-silk; one large cover for a dharmarājika [a type of *stupa*, a dome structure deemed sacred by Buddhist monks.—S.U.] of red earth; a second large cover for a dharmarājika of dark earth; a third large cover for a . . . of dark earth; one left and right . . . of . . . hair; one thick . . . for washing; a . . . of 17 ounces . . . ; one . . . ; two . . . ; one . . . for book leather; . . . one silver cup; a new . . . ; one goblet made of vasaka wood; one . . . ; one full perfume purse; one purse of camel-skin; five . . . ; one . . . ; one large . . . and one small; one spoon; one . . . of felt, filled with . . . ; three ropes; and a container for . . . things.

The reverend Ratnavṛkṣa's akṣara. Praketu's akṣara [An *akṣara* is an identifying signature mark.—S.U.]. The witness Kvāṃ Ṣīthau's akṣara. The witness Būyunä Śauśū Śvaunaka's akṣara.

[signed]

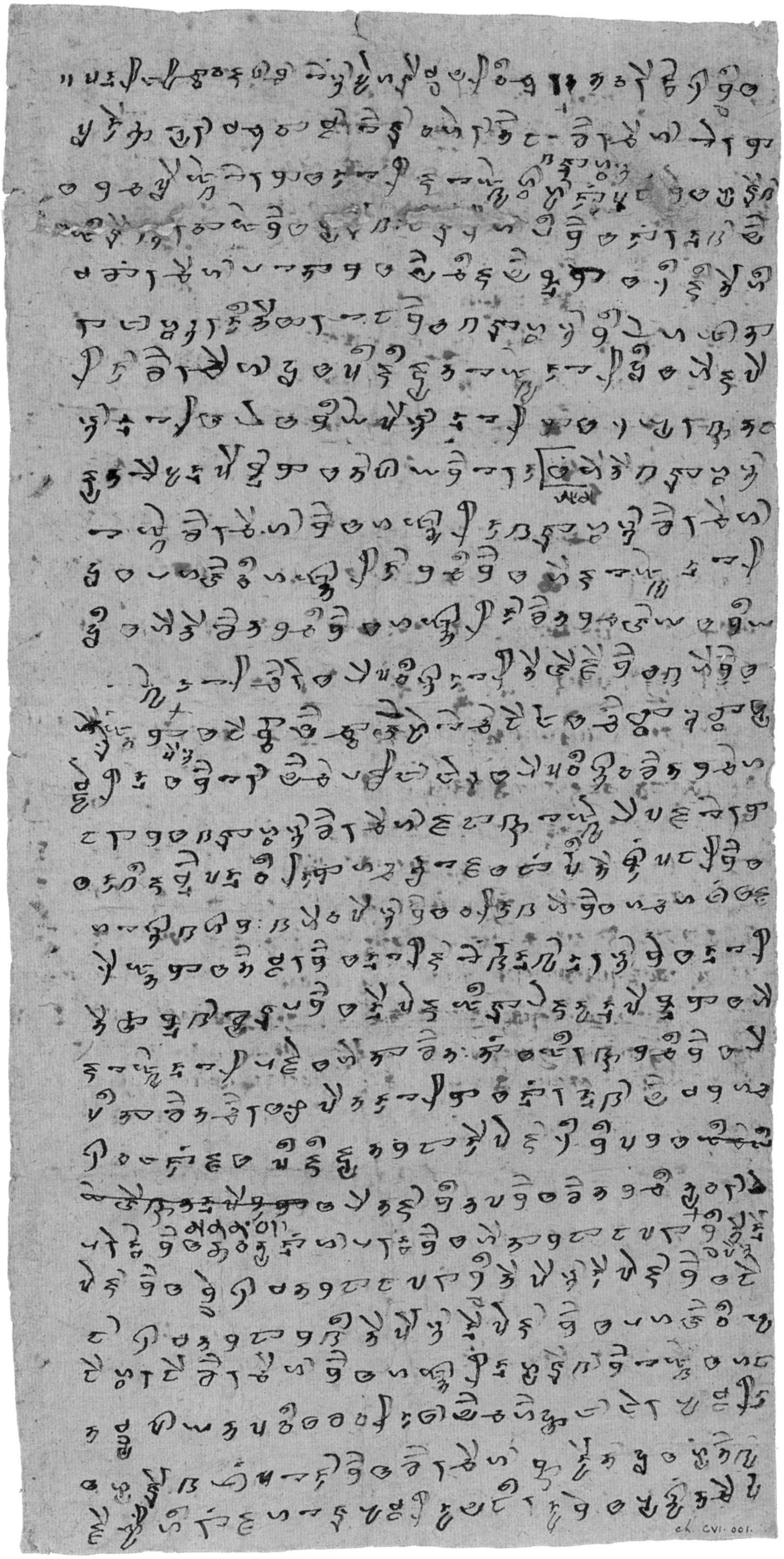
ch. CVI. 001.

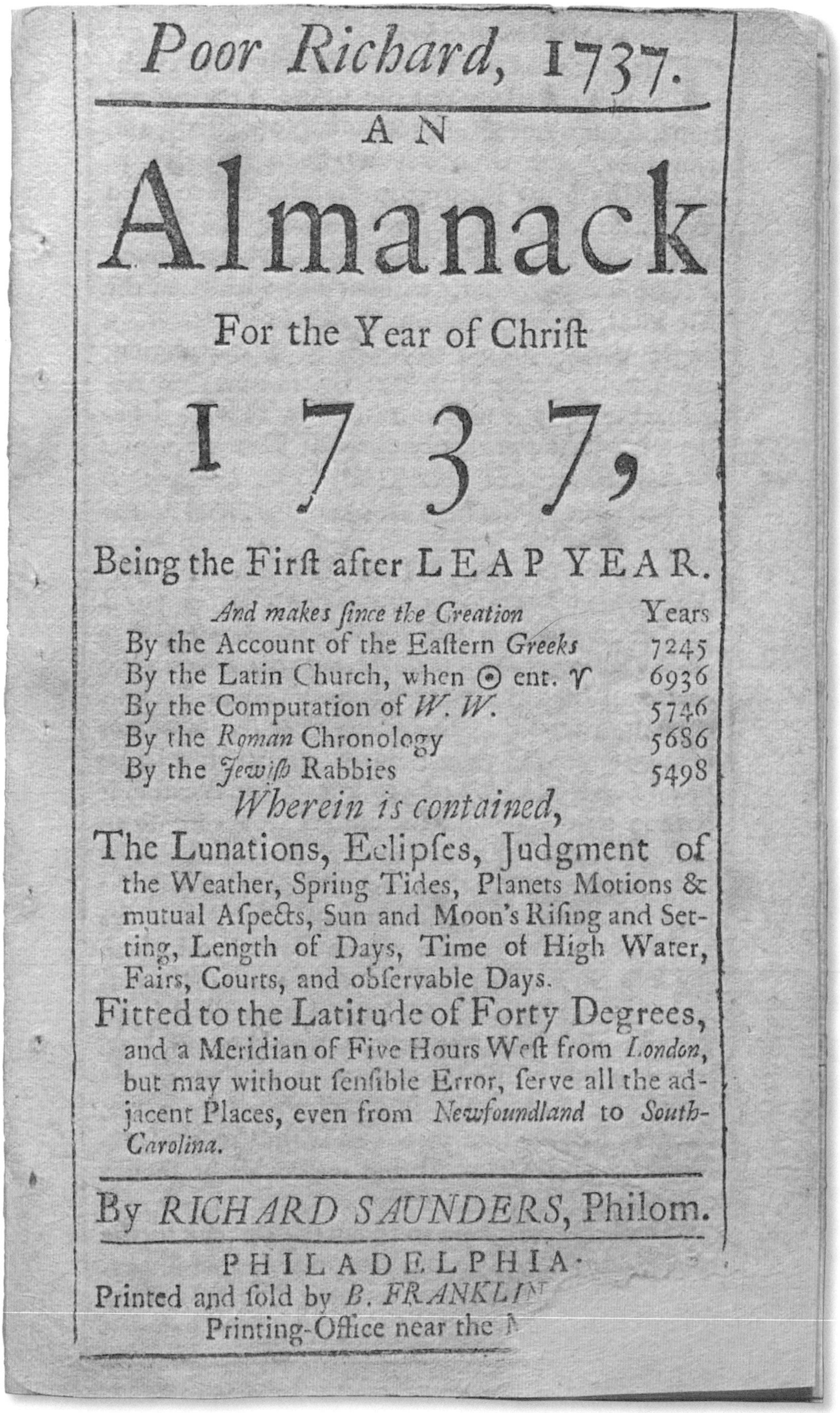
Poor Richard, 1737.

AN

Almanack

For the Year of Chriſt

1737,

Being the Firſt after LEAP YEAR.

And makes ſince the Creation	Years
By the Account of the Eaſtern *Greeks*	7245
By the Latin Church, when ☉ ent. ♈	6936
By the Computation of *W. W.*	5746
By the *Roman* Chronology	5686
By the *Jewiſh* Rabbies	5498

Wherein is contained,

The Lunations, Eclipſes, Judgment of the Weather, Spring Tides, Planets Motions & mutual Aſpects, Sun and Moon's Riſing and Setting, Length of Days, Time of High Water, Fairs, Courts, and obſervable Days.

Fitted to the Latitude of Forty Degrees, and a Meridian of Five Hours Weſt from *London*, but may without ſenſible Error, ſerve all the adjacent Places, even from *Newfoundland* to *South-Carolina*.

By *RICHARD SAUNDERS*, Philom.

PHILADELPHIA·
Printed and ſold by *B. FRANKLI*
Printing-Office near the

List No. 009

THE DRINKERS DICTIONARY

BENJAMIN FRANKLIN
January 13, 1737

Long before he entered government, the indefatigable Benjamin Franklin (1706–1790) co-owned the most popular newspaper in the colonies. And he frequently contributed to it, often under aliases such as Poor Richard (also the creator of the best-selling annual *Poor Richard's Almanack*). In 1737, Franklin printed an extensive and thoroughly entertaining "Drinkers Dictionary"—essentially a list of 228 synonyms, all being used in local taverns at the time to describe the state of being drunk.

Nothing more like a Fool than a drunken Man. Poor Richard.

'Tis an old Remark, that Vice always endeavours to assume the Appearance of Virtue: Thus Covetousness calls itself *Prudence*; *Prodigality* would be thought *Generosity*; and so of others. This perhaps arises hence, that, Mankind naturally and universally approve Virtue in their Hearts, and detest Vice; and therefore, whenever thro' Temptation they fall into a Practice of the latter, they would if possible conceal it from themselves as well as others, under some other Name than that which properly belongs to it.

But DRUNKENNESS is a very unfortunate Vice in this respect. It bears no kind of Similitude with any sort of Virtue, from which it might possibly borrow a Name; and is therefore reduc'd to the wretched Necessity of being express'd by distant round-about Phrases, and of perpetually varying those Phrases, as often as they come to be well understood to signify plainly that a MAN IS DRUNK.

Tho' every one may possibly recollect a Dozen at least of the Expressions us'd on this Occasion, yet I think no one who has not much frequented Taverns would imagine the number of them so great as it really is. It may therefore surprize as well as divert the sober Reader, to have the Sight of a new Piece, lately communicated to me, entitled

THE DRINKERS DICTIONARY.

A

He is Addled,
He's casting up his Accounts,
He's Afflicted,
He's in his Airs.

B

He's Biggy,
Bewitch'd,
Block and Block,
Boozy,
Bowz'd,
Been at Barbadoes,
Piss'd in the Brook,
Drunk as a Wheel-Barrow,
Burdock'd,
Buskey,
Buzzey,
Has Stole a Manchet out of the Brewer's Basket,
His Head is full of Bees,
Has been in the Bibbing Plot,

Has drank more than he has bled,
He's Bungey,
    As Drunk as a Beggar,
He sees the Bears,
He's kiss'd black Betty,
He's had a Thump over the Head with Sampson's Jawbone,
He's Bridgey.

C

He's Cat,
    Cagrin'd,
    Capable,
    Cramp'd,
    Cherubimical,
    Cherry Merry,
    Wamble Crop'd,
    Crack'd,
    Concern'd,
    Half Way to Concord,
Has taken a Chirriping-Glass,
    Got Corns in his Head,
    A Cup too much,
    Coguy,
    Copey,
He's heat his Copper,
He's Crocus,
    Catch'd,
He cuts his Capers,
He's been in the Cellar,
He's in his Cups,
    Non Compos,
    Cock'd,
    Curv'd,
    Cut,
    Chipper,
    Chickery,
    Loaded his Cart,
He's been too free with the Creature,
Sir Richard has taken off his Considering Cap,
He's Chap-fallen.

D

He's Disguiz'd,
He's got a Dish,
    Kill'd his Dog,

Took his Drops,
It is a Dark Day with him,
He's a Dead Man,
Has Dipp'd his Bill,
He's Dagg'd,
He's seen the Devil.

E

He's Prince Eugene,
Enter'd,
Wet both Eyes,
Cock Ey'd,
Got the Pole Evil,
Got a brass Eye,
Made an Example,
He's Eat a Toad and half for Breakfast,
In his Element.

F

He's Fishey,
Fox'd,
Fuddled,
Sore Footed,
Frozen,
Well in for 't,
Owes no Man a Farthing,
Fears no Man,
Crump Footed,
Been to France,
Flush'd,
Froze his Mouth,
Fetter'd,
Been to a Funeral,
His Flag is out,
Fuzl'd,
Spoke with his Friend,
Been at an Indian Feast.

G

He's Glad,
Groatable,
Gold-headed,
Glaiz'd,
Generous,

Booz'd the Gage,
As Dizzy as a Goose,
Been before George,
Got the Gout,
Had a Kick in the Guts,
Been with Sir John Goa,
Been at Geneva,
Globular,
Got the Glanders.

H

Half and Half,
Hardy,
Top Heavy,
Got by the Head,
Hiddey,
Got on his little Hat,
Hammerish,
Loose in the Hilts,
Knows not the way Home,
Got the Hornson,
Haunted with Evil Spirits,
Has Taken Hippocrates grand Elixir.

I

He's Intoxicated,
Jolly,
Jagg'd,
Jambled,
Going to Jerusalem,
Jocular,
Been to Jerico,
Juicy.

K

He's a King,
Clips the King's English,
Seen the French King,
The King is his Cousin,
Got Kib'd Heels,
Knapt,
Het his Kettle.

L

He's in Liquor,
Lordly,
He makes Indentures with his Leggs,
Well to Live,
Light,
Lappy,
Limber.

M

He sees two Moons,
Merry,
Middling,
Moon-Ey'd,
Muddled,
Seen a Flock of Moons,
Maudlin,
Mountous,
Muddy,
Rais'd his Monuments,
Mellow.

N

He's eat the Cocoa Nut,
Nimptopsical,
Got the Night Mare.

O

He's Oil'd,
Eat Opium,
Smelt of an Onion,
Oxycrocium,
Overset.

P

He drank till he gave up his Half-Penny,
Pidgeon Ey'd,
Pungey,
Priddy,
As good conditioned as a Puppy,
Has Scalt his Head Pan,
Been among the Philistines,

In his Prosperity,
He's been among the Philippians,
He's contending with Pharaoh,
Wasted his Paunch,
He's Polite,
Eat a Pudding Bagg.

Q

He's Quarrelsome.

R

He's Rocky,
Raddled,
Rich,
Religious,
Lost his Rudder,
Ragged,
Rais'd,
Been too free with Sir Richard,
Like a Rat in Trouble.

S

He's Stitch'd,
Seafaring,
In the Sudds,
Strong,
Been in the Sun,
As Drunk as David's Sow
Swampt,
His Skin is full,
He's Steady,
He's Stiff,
He's burnt his Shoulder,
He's got his Top Gallant Sails out,
Seen the yellow Star,
As Stiff as a Ring-bolt,
Half Seas over,
His Shoe pinches him,
Staggerish,
It is Star-light with him,
He carries too much Sail,
Stew'd,
Stubb'd,

Soak'd,
Soft,
Been too free with Sir John Strawberry,
He's right before the Wind with all his Studding Sails out,
Has Sold his Senses.

T

He's Top'd,
Tongue-ty'd,
Tann'd,
Tipium Grove,
Double Tongu'd,
Topsy Turvey,
Tipsey,
Has Swallow'd a Tavern Token,
He's Thaw'd,
He's in a Trance,
He's Trammel'd.

V

He makes Virginia Fence, Valiant,
Got the Indian Vapours.

W

The Malt is above the Water,
He's Wise,
He's Wet,
He's been to the Salt Water,
He's Water-soaken,
He's very Weary,
Out of the Way.

The Phrases in this Dictionary are not (like most of our Terms of Art) borrow'd from Foreign Languages, neither are they collected from the Writings of the Learned in our own, but gather'd wholly from the modern Tavern-Conversation of Tiplers. I do not doubt but that there are many more in use; and I was even tempted to add a new one my self under the Letter B, to wit, *Brutify'd*: But upon Consideration, I fear'd being guilty of Injustice to the Brute Creation, if I represented Drunkenness as a beastly Vice, since, 'tis well-known, that the Brutes are in general a very sober sort of People.

THE LEXICON OF PROHIBITION

EDMUND WILSON
1927

In 1927, almost two hundred years after Benjamin Franklin published *The Drinkers Dictionary* (see List No. 009), American literary critic Edmund Wilson followed suit by printing *The Lexicon of Prohibition*, a list of terms for drunkenness, arranged, he explained, "in order of the degrees of intensity of the conditions which they represent, beginning with the mildest stages and progressing to the more serious."

lit
squiffy
oiled
lubricated
owled
edged
jingled
piffed
piped
sloppy
woozy
happy
half-screwed
half-cooked
half-shot
half seas over
fried
stewed
boiled
zozzled
sprung
scrooched
jazzed
jagged
canned
corked
corned
potted
hooted
slopped
tanked
stinko
blind
stiff
under the table
tight
full
wet
high
horseback
liquored
pickled
ginned
shicker (Yiddish)
spifflicated
primed
organized
featured
pie-eyed
cock-eyed
wall-eyed
glassy-eyed
bleary-eyed
hoary-eyed
over the Bay
four sheets in the wind
crocked
loaded
leaping
screeching
lathered
plastered
soused
bloated
polluted
saturated
full as a tick
loaded for bear
loaded to the muzzle
loaded to the plimsoll mark
wapsed down
paralyzed
ossifed
out like a light
passed out cold
embalmed
buried
blotto
lit up like the sky
lit up like the Commonwealth
lit up like a Christmas tree
lit up like a store window
lit up like a church
fried to the hat
slopped to the ears
stewed to the gills
boiled as an owl
to have a bun on
to have a slant on
to have a skate on
to have a snootfull
to have a skinful
to draw a blank
to pull a shut-eye
to pull a Daniel Boone
to have a rubber drink
to have a hangover
to have a head
to have the jumps
to have the shakes
to have the zings
to have the heeby-jeebies
to have the screaming-meemies
to have the whoops and jingles
to burn with a low blue flame

Some of these, such as *loaded* and *full*, are a little old-fashioned now; but they are still understood. Others, such as *cock-eyed* and *oiled*, which are included in the Drinker's Dictionary compiled by Benjamin Franklin (and containing two hundred and twenty-eight terms) seem to be enjoying a new popularity. It is interesting to note that one hears nowadays comparatively rarely of people going on *sprees*, *toots*, *tears*, *jags*, *bats*, *brannigans* or *benders*. All these terms suggest, not merely extreme drunkenness, but also an exceptional occurrence, a violent breaking away by the drinker from the conditions for his normal life. It is possible that their partial disappearance is to be accounted for by the fact that this kind of fierce protracted drinking has now become universal, a familiar feature of social life, instead of a disreputable escapade. On the other hand, the vocabulary of social drinking, as exemplified by the above list, seems to have become particularly rich: one gets the impression that more nuances are nowadays discriminated than was the case before prohibition. Thus, *fried*, *stewed*, and *boiled* all convey distinctly different ideas; and *cock-eyed*, *plastered*, *owled*, *embalmed*, and *ossified* bring into play quite different images. *Wapsed down* is a rural expression, also used in connection with crops which have been ruined by a storm; *featured* is a theatrical word, which applies to a stage at which the drinker is stimulated to believe strongly in his ability to sing a song, to tell a funny story or to execute a dance; *organized* is properly applied to a condition of thorough preparation for the efficient conduct of a formidable evening; and *blotto*, of English origin, denotes a condition of bland unconsciousness.

List No. 011

BILL OF MORTALITY

E. COTES
August 1665

In the summer of 1665, London residents began to drop like flies as the Great Plague swept across the city, killing 68,596 people, young and old. In fact, that number covers only recorded deaths; the actual total is thought to be close to 100,000. At the time, weekly Bills of Mortality were circulated on which the last seven days' death toll was reported, broken down to show causes of death. The example seen here relates to the week beginning August 15 of that year, as the plague's grip tightened, a period during which 3,880 people perished. And here is a glossary for the benefit of those who have never heard of such grimly named ailments as Kingsevil and Strangury.

Glossary:

Childbed: Mothers who died following childbirth, usually from infection

Chrisomes: Infants who died in their first month

Consumption: Those who died of tuberculosis

Dropsie: Enlargement of organs due to build-up of fluids

Fistula: An abnormal channel or passage, a hole, that can form between organs

Flux: Dysentery

Imposthume: Abscess

Kingsevil: Lymphadenopathy of the neck

Quinsie: A throat abcess

Rising of the Lights: Lung disease

Scowring: Dysentry

Spotted fever and Purples: Meningitis

Stone: Gallstones

Strangury: Painful urination

Surfeit: Overeating

Teeth: Infants who have died during teething

Tiffick: Asthma/tuberculosis

And the Assize of Bread set forth by Order of the Lord Mayor and Court of Aldermen printed at the bottom of the Bills of Mortality was essentially a statute that regulated the local weight and price of bread each week.

The Diseases and Casualties this Week.

Abortive	6
Aged	54
Apoplexie	1
Bedridden	1
Cancer	2
Childbed	23
Chrisomes	15
Collick	1
Consumption	174
Convulsion	88
Dropsie	40
Drowned 2, one at St. Kath-Tower, and one at Lambeth	2
Feaver	353
Fistula	1
Flox and Small-pox	10
Flux	2
Found dead in the Street at St. Bartholomew the Less	1
Frighted	1
Gangrene	1
Gowt	1
Grief	1
Griping in the Guts	74
Jaundies	3
Imposthume	18
Infants	21
Kild by a fall down stairs at St. Thomas Apostle	1

Kingsevil	10
Lethargy	1
Murthered at Stepney	1
Palsie	2
Plague	3880
Plurisie	1
Quinsie	6
Rickets	23
Rising of the Lights	19
Rupture	2
Sciatica	1
Scowring	13
Scurvy	1
Sore legge	1
Spotted Feaver and Purples	190
Starved at Nurse	1
Stilborn	8
Stone	2
Stopping of the stomach	16
Strangury	1
Suddenly	1
Surfeit	87
Teeth	113
Thrush	3
Tissick	6
Ulcer	2
Vomiting	7
Winde	8
Wormes	18

Christned { Males — 83, Females — 83, In all — 166 }

Buried { Males — 2656, Females — 2663, In all — 5319 } Plague — 3880

Increased in the Burials this Week — 1289

Parishes clear of the Plague — 34. Parishes Infected — 96

The Assize of Bread set forth by Order of the Lord Maior and Court of Aldermen,

A penny Wheaten Loaf to contain Nine Ounces and a half, and three half-penny White Loaves the like weight.

List No. 012

GEORGE WASHINGTON'S SLAVES

GEORGE WASHINGTON
April 1788

When he was eleven years old, future Founding Father and the first-ever US President, George Washington, became the owner of ten slaves, inherited from his father. When Washington died fifty-six years later, over three hundred slaves lived on his estate, Mount Vernon. The list seen here was written in 1788 and details those "blacks [that he owned] above 12 years of age."

List of taxable property belonging to General Washington in Truro Parish.
April 1788

Blacks above 12 years of age.

Will
Frank
Auston
Hercules
Nathan
Giles
Joe
Paris
Gunner
Boatswain
Sam
Anthony
Tom
Will
Isaac
James
Sambo
Tom Nookes
Nat
George

Simms
Joe
Jack
Bristol
Peter
Peter
Scumburg
(past labor)
Frank
Jack
Betty (past
service)
Doll
Jenney
Charlotte
Sall
Caroline
Sall Rass
Dorchia
Alice
Myrtilla
Kitty
Moll

Billy – undr 16
Joe . . . "
Christopher – "
Cyrus – "
Uriah – "
Godferry – "
Sinah – "
Mima – "
Lylla – "
Oney – "
Anna – "
Beck – "
Virgin – "
Patt – "
Will
Will
Charles
Gabriel
Jupiter
Nanney
Kate
Sarah
Alice
Nanny

Peg
Sackey
Darcus
Amy
Nancy
Molly undr 16
Morris
Robin
Adam
Jack
Jack
Dick
Ben
Matt
Morris
Brunswick
(past service)
Hannah
Lucy
Moll
Jenny
Silla
Charity
Betty
Peg
Sail
Grace
Sue
Agga Undr 16

Will
Paul
Abraham
Paschal
Rose
Sabeen
Lucy
Delia
Daphne
Grace
Tom – undr
16
Moses – "
Isaac – "
Sam Kit
London
Cæsar
Cupid
Paul
Betty
Doll
Lucy
Lucy
Flora
Fanny
Rachael
Jenney
Edy
Daphne

98 Horses
4 Mules
1 Covering Horse @ 2 Guineas
1 Chariot

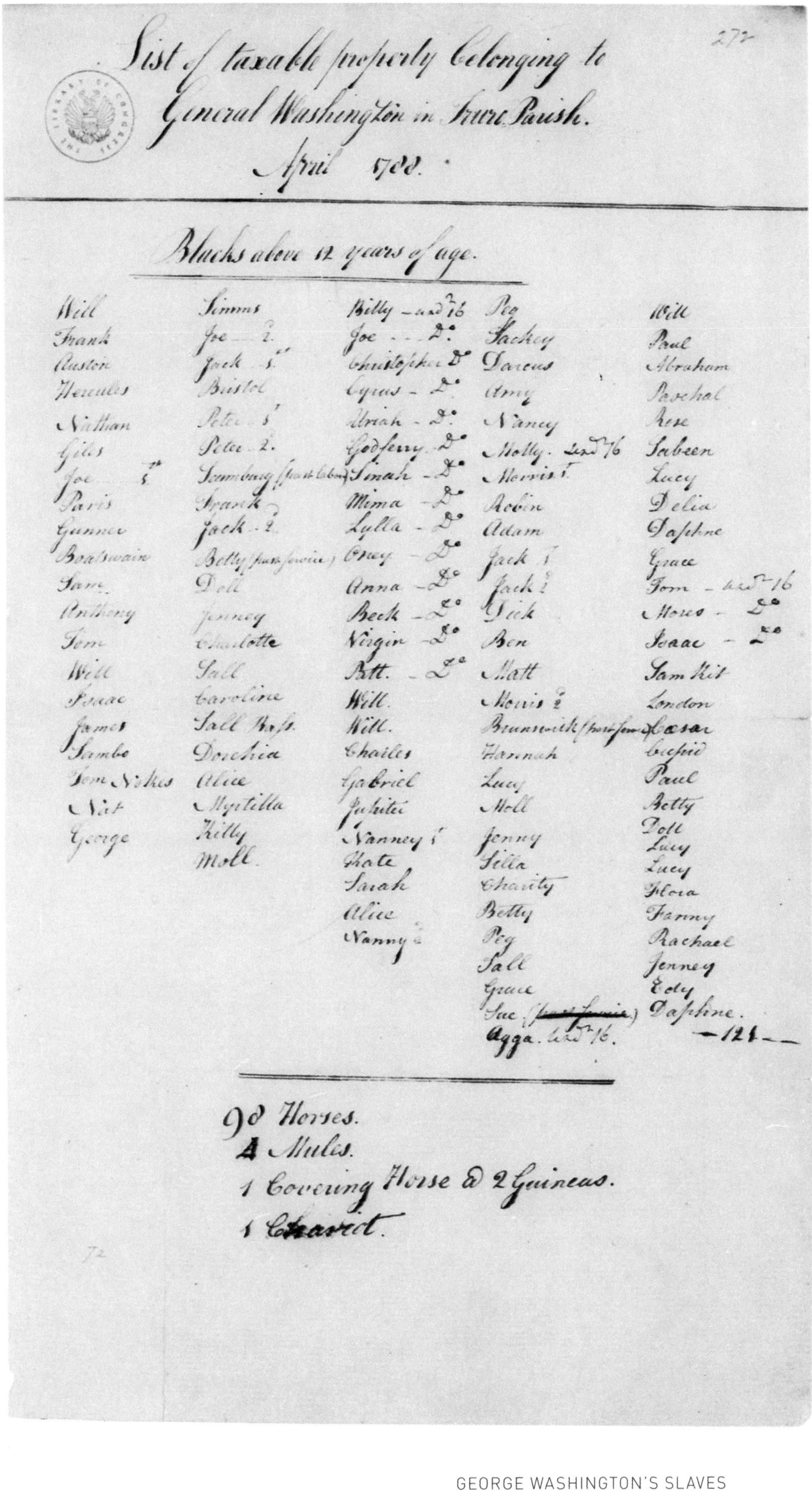

272

List of taxable property belonging to General Washington in Truro Parish. April 1788.

Blacks above 12 years of age.

Will	Simms	Billy — und. 16	Peg	Will
Frank	Joe 2	Joe — Do.	Sackey	Paul
Auston	Jack 1st	Christopher Do.	Darcus	Abraham
Hercules	Bristol	Cyrus — Do.	Amy	Paschal
Nathan	Peter 1	Uriah — Do.	Nancy	Rose
Giles	Peter 2.	Godfrey Do.	Molly. und. 16	Sabeen
Joe 1st	Sambury (past labour)	Sinah — Do.	Morris 1	Lucy
Paris	Frank	Mima — Do.	Robin	Delia
Gunner	Jack 2.	Lylla — Do.	Adam	Daphne
Boatswain	Betty (past service)	Oney — Do.	Jack 1	Grace
Sam	Doll	Anna — Do.	Jack 2	Tom — und. 16
Anthony	Jenney	Beck — Do.	Dick	Moses — Do.
Tom	Charlotte	Virgin — Do.	Ben	Isaac — Do.
Will	Sall	Patt. — Do.	Matt	Sam Kit
Isaac	Caroline	Will.	Morris 2	London
James	Sall Bass.	Will.	Brunswick (past service)	Caesar
Sambo	Dorchia	Charles	Hannah	Cupid
Tom Nokes	Alice	Gabriel	Lucy	Paul
Nat	Myrtilla	Jupiter	Moll	Betty
George	Kitty	Nanney 1	Jenny	Doll
	Moll.	Kate	Silla	Lucy
		Sarah	Charity	Lucy
		Alice	Betty	Flora
		Nanny 2	Peg	Fanny
			Sall	Rachael
			Grace	Jenney
			Sue (~~past service~~)	Edy
			Agga. und. 16.	Daphne.
				—121—

98 Horses.
4 Mules.
1 Covering Horse & 2 Guineas.
1 Chariot.

72

List No. 013

THE COWBOY CODE

GENE AUTRY
1948

For thirty years from the early 1930s, thanks to a hit CBS Radio show, numerous television and film appearances, and an illustrious country music career, American entertainer Gene Autry was known to millions of fans as the Singing Cowboy. In 1948, aware that many impressionable youngsters were keen to emulate his public persona, Autry came up with, and then promoted, the Cowboy Code—a list of ten rules which, if followed, would hopefully keep his admirers on the straight and narrow.

1. The Cowboy must never shoot first, hit a smaller man, or take unfair advantage.
2. He must never go back on his word, or a trust confided in him.
3. He must always tell the truth.
4. He must be gentle with children, the elderly, and animals.
5. He must not advocate or possess racially or religiously intolerant ideas.
6. He must help people in distress.
7. He must be a good worker.
8. He must keep himself clean in thought, speech, action, and personal habits.
9. He must respect women, parents, and his nation's laws.
10. The Cowboy is a patriot.

List No. 014

ADVICE TO CHICK ROCKERS

CHRISSIE HYNDE
1994

Having fronted the Pretenders since 1978, Chrissie Hynde is well placed to offer young women guidance on the subject of female success in rock music. In 1994 she did exactly that with her "Advice to Chick Rockers," a list subsequently printed in the teen magazine *Mouth 2 Mouth*.

1. Don't moan about being a chick, refer to feminism or complain about sexist discrimination. We've all been thrown down stairs and fucked about, but no one wants to hear a whining female. Write a loosely disguised song about it instead and clean up ($).

2. Never pretend you know more than you do. If you don't know chord names, refer to the dots. Don't go near the desk unless you plan on becoming an engineer.

3. Make the other band members look and sound good. Bring out the best in them; that's your job. Oh, and you better sound good, too.

4. Do not insist on working with "females"; that's just more b.s. Get the best man for the job. If it happens to be a woman, great—you'll have someone to go to department stores with on tour instead of making one of the road crew go with you.

5. Try not to have a sexual relationship with the band. It always ends in tears.

6. Don't think that sticking your boobs out and trying to look fuckable will help. Remember you're in a rock and roll band. It's not "fuck me," it's "fuck you!"

7. Don't try to compete with the guys; it won't impress anybody. Remember, one of the reasons they like you is because you don't offer yet more competition to the already existing male egos.

8. If you sing, don't "belt" or "screech." No one wants to hear that shit; it sounds "hysterical."

9. Shave your legs, for chrissakes!

10. Don't take advice from people like me. Do your own thing always.

ROGET'S THESAURUS

PETER ROGET
1805

Born in 1779, British physician Peter Roget had a somewhat difficult childhood during which he was forced to deal with the deaths of close family members and the mental health problems of others in quick succession. Perhaps such a chaotic and challenging upbringing caused his obsession with an activity as neat and ordered as list-making. Around 1800, in part to fend off depression, he began to write the biggest list of all: his now legendary thesaurus. By 1805 the first draft, entirely handwritten and containing 15,000 words, was complete. It was finally published forty-seven years later as *Thesaurus of English Words and Phrases Classified and Arranged so as to Facilitate the Expression of Ideas and Assist in Literary Composition.* It went through twenty-eight printings before Roget's death in 1869; and, as *Roget's Thesaurus,* it hasn't been out of print since. This page, headed "Existence" and beginning with "Ens," the Latin for "exist," was the very first entry of that initial draft.

Existence

Ens, entity, being, exist.ce Essence, quintess.ce, quidess.ce Nature thing substance course World. frame position constitution Reality, (v. truth) actual, exist.ce — fact, course of things, under y sure extant, present	Nonentity, nullity, nihility nonexist.ce noth.g nought void, zero, cypher blank empty unsubstantial Unreal, ideal, imaginary visionary, fabulous, fictitious, supposititious absent, shadow: dream phantom, phantasm
Positive, affirmation absolute Intrinsic substantive inherent	Negation, virtual, extrinsic Potential. adjective

To be, exist, obtain, stand
pass, subsist, prevail, lie
— on foot, on y tapis

To constitute, form, compose, to consist of
scope, habitude, temperament
State, mode of exist.ce condition, nature, constitut.n habit.
place

Affection, predicament, situate.n posit.n posture contingency
Circumstances, case, plight, trim, tune, — point, degree
Juncture, conjuncture, pass, emergency, exigency.

Mode, manner, style, cast, fashion, form, shape

strain, way, degree. — tenure, terms, tenor
footing, character, capacity

Relation-ship, affinity, alliance, analogy, filiat.n (v. connect.n)

Reference, about, respect.g, regard.g, concerning, touching

in point of, as to. — pertaining to, belong.g applicable to
relatively, according to.

Comparable, commensurate incomp.ble income.te — ble,

correspondent — able, irreconciliable, disendant
accordant

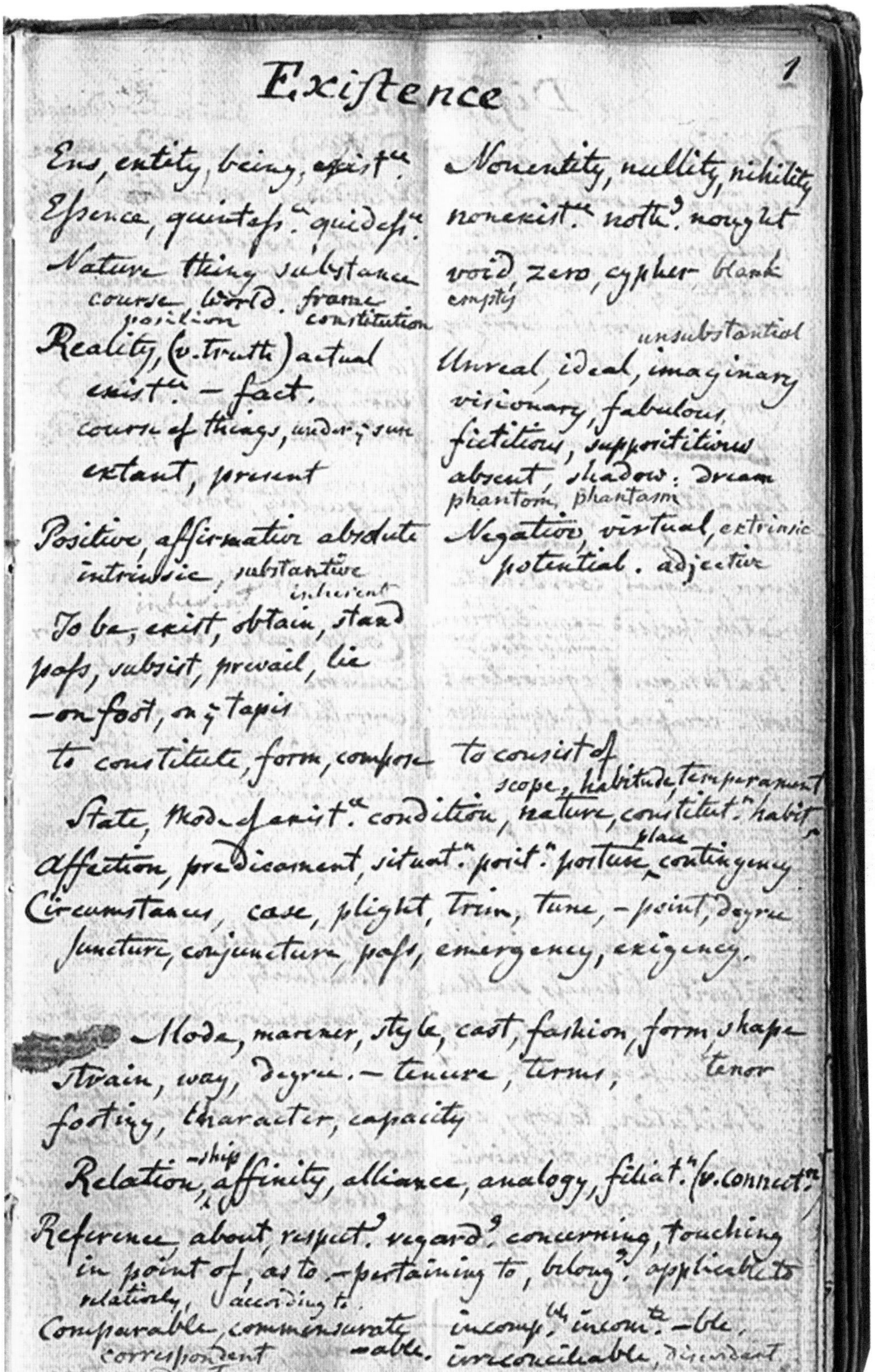
Existence
1
Ens, entity, being, existce.
Essence, quintessce quidessce
Nature thing substance
course world. frame
position constitution
Reality, (v. truth) actual
existce. — fact.
course of things, under ye sun
extant, present
Nonentity, nullity, nihility
nonexistce. nothg. nought
void, zero, cypher blank
empty
unsubstantial
Unreal, ideal, imaginary
visionary, fabulous,
fictitious, supposititious
absent, shadow: dream
phantom, phantasm
Positive, affirmative absolute
intrinsic, substantive
inherent
Negative, virtual, extrinsic
potential. adjective
To be, exist, obtain, stand
pass, subsist, prevail, lie
— on foot, on ye tapis
to constitute, form, compose
to consist of
scope, habitude, temperament
State, Mode of existce. condition, nature, constitutn. habit
place
Affection, predicament, situatn. positn. posture, contingency.
Circumstances, case, plight, trim, tune, — point, degree
Juncture, conjuncture, pass, emergency, exigency.
Mode, manner, style, cast, fashion, form, shape
strain, way, degree. — tenure, terms, tenor
footing, character, capacity
-ship
Relation, affinity, alliance, analogy, filiatn. (v. connectn.
Reference, about, respectg. regardg. concerning, touching
in point of, as to, — pertaining to, belongg. applicable to
relatively, according to.
Comparable, commensurate -able.
correspondent
accordant
incomple. incomte. -ble,
irreconcilable, discordant

List No. 016

HEINLEIN'S PREDICTIONS

ROBERT HEINLEIN
1949

Robert Heinlein (1907–1988) was one of the great science fiction novelists and author of numerous best-selling books. Named the first Science Fiction Writers Grand Master in 1975, he was the recipient of many other awards during his career. In 1949 he compiled a list of predictions for the year 2000. They were eventually published in February 1952, in *Galaxy* magazine.

So let's have a few free-swinging predictions about the future. Some will be wrong—but cautious predictions are *sure* to be wrong.

1. Interplanetary travel is waiting at your front door, c.o.d. It's yours when you pay for it, which the government is doing at least on an experimental basis.

2. Contraception and control of disease is revising relations between sexes to an extent that will change our entire social and economic structure.

3. The most important military fact of this century is that there is no way to repel an attack from space.

4. It appears utterly impossible that the United States will start a "preventive war." We will fight when attacked, either directly or in a territory we have guaranteed to defend.

5. In fifteen years the housing shortage will be solved by a "breakthrough" into new technology which will make every house now standing as obsolete as outdoor privies. The housing is taken as a matter of course on the tenth day.

6. We'll all be getting a little hungry by and by.

7. The cult of the phony in art will disappear. So-called "modern art" will be discussed only by psychiatrists.

8. Freud will be classed as a pre-scientific, intuitive pioneer, and psychoanalysis will be replaced as a growing, changing "operational psychology" based on measurement and prediction.

9. Cancer, the common cold, and tooth decay will all be conquered. The revolutionary new problem in medical research will be to accomplish "regeneration," i.e., to enable a man to grow a new leg, rather than fit him with an artificial limb.

10. By the end of this century mankind will have explored this Solar System, and the first ship intended to reach the nearest star will be abuilding.

11. Your personal telephone will be small enough to carry in your handbag. Your house telephone will record messages, answer simple queries, and transmit vision.

12. Intelligent life of some sort will be found on Mars.

13. A thousand miles an hour at a cent a mile will be commonplace; short hauls will be made in evacuated subways at extreme speed.

14. A major objective of applied physics will be to control gravity.

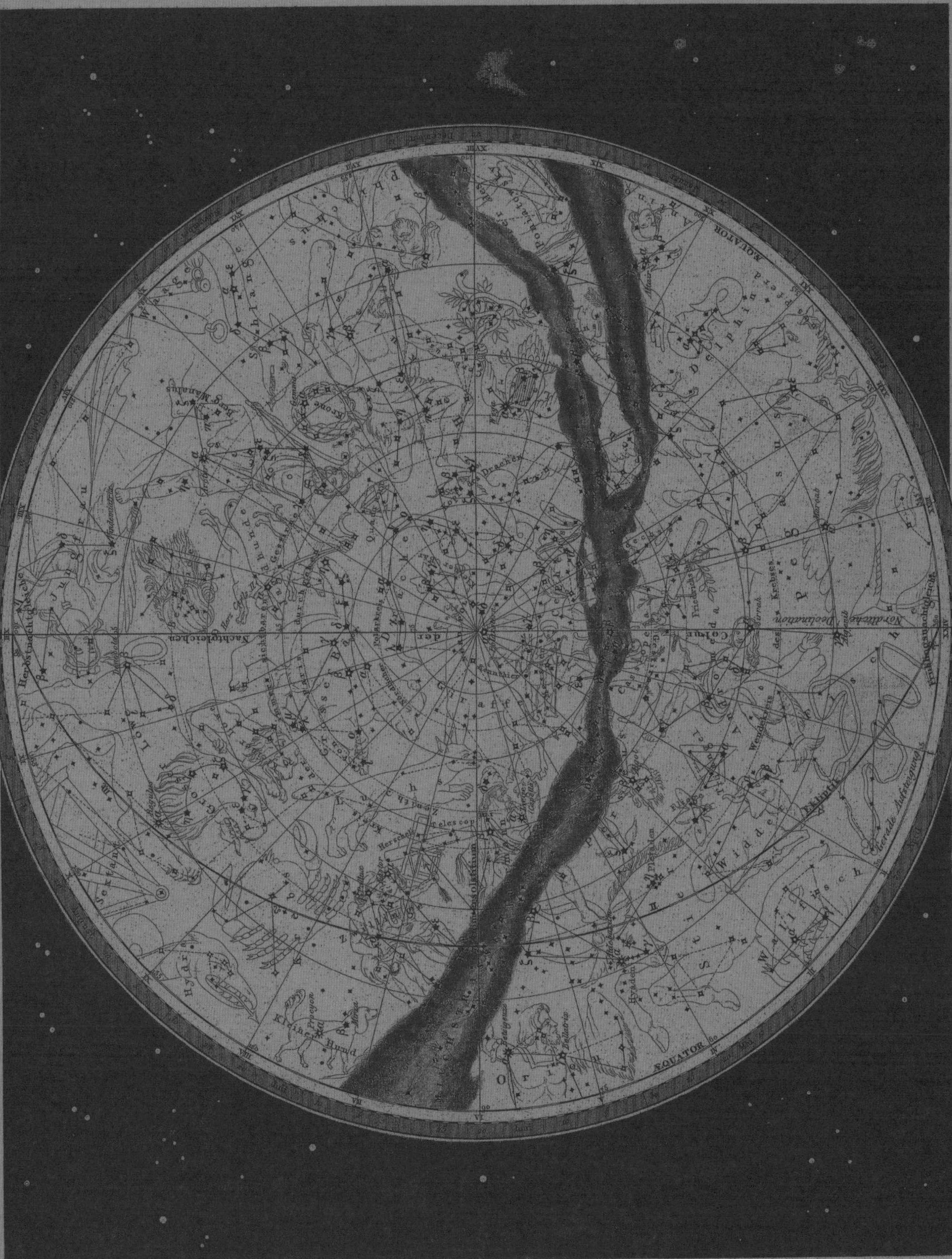
EQUATOR
Kleiner Hund
Procyon
Ekliptik
Gerade Aufsteigung
Nördliche Declination
Herbstnachtgleiche
Sextant
Hydra
Widder
Giraffe

15. We will not achieve a "world state" in the predictable future. Nevertheless, Communism will vanish from this planet.

16. Increasing mobility will disenfranchise a majority of the population. About 1990 a constitutional amendment will do away with state lines while retaining the semblance.

17. All aircraft will be controlled by a giant radar net run on a continentwide basis by a multiple electronic "brain."

18. Fish and yeast will become our principal sources of proteins. Beef will be a luxury; lamb and mutton will disappear, because sheep destroy grazing land.

19. Mankind will *not* destroy itself, nor will "civilization" be wiped out.

Here are things we *won't* get soon, if ever:
Travel through time.
Travel faster than the speed of light.
Control of telepathy and other E.S.P. phenomena.
"Radio" transmission of matter.
Manlike robots with manlike reactions
Laboratory creation of life
Real understanding of what "thought" is and how it is related to matter.
Scientific proof of personal survival after death.
Nor a permanent end to war. (I don't like that prediction any better than you do.)

THE DREAM BOOK

AUTHOR UNKNOWN
Circa 1220 BC

Discovered in the ancient Egyptian village of Deir el-Medina and dating back to approximately 1220 BC and the reign of Ramesses II, this intriguing papyrus document contains what is known as the Dream Book—a list, written in Middle Egyptian hieratic by an unknown scribe, which offers interpretations for a wide variety of dream scenarios and classifies each as either good or bad. The list seen here (there's a letter on the other side) is likely to have been copied from an earlier version and is now held at the British Museum.

Auspicious dreams:

IF A MAN SEES HIMSELF IN A DREAM:

sitting in a garden in the sun	GOOD: it means pleasure
demolishing a wall	GOOD: it means purification from evil
[eating] excrement	GOOD: consuming his property in his house
mating with a cow	GOOD: spending a happy day in his house
eating crocodile-[meat]	GOOD: [becoming] an official among his people
offering water (?)	GOOD: it means prosperity
drowning in the river	GOOD: it means purification from every evil
sleeping on the ground	GOOD: consuming his property
seeing carobs (?)	GOOD: finding a happy life
[seeing] the moon shining	GOOD: pardoning him by his god
veiling himself . . .	GOOD: his enemies flee before him
falling . . .	GOOD: it means prosperity
sawing wood	GOOD: his enemies are dead
burying an old man	GOOD: it means prosperity
cultivating vegetables	GOOD: it means finding victuals

Inauspicious dreams:

IF A MAN SEES HIMSELF IN A DREAM:

seizing one of his own legs	BAD: a report about him by those who are yonder (i.e. the dead)
seeing himself in a mirror	BAD: it means another wife
god has dispelled his weeping for him	BAD: it means fighting
while he sees himself suffering (in) his side	BAD: extracting his property from him
eating hot meat	BAD: it means not being found innocent
shod with white sandals	BAD: it means roaming the earth
eating what he abominates	BAD: it means a man eating what he abominates in ignorance
copulating with a woman	BAD: it means mourning
he is bitten by a dog	BAD: he is touched by magic
he is bitten by a snake	BAD: it means the arising of words against him
measuring barley	BAD: it means the arising of words against him
writing on a papyrus	BAD: reckoning his wrongs by his god
stirring up his house	BAD: [it means] being ill
suffering through another's spell (?)	BAD: it means mourning
being a steersman in a ship	BAD: every time he is judged, he will not be found innocent
his bed catching fire	BAD: it means driving away his wife

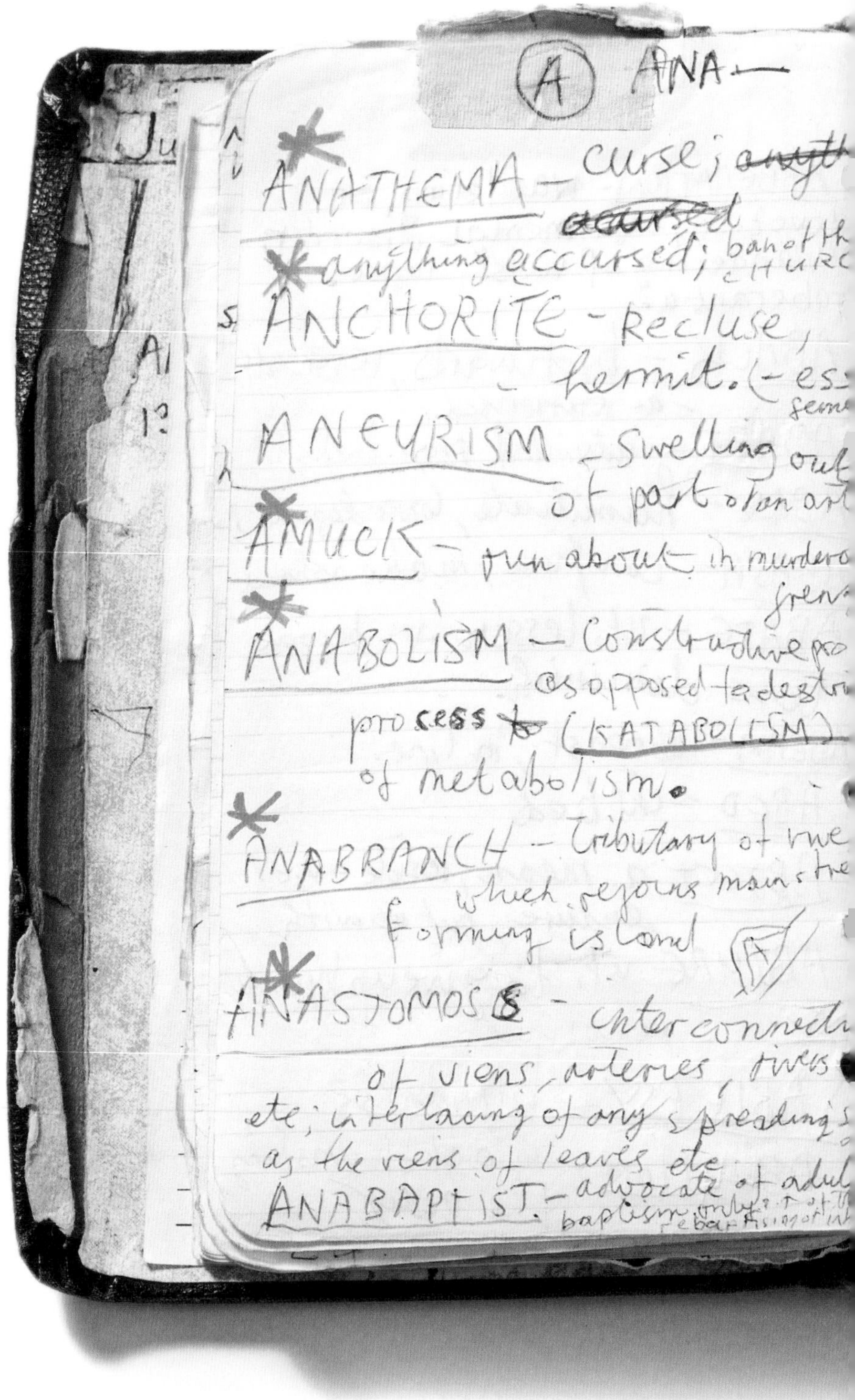

NICK CAVE'S HANDWRITTEN DICTIONARY

NICK CAVE
1984

Nick Cave is a lover of lists. As someone who for decades has spent his time writing songs, screenplays, and novels, he also has a mild obsession with language. And so Cave sometimes writes, by hand, personal dictionaries filled with notable words—those words which for some reason need to be committed to paper, filed away for future use. Here is a page taken from just one well-thumbed example, penned in 1984 as he traveled in Berlin, where he would move the following year with his band, the Bad Seeds.

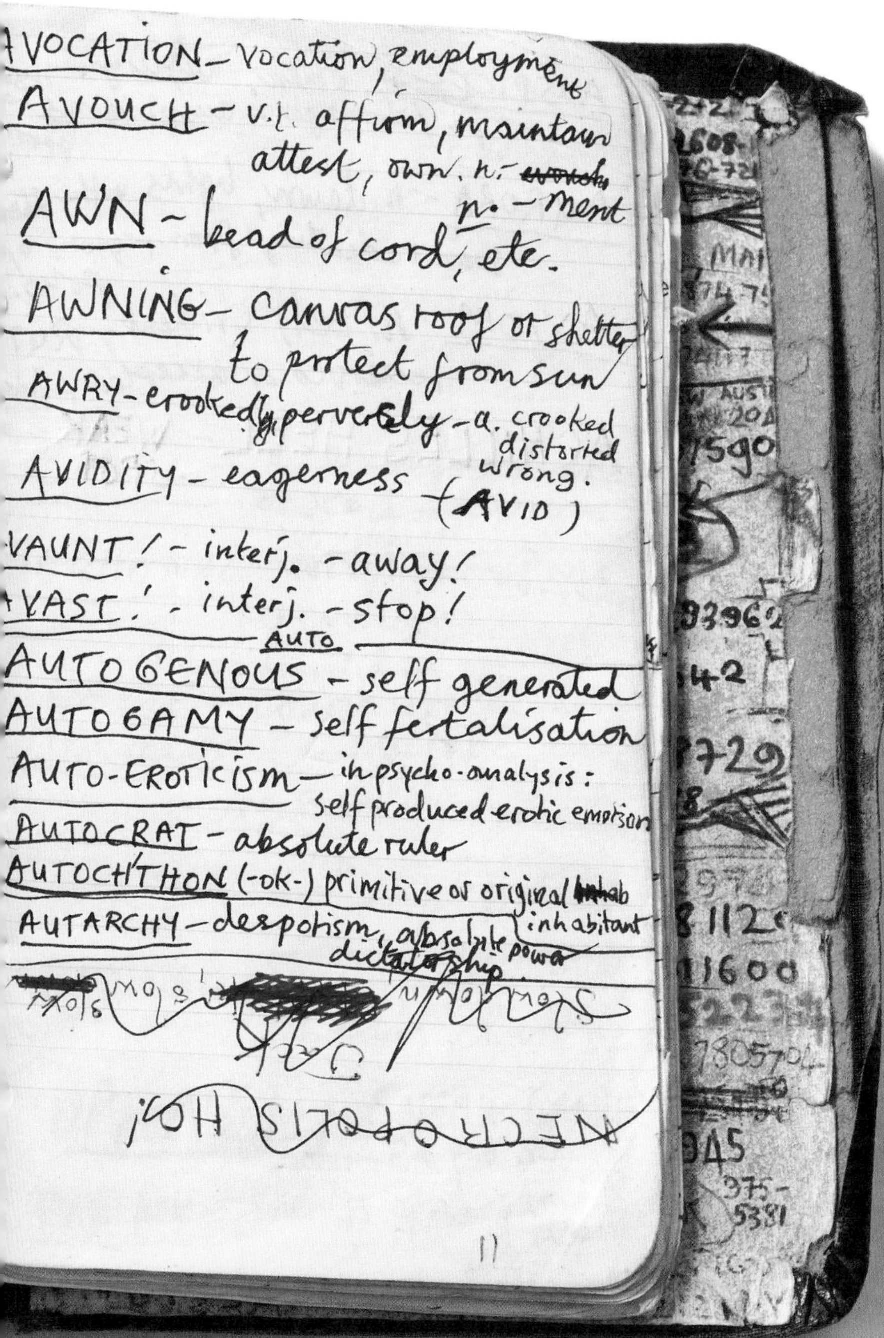
AVOCATION – vocation, employment
AVOUCH – v.t. affirm, maintain attest, own. n. – ment
AWN – bead of cord, etc.
AWNING – canvas roof or shelter to protect from sun
AWRY – crookedly, perversely – a. crooked distorted wrong.
AVIDITY – eagerness (AVID)
AVAUNT! – interj. – away!
AVAST! – interj. – stop!
AUTO
AUTOGENOUS – self generated
AUTOGAMY – self fertalisation
AUTO-EROTICISM – in psycho-analysis: self produced erotic emotion
AUTOCRAT – absolute ruler
AUTOCHTHON (-ok-) primitive or original inhabitant
AUTARCHY – despotism, absolute power dictatorship.
11

List No. 019

THE FIFTY DWARFS

DISNEY

Mid-1930s

In 1812, German storytellers the Brothers Grimm published *Snow White*, one of the most famous fairy tales in history and the basis for a wildly successful big-screen adaptation by Walt Disney Productions. Over a century later, as they began work on the animated version in 1934, the writing team at Disney compiled the following list of potential names for a group of characters whom the Brothers Grimm had chosen to leave nameless: the seven dwarfs. As we now know, Bashful, Grumpy, Happy, Sleepy, and Sneezy were picked from this shortlist; Dopey and the name of their leader, Doc, were chosen at a later date. Following the release of *Snow White and the Seven Dwarfs* in 1937, the film received an honorary Academy Award® comprising one full-size and seven miniature Oscars®.

Awful

Bashful

Biggo-Ego

Biggy

Biggy-Wiggy

Blabby

Busy

Chesty

Crabby

Cranky

Daffy

Dippy

Dirty

Dizzy

Doleful

Dumpy

Flabby

Gabby

Gaspy

Gloomy

Goopy

Graveful

Grumpy

Happy

Helpful

Hoppy

Hotsy

Hungry

Jaunty

Jumpy

Lazy

Neurtsy

Nifty

Puffy

Sappy

Scrappy

Shifty

Silly

Sleepy

Snappy

Sneezy

Sneezy-Wheezy

Snoopy

Soulful

Strutty

Tearful

Thrifty

Weepy

Wistful

Woeful

List No. 020

WARTIME GOLF RULES

RICHMOND GOLF CLUB
1940

As the Battle of Britain was being fought in the skies overhead in 1940, a bomb fell on an outbuilding belonging to Richmond Golf Club in Surrey, England, which luckily caused no deaths. As a result, the club's owners (rather than halt future rounds of golf) stiffened their upper lips and issued a rather unusual list of temporary golf rules to all members that took into account the potentially life-threatening conditions on the course.

1. Players are asked to collect Bomb and Shrapnel splinters to save these causing damage to the Mowing Machines.

2. In Competitions, during gunfire or while bombs are falling, players may take cover without penalty for ceasing play.

3. The positions of known delayed action bombs are marked by red flags placed at a reasonably, but not guaranteed, safe distance therefrom.

4. Shrapnel and/or bomb splinters on the Fairways, or in Bunkers within a club's length of a ball, may be moved without penalty, and no penalty shall be incurred if a ball is thereby caused to move accidentally.

5. A ball moved by enemy action may be replaced, or if lost or destroyed, a ball may be dropped not nearer the hole without penalty.

6. A ball lying in a crater may be lifted and dropped not nearer the hole, preserving the line to the hole, without penalty.

7. A player whose stroke is affected by the simultaneous explosion of a bomb may play another ball from the same place. Penalty one stroke.

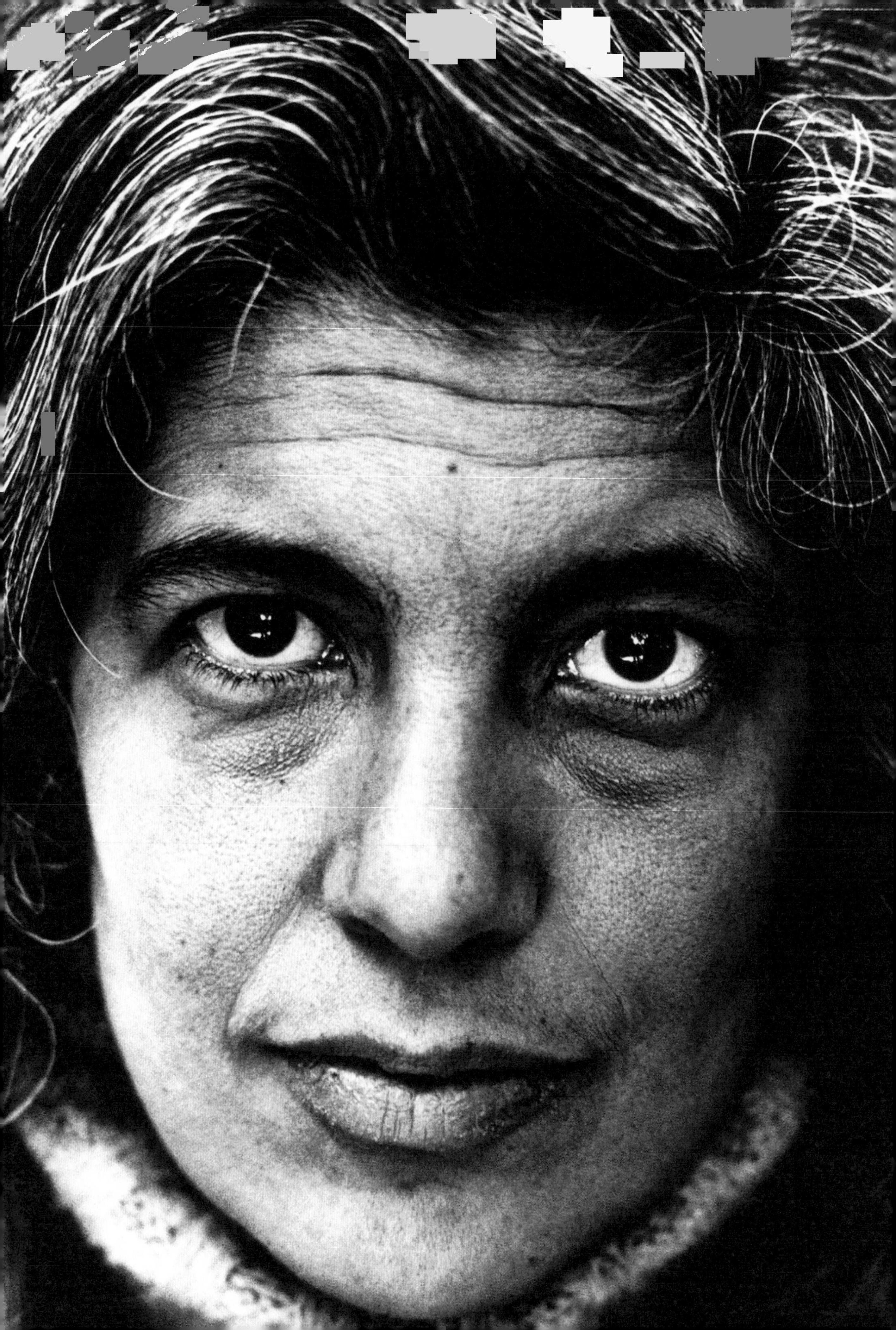

List No. 021

RULES OF PARENTING

SUSAN SONTAG
September 1959

Susan Sontag was one of the most important intellectuals of the last century, a critical essayist and celebrated author whose work never failed to stimulate debate. In September 1952, at nineteen years of age, she had her first and only child, David, with her husband, Philip Rieff. Her son went on to edit his mother's journals after her death in 2004. On a page of one of those journals can be found this list of parenting rules, written by Sontag seven years after she gave birth.

1. Be consistent.

2. Don't speak about him to others (e.g., tell funny things) in his presence. (Don't make him self-conscious.)

3. Don't praise him for something I wouldn't always accept as good.

4. Don't reprimand him harshly for something he's been allowed to do.

5. Daily routine: eating, homework, bath, teeth, room, story, bed.

6. Don't allow him to monopolize me when I am with other people.

7. Always speak well of his pop. (No faces, sighs, impatience, etc.)

8. Do not discourage childish fantasies.

9. Make him aware that there is a grown-up world that's none of his business.

10. Don't assume that what I don't like to do (bath, hairwash) he won't like either.

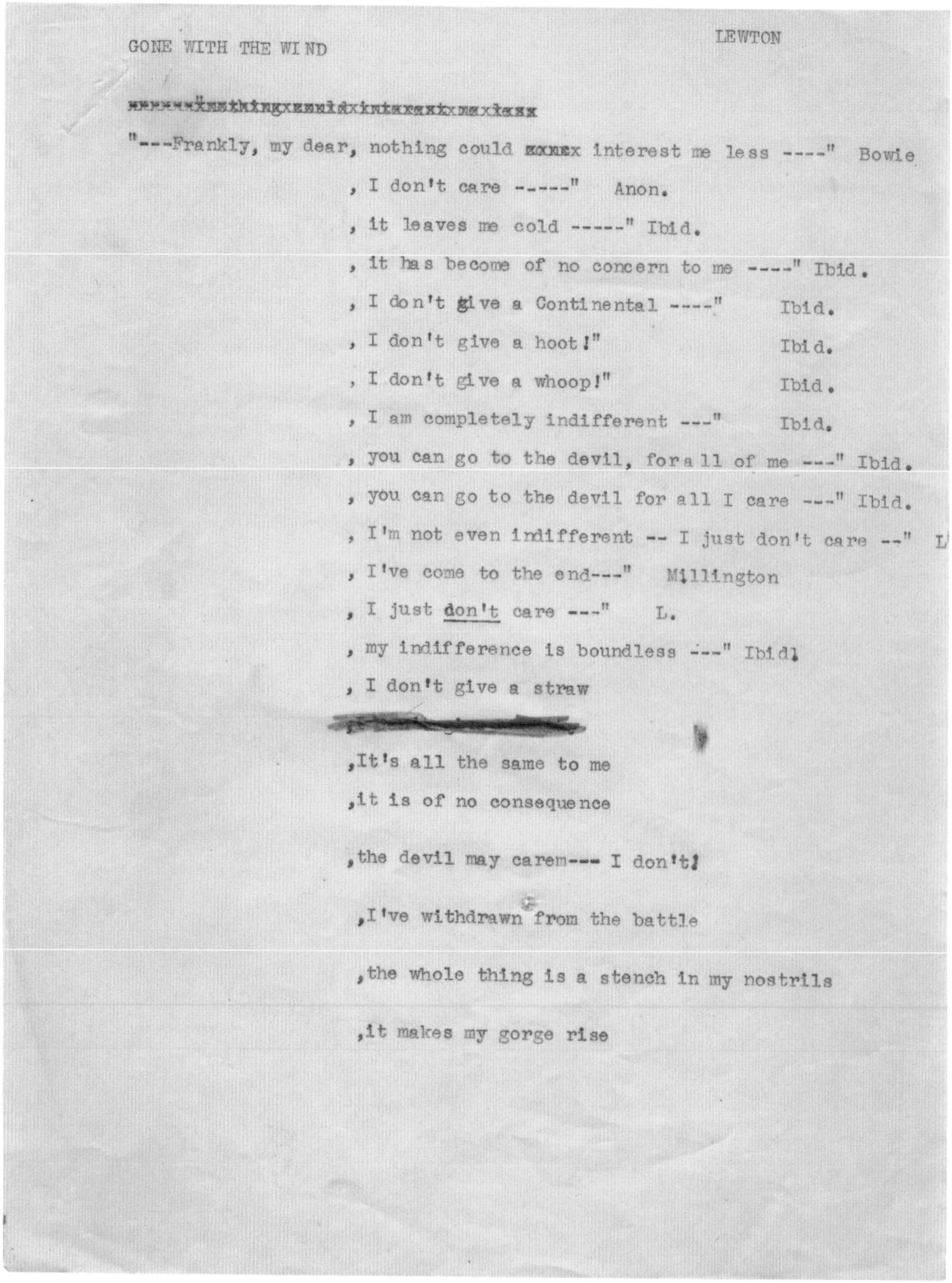

GONE WITH THE WIND LEWTON

~~xxxxxx"xnothingxcouldxinterestxmexless~~

"---Frankly, my dear, nothing could xxxxx interest me less ----" Bowie

, I don't care -----" Anon.

, it leaves me cold -----" Ibid.

, it has become of no concern to me ----" Ibid.

, I don't give a Continental ----" Ibid.

, I don't give a hoot!" Ibid.

, I don't give a whoop!" Ibid.

, I am completely indifferent ---" Ibid.

, you can go to the devil, forall of me ---" Ibid.

, you can go to the devil for all I care ---" Ibid.

, I'm not even indifferent -- I just don't care --" L

, I've come to the end---" Millington

, I just <u>don't</u> care ---" L.

, my indifference is boundless ---" Ibid.

, I don't give a straw

[redacted]

,It's all the same to me

,it is of no consequence

,the devil may carem--- I don't!

,I've withdrawn from the battle

,the whole thing is a stench in my nostrils

,it makes my gorge rise

FRANKLY, MY DEAR . . .

SELZNICK INTERNATIONAL PICTURES
1939

Few lines in cinema history are as famous as *Gone with the Wind*'s "Frankly, my dear, I don't give a damn"—a response given by Rhett Butler to Scarlett O'Hara's question, "Where shall I go? What shall I do?" In 2005, the American Film Institute named Rhett Butler's line the Greatest Movie Quote of All Time. But it could have been so different. Two months before the film's release, American censors deemed the word *damn* to be offensive and asked for it to be removed. The decision was reversed just weeks later due to a quick amendment to the Production Code by the board of the Motion Picture Association. Before that change was made, however, with the word *damn* temporarily banished, the film's producers prepared a list of alternatives.

List No. 023

DON SALTERO'S COFFEE HOUSE

DON SALTERO
Circa 1700

In 1695 a coffeehouse by the name of Don Saltero's opened at No. 18 Cheyne Walk in London's Chelsea. It drew crowds from far and wide, less for its refreshments than for the hundreds of intriguing objects and oddities that lined its walls, shelves, and ceiling. These "cabinets of curiosities" were curated by James Salter, the establishment's founder and formerly a servant to Sir Hans Sloane, and expanded upon a collection given to Salter by Sloane (the bulk of whose collection would become the British Museum). Souvenirs from all corners of the globe filled the coffeehouse; and these artifacts surely captured the attention of all who entered. On crossing the threshold of Don Saltero's, visitors were handed a copy of *A Catalogue of the Rarities to be Seen at Don Saltero's Coffee-House in Chelsea*, a guide book of which forty editions were printed over the years, all containing lists of eclectic objects such as this one.

On the Wainscot round the Room, beginning on the Piers between the Windows.

1 A Soland goose from the north of Scotland
2 A fine large hawk
3 A piece of the sugar cane, 8 feet long
4 A curious hydrometer, or weather gage
5 The bill and craw of a pelican
6 A curious skin of a snake, six feet and a half long
7 The claws of a lobster of a surprising largeness
8 A sea fan
9 Sea weeds
10 A maucauco from the East-Indies
11 The foal of a Zebra African wild ass
12 The skeleton of a cat
13 A Chinese idol
14 The pizzle of a whale
15 The head and paws of a Greenland bear
16 A sheet of paper made of silk, 12 feet long, 4 feet and a half wide, from China
17 A string of large Romish beads
18 A petrified child
19 A Guiney deer
20 A wooden shoe that was put under the speaker's chair in the reign of K. James II.
21 The King of Widdaw's staff
22 The ear of an elephant
23 Pipes found in Gloucester
24 A print of the fly cap monkey
25 Ditto of a fine lizard, coloured from the life
26 Ditto of the dead warrant for the beheading of King Charles the First
27 Ditto of a flying squirrel, coloured from the life
28 Ditto of the Brasilian pye, or toucan, coloured from life
29 A sea horse's pizzle, of which cramp rings are made
30 A large otter
31 A surprising horn of an urus, or buffaloe
*31 The cobler's awl, plover
32 A fine horned owl
33 A Chinese pheasant
*34 Chinese instrument of wind music made of reeds
34 Two fine mussel shells, 2 foot long, from Portmahon
35 The rhinoceros's horn
36 The model of a mill with an overshot wheel, which works with sand (as the large ones do by water) most curiously contrived, and made in a bottle: the stopper of the bottle is most wonderfully contrived in being fastened in the inside of the bottle with cross bars and spring bolts, with various things hanging to each end of every bolt, and yet so tight as not to admit of one grain of sand to escape.

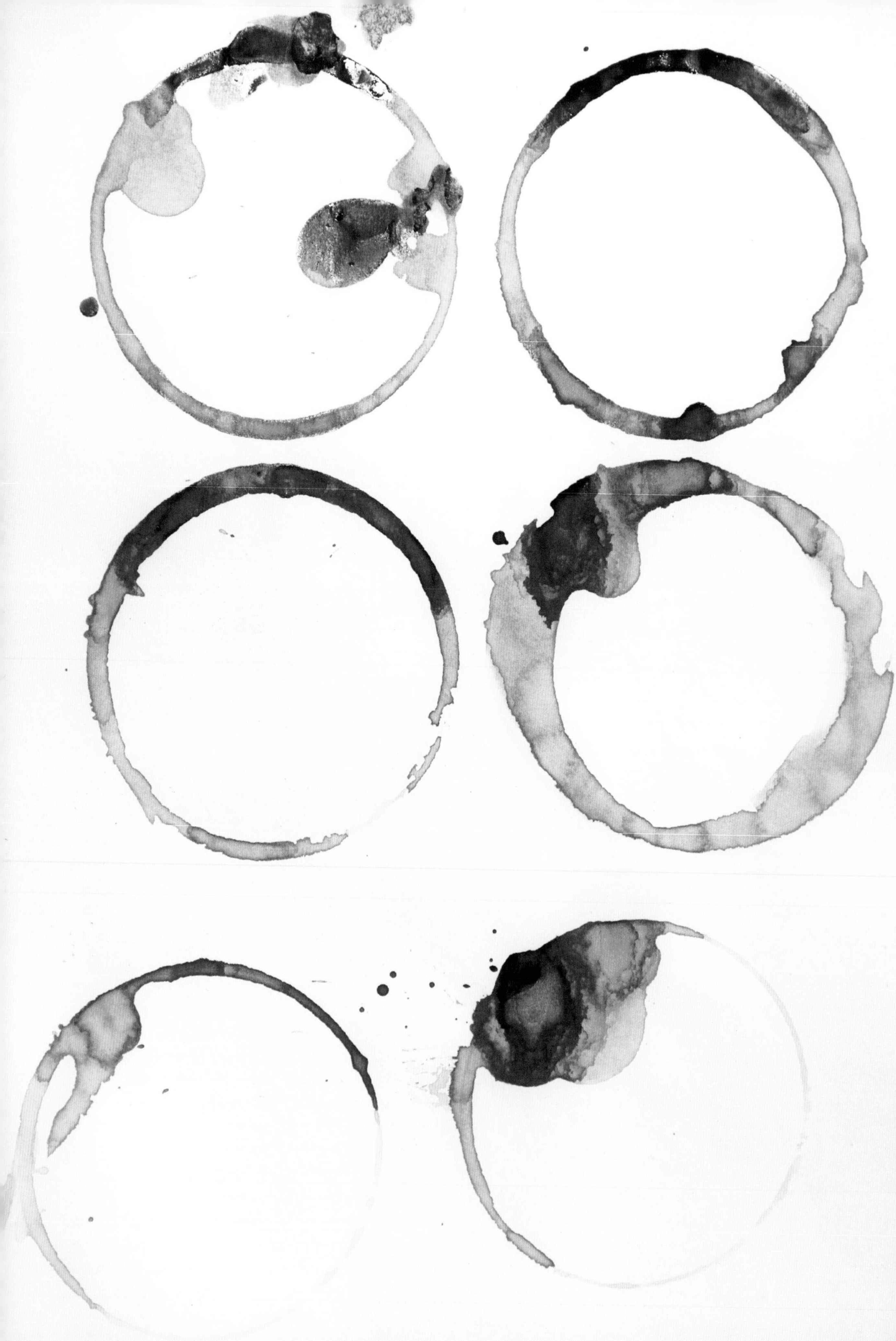

37 The horns of a West-India stag
38 A Spanish apparatus, or belt to prevent cuckoldom, commonly called a Spanish padlock
39 A Romish bishop's crosier
40 The horn of a sea unicorn, 7 foot and a half long
41 A friar's discipline
42 A Staffordshire almanack, in use when the Danes were in England
43 A coffin of slate for a friar's bones, finely carved all over
44 A joint of the back bone of a whale
45 An iron bolt, shot red-hot at fort William by the rebels, 1745
46 The paws of a Russian bear
47 A large star fish
48 The paws of a seal
49 A piece of the keel of a ship eat by the worms
50 The head of a manatee, or sea-cow
51 The lance of Tow-How Sham, king of the Darien Indians, with which he killed six Spaniards, and took a tooth out of each head, and put it in his spear as a trophy of victory
52 The skin of a snake, ten feet and a half long, an excellent hydrometer
53 The foot of an elk
54 The head and tusks of a moss or sea lion
55 The head of a roe-buck from Scotland
56 The fin of a shark
57 A chopchin with which the Chinese cut their gold sympum, or Chinese board
58 A soull cap found in the hat of a French officer, when taken at the battle of Dettingen
*58 The grinder of an elephant
59 The tooth of a whale
60 Bastinadoe from China
61 An Indian sword of war, always left in the field of battle by the conqueror
62 An Indian leaf of the tree palmeta, used by the natives as a fan
63 An almanack for a blind man
64 A Moco fan
65 The head and horns of an antelope
66 The belt and pouches, shoe, and other ornaments of Tow How-Sham, king of the Darien Indians
67 A pair of Tartar lady's shoes
68 The coronation-shoes of King William III.
69 A pair of Tripoly stockings
70 A Turkish quiver for arrows
*71 A curious brass Cremona violin
71 A pair of maucasons or shoes from Hudson's Bay
72 A shirt of mail wore by the knights templars
73 A Chinese stocking
74 Queen Elizabeth's stirrup
75 A Chinese boot
76 The jaws of a shark with 280 teeth
77 A scaly coat of mail
78 A pair of Turkish women's shoes
79 A pair of Chinese women's shoes
80 Q. Catherine's wedding shoes, q. of Charles II.
81 A pair of Turkish men's shoes

82 A Turkish slipper
83 A pair of Chinese men's shoes
84 A pair of Spanish lady's shoes
85 A pair of brashalls to play at ballon, a game used in Italy
86 A curious wooden fan
87 A curious model of a church
88 A print of the maucauco, with some weeds from the gulph of Florida
89 The Lord's Prayer, the Creed, the ten Commandments, the prayers for the king and the royal family, and the 21st psalm; all wrote in the bust of king George
90 A very curious triform picture of king Charles I. and his two sons
91 A dried cat
92 A Turkish bow
93 The root of a tree in the shape of a hog
94 The head of a badger
95 The saw of a saw fish
96 King Henry the Eighth's coat of mail
97 A pair of gauntlets
98 Knives of the Cannibal Indians
99 An Indian bow and arrows
100 Two javelins
101 A Negro boy's cap made of rats skins
102 Snow shoes
103 A Chinese waistcoat, to prevent sweating
104 A Scots Highlander's target
105 A coat made of the bark of a tree
106 A whip from Archangel
107 A Mailay's hat
108 Queen Elizabeth's chambermaid's hat
109 The target of Tee-Yee-Neen-Ho-Ga-Row, Indian emperor of the Six Nations
110 Queen Elizabeth's work-basket
111 A Bohemian hat
112 A curious print, that changes, viz. from a man to a woman
113 A moving picture of Hudibras and the conjurer
114 Ditto of the bottle-conjurer
115 Ditto of a bashful widow
116 Two young tarapins, or land turtles
117 Two fine large ostrich-eggs
118 The shell sun fish
119 The egg of an ostrich, curiously carved
120 The star-fish
121 A bucaneer's staff
122 A Barbary spur
123 King Henry the Eighth's spurs
124 A print of the scarlet manakin from Surinam, coloured from life
125 Two Madagascar lances
126 An Indian bow
127 A Turkish pistol
128 A pistol with four barrels, taken from the French at the siege of Namur
129 Four Indian arrows, extraordinarily bearded
130 Two ancient broad arrows of Robin Hood
131 Two small poisoned arrows with bearded points
132 Oliver Cromwel's broad sword

133 A Spanish spadoe
134 King James's coronation sword
135 King William's ditto
136 A Scots dusk
137 Two poisoned daggers of great antiquity
138 A Mallay's Creese
139 A travelling clock, which is thirty-six hours going down. N. B. In common clocks the hand goes round, and the dial keeps its place; but in this the dial goes round and the hand keeps its direction
140 A spur of state from Mexico, taken in the Acapulco ship by admiral Anson
141 The flaming sword of William the Conqueror
142 A print of the Zebra, or African wild ass, coloured from life
143 A starved cat found between the walls of Westminster-abbey when repairing
144 The horns of an antelope
145 A fine large tarapin, or land-turtle
146 An antique chissel
147 A fine East-India bow and arrows, the arrows headed with poison, to shoot birds with
148 An Indian tomohawk, taken in the field of battle before Quebec
149 Fine lace imitated in paper
150 The head of the rhinoceros bird
151 The head of the spatula bird
152 The tooth of a sea-horse

NURSERY RHYME VIOLENCE

GEOFFREY HANDLEY-TAYLOR
1952

In 1952, having analyzed two hundred traditional nursery rhymes, British writer Geoffrey Handley-Taylor concluded in his book *A Selected Bibliography of Literature Relating to Nursery Rhyme Reform* that approximately half of those rhymes personified "all that is glorious and ideal for the child," but that the "remaining 100 rhymes harbour unsavoury elements." He then illustrated the latter point by way of this list, in which he tallied all instances of violence found in said nursery rhymes.

8 allusions to murder (unclassified)
2 cases of choking to death
1 case of death by devouring
1 case of cutting a human being in half
1 case of decapitation
1 case of death by squeezing
1 case of death by shriveling
1 case of death by starvation
1 case of boiling to death
1 case of death by hanging
1 case of death by drowning
4 cases of killing domestic animals
1 case of body snatching
21 cases of death (unclassified)
7 cases relating to the severing of limbs
1 case of the desire to have a limb severed
2 cases of self-inflicted injury
4 cases relating to the breaking of limbs
1 allusion to a bleeding heart
1 case of devouring human flesh
5 threats of death
1 case of kidnapping
12 cases of torment and cruelty to human beings and animals
8 cases of whipping and lashing
3 allusions to blood
14 cases of stealing and general dishonesty
15 allusions to maimed human beings and animals
1 allusion to undertakers
2 allusions to graves
23 cases of physical violence (unclassified)
1 case of lunacy
16 allusions to misery and sorrow
1 case of drunkenness
4 cases of cursing
1 allusion to marriage as a form of death
1 case of scorning the blind
1 case of scorning prayer
9 cases of children being lost or abandoned
2 cases of house burning
9 allusions to poverty and want
5 allusions to quarreling
2 cases of unlawful imprisonment
2 cases of racial discrimination

RACKHAM.

GIURO DI ESSERE FEDELE "A COSA NOSTRA" SE DOVESSI TRADIRE LE MIE CARNI DEVONO BRUCIARE -- COME BRUCIA QUESTA IMMAGINE.

DIVIETI E DOVERI.

NON CI SI PUO' PRESENTARE DA SOLI AD UN'ALTRO AMICO NOSTRO - SE NON E' UN TERZO A FARLO.

NON SI GUARDANO MOGLI DI AMICI NOSTRI.

NON SI FANNO COMPARATI CON GLI SBIRRI.

NON SI FREQUENTANO NE'TAVERNE E NE'CIRCOLI.

SI E' IL DOVERE IN QUALSIASI MOMENTO DI ESSERE DISPONIBILE A COSA NOSTRA.ANCHE SE CE LA MOGLIE CHE STA PER PARTORIRE.

SI RISPETTANO IN MANIERA CATEGORICA GLI APPUNTAMENTI.

SI CI DEVE PORTARE RISPETTO ALLA MOGLIE.

QUANDO SI E' CHIAMATI A SAPERE QUALCOSA SI DOVRA' DIRE LA VERITA'.

NON CI SI PUO' APPROPRIARE DI SOLDI CHE SONO DI ALTRI E DI ALTRE FAMIGLIE.

CHI NON PUO' ENTRARE A FAR PARTE DI COSA NOSTRA.

CHI HA UN PARENTE STRETTO NELLE VARIE FORZE DELL'ORDINE.

CHI HA TRADIMENTI SENTIMENTALI IN FAMIGLIA.

CHI HA UN COMPORTAMENTO PESSIMO - E CHE NON TIENE AI VALORI MORALI.

THE MAFIA DECALOGUE

THE MAFIA
Date Unknown

Salvatore Lo Piccolo was on the run for twenty-four years. When finally arrested in 2007, he was, it is believed, head of the Sicilian Mafia, the world's most famous criminal organization and his "family" for decades. As with most families, the Mafia has rules. However, it wasn't until after Lo Piccolo's capture that Italian police discovered in his hideout a document now known as the "Mafia Decalogue," and these rules were unveiled for the world to see. Here is a translation of the *Divieti e Doveri* of the Cosa Nostra.

I SWEAR TO BE FAITHFUL TO THE COSA NOSTRA. IF I BETRAY MY FLESH MUST BURN — AS THIS IMAGE BURNS.

RIGHTS AND DUTIES

NO ONE CAN PRESENT HIMSELF DIRECTLY TO ANOTHER OF OUR FRIENDS. THERE MUST BE A THIRD PERSON TO DO IT.

NEVER LOOK AT THE WIVES OF FRIENDS.

NEVER BE SEEN WITH COPS.

DON'T GO TO PUBS AND CLUBS.

ALWAYS BEING AVAILABLE FOR COSA NOSTRA IS A DUTY — EVEN IF YOUR WIFE IS ABOUT TO GIVE BIRTH.

APPOINTMENTS MUST ABSOLUTELY BE RESPECTED.

WIVES MUST BE TREATED WITH RESPECT.

WHEN ASKED FOR ANY INFORMATION THE ANSWER MUST BE THE TRUTH.

MONEY CANNOT BE APPROPRIATED IF IT BELONGS TO OTHERS OR TO OTHER FAMILIES.

INDIVIDUALS WHO CANNOT BE PART OF THE COSA NOSTRA

ANYONE WHO HAS A CLOSE RELATIVE IN THE POLICE.
ANYONE WITH A TWO-TIMING RELATIVE IN THE FAMILY.
ANYONE WHO BEHAVES BADLY AND DOESN'T HOLD TO MORAL VALUES

Walt Disney PICTURES

INTER-OFFICE COMMUNICATION

P411B

TO ANIMATION DEPARTMENT DATE February 13, 1986

FROM Peter Schneider EXT. 2630 SUBJECT

Along with the new title for "Basil of Baker Street" it has been decided to re-name the entire library of animated classics. The new titles are as follows...

"SEVEN LITTLE MEN HELP A GIRL"

"THE WOODEN BOY WHO BECAME REAL"

"COLOR AND MUSIC"

"THE WONDERFUL ELEPHANT WHO COULD REALLY FLY"

"THE LITTLE DEER WHO GREW UP"

"THE GIRL WITH THE SEE-THROUGH SHOES"

"THE GIRL IN THE IMAGINARY WORLD"

"THE AMAZING FLYING CHILDREN"

"TWO DOGS FALL IN LOVE"

"THE GIRL WHO SEEMED TO DIE"

"PUPPIES TAKEN AWAY"

"THE BOY WHO WOULD BE KING"

"A BOY, A BEAR AND A BIG BLACK CAT"

"ARISTOCATS"

"ROBIN HOOD WITH ANIMALS"

"TWO MICE SAVE A GIRL"

"A FOX AND A HOUND ARE FRIENDS"

"THE EVIL BONEHEAD"

And of course our latest classic destined to win the hearts of the american public...

"THE GREAT MOUSE DETECTIVE"

SEVEN LITTLE MEN HELP A GIRL

ED GOMBERT

February 13, 1986

When, in early 1986, Disney executives decided to change the title of their upcoming animated feature from *Basil of Baker Street* to the more self-explanatory *The Great Mouse Detective*, its production team was less than pleased. One animator in particular, Ed Gombert, harnessed his displeasure to comical effect by creating, and circulating, this fake memo purportedly from then head of department, Peter Schneider. On it, a list of Disney's back catalog, renamed in a similarly bland style. The list was so popular that it soon reached a very unimpressed Jeffrey Katzenberg, then CEO of Disney, who, after questioning an entirely innocent Schneider, tried and failed to uncover the identity of its creator. To make matters worse, a copy then found its way to the *LA Times*. To Disney's dismay the movie's name was suddenly on everyone's lips, albeit for the wrong reasons.

For Characters Who Don't Dig Jive Talk:

A Really In There Solid Chick	An Attractive Young Girl
A Shape In A Drape	Looks Good In Clothes
Ball All Night	An All Night Party
Bring Him	Embarrass Him
Cat	A Jive Fan
Clipster	A Confidence Man
Cut on Down, Cut Out	To Leave
Dig Those Mellow Kicks	Knows How To Live
Dig What I'm Puttin' Down	Pay Attention
Drifter	Floater
Fall In On That Mess	Play That Thing
Fall On Down	Meander
Freakish High	To Get High As A Kite
Get Straight	Work It Out, Make A Deal
Good For Nothin' Mop	No Good Woman
Groovy Little Stash	Cozy Spot
Hipsters	Characters Who Like Hot Jazz
Hold Back The Dawn	Go On This Way Forever
Hype You For Your Gold	Take You For The Bank Roll
I'm Hippn' You Man	Putting You Wise
Joint Is Jumpin'	Place Full Of Customers
Juices	Liquor
Layin' It On You Straight	Telling You The Truth
Like A Motherless Child	Sedate
Lush Yourself To All Ends	Get Very Drunk
Out Of The World Mellow Stage	To Get Ecstatically Drunk
Pitch A Ball	Have A Good Time
Really In There	Knows The Answers
Same Beat Groove	Bored
A Square	Cornfed
Solid Blew My Top	Went Crazy
Solid Give Me My Kicks	Had Lots of Fun
Solid Stud	Influential man in the entertainment field
His Story is Great	A Successful Man About Town
Take It Slow	Be Careful
Your Stickin'	Flush, Carrying A Bankroll

Made in U. S. A.

FOR CHARACTERS WHO DON'T DIG JIVE TALK

HARRY GIBSON

1944

New York pianist Harry Gibson (1915–1991) was something of an anomaly: an eccentric and frantic musician, he wowed audiences in the jazz clubs of Manhattan with his musical energy, before evolving into a rock and roller in later years. His constant use of jive talk stemmed from his years growing up near Harlem. The list seen here—a beginner's guide to his dialect of choice—was printed on the inside cover of his album *Boogie Woogie in Blue*, released in 1944, the same year he coined the word *hipster*.

List No. 028

EINSTEIN'S DEMANDS

ALBERT EINSTEIN
1914

By 1914, theoretical physicist Albert Einstein's marriage to his wife of eleven years, Mileva Marić, whom he had met as a fellow student at Zurich Polytechnic, was fast deteriorating. Realizing there was no hope for their relationship on a romantic level, Einstein proposed that they remain together for the sake of their two young sons, Hans Albert and Eduard, but only if she agreed to the following list of conditions. Mileva accepted the conditions, but to no avail. A few months later she left her husband in Berlin and moved, with their two boys, back to Zurich. After living apart for five years, they divorced in 1919. That same year, Einstein married his cousin Elsa Löwenthal. Mileva Marić would never remarry.

Conditions.

A. You will make sure
1. that my clothes and laundry are kept in good order;
2. that I will receive my three meals regularly *in my room*;
3. that my bedroom and study are kept neat, and especially that my desk is left for *my use only*.

B. You will renounce all personal relations with me insofar as they are not completely necessary for social reasons. Specifically, you will forego
1. my sitting at home with you;
2. my going out or traveling with you.

C. You will obey the following points in your relations with me:
1. you will not expect any intimacy from me, nor will you reproach me in any way;
2. you will stop talking to me if I request it;
3. you will leave my bedroom or study immediately without protest if I request it.

D. You will undertake not to belittle me in front of our children, either through words or behavior.

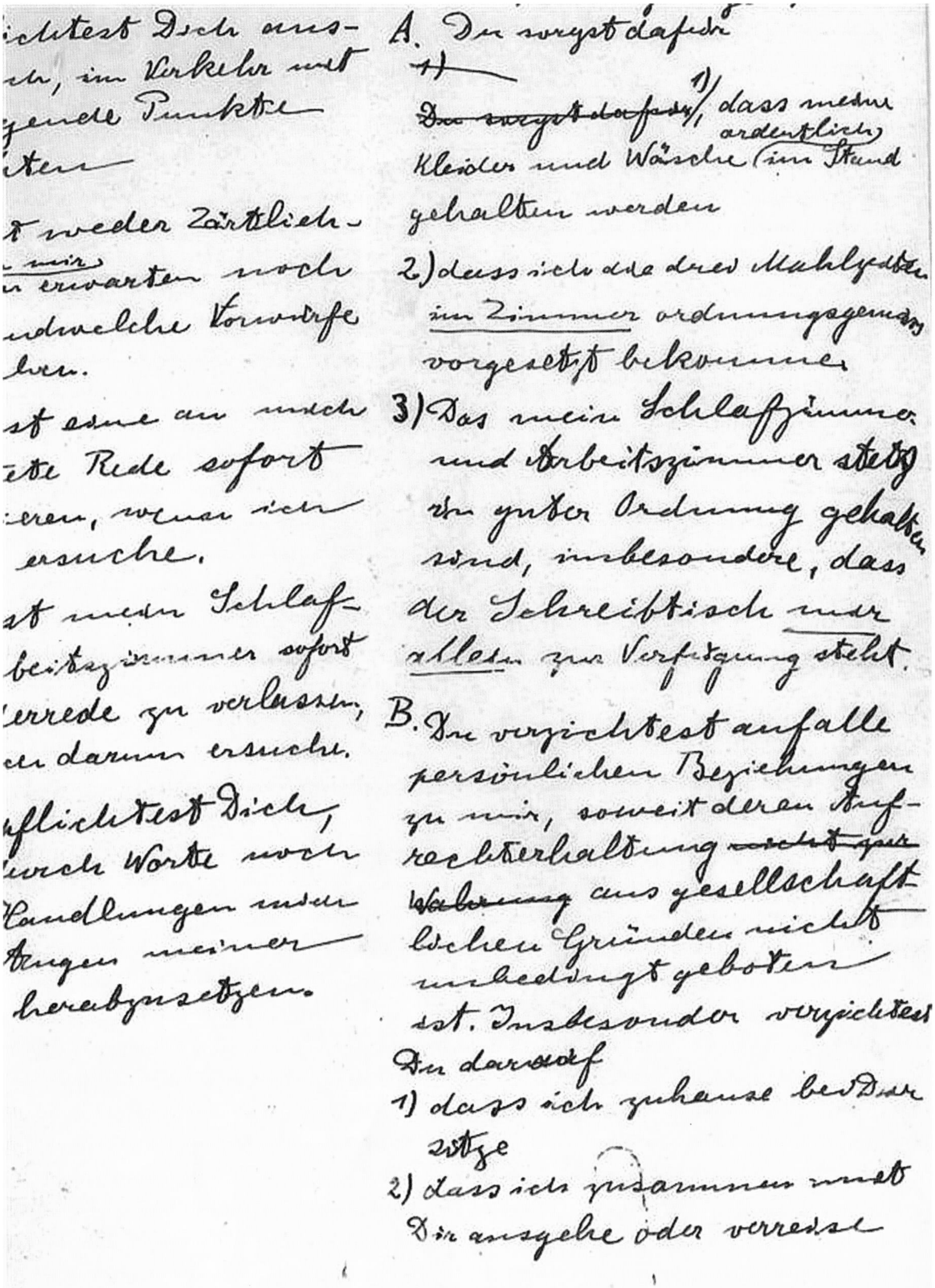

…ichtest Dich aus-
…ch, im Verkehr mit
…gende Punkte
…lten
…t weder Zärtlich-
…n mir erwarten noch
…ndwelche Vorwürfe
…chen.
…st eine an mich
…tete Rede sofort
…eren, wenn ich
… ersuche.
…st mein Schlaf-
…beitszimmer sofort
…erredе zu verlassen,
…ich darum ersuche.
…pflichtest Dich,
…durch Worte noch
…Handlungen in den
…Augen meiner
…herabzusetzen.

A. Du sorgst dafür
~~1)~~
~~Du sorgst dafür~~ 1) dass meine Kleider und Wäsche ordentlich im Stand gehalten werden
2) dass ich die drei Mahlzeiten im Zimmer ordnungsgemäss vorgesetzt bekomme.
3) Dass mein Schlafzimmer und Arbeitszimmer stets in guter Ordnung gehalten sind, insbesondere, dass der Schreibtisch mir allein zur Verfügung steht.
B. Du verzichtest auf alle persönlichen Beziehungen zu mir, soweit deren Aufrechterhaltung ~~nicht zur Wahrung~~ aus gesellschaftlichen Gründen nicht unbedingt geboten ist. Insbesondere verzichtest Du darauf
1) dass ich zuhause bei Dir sitze
2) dass ich zusammen mit Dir ausgehe oder verreise

Ecole Des 3 Gourmandes

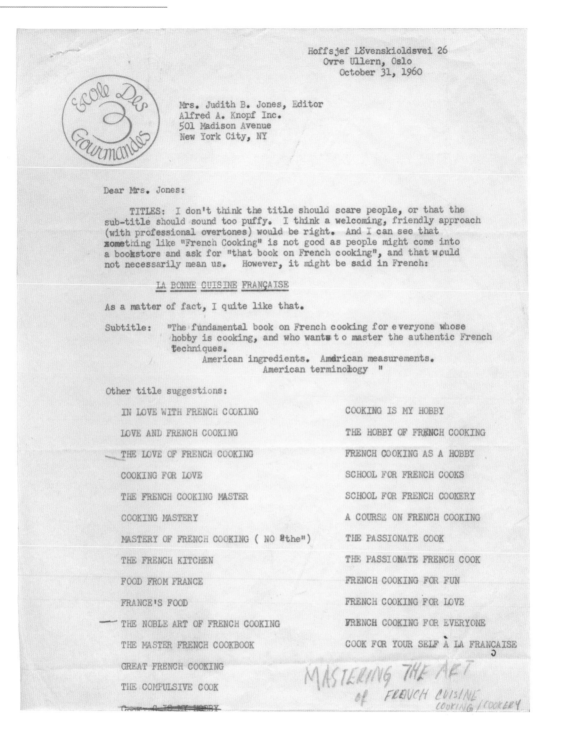

Hoffsjef Lövenskioldsvei 26
Ovre Ullern, Oslo
October 31, 1960

Mrs. Judith B. Jones, Editor
Alfred A. Knopf Inc.
501 Madison Avenue
New York City, NY

Dear Mrs. Jones:

TITLES: I don't think the title should scare people, or that the sub-title should sound too puffy. I think a welcoming, friendly approach (with professional overtones) would be right. And I can see that something like "French Cooking" is not good as people might come into a bookstore and ask for "that book on French cooking", and that would not necessarily mean us. However, it might be said in French:

<u>LA BONNE CUISINE FRANÇAISE</u>

As a matter of fact, I quite like that.

Subtitle: "The fundamental book on French cooking for everyone whose hobby is cooking, and who wants to master the authentic French techniques.
American ingredients. American measurements.
American terminology "

Other title suggestions:

IN LOVE WITH FRENCH COOKING	COOKING IS MY HOBBY
LOVE AND FRENCH COOKING	THE HOBBY OF FRENCH COOKING
— THE LOVE OF FRENCH COOKING	FRENCH COOKING AS A HOBBY
COOKING FOR LOVE	SCHOOL FOR FRENCH COOKS
THE FRENCH COOKING MASTER	SCHOOL FOR FRENCH COOKERY
COOKING MASTERY	A COURSE ON FRENCH COOKING
MASTERY OF FRENCH COOKING (NO "the")	THE PASSIONATE COOK
THE FRENCH KITCHEN	THE PASSIONATE FRENCH COOK
FOOD FROM FRANCE	FRENCH COOKING FOR FUN
FRANCE'S FOOD	FRENCH COOKING FOR LOVE
— THE NOBLE ART OF FRENCH COOKING	FRENCH COOKING FOR EVERYONE
THE MASTER FRENCH COOKBOOK	COOK FOR YOUR SELF À LA FRANÇAISE
GREAT FRENCH COOKING	MASTERING THE ART of FRENCH CUISINE COOKING / COOKERY
THE COMPULSIVE COOK	
~~COOKING IS MY HOBBY~~	

MASTERING THE ART OF FRENCH COOKING

JULIA CHILD
October 31, 1960

As the author of more than a dozen best-selling cookbooks and the host of numerous successful television cooking shows, Julia Child was responsible for inspiring millions of Americans to be more creative in the kitchen. It was her first book, however, that made the biggest impact. Published in 1961 to rave reviews, its strong sales continue to this day. The prior fall, Julia Child wrote her editor at Knopf with a list of potential titles for her debut. Judith Jones tells the story that when the title *Mastering the Art of French Cooking* was eventually chosen and she presented it to Alfred Knopf himself, he said, "Mrs. Jones, you can't have a title with a gerund in it! That's ridiculous. If this book sells with that title, I'll eat my hat."

List No. 030

ROLL OF MISSING MEN

CLARA BARTON
1865

As she worked tirelessly to care for soldiers and provide those at the frontline with medical supplies during the American Civil War, volunteer Clara Barton (1821–1912) became known as the "Angel of the Battlefield" for her good deeds, which continued as the war came to an end. Requesting permission from Abraham Lincoln, she set up the Office of Correspondence with the Friends of the Missing Men of the United States Army, through which she and a small staff replied to the thousands of frantic, unanswered letters from those awaiting word on their absent loved ones. Before long, with no such system already in place, Barton drew up a list of missing persons and had it printed in newspapers all over the country. The list seen here, accompanied by a letter from Barton, reproduced to the right, was the first; many more followed.

A few years later, Clara Barton founded the American Red Cross.

WASHINGTON, D. C., *June* 1, 1865.

Soldiers and Brothers:

Please examine this Roll; and if you know what became of any man here named, or have facts of interest to surviving friends, communicate the same to me by letter, as soon as possible, with your address in full.

If any one sees his own name, or that of a comrade whom he *knows* to be living, please inform me, that it may be withheld from future rolls.

Letters of inquiry for missing soldiers may be brief—should contain the name, regiment, company, and State to which they belonged, with the full address of the writer, plainly written.

Attention will no longer be confined to those who have been prisoners, but an effort will be made to ascertain the fate of *all* missing men of the United States army during the war.

If any letter of inquiry fails to receive an answer, please write again. No apologies are necessary, and no letter will be neglected.

CLARA BARTON

Address—
Miss Clara Barton,
Washington, D. C.

Please paste in a safe and conspicuous place.

ROLL OF MISSING

TO RETURNED SOLDIERS AND OTHERS.

WASHINGTON, D. C., *June* 1, 1865.

SOLDIERS AND BROTHERS:

Please examine this Roll; and if you know what became of any man here named, or have facts of interest to surviving friends, communicate the same to me by letter, as soon as possible, with your address in full.

If any one sees his own name, or that of a comrade whom he *knows* to be living, please inform me, that it may be withheld from future rolls.

Letters of inquiry for missing soldiers may be brief—should contain the name, regiment, company, and State to which they belonged, with the full address of the writer, plainly written.

Attention will no longer be confined to those who have been prisoners, but an effort will be made to ascertain the fate of *all* missing men of the United States army during the war.

If any letter of inquiry fails to receive an answer, please write again. No apologies are necessary, and no letter will be neglected.

CLARA BARTON.

Address—
Miss CLARA BARTON,
Washington, D. C.

OFFICERS.

Andrews, E. E., col., surg. 68th U. S. inf.
Bennett, ——, capt., co. C, 210th Pa. inf.
Bingham, Leonard P., 1st lieut., co. G, 17th Vt.
Bullard, Stephen H., maj., co. —, — Mich. cav.
Butler, Frank, lieut., co. —, 51st N. Y. inf.
Caton, Milo, capt., co. H, 21st Ohio inf.
Chalmers, Hugh, 2d lt., co. E, 146th N. Y. inf.
Fish, George W., lieut., co. —, 3d Ohio inf.
Harlow, I. T., capt., co. —, 31st Me.
Harris, S. T., capt., co. —, 3d Tenn. cav.
Hunter, A. M., lt., co. —, 1st Tenn. (col.) art'y.
Hyde, Horace A., lieut., co. B, 1st Vt. cav.
Miller, Levis, capt., co. L, 6th Pa. cav.
Peirce, Garden L., lt., co. C., 112th N. Y. inf.
Saxton, Luther W., capt., co. A, 54th Ohio inf.
Sears, D. C., lieut., co. B, 94th N. Y. inf.
West, Charles H., jr., lt., co. C, 8th N. Y. H. A.
Wilder, George O., lieut., co. —, 15th Mass. inf.

REGULARS.

Corliss, Amos, 17th inf.
Chamberlin, Oscar D., co. F, 19th inf.
Cummings, John, co. F, 12th inf.
Corbin, Bloomer C., co. C, 16th inf.
Cisva, Samuel A., co. E, 11th inf.
Davis, Robert, co. A, 12th inf.
Fields, Charles F., co. A, 12th inf.
Farrar, Charles, co. A, 12th inf.
Tregaskis, Richard Alfred, co. B, 14th inf.
Heller, Daniel, co. —, 15th inf.
Lindsay, Herbert W. co. C, 12th inf.
Mitchell, John, co. G, 11th inf.
Martin, Seth, co. E, 16th inf.
McCord, George W., co. C, 14th inf.
O'Neill, John, co. A, 4th inf.
Patch, Frank T., co. G, 18th inf.
Seaton, Thomas M., co. G, 18th inf.
Tennison, John, co. E, 14th inf.
Vantarol, Rurel, co. —, 18th inf.
Wilson, Joseph, co. G, 14th inf.
Wickham, Horace, serg., co. F, 2d inf.
Young, Silas D., co. A, 19th inf.

Conrad, Peter S., co. —, 5th cav.
Dietrich, Peter, co. I, 6th cav.
Eisele, Henry, co. H, 6th cav.
Kane, Emmett, co. E, 1st cav.
Michelbach, Henry, co. G, 5th cav.
Olinger, Charles, co. M, 1st cav.

Clarence ——, co. D, 1st art.
Devlin, Robert, bat. B, 1st art.
Gould, Charles H., bat. D, 1st s. s.
Jenks, Melville, bat. D, 7th art.
Flamer, Jeremiah, co. B, 26th col. troops.

STATE OF MAINE.

Arnold, John S., co. C, 8th vol.
Bancroft, Columbus, co. D, 16th vol.
Burnell, Henry L., corp., co. I, 8th vol.
Chadbourn, Nathan, sergt., co. F, 32d vol.
Douglass, C. H., co. A, 17th vol.
Flanders, Lewis G., co. E, 20th vol.
Gilchrist, George, co. B or E, 31st vol.
Ham, John L., sergt., co. D, 32d vol.
Hutchins, Enos, co. E, 8th vol.
Hodges, Charles E., co. D, 11th vol.
Heald, Perham, co. A, 19th vol.
Johnson, Chas. W., corp., co. G, 32d vol.
Kench, Nelson H., co. E, 8th vol.
Williams, Luke B., co. H, 3d vol.
McCann, Alexander, co. C, 6th vol.
Norton, Joseph O., co. I, 19th vol.
Overlock, Alden, co. G, 8th vol.
Pitman, Eli, co. G, 31st vol.
Parker, Samuel D., co. E, 12th vol.
Stevens, James Orator, co. F, 19th vol.
Thomas, George W., co. C, 4th vol.
Turner, Chas. C., co. E, 4th vol.
Thayer, Adin B., co. B, 16th vol.
Taylor, John U., co. F., 32d vol.
Tuttle, Lewis, co. F, 32d vol.
Tuttle, Davis, co. F, 32d vol.
Vinal, Wester S., co. I, 19th vol.
Wills, Isaac T., co. B, 7th vol.
Worthing, Elmar W., co. K, 19th vol.
Young, Delance, co. C, 8th vol.
Hills, Andrew J., co. M, 20th cav.
Perkins, Thomas H., co. H, 1st cav.
Whitney, Thos. C., co. A, 1st cav.
Chadbourne, Albert, bat. E, 1st heavy art.
Stover, Alvin H. P., 1st bat.
Wentworth, Caleb, co. F, 32d vol.

STATE OF NEW HAMPSHIRE.

Ames, John G., co. F, 2d vol.
Berry, James, co. K, 9th vol.
Brennan, John, co. A, 13th vol.
Clarke, Chas. C., co. L, 1st cav.
Danforth, Charles B., co. —, 7th vol.
Gilman, George W., co. H, 9th vol.
Hayes, James W., co. H, 9th vol.
Haven, Benjamin F., co. K, 9th vol.
Johnson, Albert O., co. —, 5th vol.
Kingsbury, Harlan P., co. K, 9th vol.
Lowe, Leonard, co. I, 9th vol.
Lester, William G., co. G, 5th art.
Phelps, George M., co. G, 3d vol.
Parsons, William Henry, co. B, 11th vol.
Spaulding, Fernando C., co. K, 4th vol.
Smith, Nathaniel, co. G, 5th vol.
Smith, Walter W., co. K, 6th vol.
Vincent, Rupert, co. H, 3d vol.
Willey, Edward, co. I, 6th vol.

STATE OF VERMONT.

Aiken, William A., co. A, 11th vol.
Avery, Frederick B., co. C, 3d vol.
Ball, Loel, co. D, 4th vol.
Hunt, Bradbury A., co. K, 10th vol.
Bailey, Henry C., co. A, 5th vol.
Barber, William H., co. C, 11th vol.
Bishop, Emerson, co. E, 11th vol.
Chapin, H. C., co. F, 4th vol.
Cole, Felix G., co. A, 4th vol.
Camp, Henry, co. A, 4th vol.
Crow, Henry, co. C, 5th vol.
Cheever, Moses R., co. G, 4th vol.
Chamberlin, Converse P., co. A, 6th vol.
Conly, Frank, co. B, 5th vol.
Davis, Leander, co. K, 10th vol.
Downer, Russel L., co. B, 5th vol.
Elkins, Moses M., co. F, 11th vol.
Forrest, Silas, co. I, 3d vol.
Fairchild, G. L., co. A, 11th vol.
Gorham, Hiram I., co. I, 4th vol.
Gelo, Aiken, co. B, 3d vol.
Himes, George C., co. F, 10th vol.
Hosmer, Francis J., co. I, 4th vol.
Ingleston, William H., co. E, 6th vol.
Kendall, Wallace, co. A, 4th vol.
Lumsden, Calvin E., co. D, 4th vol.
Melcher, William, co. F, 9th vol.
Martindale, George W. H., co. L, 11th vol.
Phillips, William H., co. —, 12th vol.
Page, Edgar W., co. I, 4th vol.
Perry, Adolphus B., co. H, 4th vol.
Robbins, George, co. F, 11th vol.
Ryerson, William, co. F, 4th vol.
Reid, Norman B., co. H, 10th vol.
Richardson, Charles E., co. E, 2d vol.
Smith, Moses G., co. A, 4th vol.
Smith, Able B., co. D, 4th vol.
Scott, Royal O., co. F, 4th vol.
Stevens, Winthrop, co. F, 4th vol.
Slate, Henry W., co. D, 17th vol.
Sartwell, William E., co. L, 11th vol.
Stewart, Edwin W., co. A, 11th vol.
Scribner, Walter, co. G, 4th vol.
Smith, H. C., co. —, 9th vol.
Twiss, George S., co. F, 11th vol.
Tinkham, Clarence G., co. H, 11th vol.
Tucker, Milo, co. G, 9th vol.
Williams, Ezra G., co. G, 4th vol.
Wakefield, Joseph H., co. H, 4th vol.
Whitney, Varnum B., co. H, 1st heavy art.

Abbott, Horace M., co. D, 1st cav.
Blood, Frank J., co. K, 1st cav.
Badger, Alphonso H., co. D, 1st cav.
Butts, Harvey R., co. E, 1st cav.
Chamberlin, Wm. A., co. I, 1st cav.
Fay, Ramson Y., co. E, 1st cav.
Gilligan, Patrick C., co. D, 1st cav.
Hinds, Justin G., co. D, 1st cav.
Howard, David E., co. F, 1st cav.
Jenne, Harvey A., co. D, 1st cav.
Labonta, Henry, co. —, 1st cav.
Labonta, Lewis, co. D, 6th vol.
Morgan, Charles H., co. M, 11th cav.
Tupper, Hiram E., co. K, 1st cav.
Watson, William G., co. L, 1st cav.
Fleury, Allen S., battery K, 1st heavy art.
Hall, Charles C., battery A, 1st heavy art.
Keyes, Howard, battery K, 1st heavy art.
Kidder, Joseph, battery F, 11th heavy art.
Macomber, Orlando, battery K, 1st heavy art.
Willey, Chester S., battery A, 1st heavy art.
Bidwell, Emory S., co. B, 5th vol.
Wardner, Oel, co. B, 1st vol.

STATE OF MASSACHUSETTS.

Acker, Eldridge, co. E, 20th inf.
Ashworth, John, co. E, 1st inf.
Bartlett, Charles H., co. —, 15th inf.
Ball, Daniel E., co. C, 27th inf.
Bullen, Joseph W., co. C, 40th inf.
Bardwell, Orange, co. F, 37th inf.
Buffer, Elliot D., co. A, 34th inf.
Borniss, William H., co. H, 10th inf.
Bartlett, Will A., co. A, 27th inf.
Britt, Oscar C., co. C, 27th inf.
Chickering, Henry G., co. E, 34th inf.
Champney, Preston A., co. D, 25th inf.
Carroll, Robert, co. D, 34th inf.
Cooley, Milo H., co. F, 27th inf.
Carl, Robert, co. D, 34th inf.
Curtis, David B., co. G, 57th inf.
Dow, Albert W., co. K, 57th inf.
Dunn, James, co. A, 19th inf.
Dickerman, Charles C., co. D, 39th inf.
Elsbree, Frederick C., co. B, 7th inf.
Emmons, Chancey L., co. C, 27th inf.
Emerson, George O., co. B, 21st inf.
Elsbree, Frederick O., co. C, 7th inf.
Estee, Sidney, co. H, 27th inf.
Eddy, Lafayette, co. F, 34th inf.
Frost, Charles C., co. K, 18th inf.
Fellows, Joseph E., co. E, 15th inf.
Field, Edgar, co. F, 37th inf.
Frissell, Henry A., co. G, 15th inf.
Fuller, Herbert N., co. E, 15th inf.
Fitzpatrick, Michael, co. A, 25th inf.
Gould, Oscar Emory, co. E, 23d inf.
Greenough, Archibald, co. C, 24th inf.
Howard, William F., co. I, 57th inf.
Hubbard, Calvin, co. G, 36th inf.
Harbock, Horace P., 22d co. 2d sharp-shooters.
Hemenway, Elbert O., co. K, 39th inf.
Hurlburt, Charles H., co. C, 15th inf.
Jennisson, R. B., co. G, 36th inf.
Labombard, Peter, co. E, 57th inf.
Lucier, Raymond, co. F, 59th inf.
Lyman, Charles Austin, co. —, 27th inf.
Little, John, co. G, 20th inf.
Lacky, John, co. —, 19th inf.
Mahr, George W., co. E, 18th inf.
Mandell, A. S., co. H, 36th inf.
Moulten, H. Harrison, co. F, 15th inf.
McWilliams, William, co. D, 17th inf.
Martin, Edward, co. B, 56th inf.
Newcomb, Bryant, co. E, 32d inf.
Packard, Merrick E., co. C, 27th inf.
Plimpton, Emerson F., co. F, 56th inf.
Peckham, Henry Samuel, co. E, 59th inf.
Peckham, Anson P., co. —, 15th inf.
Phipps, Mahen M., co. C, 27th inf.
Richards, John Henry, co. —, 57th inf.
Roberts, James, co. I, 18th inf.
Ripley, Brigham S., co. C, 27th inf.
Roake, John M, co. D, 34th inf.
Smith, Henry, co. —, 15th inf.
Southwick, Josiah M, co. G, 18th inf.
Shaw, Charles S., co. C, 15th inf.
Stevens, Elbridge, co. A, 39th inf.
Morrison, J. T., co. C, 39th inf.
Sisson, Sauford A., co. D, 40th inf.
Swift, Perez, co. D, 40th inf.
Stuart, James A., co. H, 11th inf.
Sawyer, John, co. F, 33d inf.
Thurston, John A, co. E, 15th inf.
Vilbert, George L., co. H, 15th inf.
Wood, Myron R., co. E, 36th inf.
Woffenden, Samuel, co. C, 27th inf.
Woffenden, John William, co. C, 27th inf.
Wilder, Charles S., co. A, 21st inf.
Willington, George F., co. H, 15th inf.
Weatherell, Andrew M., co. C, 27th inf.

Barnes, Newman, co. M, 2d cav.
Clary, James W., co. G, 1st cav.
Davis, Thomas B., co. H, 1st cav.
Hunt, Jesse Edward, co. I, 2d cav.
Merrill, Perry O., co. —, 1st cav.
Raymond, Walter L., co. L, 1st cav.
Raymond, Frederick M, co. E, 1st cav.
Sanborn, George B., co. B, 2d cav.
Smith, Oliver A., co. —, 2d cav.
Vinton, Harvey L., co. G, 1st cav.
White, B. F., co. F, 1st cav.

Atwood, Charles H., co. G, 2d heavy art.
Brewer, John, co. D, 1st heavy art.
Chalk, Henry T., co. I, 1st heavy art.
Clark, Horace Lee, co. —, 2d heavy art.
Curtis, Francis C., co. E, 1st heavy art.
Dow, Henry A., co. E, 1st heavy art.
Davis, Corbin, co. E, 1st heavy art.
Davis, John E., co. E, 1st heavy art.
Miller, Lysander, co. G, 2d heavy art.
Redfield, Gleason Timothy, co. —, 10th bat.
Walton, Joseph H., co. F, 1st bat.
Perkins, Franklin, co. I, 1st bat.
Shirley, William H., co. I, 1st bat.
Ward, William, co. I, 1st bat.
Savage, Edward, co. E, 34th inf.

STATE OF RHODE ISLAND.

Delanah, Charles B., co. G, 1st cav.
Taylor, Herbert, co. I, 1st cav.
West, Hiram, co. A, 1st cav.
Dunlapp, George, co. E, 5th art.
Edwards, George H., bat. A, 3d light art.

STATE OF CONNECTICUT.

Besancon, Pierre, co. D, 14th inf.
Barriage, G. Deming, co. G, 16th inf.
Billings, Sanford M., co. —, 21st inf.
Crossley, Benjamin, co. G, 8th inf.
Clark, John S., co. D, 6th inf.
Converse, Joel T., co. D, 1[illegible]th inf.
Colburn, Jonathan S., co. [illegible], 18th inf.
Creighton, George, co. G, [illegible]6th inf.
Davis, I. Corbin, co. G, 18th inf.
Donison, George E., co. F, 16th inf.
Hamilton, H. Neff, co. B, 1[illegible]th inf.
Hintz, Henry, co. E, 16th inf.
Jackman, Calvin, co. B, 7th inf.
Lyon, Olins Levi, co. E, 12th inf.
Kinne, Martin V. B., co. G, 21st inf.
Moger, Auran J., co. I, 10th inf.
McNeil, Alexander, co. —, 14th inf.
Nichols, Michael, co. I, 7th inf.
Pratt, Albert G., co. G, 7th inf.
Quingley, Patrick, co. E, 7th inf.
Quingley, Edward H., co. B, 17th inf.
Richards, Charles I., co. A, 18th inf.
Sutliff, Elbert, co. K, 16th inf.
Upson, Charles A., co. C, 14th inf.
Walton, Bernard, co. —, 14th inf.
Walling, James, jr., co. E, [illegible]th inf.
Whitney, George F., co. I, 16th inf.
Whaley, Edward, co. B, 17th inf.
Wood, Charles H., co. D, 7th inf.

Adams, L. A., co. A, 1st cav.
Brown, Charles H., co. H, 1st cav.
Bolley, Orin T., co. —, 1st cav.
Crandall, Myron, H., co. L, 1st cav.
Canfield, Benjamin, co. I, 1st cav.
Greenough, Henry Waldo, co. D, 1st cav.
Olena, Rollin L., co. E, 1st cav.
Starkweather, Eugene W., co. L, 1st cav.
Tyler, L. E., co. —, 1st cav.
Weaver, John N., co. I, 1st cav.
Downs, Amasiah, co. K, 2d heavy art.
Fitzgerald, Matthew, co. E, 2d heavy art.

STATE OF NEW YORK.

Avery, John, co. D, 146th inf. vol.
Ambrose, Edward F., co. G, 108th inf.
Aiken, Wm., co. I, 147th inf.
Ashford, G. G., co. —, 146th inf.
Armstrong, Edgar G., co. C, 109th inf.
Amos, Robert, co. E, 47th inf.
Burke, Timothy, co. B, 97th inf.
Bigelow, L. R., co. —, 85th inf.
Burlingame, M. A., co. —, 97th inf.
Bennett, George A., co. G, 51st inf.
Bryant, L. A., co. —, 146th inf.
Ballard, Joseph, co. K, 147th inf.
Barger, Lowry, co. F, 154th inf.
Bolton, Noble, co. —, 111th inf.
Braner, Horatio, co. D, 152d inf.
Boyd, Duncan W., co. C, 124th inf.
Briggs, Miles, co. K, 90th inf.
Barny, George, co. —, 86th inf.
Bishop, Samuel H., co. A, 156th inf.
Barny, John, co. —, 85th inf.
Briggs, James E., co. B, 108th inf.
Barger, L. D., co. F, 154th inf.
Boynton, Thomas, co. C, 188th inf.
Burbanks, Jacob D., co. D, 85th inf.
Bush, J. W., co. E, 76th inf.
Bale, Joshua W., co. A, 76th inf.
Buffum, Lewis, serg., co. K, 100th inf.
Benton, D. L., co. B, 76th inf.
Brown, A. E., co. C, 152d inf.
Brown, George, co. A, 5th inf.
Bekon, James A., co. H, 90th inf.
Boucher, Milon, co. H, 86th inf.
Barr, ——, co. C, 140th inf.
Baker, William, co. C, 95th inf.
Bellwa, William, co. E, 140th inf.
Bulkley, Edwin A., co. E, 97th inf.
Barton, Jonathan, co. D, 118th inf.
Bannister, A. J., co. D, 64th inf.
Beals, Edward A., co. C, 85th inf.
Cushman, A. P., co. H, 100th inf.
Carter, Henry A. co. A, 179th inf.
Church, Delos, co. I, 72d vol.
Carter, Henry A., co. A, 179th inf.
Canfield, Aug. W., co. D, 86th inf.
Catford, James, co. H, 13th inf.
Carson, James, 1st serg., co. D, 140th inf.
Clay, Thomas, serg., co. H, 125th inf.
Curtis, Wm. H., co. I, 146th inf.
Campbell, Jno. F., co. A, 147th inf.
Conklin, Elijah D., corp., co. —, 120th inf.
Compton, Charles W., co. —, 121st inf.
Coon, Harvey, co. A, 90th inf.
Chidester, Albert, co. H, 109th inf.
Corwin, James C., co. C, 111th inf.
Coary, Dennis, co. A, 164th inf.
Coburn, Amasa, co. H, 106th inf.
Conklin, A. J., co. —, 120th inf.
Church, William P., co. C, 42d inf.
Clark, Oliver P., co. B, 94th inf.
Dermot, Peter, co. H, 146th inf.
Dumont, Peter L., serg., co. A, 146th inf.
Dyke, Albert, co. I, 85th inf.
Dalton, S. P., co. K., 22d inf.
Dimmick, Samuel S., co. K, 40th inf.
Durham, R. H., co. H, 123d inf.
Duff, James F., co. C, 146th inf.
Donnis, Henry G., co. D, 156th inf.
Duel, Myron A, co. E, 142d inf.
Dimmond, Frederick, co. E, 146th inf.
Duncan, David, co. K, 169th inf.
Devenhoff, I. Dorr, co. B, 121st inf.
Drake, George N. L., co. G, 121st inf.
Dillon, William H., co. B, 146th inf.
Denno, William, co. A, 98th inf.
Drayton, William, co. F, 51st inf.
Doughty, Edwin F., co. A, 48th inf.
Evans, Franklin, co. D, 140th inf.
Eldred, Addison M., co. E, 52d inf.
Eddy, John C., co. E, 112th inf.
Earl, William, co. —, 60th inf.
Farley, Thomas, co. K, 148th inf.
Fleegar, Henry, co. C., 47th inf.
Fish, Hosea, co. A, 179th inf.
Finch, Thomas B., 1st serg., co. C, 108th inf.
Forges, William, co. I, 40th inf.
Fralick, William, serg., co. I, 97th inf.
Fisher, H. C., co. —, 69th inf.
Fuller, Nelson T., co. E, 51st inf.
Forger, William, jr., co. —, 40th inf.
Farrar, Charles, co. A, 12th inf.
Fairfax, Charles, co. A, 111th inf.
Garner, Charles M., co. I, 97th inf.
Garrett, S. J., co. D, 146th inf.
Graves, S. G., co. H, 20th inf.
Graves, William T., co. H, 20th inf.
Graves, Robert T., co. F, 146th inf.
Goffe, John W., co. G, 146th inf.
Goodman, B. F., serg., co. B, 57th inf.
Gardner, Charles, co. I, 97th inf.
Hillis, Joseph, co. D, 167th inf.
Hart, William, co. B, 94th inf.
Horton, Nathan S., co. —, 49th inf.
Hecker, George, co. —, 40th inf.
Holley, Theodore W., co. —, 76th inf.
Hayes, John, co. K, 140th inf.
Hudson, William T., co. K, 85th inf.
Hudson, John A., co. A, 148th inf.
Hyer, Albert, co. A, 157th inf.
Haner, Stephen, serg., co. C, 109th inf.
Holloway, Jos. H., co. D, 146th inf.
Hadsall, Isaiah, co. B, 146th inf.
Hunter, William, co. E, 162d inf.
Holmes, Eugene S., co. K, 117th inf.
Hodges, Charles, co. G, 121st inf.
Hughes, George, ord. serg., co. C, 89th inf.
Henry, James, serg., co. I, 76th inf.
Hecker, George, co. —, 40th inf.
Hermans, F. C., co. A, 20th inf.
Hayward, S. S., co. C, 67th inf.
Haner, David, co. G, 134th inf.
Hyne, William, co. D, 140th inf.
Hudson, John, co. A, 148th inf.
Hugh, E. G., co. C, 140th inf.
Howard, John, co. H, 111th inf.
Howard, Leverett, 118th inf.
Howell, William H., corp., co. E, 124th inf.
Irish, E. W., 1st serg., co. C, 85th inf.
Johnson, James T, co. A, 104th inf.
Jones, David W., co. C, 115th inf.
Johnson, E. W., co. —, 50th eng.
Johnson, Thomas A., co. K, 179th inf.
Jones, Ezra C., co. E, 147th inf.
Johnston, William, co. —, 140th inf.
Jones, Daniel W., co. C, 115th inf.
Jones, George, co. —, 100th inf.
Jerome, James, co. F, 111th inf.
Kelley, Lutheran, co. —, 149th inf.
Kelley, Thomas, co. —, 59th inf.
Keating, Michael, co. A, 146th inf.
Keeler, Elijah K., co. C, 76th inf.
Knight, Arthur F., co. F, 117th inf.
Kessler, John A., co. B, 149th inf.
Kidder, William, co. H, 8th inf.
Keating, Thomas, co. L, 83d inf.
Lach, William, co. E, 100th inf.
Lynch, Joseph, co. A, 117th inf.
Leroy, Lineberg, co. —, 128th inf.
Lougee, John L., co. H, 159th inf.
Lansdell, Joseph, co. A, 95th inf.
Latham, Sylvester, co. I, 96th inf.
Lutton, Thomas, co. —, 95th inf.
Loll, Gaylor, co. C, 152d inf.
Lull, G. H., co. H, 152d inf.
La Boiteaux, Wm., co. D, 148th inf.
Miller, Samuel W., co. K, 131st inf.
McNeill, D. C., serg., co. E, 159th inf.
McPherson, Alex., co. G, 121st inf.
Madan, Wm. H., co. G, 162d inf.
Morey, Wm. D., co. F, 152d inf.
Mailer, James R., serg., co. B, 134th inf.
Mills, Jay J., co. E, 85th inf.
Marsh, Chas. R., co. E, 142d inf.
Maurice, Pigotte, co. K, 170th inf.
McCormick, John, serg., co. A, 162d vol.
Merrill, M. C., co. G, 118th vol.
McElroy, Wm., co. B, 121st vol.
Main, Wm. Oscar, co. A, 85th vol.
Merkle, Jos., co. A, 1st vol. Excel. brig.
Morgan, D. V. B., co. E, 93d vol.
McQuilkins, Thos., co. I, 1st vol.
May, Horace, co. D, 118th vol.
McMichael, James, co. H, 66th vol.
Murphy, Peter, co. K, 74th vol.
Martin, Albert G., co. B, 16th vol.
McOmber, Otis, co. B, 76th vol.
Marsh, Edwin T., co. I, 140th vol.
Norwicke, A. J., corp., co. B, 156th vol.
Northrop, J. B., co. —, 111th vol.
Nelson, John H., co. D, 14th vol.
Ogden, Stephen T., co. G, 111th vol.
Olmstead, J. W., co. —, 69th vol.
Prosser, E. W., co. A, 64th vol.
Peters, George, co. A, 111th vol.
Parsons, Warren B., co. E, 64th vol.
Rodney, Pusho, co. I, 51st vol.
Persons, Henry, co. C, 40th vol.
Poor, Elijah, co. —, 92d vol.
Page, Ozias D., co. F, 146th vol.
Porter, Geo. A., co. K, 14th vol., Brooklyn.
Potter, Henry, co. E, 48th vol.
Quackenbush, George, co. —, 94th vol.
Reiley, John J., co. C, 69th vol.
Remington, Henry, co. C, 122d vol.
Reeve, George, co. C, 152d vol.
Ripley, Fras. A., serg. co. C, 152d vol.
Rickett, Wm., co. F, 97th vol.
Rockafeller, W. E., co. D, 85th vol.
Russell, Geo. R., co. D, 117th vol.
Radley, John, co. C, 152d vol.
Rockwell, Eldridge, co. I, 42d vol.
Stone, Alvat B., co. A, 94th vol.
Seymour, Fred., co. D, 156th vol.
Scheidler, George, co. F, 97th vol.
Snyder, K. L., co. D, 85th vol.
Smith, George, co. K, 111th vol.
Smith, Andrew, co. F, 160th vol.
Sherwood, Jones, co. G, 70th vol.
Sergent, Stanly, co. C, 152d vol.
Sherman, A. E., co. A, 117th vol.
Smith, William S., co. —, 85th vol.
Seward, A. R., co. D, 76th vol.
Scholl, Henry, co. —, 146th vol.
Smalley, George D., co. H, 140th vol.
Stockwell, Lewis, co. H, 97th vol.
Seiler, Jno. T., co. F, 140th vol.
Sleeger, Geo. B., co. A, 94th vol.
Schott, Henry, co. —, 146th vol.
Sampson, Thomas S., co. G, 92d inf.
Snook, James S., co. A, 51st inf.
Stevens, Wm. Thomas, co. I, 99th inf.
Smith, James, co. K, 104th inf.
Stannard, W. W., co. D, 118th inf.
Shearman, A. R., co. F, 179th inf.
Salyer, Simeon, co. C, 126th inf.
Swanson, James, co. E, 146th inf.
Smith, George, co. K, 111th inf.
Stevens, F. L., serg. 72d, con'd with 120th inf.
Shuyler, Henry S., co. I, 86th inf.
Tidd, Samuel V., co. K, 124th inf.
Taylor, Stephen, co. G, 97th inf.
Tilford, Braton P., co. F, 149th inf.
Taylor, Thomas J., co. B, 93d inf.
Thomas, James L., co. A, 104th inf.
Trousdell, Wm. J., co. I, 140th inf.
Taylor, Levi, co. H, 69th inf.
Taylor, Adney, co. H, 69th inf.
Tuttle, James C., co. D, 16th inf.
Taylor, Charles, co. F, 115th inf.
Taylor, Lorenzo D., co. D, 141st inf.
Teruilliger, Nelson, co. C, 120th inf.
Taylor, S. B., co. K, 147th inf.
Upham, Jared Jewel, 85th inf.
Vorhis, Jacob, co. F, 104th inf.
Vannasdall, Wesley D., co. A, 115th inf.
Van Blarcom, Isaac, co. D, 95th inf.
Van Schuyver, George, co. G, 108th inf.
Van Arman, Charles E., co. H, 69th inf.
Vantine, G. G., co. F, 106th inf.
Vale, Adrian, serg., co. D, 176th inf.
Williams, John, drummer, 226th inf.
Wellen, Augustus P., co. B, 100th inf.
Witter, Wm. Owen, co. I, 49th inf.
Williams, John H., co. C, 58th inf.
Webster, Elwood, co. K, 76th inf.
Westcott, Henry C., co. F, 118th inf.
Wiley, James, co. B, 59th inf.
West, Wm. W., co. D, 157th inf.
Woodward, Oran B., co. I, 111th inf.
Wolf, John, co. E, 111th inf.
White, George W., co. F, 104th inf.
Wilson, Robert, co. A, 117th inf.
Weller, John J., co. E, 63d inf.
Wiser, M. L., co. F, 90th inf.
Waldron, Nelson, co. K, 176th inf.
Wallace, Thomas, serg., co. G, 164th inf.
Whitten, Joseph G., co. I, 120th inf.
Wolfe, Cristian A., co. D, 132d inf.
Warren, Nathan T., co. I, 105th inf.
Williams, A. B., serg., co. D, 111th inf.
White, H. G., co. A, 94th inf.
Williams, Lyman W., co. F, 121st inf.
Wilson, James, co. K, 132d inf.
Webb, Lewis M., co. F, 147th inf.
White, Lois, co. D, 156th inf.
Yeta, Charles, co. A, 121st inf.

Alexander, Ephraim, jr., co. —, 15th cav.
Atwell, Theodore, serg., co. M, 6th cav.
Bentley, Washington, co. —, 25th cav.
Bishop, Chester, corp., co. B, 10th cav.
Borst, Edwin, co. B, 5th cav.
Breese, Niles, co. H, 3d cav.
Barr, John, serg., co. F, 10th cav.
Bowman, Byron J., co. E, 10th cav.
Briggs, Benjamin T., co. F, 12th cav.
Bacon, Lyman, co. E, 8th cav.
Burke, John, co. D, 2d cav.
Boyce, Ambrose A., co. I, 3d cav.
Bixby, Daniel C., co. —, 5th cav.
Bress, N. D., co. H, 3d cav.
Bayliss, Edward, co. C, 24th cav.
Bootey, John C., co. C, 9th cav.
Baker, Lamont M., serg., co. G, 24th cav.
Bronsom, Marcus D., co. B, 6th cav.
Barr, John, serg., co. F, 10th cav.
Borden, Holland, corp., co. —, 3d cav.
Baker, Josiah, co. M, 15th cav.
Boorman, John H, co. D, 1st cav.
Bingham, Charles Elmer, co. D, 5th cav.
Coleman, James H., serg., co. C, 3d cav.
Caly, Herschell, co. L, 21st cav.
Cremer, Martin, co. F, 15th cav.
Chase, Samuel, co. L, 2d cav.
Carpenter, John, co. C, 22d cav.
Dougherty, William, co. B, 5th cav.
Dowes, Thomas, serg., co. K, 22d cav.
Davis, Henry T., co. G, 5th cav.
Evens, Luke, co. G, 22d cav.
Estes, E. M., co. —, 3d cav.
Elmendorf, Alex. F, co. —, 2d Harris light cav.
Farnham, Charles F., co. G, 5th cav.
Farnham, Frederic, co. F, 6th cav.
Failing, Milton M., co. C, 8th cav.
Gleason, Harrison D., co. M, 22d cav.
Garrigan, Edward C., co. F, 2d cav.
Gorton, Cornelius, co. B, 5th cav.
Gifford, Edwin M., co. A, 3d cav.
Getman, David, co. I, 10th cav.
Hazen, John M., co. G, 5th cav.
Hubbard, John, co. —, 8th cav.
Hughes, John H., serg., co. B, 24th cav.
Harvey, Barton J., co. D, 8th cav.
Huson, George B., co. —, 22d cav.
Hecks, Fred., co. —, 5th cav.
Hill, Andrew J., co. M, 15th cav.
Hopson, Sidney P., 6th cav.
Jackson, John W., co. F, 5th cav.
Kerk, Edw., co. —, 18th cav.
Kenney, Michael, co. F, 12th cav.
Keys, Davenport, co. B, 5th cav.
Lamson, Henry, co. M, 15th cav.
LaGrange, Caspar, co. G, 10th cav.
Latham, Eldridge P., serg., co. H, 6th cav.
Lyon, Charles, co. K, 21st cav.
Munroe, George, co. F, 5th cav.
Miner, William B., co. —, 4th cav.
Mix, Albert J., co. A, 12th cav.
Morgan, Edwin L., co. F, 12th cav.
Main, Milo A., co. G, 10th cav.
Moohler, John, co. E, 2d cav.
Monroe, George, co. K, 4th cav.
Miller, Rockwell L., co. C, 5th cav.
Minor, Henry, serg., co. E, 5th cav.
Mahan, Benjamin F., co. K, 5th cav.
McMinn, Clarence L., co. E, 3d cav.
Norton, Ashbel, co. M, 15th cav.
Niemann, William H., serg., co. F, 5th
Patterson, Orin, co. E, 24th cav.
Perine, Joseph L., co. D, 25th cav.
Pratt, George B., co. D, 10th cav.
Pread, Simeon G., co. D, 13th cav.
Raymond, William O., co. L, 8th cav.
Ray, George G., co. D, 2d cav.
Rustin, James W., co. D, 8th cav.
Riggs, Hiram M., co. D, 13th cav.
Rossett, Edward, co. —, 5th cav.
Smith, Robert H., corporal, co. E, 3d
Smith, William P., co. D, 5th cav.
Smith, Volney L., co. K, 4th cav.
Smith, Charles, serg., co. E, 9th cav.
Southworth, Robert, serg., co. E, 22d
Smith, James, co. M, 20th cav.
Smith, James A., co. H, 22d cav.
Salisbury, Edwin, co. D, 16th cav.
Segar, Edwin, co. F, 8th cav.
Stearns, Alvin, co. D, 6th cav.
Smith, Leroy S., lieut., co. G, 14th cav.
Terry, Scudder H., co. K, 13th cav.
Taylor, Alexander, co. —, 5th cav.
Trussler, J. C., serg., co. F, 9th cav.
Winnett, Jos. A., co. —, 8th cav.
Woodhull, David F., co. E, 8th cav.
White, Martin, co. I, 18th cav.
Whipple, Marion D., co. D, 22d cav.
Watson, Thomas, co. —, 22d cav.
Warner, Adna M., co. A, 8th cav.
Wynkoop, Guy, co. H, 10th cav.
Youngs, G. C., co. H, 22d cav.
Heath, Jarius P., co. D, 2d vet. cav.
Johnson, George W., co. H, 1st vet. ca
Jones, John B., co. D, 1st vet. cav.
Roe, Henry, co. F, 1st vet. cav.
Bowen, Wm. B., co. H, 1st N. Y. drag.
Buckley, Samuel F., co. —, 2d mounted
Jones, William, co. F, 2d mounted rifles
Ames, James R., co. I, 14th heavy art.
Allen, David H., co. A, 4th heavy art.
Baily, Robert, co. —, 8th heavy art.
Bayne, Henry C., co. A, 8th heavy art.
Bayne, George W., co. A, 8th heavy ar
Brown, Oscar, co. A, 9th heavy art.
Boss, George T., co. D, 9th heavy art.
Blodget, A. T., co. H, 4th heavy art.
Barbey, John, co. L, 2d heavy art.
Bodell, George D., 12th battery.
Brown, Edwin F., corp., co. A, 8th hea
Burr, Frank H., co. —, 2d heavy art.
Brown, James Ira, co. H, 5th heavy art.
Bishop, Cassius M. C., co. M, 7th heavy
Blodgett, Frederick, co. D, 5th heavy a
Clark, Ira A., co. —, 8th heavy art.
Carloss, Edwin M., serg., co. L, 14th he
Calvert, Walter L., co. I, 8th heavy art
Cole, Edgar, co. B, 14th heavy art.
Cross, Asa, co. M, 4th heavy art.
Cook, Frank, co. F, 4th heavy art.
Church, Zenas E., co. C, 4th heavy art.
Crosby, Horace M., co. B, 5th heavy ar
Downs, Valentine J., co. A, 2d heavy a
Dewitt, John H., co. —, 9th heavy art.
Dunham, Russell, co. C, 8th heavy art.
Drew, Hiram, co. F, 4th heavy art.
Devendorf, Rudolph, co. L, 2d heavy a
Dygert, Warner N., co. D, 2d heavy ar
Ellis, William, co. E, 2d heavy art.
Fay, John W., co. A, 7th heavy art.
Foley, Thomas, co. E, 2d heavy art.
Fish, Lester N., co. H, 7th heavy art.
Foster, Charles S., co. I, 7th heavy art.
Faulkner, Richard, co. E, 8th heavy art.
Garfield, George, co. H, 7th heavy art.
Gerald, Frederick, co. E, 8th heavy art
Gillett, William, co. I, 8th heavy art.
Houghtaling, Jacob H., co. E, 7th heav
Holmes, Wm. S., co. K, 8th heavy art.
Hertsberg, Otto, co. E, 8th heavy art.
Jaffers, Benjamin, co. D, 9th heavy art.
Jones, David, co. —, 9th heavy art.
Johnson, George W., co. —, 8th heavy
Kenyon, Franklin A., co. —, 8th heavy
Kahle, Christian, co. D, 8th heavy art.
Lyon, James, 5th independent battery.
Leonard, Chas. H., co. A, 7th heavy art
Longstaff, John Wm., co. B, 8th heavy
Loomis, John, co. M, 14th heavy art.
Lester, Wm. C, co. G, 5th heavy art.
Laduc, Ambrose, co. E, 9th heavy art.
Laflare, John, co. A, 14th heavy art.
Lake, Romantus, co. B, 4th heavy art.
Lock, John B., serg., co. L, 7th heavy
McCollum, Melvin C., co. F, 8th heavy
Marsh, Chas., co. H, 4th heavy art.
Marcellus, Lewis, co. A, 9th heavy art.
Murray, James E. co. D, 8th heavy art.
Mosier, Edward, co. E, 9th heavy art.
McConnell, Evi, co. E, 9th heavy art.
Moshure, Abijah, co. G, 7th heavy art.
Martindale, Wm. J., 5th heavy art.
Owen, Chas. G., co. M, 14th heavy art.
Pearson, James, co. E, 8th heavy art.
Parker, Orren F., co. A, 8th heavy art.
Phelps, G. S., co. A, 14th heavy art.
Pope, Joseph, co. K, 2d heavy art.
Rumsey, George W, co. F, 5th heavy ar
Richards, Jas. M., co. H, 5th heavy art.
Rogers, Amos, co. I, 7th heavy art.
Rose, Adelbert, co. H, 5th heavy art.
Reily, Henry, 15th heavy art.
Rose, Elsler, co. H, 4th heavy art.
Rawson, Porter D., 24th battery.
Stiles, Geo. W., co. I, 7th heavy art.
Stapleton, Richard, co. G, 7th heavy art.
Simmons, Almon B., co. H, 8th heavy ar
Spaulding, Mortimer, co. B, 14th heavy
Sykes, N. B., co. H, 4th heavy art.
Smith, John D., co. G, 4th heavy art.
Scheidler, George, co. F, 17th New Yor
Satterlee, John, co. E, 4th heavy art.
Thornton, Judson M., co. L, 14th heavy
Toll, Reinhard, co. C, 14th heavy art.
Travis, Harrison, co. G, 4th heavy art.
Thomas, John E., co. H, 5th heavy art.
Tucker, James, co. C, 9th heavy art.
Way, David, co. D, 9th heavy art.
Waring, William E, co. A, 4th heavy ar
Wilson, Simon, 4th heavy art.
Whritemour, Marcus, co. M, 15th heavy
Woolsey, John, 24th bat.
Wright, John W., co. L, 2d heavy art.
Watson, James, 8th heavy art.
Watts, William, co. D, 8th heavy art.
Weldon, John, co. E, 7th heavy art.

STATE OF NEW JERSEY

Arnold, Edwin B., co. —, 33d inf.
Bailey, William B., co. C, 15th inf.
Bloodgood, Augustus, co. —, 11th inf.
Dickerson, William C., co. D, 15th inf.
Dougherty, John W., co. H, 7th inf.
Dunn, George W., co. F, 1st inf.

MEN.—NO. 1.

gbert, James co. B, 15th inf.
innon, James, co. I, 11th inf.
riggs, Thomas, co. —, 33d inf.
oward, Thomas H., co. H, 10th inf.
yde, Wilson, co. B, 38th inf.
ipsey, Jacob M., co. I, 10th inf.
ovell, W. F. co. D, 1st inf.
inion, Jacob P., co. B, 15th inf.
uchmore, Elias D., co. C, 14th inf.
iller, Henry, co. B, 38th inf.
oid, JoT., co. D, 14th inf.
hipley, Andrew J., co. C, 8th inf.
horne, Charles D., co. E, 10th inf.
urner, Peter, co. K, 4th inf.
ells, Charles J., co. C, 10th inf.
oods, W. S., co. D, 1st inf.
right, W. H., co. K, 1st inf.
ilson, Harrison, co. E, 10th inf.

arrie, W. J., co. —, 2d cav.
oerd, Ernest, co. —, 3d cav., hussars.
alines, Edward, co. M, 2d cav.
elick, George A., co. E, 2d cav.
cPeck, Henry P., co. B, 1st cav.
eterson, Henry, co. H, 3d cav.
ill, Charles W., co. M, 3d cav.
illiams, Charles J., co. L, 1st cav.

PENNSYLVANIA.

ikman, William, co. F, 116th vol.
nthony, J. C., co. A, 56th vol.
xtell, J. G., co. A, 145th vol.
ndrew, David W., co. D, 26th vol.
vers, Samuel, co. D, 62d vol.
utton, Charles, co. B, 149th vol.
ack, Samuel N., co. F, 106th vol.
gelow, Charles A. W., co. F, 53d vol.
chtell, Isaac, co. A, 184th vol.
ickley, William, co. B, 90th vol.
wer, George W., co. K, 103d vol.
iggs, Theron T., co. B, 145th vol.
ardick, Charles W., co. C, 145th vol.
ryer, S. P., co. I, 111th vol.
nd, ——, co. I, 183d vol.
ce, James, co. —, 149th vol.
rnes, Walter, co. G, 119th vol.
urton, Joseph N., co. A, 61st vol.
rnes, H. J., co. A, 57th vol.
ock, Jacob, co. F, 103d vol.
nnett, Byron, co. —, 141st vol.
rns, John, co. A, 83d vol.
nder, Flavius G., co. C, 77th vol.
ubaker, Benjamin, co. D, 79th vol.
ppersmith, Jno. P., co. I, 145th vol.
iswell, Sherman M., co. B, 103d vol.
pp, William, co. I, 143d vol.
ampbell, Amos, co. C, 11th vol.
ark, John, co. G, 103d vol.
onley, M. L., co. E, 138th vol.
wan, Espy, co. G, 191st vol.
sserly, Thomas, co. G, 191st vol.
ampbell, Knox G., co. G, 191st vol.
rbet, James, co. H, 99th vol.
amberlain, James, co. H, 107th vol.
emens, Wm. D., co. B, 88th vol.
oley, Wm., co. B, 95th vol.
lebaugh, Wm., co. K, 69th vol.
rr, Wm., co. E, 149th vol.
ehl, Espy, co. D, 55th vol.
mpsey, John H., co. A, 63d vol.
x, Edwin, co. C, 83d vol.
ck, James, co. —, 79th vol.
inlap, S. A., co. I, 103d vol.
orulf, Elen, co. F, 116th vol.
efibaugh, Wm. H., co. E, 138th vol.
efibaugh, Jno. W., co. A, 184th vol.
elaney, Matthew, co. B, 51st vol.
avidson, Alex., co. G, 191st vol.
alo, Solomon, co. D, 148th vol.
umm, Michael H., co. C, 85th vol.
aved, George C., co. C, 81st vol.
irenfeld, J. M., co. D, 184th vol.
oerhart, James W., co. G, 191st vol.
xes, Ezekiel, co. E, 103d vol.
linger, John, co. I, 107th vol.
okendorff, George R., co. A, 157th vol.
ben, William, co. I, 69th vol.
sters, David, co. D, 148th vol.
sters, Francis W., co. A, 13th vol.
sters, Henry, co. A, 13th vol.
ood, George W., co. H, 148th vol.
uley, Joseph, co. F, 48th vol.
ay, Stephen, co. —, 106th vol.
oster, Frank, co. H, 143d vol.
sher, John, co. I, 85th vol.
ass, John T., co. D, 22d vol.
ilbert, Henry, co. F, 53d vol.
reen, W. Henry D., co. K, 141st vol.
oc, W. H. L., co. H, 45th vol.
nyst, J. W., co. I, 57th vol.
reen, Joseph F., co. H, 105th vol.
rim, Henry, co. K, 48th vol.
ibson, David, co. A, 55th vol.
ordon, Robert, co. G, 69th vol.
ouston, Will., co. D, 10th vol.
ant, John T., co. K, 55th vol.
yatt, Thomas J., co. K, 118th vol.
yatt, James W., co. H, 118th vol.
ershey, Abraham L., co. G, 2d vol.
all, John, co. B, 100th vol.
ll, Wilson S., co. D, 141st vol.
ll, Charles F., co. C, 72d vol.
orn, Robert, co. I, 111th vol.
ousel, William P., co. —, 190th vol.
ess, Levi, co. —, 118th vol.
aisley, F. A., co. G, 191st vol.
aley, James B., co. —, 100th vol.
ost, Jacob, co. G, 83d vol.
unter, John, co. —, 155th vol.
endershot, David, co. E, 143d vol.
owye, Matthew, co. E, 141st vol.
amilton, John E., co. H, 188th vol.
agan, George, co. —, 199th vol.
udson, Thomas E., co. K, 48th vol.
all, John, co. B, 100th vol.
awk, Michael, co. F, 103d vol.
hnson, James E., co. I, 45th vol.
nes, James, co. K, 9th vol.
ohnson, Harris, co. I, 45th vol.
linger, Ephraim, co. H, 148th vol.
uckey, David, co. A, 184th vol.
elly, Henry, co. F, 138th vol.
oyser, Jacob, co. B, 148th vol.
orskossky, Julius, co. H, 50th vol.
oox, James, co. A, 184th vol.
ratzer, H., co. F, 76th vol.
insley, Nathan P., co. H, 145th vol.
ell, Jordan, co. F, 118th vol.
arns, Jacob J., co. K, 149th vol.
ing, John L., co. E, 118th vol.
ers, John Oliver, co. F, 100th vol.
olley, George W., co. I, 101st vol.
ophart, Samuel, co. C, 77th vol.
ing, Daniel, co. E, 84th vol.
neep, Peter, co. —, 149th vol.
ayton, Samuel, co. A. 184th vol.
oarn, Adam, co. E, 11th vol.
ake, Fred., co. F, 106th vol.
ather, Burton K., co. —, 52d vol.
etteer, Alfred W., co. —, 77th vol.
vingston, George W., co. H, 190th vol.
o, George W., co. I, 67th vol.

Munsell, Harvey M., co. C, 99th vol.
Metcalf, Wm. H., co. —, 87th vol.
McGuire, Richard P., co. A, 55th vol.
Morse, Levi, co. F, 141st vol.
Meinhard, Ferdinand, co. H, 50th vol.
McCoy, A. J., co. I, 103d vol.
McCoy, Shannon, co. F, 138th vol.
Masters, ——, co. —, 143d vol.
McDowell, John S., co. F, 77th vol.
Miller, Orlando O., co. B, 145th vol.
McKee, Charles W., co. H, 191st vol.
Marguis, Edwin, co. C, 63d vol.
Miller, Herman K, co. H, 148th vol.
McKinnon, John Y., co. H, 53d vol.
Marks, William H., co. D, 118th vol.
Morton, George H., co. I, 118th vol.
Moody, Oscar A., co. G, 150th vol.
Morris, William, co. G, 77th vol.
Matthews, F. A., co. C, 148th vol.
McCarthy, David, co. D, 68th vol.
Musser, John, co. D, 77th vol.
Moore, Joseph H., co. E, 72d vol.
Malone, Albert M., co. E, 106th vol.
Mellon, William, co. A., 106th vol.
Meldrum, John C., co. C, 184th vol.
McConnell, Philip J., co. I, 55th vol.
Martin, Alvin A., co. D, 53d vol.
Moorhead, Howard S., co. H, 101st vol.
McNess, John H., co. E, 100th vol.
McGill, George, co. K, 45th vol.
Neal, George B., co. G, 188th vol.
Noble, James H., co. D, 73d vol.
Ober, David S., co. A, 184th vol.
Obonnor, Hugh J., co. A, 49th vol.
Oliver, George C., co. D, 111th vol.
Oler, James, co. D, 101st vol.
Orbin, Thomas, co. B, 85th vol
Potter, James O., co. G, 53d vol.
Purdy, William, co. H, 140th vol.
Potter, Benj. F., co. I, 148th vol.
Pierce, Byron, co. K, 141st vol.
Parent, Philip, co. —, 45th vol.
Purcell, Patrick, co. K, 101st vol.
Phipps, Joseph A., co. E. 57th vol.
Parker, William H., co. D, 102d vol.
Quanee, Charles H., co. B, 145th vol.
Rauch, Simon, co. E, 148th vol.
Rhinehardt, Samuel, co. I, 107th vol.
Russell, Ernest F, co. I, 141st vol.
Rhodes, William H, co. I, 145th vol.
Riddell, Royal W., co. C, 145th vol.
Raynolds, Charles R., co. H, 145th vol.
Rowland, Masters, co. F, 111th vol.
Sandt, Edward, co. A, 47th vol.
Smith, Wilbur, co. I, 82d vol.
Smith, William, co. F, 84th vol.
Surdam, Francis, co. D, 53d vol.
Scoutan, Lewis, co. F, 53d vol.
Smith, Job, co. A, 140th vol.
Starks, Charles T, co. —, 149th vol.
Stotler, Thomas, co. —, 101st vol.
Shirk, John H., co. —, 79th vol.
Scavercoll, James, co. K, 141st vol.
Shaffer, John, co. —, 57th vol.
Steel, Joseph, co. B, 191st vol.
Sayre, James, co. I, 10th vol.
Steere, Charles, co. E, 95th vol.
Sharp, Martin L., co. F, 100th vol.
Sheriff, Charles F., co. K, 100th vol.
Stevens, George H, co. G, 77th vol.
Sorber, Andrew, co. F, 53d vol.
Trout, Jacob W., co. K, 138th vol.
Turner, James W., co. A, 211th vol.
Teeter, Christian S., co. A, 184th vol.
Tripp, George W., co. E, 143d vol.
Tillotson, Perry H., co. K, 57th vol.
Thompson, Joseph S., co. H, 183d vol.
Thompson, Cowden, co. I, 10th vol.
Truman, W. W., co. G, 191st vol.
Vancuren, Edward, co. C, 145th vol.
Vail, Gilbert B., co. G, 77th vol.
Vail, Merritt J., co. B, 143d vol.
Ward, Samuel, co. E, 135th vol.
Walker, Houston, co. E, 100th vol.
Wolford, Wm., co. B, 149th vol.
Wickerham, W. H. H., co. D, 22d vol.
Wilber, Louis W., co. D, 106th vol.
Warner, Edwin A., co. D, 85th vol.
Woodcock, Thomas, co. E, 183d vol.
Welch, Robert, co. I, 101st vol.
Wright, Edmund S., co. A, 184th vol.
Williams, John E., co. B, 62d vol.
Wilson, James, co. K, 83d vol.
Wheaton, Ambrose H., co. G, 53d vol.
Wilkinson, John, co. I, 45th vol.
Weeks, Caradon Q., co. F, 75th vol.
Wolford, William H., co. B, 149th vol.
Whitson, Henry, co. H, 53d vol.
Whitney, Orange P., co. H, 187th vol.
Young, John, co. —, 149th vol.
Young, John, co. C, 45th vol.
Young, Philip S., co. H, 101st vol.

Aikelo, John J., co. H, 5th cav.
Austin, Edward, co. F, 20th cav.
Black, James A., co. D, 14th cav.
Bryan, William C., co. D, 5th cav.
Beardsley, Luther, co. L, 12th cav.
Baker, Willard, co. L, 12th cav.
Bevens, Robert, co. I, 20th cav.
Brady, Michael, co. M, 5th cav.
Brosins, Amos P., co. K, 14th cav.
Cormer, Abner P., co. B, 4th cav.
Campbell, Thomas F, co. B, 4th cav.
Coleman, J. L., co. K, 18th cav.
Davis, James, co. I, 5th cav.
Deming, Charles W., co. D, 16th cav.
Dyer, Joshua E., co. D, 5th cav.
Evans, Samuel F., co. F, 7th cav.
Ellis, Enos, co. I, 11th cav.
Foot, Charles, co. G, 20th cav.
Fuller, Henry, co. M, 13th cav.
Gillmore, Robert A., co. —, 12th cav.
George, Thomas, co. B, 18th cav.
Gass, John T., co. C, Ringgold battalion.
Gates, Jacob S. C., co. D, 13th cav.
Geary, G. S., co. D, 4th cav.
Havens, John, co. L, 19th cav.
Hottenstein, George W., co. I, 18th cav.
Hennigh, Nathan L. H., co. A, 14th cav.
Hart, Isaac, co. B, 17th cav.
Havlin, Mathew M., co. D, 4th cav.
Ivory, Thomas, co. G, 12th cav.
Jones, Henry P., co. B, 2d cav.
Kelley, George W., co. K, 18th cav.
Lane, Amos P., co. E, 6th cav.
Levan, John, co. G, 8th cav.
Miller, Levis, serg., co. L, 6th cav.
Morgret, William, co. K, 18th cav.
McCray, Charles E., co. B, 12th cav.
Mugot, John, co. K, 18th cav.
Miller, Hamlin B., co. I, 14th cav.
McFadden, Lewis, co. I, 4th cav.
Mulaby, Aaron H., co. B, 7th cav.
Meekley, Eli, co. E, 17th cav.
Miller, Lewis, co. L, 6th cav.
Myers, Joseph M., co. D, 13th cav.
McCoy, Isaac A., co. A, 9th cav.
Mastezatt, Charles A., co. D, 14th cav.
Meredith, Alfred A., co. A, 22d cav.
McCoy, Alexander, co. A, 9th cav.

Meredith, Alfred A., co. A, 22d cav.
Norris, John G., co. —, 17th cav.
Neifergold, Henry, co. A, 14th cav.
Nagel, George W., co. —, 18th cav.
Norris, Simon, co. G, 16th cav.
Odenheimer, John M., co. —, 6th cav.
Oliver, Adam E., co. D, 17th cav.
Penepacker, Benj. F., co. F, 12th cav.
Ramsey, Milton G., co. —, 17th cav.
Rudd, William, co. H, 20th cav.
Robbins, James, co. M, 2d cav.
Ruper, Emanuel, co. C, 14th cav.
Rees, David T., co. A, 7th cav.
Sellers, John T., co. E, 2d cav.
Smith, Samuel A., co. K, 14th cav.
Smith, James L., co. A, 13th cav.
Swearer, George N., co. H, 13th cav.
Schmidt, Charles L., co. B, 5th cav.
Shields, William, co. —, 5th cav.
Schlearback, Conrad, co. —, 4th cav.
Snowden, John W., co. E, 2d cav.
Scott, Andrew J., co. D, 14th cav.
Smith, Dennis, co. A, 18th cav.
Sanderson, Wm. E., co. I, 2d cav.
Sargent, C. B., co. F, 14th cav.
Siebert, John, co. B, 5th cav.
Watkins, Andrew, co. —, 18th cav.
Woodburn, James S., co. F, 13th cav.
White, George, co. C, 1st cav.
Wallace, Frank, co. F, 2d cav.
Walker, James W., co. —, 7th cav.
White, Joseph, co. A, 17th cav.
Wright, Jacob, co. B, 12th cav.
Young, George H., co. F, 5th cav.
Bail, Joseph I., co. F, 2d heavy art.
Bird, George, co. F, 2d heavy art.
Beaner, Simon J., co. H, 55th heavy art.
Crawford, Sylvester, co. D, 2d heavy art.
Claybaugh, Geo. W., co. —, heavy art.
Hartwick, John, co. C, 112th heavy art.
Hansinger, Aaron, co. D, 2d heavy art.
Irvin, Charles, co. G, 2d heavy art.
Miller, Eden, co. K, 2d heavy art.
Ormsby, C. M., co. G, 2d heavy art.
Ordning, George, co. C, 112th heavy art.
Rogers, Jeremiah B., co. K, 2d heavy art.
Simpson, John D., co. C, 2d heavy art.
Towson, Jeremiah B., co. A, 3d heavy art.
Wood, James M., co. —, 2d heavy art.
Wood, George H., co. C, 2d heavy art.
Bragg, Lucian G., co. E, 2d reserves.
Belcher, Geo. W., co. E, 2d reserves.
Davison, Garrett, co. —, 9th reserves.
Huston, Wm. S., co. D, 10th reserves.
Hinkel, Jonas, co. C, 7th reserves.
Jayne, S. W., co. C, 6th reserves.
Lathrop, Halsey, co. C, 6th reserves.
Laino, John, co. D, 10th reserves.
Laughten, Robert E., co. A, 10th reserves.
McCurdy, John G., co. B, 10th reserves.
McCahon, James, co. D, 10th reserves.
McPark, Robert, co. D, 10th reserves.
Margut, Mathia, co. D, 6th reserves.
McCloy, John, co. F, 11th reserves.
Otto, John, co. F, 7th reserves.
Seaton, M. A., co. G, 9th reserves.
Stansbury, Y. S., co. H, 12th reserves.
Smith, G. W., co. H, 5th reserves.
Welty, Jacob W., co. H, 7th reserves.
Woodburn, Jos. D., co. G, 7th reserves.
Williamson, Alvin, co. G, 11th reserves.

Buchanan, Julius, co. I, 1st rifles.
Gillespie, James, co. K, 1st rifles.
McClintock, James P., co. C, 1st rifles.
McDowell, B. C., co. I, 1st rifles.
Mulleson, John H., co. —, 1st rifles.
Roberts, Frederick T., co. —, 1st rifles.
Snyder, Jacob, co. E, 1st rifles.
Sickles, C. T., co. K, 1st rifles.

STATE OF DELAWARE.

Maxworthy, George W., co. D, 2d vol.
Rhine, Joseph, co. G, 1st vol.
Thorn, Henry T., co. D, 2d vol.

STATE OF MARYLAND.

Duke, Cornelius, co. K, 5th vol.
Gorman, Stephen, co. D, 1st vol.
Goriff, J. C., co. —, 1st vol.
Hitchins, Joseph H., co. —, 2d vol.
King, Albert, co. H, 3d vol.
King, William J., co. H, 3d vol.
Martin, Loos, co. A, 1st vol.
Mervine, John, co. H, 2d vol.
Poffinbarger, Charles, co. A, 7th vol.
Rohrer, W. H., co. —, 1st vol.
Seeger, Charles, co. F, 6th vol.
Wehn, George C., co. D, 7th vol.

DISTRICT OF COLUMBIA.

Boissonnault, M. F., co. H, 1st cav.
Cushing, James B., co. I, 1st cav.
Giddings, Henry, co. B., 1st cav.
Jones, John, co. L, Baker's cav.
Maffit, E. C., co. I, 1st cav.
Overlock, R. L., co. G, 1st cav.
Smith, William E., co. I, 1st cav.
Shafer, Frederick, co. —, 1st cav.
Tibbetts, John, co. I, 1st cav.

STATE OF OHIO.

Allen, A. B., co. C, 121st reg.
Allen, Albert B., co. C, 19th reg.
Alward, Alfred L., co. B, 135th reg.
Amour, W. Henry, co. H, 34th, after m't'd inf.
Brown, James E., co. C, 93d reg.
Brown, Henry H., co. A, 41st reg.
Beard, Osro R., co. —, 123d reg.
Blocher, Henry D, co. E, 104th reg.
Batley, George, co. C, 124th reg.
Cowels, George, 10th 60.
Crane, John B., co. D, 100th reg.
Connally, John, co. H, 103d reg.
Cahill, Wm. F., co. A, 51st reg.
Cram, John B, co. D, 100th reg.
Cary, Asa, co. E, 21st reg.
Cayle, James P., co. G, 2d reg.
Clay, Oliver D., co. G, 122d reg.
Coit, Eureka, co. C, 123d reg.
Davis, Clinton W., co. K, 95th reg.
Dodge, David B, co. H, 100th reg.
Duffy, James, co. H, 45th reg.
Ells, Henry M, co. G, 10th reg.
Ewing, David, co. D, 135th reg.
Gurnsey, Chas. W., co. E, 72d reg.
Hillyer, John H., co. F, 98th reg.
Harsh, Christian, co. C, 126th reg.
Henderson, David, co. H, 122d reg.
King, John P., co. C, 72d reg.
Kerr, Andrew, co. I, 13th reg.
Joselyn, Alfred A., co. A, 122d reg.
Johnson, Samuel G., co. G, 177th reg.
Lee, H. D., 32d reg.
McPurdy, James, co. K, 13th reg.
McCollum, Jas. Madison, co. K, 4th reg.
McNaury, F. G., co. K, 126th reg.
Maher, Patrick, co. E, 4th reg.
Moorehead, Josiah, co. A, 102d reg.
McPurdy, James, co. K, 13th reg.
Moore, Chas., co. E, 19th reg.
Preshan, James A., co. C, 116th reg.

Patterson, Adolphus G., co. H, 19th reg.
Parsons, George F., co. A, 124th reg.
Philips, V. B., co. H, 100th reg.
Paisley, James, co. —, 65th reg.
Rowson, Rasha, co. H, 103d reg.
Riddick, Robert G., co. —, 197th reg.
Rich, Solomon, co. H, 116th reg.
Sloan, Alexander A. co. D, 34th reg.
Sweet, Myron co. F, 49th reg.
Stark, Gilbert J, co. —, 32d reg.
Shaw, Delos, co. E, 103d reg.
Sheppard, Thomas J., co. E, 97th reg.
Stair, John, co. H, 100th reg.
Smith, B. P., co. A, 105th reg.
Stowe, Oserald F., co. G, 31st reg.
Schreiner, John, co. K, 101st reg.
Touesdale, Henry, co. H, 2d reg.
Tullis, Lindley, co. C, 24th reg.
Vail, Samuel, co. A, 49th reg.
Ward, Hiram, co. A, 103d reg.
Woodruff, William, co. —, 102d reg.
Welsh, William C., co. —, 105th reg.
Wheeler, Caleb C., co. —, 122d reg.
Withington, Thomas M., co. —, 72d reg.
Warren, Haddock, co. B, 116th reg.
Zuber, John M., co. B, 100th reg.

Barrett, Robert, co. G, 6th cav.
Bartges, Christian, co. F, 2d cav.
Chilsen, A. W., co. —, 45th cav.
Clayton, Noel, co. D, 4th cav.
Coats, Rufus Elisha, co. —, 2d cav.
Donaldson, Richard B., co. M, 6th cav.
Fredrick, Knodel, co. —, 3d independent cav.
Krebs, Burkhard, co. —, 3d independent cav.
Johnson, W. D., co. H, 3d cav.

Lyon L., co. B, 1st art.
Stanford, Perkins, co. A, 2d art.
Volen, Henry Leopoldi, co. K, 6th art.
Wilcox, Thomas B., company M, 4th art.

STATE OF INDIANA.

Ballinger, Robert B., co. —, 40th inf.
Burris, James M., co. F, 82d inf.
Burnes, James A., co. —, 40th inf.
Evans, Charles W., co. I, 88th inf.
Farrington, Jabes, co. —, 40th inf.
Grooms, Henry C., co. D., 13th inf.
Hawkins, Martin V., co. —, 49th inf.
Hutchinson, Joseph, co. A, 2d inf.
Kurtz, Byron, co. E or I, 75th inf.
Patter, Casimer, co. —, 20th inf.
Patter, James E., co. —, 20th inf.
Reynolds, Jeremiah, co. G, 63d inf.
Rivir, John, co. F, 30th inf.
Spicer, Buell E., co. A, 6th inf.
Spicer, William H., co. C, 6th inf.
Scorlett, J. L., co. K, 12th inf.
Shearer, Harrison, co. I, 9th inf.
West, George W., co. H, 18th inf.
Clements, Thomas J., co. B, 5th cav.
Inglish, Archibald F., co. F, 7th cav.
McCrum, James, co. —, 5th cav.
Salts, William C., co. —, 4th cav.
Wiley, Philip, co. B, 5th cav.

STATE OF ILLINOIS.

Baker, James A, co. F, 113th inf.
Belden, William P., co. B., 72d inf.
Ball, Clark J., co. I, 93d inf.
Briggs, Wills, co. G, 95th inf.
Calvert, William, co. F, 72d inf.
Carver, Edward E, co. B, 72d inf.
Cook, Archibald, co. K, 51st inf.
Caddington, Wm., co. I, 93d inf.
Dawson, Aaron, co. B, 30th inf.
Dann, Jerome B., co. K, 20th inf.
Devine, James D., co. K, 38th inf.
Gearheart, E. L., co. D, 8th inf.
Green, Samuel, co. H, 42d inf.
Henderson, John B., corp., co. G, 66th inf.
Kendall, Clinton A., co. —, 60th inf.
Maxham, H. C., co. H, 19th inf.
McCreery, John P., co. C, 119th inf.
McMurtry, John L., co. C, 116th inf.
Miller, James P., co. I, 31st inf.
Pomeroy, James Wm., co. C, 104th inf.
Ramsay, Chas. D., co. —, 14th and 15th bat.
Reid, Elwin, jr., co. K, 13th inf.
Reynolds, Dwight, co. D, 32d inf.
Rose, Lewis A., co. F, 42d inf.
Strube, Chas. H., co. D, 88th inf.
Sweetland, Chas. F., co. F, 36th inf.
Taylor, Jesse B., co. F, 112th inf.
Thomson, Robert H., co. C, 13th inf.
Whitney, Theo. F., co. G, 89th inf.
Williams, John A., co. G, 64th inf.
Ball, Eliphalet G., co. —, 9th cav.
Fairless, James A., co. G, 14th cav.
Fox, James D., co. —, 16th cav.
Jenks, Joseph P., co. I, 3d cav.
Roebuck, Russell, co. —, 16th cav.
Smith, Barney, co. G, 14th cav.
Watts, Francis, co. L, 14th cav.
Wildman, H. H., co. I, 16th cav.
Brown, George S., Bridge's bat., light art.
McRay, Wm. J., or Ja., Philip's Chicago bat.
Messick, Wm. L., co. E, 1st art.
Snow, Martin Van B., Chicago Board Trade bat.

STATE OF MICHIGAN.

Abernethy, Albert B, co. G, 11th inf.
Atwell, Levi, co. L, 1st engineers.
Brockway, Martin B., co. B, 4th inf.
Bressen, Dennis, co. A, 26th inf.
Beebe, John, co. A, 1st sharp-shooters.
Berry, Chester D., co. I, 20th inf.
Black, William, co. D, 16th inf.
Bishop, Joshua, co. —, 13th inf.
Cope, Martin, co. H, 17th inf.
Carr, Charles R., co. K, 25th inf.
Davis, Theodore T., co. D, 13th inf.
Duel, Charles E., co. D, 27th inf.
Decker, Jasper R., co. G, 1st engineers.
Ensign, James, co. A, 11th inf.
Hine, E. W., co. F, 24th inf.
Harmon, Henry, co. H, 19th inf.
Hoyt, John R., co. D, 21st inf.
Hill, Seymour E., co. B, 17th inf.
Hertsberg, William, co. G, 20th inf.
Johnson, James, co. I, 17th inf.
Johnson, Russell M., co. I, 17th inf.
Reeney, W. H. H., co. I, 1st inf.
Miller, W. H., 1st serg., co. C, 20th inf.
McLaughlin, Jas. M., co. —, 2d sharp-shooters.
Norton, Hiram, co. M, 1st engineers.
Nedean, Jacob, co. E, 17th inf.
Peer, Richard, co. H, 22d inf.
Rowley, Russell, co. I, 7th inf.
Smith, Samuel, co. H, 17th inf.
Sutherland, Mason M., co. E, 1st sharp-shooters.
Schmeid, Reuben, co. F, 21st inf.
Shepherd, Solon, co. G, 1st sharp-shooters.
Shenwood, John A., co. C, 24th inf.
Sinclair, Asa, co. F, 1st engineers.
Taylor, Isaiah, co. A, 27th inf.
Van Wert, Edwin, co. E, 3d inf.
Whelan, E. M., co. G, 14th inf.
Wakeman, Clark, co. F, 21st inf.
Willits, James B., co. A, 1st sharpshooters.
Waterbury, Aaron V., co. H, 17th inf.
Winebrenner, John, co. A, 5th inf.

Westcot, William, co. I, 7th inf.
Budd, Sebring, co. B, 1st cav.
Cummins, John W., co. L, 5th cav.
Clark, George M., co. L, 1st cav.
Duley, A. L., co. E, 7th cav.
Fitzgerald, co. C, 6th cav.
Frost, Allen M., co. G, 8th cav.
Groucher, Homer co. B, 6th cav.
Hutton, Samuel W., co. G, 9th cav.
Hathaway, Edward F., co. M, 8th cav.
Ingledue, Eber E., co. K, 9th cav.
Marshall, George N., co. M, 4th cav.
Moore, Allen, co. M, 6th cav.
McKay, B. G., co. M, 1st cav.
Preston, Benjamin, co. K, 7th cav.
Russell, Major W., co. M, 5th cav.
Ramsdell, Solomon, co. —, 6th cav.
Sherburn, Samuel, co. D, 6th cav.
Springer, Joseph, co. A, 7th cav.
Seeley, Harvey K., co. B, 6th cav.
Vincent, Albert, co. M, 1st cav.
Wilcox, Charles, co. A, 7th cav.
Willis, Henry O., co. —, 3d cav.
Wood, Charles, co. D, 11th cav.
Williams, J. D., co. I, 6th cav.

STATE OF WISCONSIN.

Brown, Edward, co. A, 13th inf.
Coburn, William A., co. A, 10th inf.
Card, Warren D, co. H, 33d inf.
Dubois, Jacob V., co. B, 36th inf.
Estey, Amos E., co. B, 21st inf.
Griggs, John A., co. —, 36th inf.
Green, L. Abner, co. I, 19th inf.
Hall, Hiram R., co. G, 13th inf.
Hitchcock, Joseph, co. K, 10th inf.
Menzies, Frederick, co. —, 5th inf.
McDonald, Isaac H., co. C, 2d inf.
Northcott, Richard, co. H, 10th inf.
Perry, Leslie, co. —, 6th inf.
Pyle, Amos M., co. K, 36th inf.
Smith, Sanford, co. E, 19th inf.
Sleeper, Hiram H., co. C, 38th inf.
Smith, Albert M., co. G, 21st inf.
Van Vickle, Walter M., co. C, 36th inf.
Webster, Alexander C., ser., co. E, 7th inf.
Wood, Walter, cor., co. A, 10th inf.
Webster, A. C., co. E, 7th inf.

Brown, Ellis, co. C, 1st cav.
Cole, Ezra H., co. H, 1st cav.
Dent, William, co. E, 1st cav.
Pillsbury, Adoniram Judson, co. H, 1st cav.
Somerville, William, co. H, 1st cav.

MINNESOTA.

Adams, Edwin H., co. H, 9th reg.
Bond, Daniel B., co. —, 1st bat.
Harney, Joseph E., co. K, 9th reg.
Ketchum, George W., co. —, 1st reg.
Mathews, Lyman, co. E, 9th reg.

STATE OF IOWA.

Baxley, David M., co. G, 35th inf.
Buckmaster, Frederick, co. K, 15th inf.
Jacobs, Josiah B., co. H, 7th inf.
Johnson, Jackson, co. —, 17th inf.
Knight, John F., co. I, 9th inf.
Knowles, Seth, co. C, 15th inf.
Lucis, Francis M., co. C, 25th inf.
Overtwiff, George, co. H, 5th inf.
Ray, William, co. —, 7th inf.
Richey, John N., co. E, 16th inf.
Tippery, William, co. K, 5th inf.
Whitten, Josiah A., co. H, 5th inf.
Whitten, John, co. H, 5th inf.
Bishard, Daniel C., co. M, 8th cav.
Dean, Henry H., co. B, 8th cav.
Frentzke, Charles, co. F, 5th cav.
Littlejohn, Leverett Junius, co. B, 4th cav.
Macy, Cyrus F., co. C, 8th cav.
Russell, W. W., co. A, 8th cav.
Wescott, Miles D., co. L, 8th cav.
Whitford, V. B., co. —, 5th cav.

STATE OF KENTUCKY

Beatty, Wm. H., serg., co. —, 15th regiment.
Cooke, Samuel H., co. H, 4th mounted inf.
Glassman, Peter, 4th cav.
Hamilton, John D., co. D, 11th cav.
Nilost, John, co. H, 6th cav.

STATE OF MISSOURI.

Owens, Owen H., co. G, 10th cav.
Doane, J. W., co. F, 1st light artillery.

VIRGINIA.

Clatter, John L., co. I, 4th.
Broughton, William, co. F, 2d mounted inf.
Howe, Lemuel B., co. I, 5th cav.
Holmes, Norris, co. —, 1st cav.
Noble, James C., co. B, 1st cav.

STATE OF WEST VIRGINIA.

Blessing, Pius, co. C, 15th inf.
Carroll, Tunis, co. E, 1st inf.
Campbell, William B., co. I, 12th inf.
Carothers, William E., co. A, 7th inf.
Hunt, Eugenius W., co. —, 12th inf.
Hunt, Philip, co. —, 12th inf.
Richter, Oscar, co. A, 1st inf.
Shup, Nicholas L., co. H, 14th inf.
Feay, William G, battery D, 1st light art.
Loring, John E., battery D, 1st light art.
Stephens, Allen, battery D, 1st light art.
Newman, Samuel G., co. —, 6th cav.

STATE OF TENNESSEE.

Barnett, John N., co. A, 2d mounted rifles.
Kirby, James M., co. K, 2d mounted rifles.
Bayles, Leroy, co. K, 2d mounted rifles.
Edwards, Ivey, co. B, 5th inf.
Willson, William K, co. —, 6th inf.
Edwards, Harry, co. B, 5th inf.
Long, J. A., co. C, 2d mounted inf.
Long, William H. H., co. C, 2d mounted inf.
Loren, Thomas J., co. H, 2d mounted inf.
Montgomery, William T., co. —, 4th inf.
Sherman, John, construction corps.
Byerly, William E. H., co. T, 10th cav.
Godsey, Samuel, co. N, 10th cav.
Montgomery, Campbell G, co. L, 1st cav.
Tate, Frank Boyd, co. M, 9th cav.
Brown, Henry, co. M, 8th cav.

MISCELLANEOUS.

Brown, Vincent, civilian.
Bradley, John, U. S. gunboat Southfield.
Butterfield, James P., laborer.
Campbell, J. B., 18th reg., 1st bat., V. R. C.
Edwards, Leonard J., U. S. ship Granite City.
Irvine, A. M., headq'rs 3d div'n 5th army corps.
Johnson, Geo. P., U. S. gunboat Nipsic.
Mollody, Patrick, marine battalion.
Rymer, Thos. F., signal officer, Charleston harbor.
Saule, Lewis H., co. A, 1st Berdan's Sharpsh's.
Sherwood, Henry, wagonmaster.
Nicholl, Jas.S., quarterm'sdep't, 1st div. 15th A. C.
Hill, James H., civilian.
Williams, James M., U. S. gunboat Southfield.
Griffin, Thomas, alias T. Smith, steamer Clifton.
Mahoney, George, steamer Clifton.

List No. 031

THE SALEM WITCHES

AUTHOR UNKNOWN
May 28, 1692

According to a witness, in January 1692, eleven-year-old Salem resident Abigail Williams and her nine-year-old cousin, Elizabeth Parris, began to behave erratically and sometimes had fits. Unable to find a medical reason for their behavior, the local doctor, William Griggs, instead blamed witchcraft, a diagnosis with which the girls agreed. Before long, other girls were also claiming to be possessed. The afflicted then began to accuse various local goodwives and others of being witches; and soon the Salem Witch Trials were in full swing. The list seen here details just some of the accused (on the left) and their accusers. The trials lasted for more than a year, during which twenty people, most of whom were deemed "witches," were executed.

Complaint of Severall May 28th 1692

Gooddy Carier of Andevor Tho: Carriers wife	Mary Walcott Abigail William
Gooddy fosdick of Maldin Goody pain: Mary Waren	Mary Walcott Mircy Lewes Abigail William Ann Putnam
Goody Read of marble head upon the hill by the meet'house	Mary Walcott Mircy Lewes Abigail William Ann Putnam
Gooddy Rice of Reding	Ed. Marshals wife Mary Walcott Abigall William
Goody How of Topsfield on Ipswich bounds	Mary Walcott Abigail Williams
Capt Hows brother wife vis Ja. Hows wife	Two women there abouts much affleted and suspect hir but canot sartainly say
Capt. Alldin complaind of a long time by	Mary Walcott Mircy Lewes Abigail Williams Ann Putnam Susana Sheldon
Wm. proctor	Mary Walcot Susana Shelden
Toothakors wife & daughter	Mary Walcot Abig. Williams
Capt. Flood	Mary Walcot Abigail Williams & the rest

As much as is legible at the foot of the list reads:

Arthur Abot lives in a by place some thing neare Maj. Appletons Farms and lives between Ip'h Topsfeild & Wenham
Complained of by Many'

Complaint of Severale May 28th 1692

goody Carrier of Andevor Tho. Carrier wife	mary walcott Abigail william
goody fosdick of maldin Goody pain: mary Waren	mary walcott mircy lewes Abigail william Ann putnam
goody Read of marble head upon ye hill by ye meeting house	mary walcott mircy lewes Abigail william Ann putnam
goody Rice of Reding	Ed. marshals wife mary walcott Abigail william
goody How of Topsfeild or Ipswich bounds Capt Hows brother wife Sir Ja. Hows wife	mary walcott Abigail williams two women there abouts much afflicted and suspect her but canot sartainly say
Capt. Alldin complaind of a long time by	Mary walcott mircy lewes Abigail williams Ann putnam Susana Sheldon
Wm. proctor	Mary. Walcot Susana. Shelden
Toothakers wife & daughter	Mary Walcot Abig. Williams
Capt flood	Mary Walcot Abigail Williams & others

Arthur Abott lives in a by place
some thing neere Majr Appletons farme
and lives betwen Ipsd. Topsfeild & Wenham

Abott yt lives betwen Ipswitch
Topsfeild and Wenham

Complaint of by
Mary [illegible]

List No. 032

J'AIME, JE N'AIME PAS

ROLAND BARTHES
1977

In his unconventional 1977 autobiography, *Roland Barthes* by Roland Barthes—a book which in itself is a list of sorts—the French sociologist, critic, and theorist presents two wonderfully evocative lists: one of things he likes, and another of things he doesn't. He then muses that such things are essentially pointless.

J'aime, je n'aime pas — I like, I don't like

I like: salad, cinnamon, cheese, pimento, marzipan, the smell of new-cut hay (why doesn't someone with a "nose" make such a perfume), roses, peonies, lavender, champagne, loosely held political convictions, Glenn Gould, too-cold beer, flat pillows, toast, Havana cigars, Handel, slow walks, pears, white peaches, cherries, colors, watches, all kinds of writing pens, desserts, unrefined salt, realistic novels, the piano, coffee, Pollock, Twombly, all romantic music, Sartre, Brecht, Verne, Fourier, Eisenstein, trains, Médoc wine, having change, *Bouvard and Pécuchet*, walking in sandals on the lanes of southwest France, the bend of the Adour seen from Doctor L.'s house, the Marx Brothers, the mountains at seven in the morning leaving Salamanca, etc.

I don't like: white Pomeranians, women in slacks, geraniums, strawberries, the harpsichord, Miró, tautologies, animated cartoons, Arthur Rubinstein, villas, the afternoon, Satie, Bartók, Vivaldi, telephoning, children's choruses, Chopin's concertos, Burgundian branles and Renaissance dances, the organ, Marc-Antoine Charpentier, his trumpets and kettledrums, the politico-sexual, scenes, initiatives, fidelity, spontaneity, evenings with people I don't know, etc.

I like, I don't like: this is of no importance to anyone; this, apparently, has no meaning. And yet all this means: *my body is not the same as yours*. Hence, in this anarchic foam of tastes and distastes, a kind of listless blur, gradually appears the figure of a bodily enigma, requiring complicity or irritation. Here begins the intimidation of the body, which obliges others to endure me *liberally*, to remain silent and polite confronted by pleasures or rejections which they do not share.

(A fly bothers me, I kill it: you kill what bothers you. If I had not killed the fly, it would have been *out of pure liberalism*: I am liberal in order not to be a killer.)

List No. 033

WORKMEN'S ABSENCES

AUTHOR UNKNOWN

Circa 1250 BC

This limestone ostracon was discovered during excavations of Deir el-Medina, an ancient Egyptian village once home to families of the workmen who built the tombs in the Valley of the Kings. It features a list of reasons for the laborers' work absences in Year 40 of Ramses II. Several are the excuses that still ring true today, such as "DRINKING WITH KHONSU"; and several are those, such as "EMBALMING HORMOSE," that somehow don't.

Huynefer: month 2 of Winter, day 7 (ILL), month 2 of Winter, day 8 (ILL), month 3 of Summer, day 3 (SUFFERING WITH HIS EYE), month 3 of Summer, day 5 (SUFFERING WITH HIS EYE), day 7 (ILL), day 8 (ILL)

Amenemwia: month 1 of Winter, day 15 (EMBALMING HORMOSE), month 2 of Winter, day 7 (OFF ABSENT), month 2 of Winter, day 8 (BREWING BEER), month 2 of Winter, day 16 (STRENGTHENING THE DOOR), day 23 (ILL), day 24 (ILL), month 3 of Winter, day 6 (WRAPPING (THE CORPSE OF) HIS MOTHER)

Inhurkhawy: month 4 of Spring, day 17 (HIS WIFE WAS BLEEDING)

Neferabu: month 4 of Spring, day 15 (HIS DAUGHTER WAS BLEEDING), day 17 (BURYING THE GOD), month 2 of Summer, day 7 (EMBALMING HIS BROTHER), day 8 (LIBATING FOR HIM), month 4 of Summer, day 26 (HIS WIFE WAS BLEEDING)

Paser: month 1 of Winter, day 25 (LIBATING FOR HIS SON), month 1 of Summer, day 27 (BREWING BEER), month 2 of Summer, day 14 (ILL), day 15 (ILL)

Pakhuru: month 4 of Summer, day 4, day 5, day 6, day 7 (ILL), day 8

Seba: month 4 of Spring, day 17 (THE SCORPION BIT HIM), month 1 of Winter, day 25 (ILL), month 4 of Winter, day 8 (HIS WIFE WAS BLEEDING), month 1 of Summer, day 25, 26, 27 (ILL), month 2 of Summer, day 2, day 3 (ILL), month 2 of Summer, day 4, day 5, day 6, day 7 (ILL)

Neferemsenut: month 2 of Winter, day 7 (ILL)

Simut: month 1 of Winter, day 18 (OFF ABSENT), month 1 of Winter, day 25 (HIS WIFE WAS . . . AND BLEEDING), month 4 of Winter, day 23 (HIS WIFE WAS BLEEDING)

Khons: month 4 of Spring, day 7 (ILL), month 3 of Winter, day 25 (ILL), month 3 of Winter, day 26 (ILL), day 27, day 28 (ILL), month 4 of Winter, day 8 (WITH HIS GOD), month 4 of Summer, day 26 (ILL), month 1 of Spring, day 14 (HIS FEAST), day 15 (HIS FEAST)

Inuy: month 1 of Winter, day 24 (FETCHING STONE FOR QENHERKHEPSHEF), month 2 of Winter day 8 (DITTO), month 2 of Winter, day 17 (OFF ABSENT WITH THE SCRIBE), month 2 of Winter, day 24 . . .

Sunero: month 2 of Winter, day 8 (BREWING BEER), month 2 of Summer, day 2 (ILL), day 3, day 4, day 5, day 6, day 7, day 8 (ILL)

Nebenmaat: month 3 of Summer, day 21 (ILL), day 22 (DITTO), month 4 of

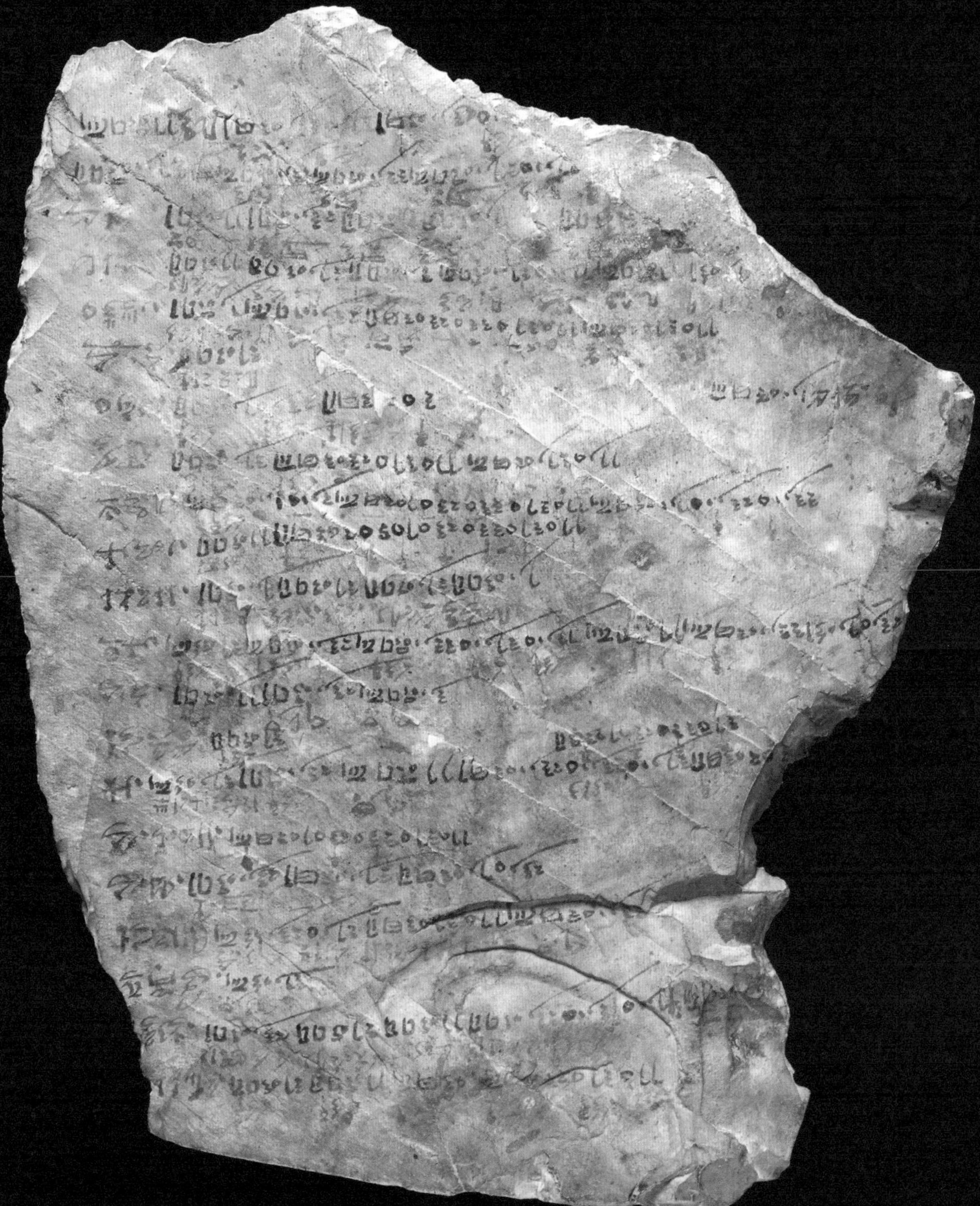

Summer, day 4 (DITTO), day 5, day 6 (DITTO), day 7, day 8 (DITTO), month 4 of Summer, day 24 (ILL), day 25 (ILL), day 26 (ILL)

Merwaset: month 2 of Winter, day 17 (BREWING BEER), month 3 of Summer, day 5 (ILL), day 7, day 8 (ILL), month 3 of Summer, day 17 (ILL), day 18 (WITH HIS BOSS)

Ramose: month 2 of Winter, day 14 (ILL), day 15 (ILL), month 2 of Summer, day 2 (MOURNING HIS SON), day 3 (ILL)

Bakenmut: month 2 of Winter, day 7 (FETCHING STONE FOR THE SCRIBE)

Rahotep: month 1 of Winter, day 14 (OFFERING TO THE GOD), month 4 of Winter, day 25 (HIS DAUGHTER WAS BLEEDING), month 2 of Summer, day 5 (WRAPPING (THE CORPSE OF) HIS SON), day 6, day 7, day 8 (DITTO), month 4 of Summer, day 7 (WITH THE SCRIBE), day 8 (WITH THE SCRIBE)

Iierniutef: month 2 of Winter, day 8 (OFF ABSENT), month 2 of Winter, day 17 (WITH THE SCRIBE), month 2 of Winter, day 23 (ILL), month 3 of Winter, day 27 (WITH THE SCRIBE), day 28 (OFF ABSENT), month 4 of Winter, day 8 (WITH THE SCRIBE), month 1 of Spring, day 14

Nakhtamun: month 1 of Winter, day 18 (BREWING BEER), month 1 of Winter, day 25 (WITH HIS BOSS), month 2 of Winter, day 13 (WITH HIS BOSS), month 2 of Winter, day 14 (WITH HIS BOSS), month 2 of Winter, day 15 (WITH HIS BOSS), month 2 of Winter, day 16 (WITH HIS BOSS), day 17, day 18 (WITH HIS BOSS), month 2 of Winter, day 24 (WITH HIS BOSS), month 3 of Winter, day 25 (WITH HIS BOSS), month 3 of Winter, day 26 (WITH HIS BOSS), month 3 of Winter, day 27 (WITH HIS BOSS), day 28 (WITH HIS BOSS), day . . . (WITH HIS BOSS), month 4 of Winter, day 8 (WITH THE SCRIBE), month 1 of Summer, day 16 (SUFFERING WITH HIS EYE), day 17 (SUFFERING WITH HIS EYE), month 1 of Summer, day 25 (ILL), day 26, day 27 (ILL)

Penduauu: month 1 of Spring, day 14 (DRINKING WITH KHONSU)

Hornefer: month 2 of Winter, day 13 (WITH HIS BOSS), day 14 (WITH HIS BOSS), day 15 (WITH HIS BOSS), month 2 of Winter (WITH HIS BOSS), day 16 (WITH HIS BOSS), day 17 (WITH HIS BOSS), day 23 (WITH HIS BOSS) . . . month . . . of Summer. . .

Hornefer: month 2 of Summer, day 10 (ILL)

Sawadjyt: month 3 of Spring, day 23 (WITH HIS BOSS), day 24 (WITH HIS BOSS), month 4 of Spring, day 16 (HIS DAUGHTER WAS BLEEDING), month 1 of Winter, day 14 (OFFERING TO THE GOD), month 1 of Winter, day 15 (DITTO), month 1 of Winter, day 24 (LIBATING TO HIS FATHER), day 25 (DITTO), day 26(?) (DITTO), day 28(?) (WITH HIS BOSS)

Sawadjyt: month 2 of Summer, day 14 (WITH HIS BOSS)

Horemwia: month 3 of Spring, day 21 (WITH HIS BOSS), day 22 (WITH HIS BOSS), month 2 of Winter, day 8 (BREWING BEER), month 3 of Summer, day 17 (ILL), day 18 (ILL), day 21 (ILL), day 22, month 2 of Summer, day 4 (WITH HIS BOSS), month 2 of Summer, day . . . (WITH HIS BOSS)

Horemwia: month 4 of Summer, day 4 (ILL), day 5 (ILL), day 6 (ILL), day 7 (ILL)

Amennakht: month 4 of Spring, day 15 (WITH HIS BOSS DITTO), day 16 (DITTO), day 17 (DITTO), month 3 of Winter, day 18 (BREWING BEER), month 2 of Summer, day 4 (WITH HIS BOSS), month 3 of Summer, day 7, day 8 (WITH HIS BOSS), month 3 of Summer, day 24, day 25, day 26 (WITH HIS BOSS)

Wadjmose: month 4 of Winter, day 23 (HIS DAUGHTER WAS BLEEDING), month 4 of Summer, day 6 (BUILDING HIS HOUSE)

Nebamentet [illegible]

Hehnekhu: month 1 of Summer, day 16 (WITH HIS BOSS), day 17 (WITH HIS BOSS), month 2 of Summer, day 7 (WRAPPING (THE CORPSE OF) HIS MOTHER), day 8 (DITTO)

Nakhy: month 1 of Spring, day 14 (WITH HIS BOSS), day 15 (DITTO)

Nakhtmin: month 1 of Winter, day 25 (LIBATING), month 2 of Winter, day 7 (FETCHING STONE FOR THE SCRIBE), month 3 of Winter, day 27 (HIS WIFE WAS BLEEDING)

Pennub: month 3 of Spring, day 21 (WITH AAPEHTI), day 22 (DITTO), day 23 (DITTO), day 24 (DITTO), month 2 of Winter, day 7 (FETCHING STONE FOR THE SCRIBE), month 2 of Winter, day 8 (FETCHING STONE FOR THE SCRIBE), day 23 (WITH THE SCRIBE), day 24 (WITH THE SCRIBE), month 3 of Winter, day 28 (BREWING BEER), month 4 of Winter, day 24 (HIS MOTHER WAS ILL), day 25 (DITTO)

Aapehti: month 3 of Spring, day 21 (ILL), day 22 (ILL), day 23 (ILL), day 24 (ILL), month 4 of Spring, day 7 (ILL), day 8 (ILL), day 15 (ILL), day 16 (ILL), month 1 of Winter, day 14 (OFFERING TO THE GOD), month 1 of Winter, day 17 (ILL), month 1 of Winter, day 18 (ILL), month 1 of Summer, day 27 (ILL)

Khaemtir: month 3 of Spring, day 21 (WITH HIS BOSS), day 22 (DITTO), day 23 (DITTO), day 24 (DITTO), month 4 of Spring, day 17 (BURYING THE GOD), month 1 of Winter, day 18 (BREWING BEER), month 3 of Summer, day 8 (ILL)

Amenmose: month 2 of Winter, day 8 (BREWING BEER)

Anuy: month 1 of Winter, day 24 (FETCHING STONE FOR THE SCRIBE), month 3 of Winter, day 28 (BREWING BEER)

Wennefer: month 1 of Winter, day 14 (OFFERING TO THE GOD), month 4 of Summer, day 4 (OFFERING TO HIS GOD)

Buqentuf: month 1 of Winter, day 17 (WITH HIS BOSS), month 1 of Winter, day 18 (BREWING BEER), month 2 of Summer, day 6 (WRAPPING (THE CORPSE OF) HIS MOTHER), day 8 (DITTO)

Manninakhtef [illegible]

Huy: month 1 of Winter, day 17 (BREWING BEER), day 18 (BREWING BEER), month 2 of Winter, day 17 (BREWING BEER), month 3 of Winter, day 27 (WITH HIS BOSS), day 28 (DITTO), month 4 of Winter, day 3 (WITH HIS BOSS), month 4 of Winter, day 7 (WITH HIS BOSS), day 8 (DITTO)

Huy: month 4 of Winter, day 24 (WITH HIS BOSS), month 4 of Summer, day 25 (DITTO), day 26 (DITTO)

. . . : month 3 of Spring, day 21 (ILL), day 22 (ILL), day 23 (ILL), day 24 (ILL), month 4 of Spring, day 7 (ILL), day 8 (ILL), month 1 of Winter, day 24 (ILL), month 2 of Winter day 8 (BREWING BEER), month 2 of Summer, day 8 (BREWING BEER)

Paherypedjet: month 3 of Spring, day 21 (WITH AAPEHTI), day 22 (DITTO), day 23 (DITTO), day 24 (DITTO), month 4 of Spring, day 7 (DITTO), day 8 (DITTO), day 15 (DITTO), day 16 (DITTO), day 17 (DITTO), month 1 of Winter, day 14 (OFFERING TO THE GOD), month 2(?) of Winter, day 13 (. . .), month 3 of Winter, day 25 (WITH KHONS MAKING REMEDIES), 26 (DITTO), month 3 of Winter, day 27 (DITTO), month 1 of Summer, day 25 (MAKING REMEDIES FOR THE SCRIBE'S WIFE), day 26 (DITTO), day 27 (DITTO), month 2 of Summer, day 2 (DITTO), day 3 (DITTO), day 4, day 5, day 6, day 7, day 8 (DITTO), month 3 of Summer, day 3 (WITH KHONS MAKING REMEDIES), day 17 (WITH HOREMWIA), day 18 (WITH HOREMWIA), day 21 (DITTO), day 22, month 4 of Summer, day 4, month 4 of Summer, day 5, day 6, day 7, day 8, day 24 (ILL), day 25, day 26, month 1 of Spring, day 15 (ILL), day 16(?) (ILL)

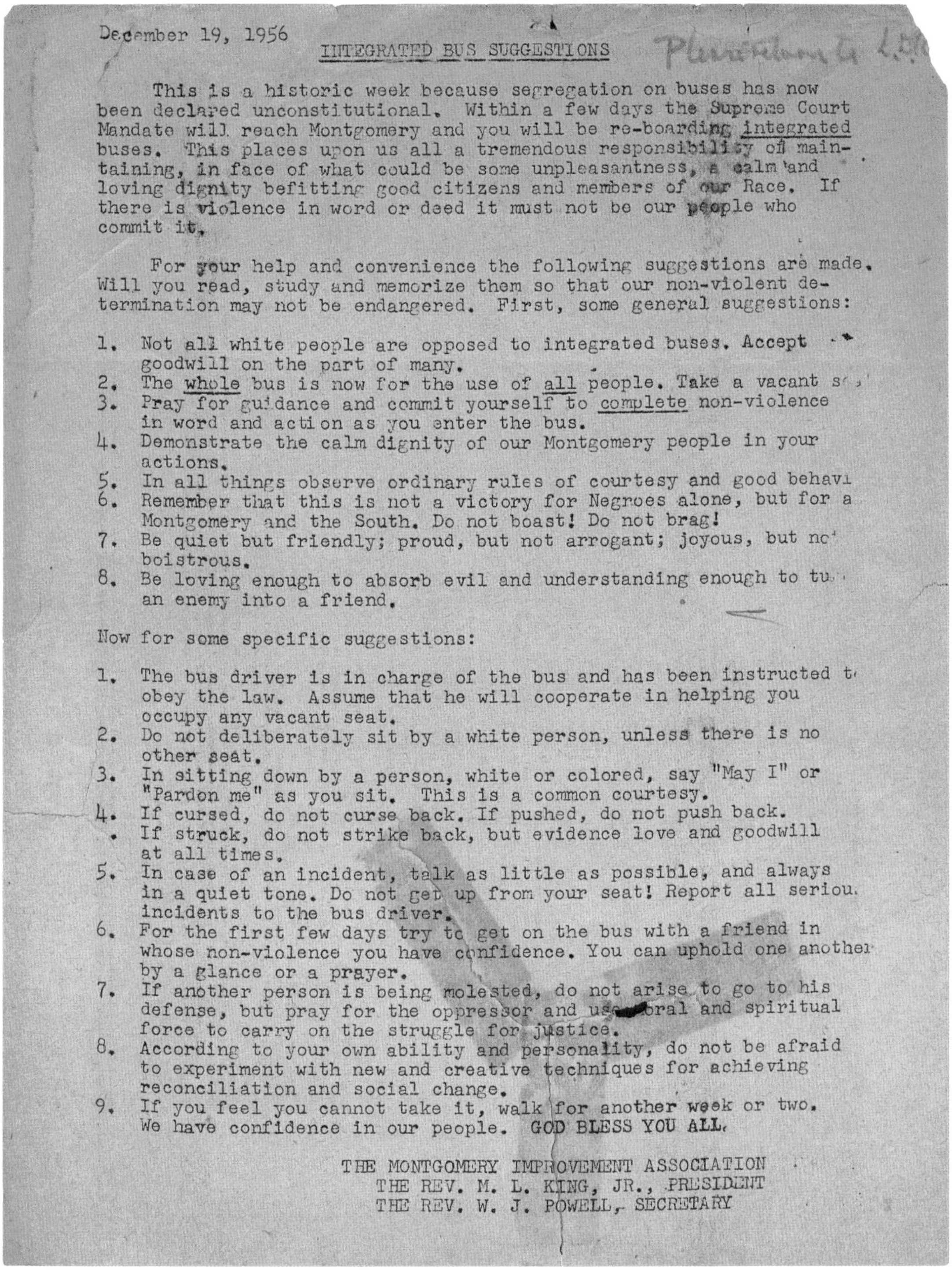

December 19, 1956

INTEGRATED BUS SUGGESTIONS

This is a historic week because segregation on buses has now been declared unconstitutional. Within a few days the Supreme Court Mandate will reach Montgomery and you will be re-boarding integrated buses. This places upon us all a tremendous responsibility of maintaining, in face of what could be some unpleasantness, a calm and loving dignity befitting good citizens and members of our Race. If there is violence in word or deed it must not be our people who commit it.

For your help and convenience the following suggestions are made. Will you read, study and memorize them so that our non-violent determination may not be endangered. First, some general suggestions:

1. Not all white people are opposed to integrated buses. Accept goodwill on the part of many.
2. The whole bus is now for the use of all people. Take a vacant s
3. Pray for guidance and commit yourself to complete non-violence in word and action as you enter the bus.
4. Demonstrate the calm dignity of our Montgomery people in your actions.
5. In all things observe ordinary rules of courtesy and good behavi
6. Remember that this is not a victory for Negroes alone, but for a Montgomery and the South. Do not boast! Do not brag!
7. Be quiet but friendly; proud, but not arrogant; joyous, but no boistrous.
8. Be loving enough to absorb evil and understanding enough to tu an enemy into a friend.

Now for some specific suggestions:

1. The bus driver is in charge of the bus and has been instructed t obey the law. Assume that he will cooperate in helping you occupy any vacant seat.
2. Do not deliberately sit by a white person, unless there is no other seat.
3. In sitting down by a person, white or colored, say "May I" or "Pardon me" as you sit. This is a common courtesy.
4. If cursed, do not curse back. If pushed, do not push back.
   - If struck, do not strike back, but evidence love and goodwill at all times.
5. In case of an incident, talk as little as possible, and always in a quiet tone. Do not get up from your seat! Report all seriou incidents to the bus driver.
6. For the first few days try to get on the bus with a friend in whose non-violence you have confidence. You can uphold one anothe by a glance or a prayer.
7. If another person is being molested, do not arise to go to his defense, but pray for the oppressor and use moral and spiritual force to carry on the struggle for justice.
8. According to your own ability and personality, do not be afraid to experiment with new and creative techniques for achieving reconciliation and social change.
9. If you feel you cannot take it, walk for another week or two. We have confidence in our people. GOD BLESS YOU ALL.

THE MONTGOMERY IMPROVEMENT ASSOCIATION
THE REV. M. L. KING, JR., PRESIDENT
THE REV. W. J. POWELL, SECRETARY

INTEGRATED BUS SUGGESTIONS

MARTIN LUTHER KING JR

December 19, 1956

On December 1, 1955, the course of history was changed when Rosa Parks refused to give up her bus seat for a white passenger and was subsequently arrested. For the next year, until racial segregation was deemed unconstitutional by the federal courts, a boycott of the public transport system took place, headed by Martin Luther King Jr. On December 19, 1956, the eve of a historic victory for those opposed to such segregation, King prepared a list of guidelines for those soon to be reboarding the buses.

List No. 035

TEN COMMANDMENTS FOR CON MEN

VICTOR LUSTIG

1936

"Count" Victor Lustig was a con man of considerable note. Born in 1890, by the 1930s he was wanted by approximately forty-five law enforcement agencies worldwide for a plethora of crimes. He had twenty-five known aliases and spoke five languages. He cunningly gained $5,000 from Al Capone, one of the most notorious and feared criminals of the age. Better still, in 1925, Lustig posed as a government official in Paris, took five businessmen on a tour of the Eiffel Tower, and then "sold" it to one of them as 7,300 tons of scrap metal. The con went so well he tried it again soon after. In 1936, Lustig wrote this list of commandments for aspiring con men. Victor Lustig would die in 1947, having been sentenced to twenty years on Alcatraz for counterfeiting.

1. Be a patient listener (it is this, not fast talking, that gets a con-man his coups).
2. Never look bored.
3. Wait for the other person to reveal any political opinions, then agree with them.
4. Let the other person reveal religious views, then have the same ones.
5. Hint at sex talk, but don't follow it up unless the other fellow shows a strong interest.
6. Never discuss illness, unless some special concern is shown.
7. Never pry into a person's personal circumstances (they'll tell you all eventually).
8. Never boast. Just let your importance be quietly obvious.
9. Never be untidy.
10. Never get drunk.

List No. 036

GOBBLEFUNK

ROALD DAHL
Early 1980s

In 1982, *The BFG* was published—a magical and wildly successful children's book in which a Big Friendly Giant blows pleasant dreams through the windows of young children. As he was creating the story, renowned author Roald Dahl set about creating a new vocabulary for the enormous protagonist: a 238-word language that he ultimately named "Gobblefunk." Words that made the cut included: "humplecrimp," "swallomp," "crumpscoddle," and, perhaps most memorably, "snozzcumber." The list you see here was written by Dahl as he brainstormed, and offers a snapshot of "Gobblefunk" in its infancy.

The Fleshlumpeating Giant

a notmucher, a squeakpip.

cronky
crinky
corky

blivver(ing)
stoching
protching
mickering (aww)

~~swish~~

~~manhugging giant~~
~~fizzlecump~~
~~bottle wart~~
gumplewink
~~swigfiddle~~
~~squiffsquiddle~~
flushbuckling
whopsy-waddling
~~pongswizzler~~
~~scumscrewer~~
bagblurter
~~fizzwiggler~~
spitzwargler
spitzwoggler
~~buzzbunger~~
bizzfizz
buzzfuzz
baghangar
bophanger
wash-hinger
spongewiggler
~~codswallop~~
~~muckfrumping~~
splatchwinkling
~~crodscollop~~
shardlelly
~~spatchwinkle~~
~~swishfiggler~~
swogglewop
gunzleswipe
pifflemutter

troggy
paggle
~~pibbling~~
~~dibbling~~
ristling
~~blunketing~~
pranky
filking
pilching
~~scoddling~~
slidger
~~squiggling~~
squibbling
squinkling
squeakling
~~squmping~~
scumping
~~scuddling~~
swiddling
~~squiffling~~
slunging
grobbled
squiffly-jumpsy

rag-rasper
~~rotrasper~~

~~scrumplet~~
squiffler
sludge
pong-ping-pong

~~jumpsy~~
dropsy
~~swipsy~~
kicksey
fruggler
~~grobswitch~~
crodswitch
kickswitch
~~grobby~~
~~lickswitch~~
dissible
sliggy

~~bunkledoodle~~
grob fatch
~~grobswitch~~
~~wimplesquiffer~~
snipply
grilky
gronky
grouty
~~cream puffnut~~

~~snog winker~~
~~ring beller~~
phizz-whizz
chidler or tottle = child
schweinwein
squinky
scud

~~squeakpip~~

he skimmed toward her.
lemons & fresh coffee

The Fleshlumpeating Giant

a rotmucher, a squeakpip.

~~manhugging giant~~

Cronky
crinky
Corky
blivver(ing)
slocking
protching
mickering (away)
Swish...

~~fizzlecump~~
~~bottlewart~~
jumplewink
~~swigpiddle~~
~~squiffsquiddle~~
flushbuckling
whopsy-waddling
~~pongswizzler~~
~~scumscewer~~
bagblaster
~~fizzwiggler~~ wigger
spitzwaggler
spitzwoggler
~~buzzburger~~
bizzfizz
buzzfuzz
baghanger
bophanger
wash-linger
spongewiggler
codswallop
~~muckfrumping~~
splatchwinkling
~~crodscollop~~
shadbelly
~~splatchwinkle~~
~~swishfiggler~~
swogglewop
gunzleswipe
pifflemuffler

Troggy
paggle
~~fibbling~~
~~dibbling~~
ristling
~~blunketing~~
prunking
filking
~~pif~~ pilching
~~scuddling~~
sludger
~~squiggling~~
squibbling
squinkling
squackling
~~scrumpling~~
scumping
~~scuddling~~
swiddling
~~squiffling~~
slunging
grobbled
squiffly-jumpsy
rag rasper
~~rotrasper~~
~~scrumplet~~
squiffler
sludge
(pong-ping-pong)

~~jumpsy~~
dropsy
~~snipsy~~
kicksey
fruggler
~~frobswitch~~
crodswitch
kickswitch
~~grobby~~
~~lickswish~~
dissible
sliggy
~~buckleboodle~~
(grob fatch)
~~frobswitch~~
~~[illegible]~~
~~snippling~~ ~~[illegible]~~
grilky
gronky
grousy
~~cream puffnut~~
~~grogwinkle~~
~~riggbelter~~
phizz-whizz
(chidler or tottle = child)
schweinwein
~~squeakpip~~

[illegible]
squinky

List No. 037

TOPICS TO BE INVESTIGATED

LEONARDO DA VINCI
1489

Leonardo da Vinci's fascination with every aspect of the human body is apparent in much of his work, his famous *Vitruvian Man* (the pen-and-ink drawing of a man whose supposedly ideal proportions were based on those discussed in the writings of Roman architect Vitruvius) being a prime example. In 1489, around the same time as he drew the *Vitruvian Man*, Leonardo wrote in one of his notebooks, from right to left as was his wont, a list of topics to be investigated in his quest to become an expert anatomist.

What nerve is the cause of movement of the eye and makes the movement of one eye draw the other

on closing the eyelids

on raising the eyelids

on lowering the eyelids

on shutting the eyes

on opening the eyes

on raising the nostrils

on opening the lips with the teeth closed

on bringing the lips to a point

on laughing

on [the expression of] wonder

describe the origin of man when he is generated in the womb

and why an infant of eight months does not live

what is sneezing

what is yawning

epilepsy

spasm

paralysis

trembling with cold

sweating

tiredness

hunger

sleep

thirst

lust

on the nerve which causes movement from the shoulder to the elbow

on movement from the elbow to the hand

from the wrist to the beginning of the fingers

from the beginning of the fingers to their middle

and from the middle to the last joint

on the nerve which causes movement of the thigh

and from the knee to the foot and from the ankle to the toes

and also to their middle

and of the rotation of the leg

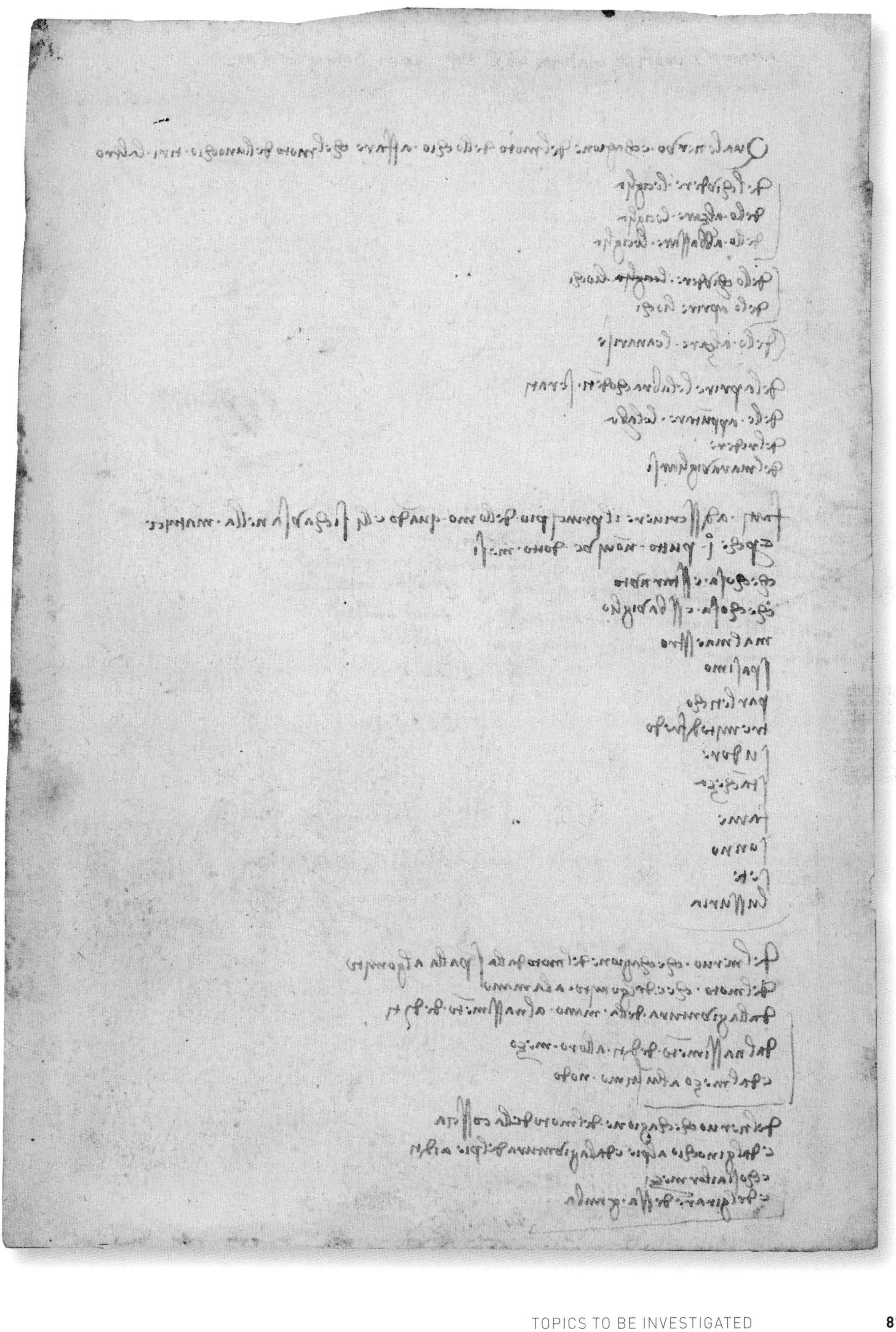

NEW YER'S GUIFTES GIUEN TO THE QUENE'S MAIESTIE

QUEEN ELIZABETH I
1578–1579

Every New Year's Day of her forty-four-year reign, from 1559 until 1603, Queen Elizabeth I would amass hundreds of gifts from members of the royal household in a tradition that had begun centuries before, but that Elizabeth actively encouraged as no other. Although it was a voluntary arrangement, almost all who served the Queen's Majesty offered her gifts, or gold. (An Elizabethan pound was roughly equivalent to $450 in today's money.) The queen even offered presents to some in return, albeit of low value and often boasting her image. After each gift exchange a list was drawn up of her highness's takings, beginning with lords and ladies, ending with her lowly staff, and signed off by the queen herself.

New Yer's Guiftes giuen to the QUENE'S MAIESTIE *at her Highnes Manor of Richmond, by these Persons whose Names hereafter do ensue, the First of January, the Yere abouesaid.*

	£.	s.	d.
By the Lady *Margret* Countes of *Darby*, a trayne gowne of tawny vellat.			
Delivered to *Rauff Hope*, Yoman of her Roobes.			
By Sir *Nicholas Bacon*, Knight, Lorde Keper of the Greate Seale of Inglande, in golde and siluer	13	6	8
By the Lorde *Burley*, Lorde High Treausorour of Inglande, in golde	20	0	0
By the Lorde Marquis of *Winchester*, in golde	20	0	0
Delivered to *Henry Sackford*, Grome.			

EARLES.

	£.	s.	d.
By therle of *Leycetour*, Master of the Horses, a verey feyer juell of golde, being a clocke fully furnished with small diamonds pointed, and a pendaunte of golde, diamonds, and rubyes, very smale; and upon eche side a lozenge diamonde, and an apple of golde enamuled grene and russet.			
Delivered to the Lady *Hawarde*.			
By therle of *Arondell*, in golde	30	0	0
By therle of *Shrewesbury*, in golde	20	0	0
By therle of *Darby*, in golde	20	0	0
By therle of *Sussex*, Lorde Chamberleyn, in golde	20	0	0
By therle of *Lincoln*, Lord Admirall of Inglande, in golde	10	0	0
Delivered to the aforesaid *Henry Sackford*.			
By therle of *Warwyck*, a juell of golde, being a very great tophas set in gold, ennamuled with 8 perles pendant.			
Delivered to the Lady *Hawarde*.			
By therle of *Bedforde*, in golde	20	0	0
Delivered to the foresaid *Henry Sackford*.			
By therle of *Oxforde*, a very feyer juell of golde, wherein is a helmet of golde and small diamonds furnished, and under the same is five rubyes, one bigger then threst, and a small diamond brokenne; and all threst of the same juell furnesshed with small diamonds.			
Delivered to the Lady *Hawarde*.			
By therle of *Rutlande*, in golde	10	0	0
By therle of *Huntingdon*, in golde	10	0	0
By therle of *Penbroke*, in golde	20	0	0
By therle of *Northumberlande*, in golde	10	0	0
By therle of *Southampton*, in golde	20	0	0
Delivered to the foresaid *Henry Sackford*.			
By therle of *Hertford*, a small peyer of writing tabells enamuled with a grashopper, all of golde, ennamuled grene on the backsyde, and a pynne of golde having a small perle at thende thereof.			

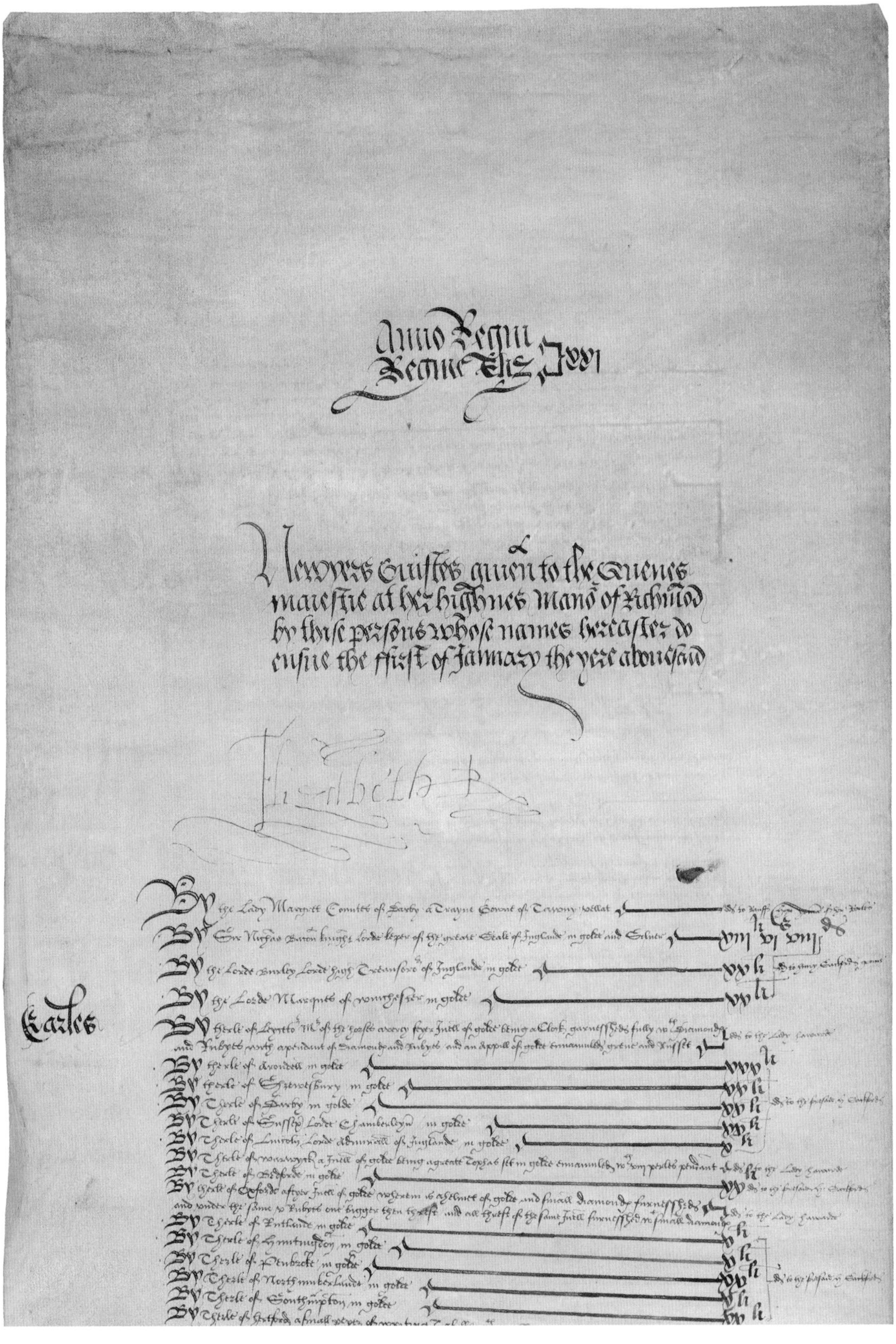
Anno Regni
Regine Eliz. xxvi

Newyeres Guiftes giuen to the Quenes
maiestie at her highnes Manor of Richmond
by theise persons whose names hereafter do
ensue the ffirst of January the yere abouesaid

Elizabeth R

By therle of *Ormonde*, a very fayre juell of golde, whearin are three large emeraldes sett in roses white and redd, one bigger than the other twoo; all the rest of the same juell garnished with roses and flowers enamuled, furnished with very smale dyamonds and rubyes; aboute the edge very smale perles; and in the bottome is parte of a flower-de-luce garnished with smale diamondes, rubyes, and one sapher, with three meane pearles pendaunte, two of them smale; the backsyde a flower-de-luce enamuled greene.
By therle of *Surr'*, a gyrdill of tawny vellat embrawdred with sede perle, the buckyll and pendant of golde.
Delivered to the Lady *Hawarde*.

Vicount.

By the Vicounte *Mountague*, in golde	10	0	0

Delivered to the foresaid *Henry Sackford*.

Duchesses, Marquisses, and Countess.

By the Duches of *Suffolke*, a lylly pot of agathe, a lylly flower going owte of it garnsshed with roses of rubyes and diamonds hanging at two small cheynes of golde.
Delivered to the Lady *Hawarde*.

By the Duches of *Somerset*, in golde and silver	18	6	8
By the Lady Marques of *Winchester*, in golde	10	0	0

Delivered to the foresaid *Henry Sackford*.
By the Lady Marques of *Northampton*, a gyrdill of golde with buckells and pendants of golde, garneshed with sparks of rubyes and diamonds, and also 10 perles set in colletts of golde.
Delivered to the Lady *Hawarde*.
By the Countes of *Shrewesbury*, a mantyll of tawny satten enbrawdred with a border of Venice golde and silver, lyned with white taphata, and faced with white satten.
By the Countes of *Warwyk*, a cap of black vellat with 13 buttons of golde, in every of them eyther a ruby or diamonde; and a knot of small perle, with a garter and a byrde upon the same; and a perle pendant.
Delivered to the foresaid *Rauf Hoope*.

By the Countes of *Sussex*, in golde	10	0	0

Delivered to the foresaid *Henry Sackford*.
By the Countess of *Bedford*, a foreparte of white satten, enbrawdred with black sylke and golde, with two feyer borders of Venice golde and sede perle enbrawdred.
Delivered to the foresaid *Rauf Hoope*.
By the Countes of *Lincoln*, a jug of marbill garnesshed with golde, per oz. 18 oz. di. qr.
Remaynyng with *John Astley*, Master of the Juells.

By the Countes of *Huntingdon*, in golde	8	0	0

Delivered to the foresaid *Henry Sackford*.
By the Countes of *Oxford*, a foreparte of a kyrtyll of white satten enbrawdred with flowers of silver, and two borders of golde and sede perle enbrawdred upon black vellat.
Delivered to the foresaid *Rauf Hoope*.

By the Countes of *Penbroke*, doager, in golde	12	0	0
By the Countes *Penbroke*, junior, in golde	10	0	0
By the Countes of *Northumberlande*, in golde	10	0	0
By the Countes of *Southampton*, in golde	10	0	0

Delivered to the foresaid *Henry Sackford*.
By the Countes of *Essex*, a greate cheyne of amber slightly garneshed with golde and small perle.
Delivered to the *Lady Hawarde*.

By the Countes of *Rutlande*, in golde	10	0	0

Delivered to the foresaid *Henry Sackford*.
By the Countes of *Kent*, doager, a mufler of purple vellat, enbrawdred with Venice and damaske golde and perle.

Delivered to Mrs. *Elizabeth Knowlls*.
By the Countes of *Kent*, junior, a foreparte of a kyrtyll network, floureshed with golde and tufts of sundry coloured sylke.
Delivered to the foresaid *Rauf Hoope*.

By the Vicecountes of *Mountague*, in golde	10	0	0

Busshops.

By the Archebusshop of *Yorke*, in golde	30	0	0
By the Busshop of *Ely*, in golde	30	0	0
By the Busshop of *Dureham*, in golde	30	0	0
By the Busshop of *London*, in golde	20	0	0
By the Busshop of *Winchester*, in golde	20	0	0
By the Busshop of *Salisbury*, in golde	20	0	0
By the Busshop of *Lincoln*, in golde	20	0	0
By the Busshop of *Norwiche*, in golde	20	0	0
By the Busshop of *Worcetour*, in golde	20	0	0
By the Busshop of *Lichfelde*, in golde and silver	8	6	8
By the Busshop of *Hereford*, in golde	10	0	0
By the Busshop of *Seint David*, in golde	10	0	0
By the Busshop of *Karlyle*, in golde	10	0	0
By the Busshop of *Bathe*, in golde	10	0	0
By the Busshop of *Peterborough*, in golde	10	0	0
By the Busshop of *Glocestour*, in golde	10	0	0
By the Busshop of *Chicester*, in golde	10	0	0
By the Busshop of *Rochester*, in golde	10	0	0

Lordes.

By the Lorde of *Burgavenny*, in golde	30	0	0

Delivered to the foresaid *Henry Sackford*.
By the Lorde *Howarde*, a lock of golde, black ennamuled, garneshed with 16 small diamonds.
Delivered to the Lady *Hawarde*.
By the Lorde *Russell*, a cawle of here, garneshed with buttons of golde, within ennamuled, and set with ragged perle.
Delivered to the Mrs. *Elizabeth Knowlls*.

By the Lorde *Riche*, in golde	10	0	0
By the Lorde *Darcy of Chyche*, in golde	10	0	0
By the Lorde *Shandowes*, in golde and silver	6	13	4
By the Lorde *North*, in golde	10	0	0
By the Lorde *Paget*, in golde	10	0	0
By the Lorde *Stafford*, in golde	10	0	0
By the Lorde *Compton*, in golde	10	0	0
By the Lorde *Norrys of Rycote*, in golde	10	0	0
By the Lorde *Lumley*, in golde	10	0	0
By the Lorde *Wharton*, in golde	10	0	0
By the Lorde *Morley*, in golde	10	0	0

Delivered to the foresaid *Henry Sackford*.

By the Lorde *Cobham*, a dublet of white satten lyned with murry, white sarcenet leyed with a pasmane of golde and sylke.

Delivered to the foresaid *Rauf Hope.*

By the Lorde *Henry Hawarde*, a juell of golde, being a ded tre with mysaltow, set at the rote with sparks of diamonds and rubys.

Baronesses.

By the Lady Baronesse *Burleigh*, 36 buttons of golde, one broken.			
Delivered to the Lady *Haward.*			
By the Lady Barones *Howarde*, Dowager, in golde	10	0	0
Delivered to the forsaid *Henry Sackford.*			
By the Lady Barones *Howard*, jun. a juell of golde, garnesshed with rubys and diamonds, and thre smale perles pendant.			
Delivered to the same Lady *Hawarde.*			
By the Lady Barones *Cobham*, a petticote of crymsen rewed with silver.			
By the Lady Barones *Dacres*, a gowne of wrought vellat.			
Delivered to the forsaid *Rauf Hope.*			
By the Lady Barones *Tayleboyes*, in golde	10	0	0
Delivered to the forsaid *Henry Sackford.*			
By the Lady Barones *Shandowes*, douger, a feyer skarf of grene sersenet enbrawdred with byrds and flowers of sylke and golde of sundry collours, frenged with Venice golde, and lyned with murry sarceonet.			
By the Lady Barones *Shandowes*, jun. a vale of black networke flurreshed with flowers of silver and a small bone lace.			
Delivered to Mrs. *Elizabeth Knowlls.*			
By the Lady Barones *Seint John Bletzelow*, in golde	10	0	0
Delivered to the forsaid *Henry Sackford.*			
By the Lady Barones *Paget*, the Lord's wyf, a pettycote of cloth of golde, stayned black and white, with a bone lace of golde and and spangells leyed lyke waves of the see.			
Delivered to the foresaid *Rauf Hope.*			
By the Barones *Paget Darce*, a small cheyne of golde, with a luer of golde hanging at it, on thone syde a white dove, and on thother syde a hawke with a button white ennamuled.			
By the Lady Barones *Cheyny*, a carcanet of golde, cont' 8 peces, with byrds and frute ennamuled.			
Delivered to the foresaid Lady *Hawarde.*			
By the Lady Barones *Awdeley*, a foreparte of a kyrtill of orenge collored satten.			
Delivered to the foresaid *Rauf Hope.*			
By the Lady Barones *Barkeley*, in golde	10	0	0
By the Lady Barones *Bookehurst*, in golde	5	0	0
By the Lady Barones *Norris*, in golde	10	0	0
Delivered to the forsaid *Henry Sackford.*			
By the Lady Barones *Sheffelde*, a kyrtyll of purple satten, with roses of white lawne enbrawdred with golde unlyned.			
Delivered to the foresaid *Rauf Hope.*			
By the Lady *Vere*, Mr. *Bartewe's* wyf, a vale oof open worke with golde and spangills.			
Delivered to Mrs. *Elizabeth Knowlls.*			
By the Lady Barones *Morley*, a pettycote of white satten all over enbrawdred with roses of golde; and 3 gards, likewyse enbrawdred, lyned with white satten, and frenged with sylke and golde.			
Delivered to the forsaid *Rauf Hope.*			

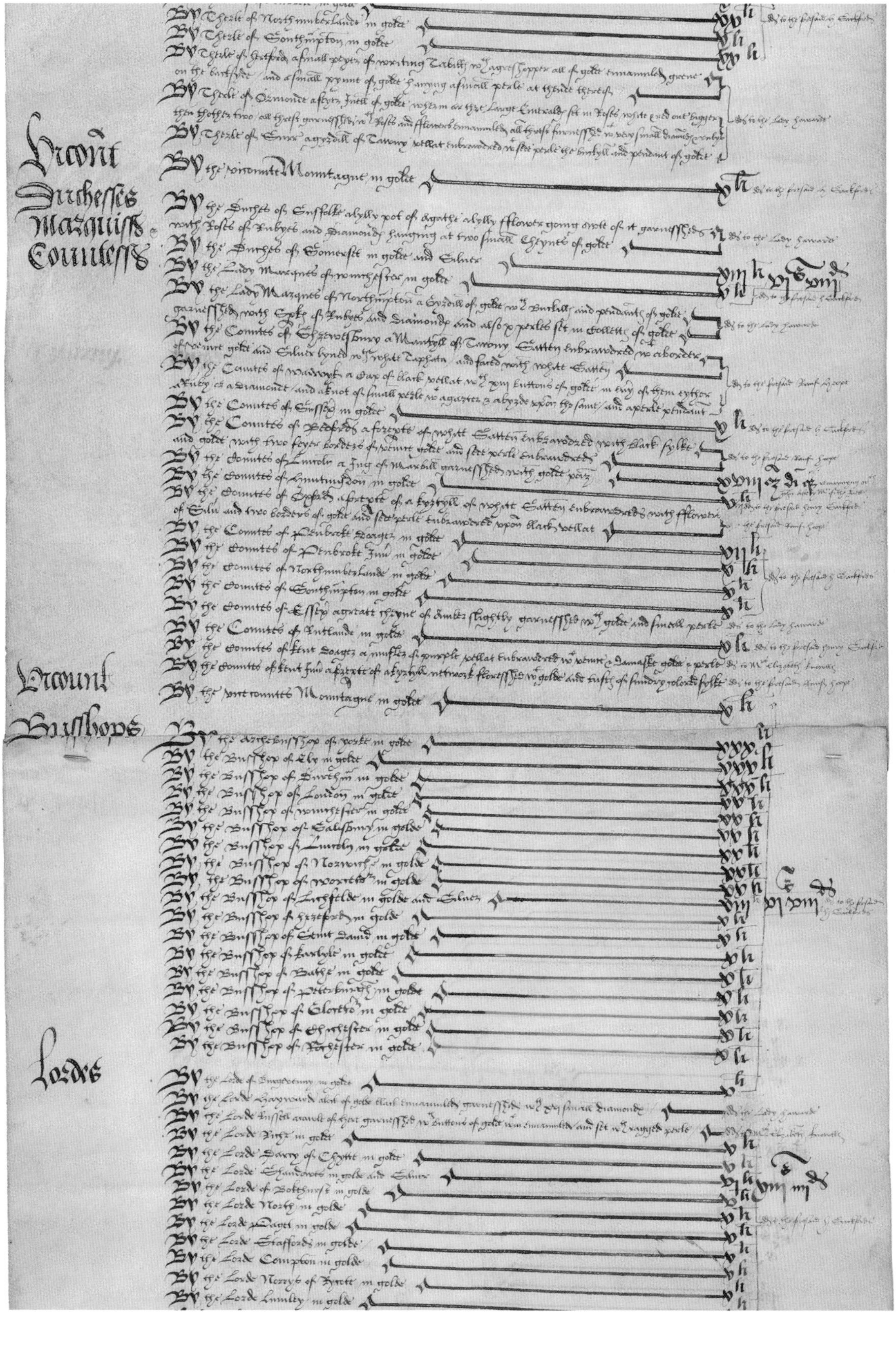

By the Lady Barrones *Wharton*, a juell of golde, wherein is a parret hanging, garnesshed with small diamonds, and a cluster of perle pendaunt lacking a ffysshe on thone syde.
Delivered to the forsaid Lady *Hawarde*

Ladies.

By the Lady *Mary Sydney*, a smock and two pillowbyers of cameryk, feyer wrought with black worke, and edged with a brode bone lace of black sylke.
Delivered to Mrs. *Skydmore*.
By the Lady *Mary Sem'*, wif to Mr. *Rogers*, a touthe-pike of golde made gonne fation.
Delivered to the foresaid Lady *Haward*.
By the Lady *Elizabeth Sem'*, alias *Knightlye*, a kyrtell of oring tawnye satten, edged with a passamayne of silver.
Delivered to the forsaid *Rauf Hope*.
By the Lady *Stafforde*, a juell of golde, being an agate garnished with golde, sett about with sparks of rubyes and diamonds, with a smale perle pendaunt.
Delivered to the forsaid Lady *Haward*.
By the Lady *Carowe*, a cusshen clothe camereke, blake worke, and frenged with Venice golde.
Delivered to Mrs. *Skydmore*.
By the Lady *Cheeke*, a foreparte of golde and silver networke.
Delivered to the forsaid *Rauf Hope*.

By the Lady *Butler*, in golde	6	0	0

Delivered to the foresaid *Henry Sackford*.
By the Lady *Heniaige*, a pomaunder gar' with golde and 12 sparks of rubies and perles pendaunt, per oz.
Delivered to the foresaid Lady *Haward*.
By the Lady *Waulsingham*, 4 paire of gloves set with buttons of golde.

Delivered to Mrs. *Elizabeth Knowlls*.
By the Lady *Drury*, a foreparte of clothe of silver, all over enbraudred with clothe of golde.

Delivered to the foresaid *Rauf Hope*.

By the Lady *Pawlet*, in golde	5	0	0

Delivered to the foresaid *Henry Sackford*.
By the Lady *Willoby*, Sir *Francis*' wif, tow pillowberes of camerike wrought allover withe carnatyon silke.
Delivered to Mrs. *Skydmore*.

By the Lady *Gresham*, in golde	10	0	0
By the Lady *Cromwell*, Sir *Henrye's* wif, in golde	5	0	0

Delivered to the forsaid *Henry Sackford*.
By the Lady *Ratclyf*, a vale of white worke with spangles, and a smale bone lace of silver, a swete bag, beinge of changeable silke, with a smale bone lace of golde.
The vale delivered to Mrs. *Elizabeth Knowlls*; and the bag to Mrs. *Skydmore*.
By the Lady *Frogmorton*, a large bag to put a pillow in of morre satten, allover enbrauderid with golde, silver, and silke of sondry collours, with 4 tassels of grene silke and golde; and a cusshen-cloth of networke, florisshed over with flowers of golde, silver, and silke of sondry collours, lyned with white satten.
Delivered to Mrs. *Skydmore*.
By the Lady *Cromwell*, Lorde *Cromwell's* wif, 3 sutes of ruffes of white cute worke, edged with a passamayne of white.
Delivered to Mrs. *Jane Bresett*.
By the Lady *Wilforde*, thre peces of lawne, wroughte with white and florisshed with golde.
Delivered to Mrs. *Skydmore*.

By the Lorde Darcy of Chyche in golde
By the Lorde Shandowes in golde and Siluer
By the Lorde of Bokhurste in golde
By the Lorde North in golde
By the Lorde Paget in golde
By the Lorde Stafforde in golde
By the Lorde Compton in golde
By the Lorde Norrys of Ricott in golde
By the Lorde Lumley in golde
By the Lorde Wharton in golde
By the Lorde Morley in golde
By the Lorde Cobham a Dublet of white Satten lyned with murry white sarcenet layde with a passamant of golde and sylke
By the Lorde Henry Haward a Juell of golde being a Crabbe with mysseltowe set at the toppe with sparks of Diamonds and Rubyes

Baronesses

By the Lady Baronesse Burleigh xxxij buttons of golde out broken
By the Lady Baronesse Hawarde Dowager in golde
By the Lady Baronesse Haward Junior a Juell of golde garnesshed with Rubys and Diamonds and thre perles pendant
By the Lady Baronesse Cobham a petticote of Crymsen Satten with Siluer
By the Lady Baronesse Darcy a gowne of wrought vellat
By the Lady Baronesse Tayleboys in golde
By the Lady Baronesse Shandowes Dowager a foreparte of grene sarcenet enbrawdered with byrdes and flowres of sylke and golde of sundry colours frenged with venice golde and lyned with murry Carsonet
By the Lady Baronesse Shandowes Junior a vale of blak network florisshed with flowres of Siluer and a small bonelace
By the Lady Baronesse Saint John Bletzlow in golde
By the Lady Baronesse Paget the Lordes wyfe a petty cote of clothe of golde stayned blak and white with a bone lace of golde and Spangills layed lyke wavys of the See
By the Baronesse Paget Carey a small cheyne of golde with a lute of golde hanging at it on thone syde a hart sett and on thotherside a hawke with a Button white ennamuled
By the Lady Baronesse Cheyny a Carcanett of golde sett with pery with byrds and fruit ennamuled
By the Lady Baronesse Audeley a foreparte of a kyrtill of Orenge collored Satten
By the Lady Baronesse Barkeley in golde
By the Lady Baronesse Bokhurste in golde
By the Lady Baronesse Norrys in golde
By the Lady Baronesse Sheffelde a kyrtill of purple Satten with roses of white lawne enbrawdered with golde unlyned
By the Lady Barret Mrs Barkleys wyfe a vale of open worke with golde and Spangills
By the Lady Baronesse Morley a pettycote of white Satten alover enbrawdered with roses of golde and iii gardes likewyse enbrawdered lyned with white Satten and frenged with sylke and golde
By the Lady Baronesse Wharton wherein is a Juell of golde a parrett hanging garnesshed with small Diamonds and a cluster of perle pendant lacking a fysshe on thonesyde

Ladies

By the Lady Mary Sydney a Smock and two pillowbyres of Camerycke sewed wrought with blak worke and edged with abrode bonelace of blak sylke
By the Lady Mary Seimour wyfe to Mr Rogers a Tothe pike of golde made gonne fashion
By the Lady Elizabeth Seimour alias knyghtley a kyrtell of Orenge Tawny Satten edged with a passamayne of Siluer
By the Lady Stafforde a Juell of golde being an Agath sett about with sparks of Rubyes and diamonds with a small perle pendant
By the Lady Carowe a Cusshen clothe Camerycke blak work and frenged with venice golde
By the Lady Cheek a foreparte of golde and siluer networke
By the Lady Butler in golde
By the Lady Hennage a pomander garnished with golde and vj sparks of Rubies and perles pendant
By the Lady Walsingham iii paire of gloves set with buttons of golde
By the Lady Drury a foreparte of clothe of siluer alover enbrawderid with clothe of golde
By the Lady Pawlet in golde
By the Lady Willoby Sir Frauncis wife two pillowberes of Camerike wroughte allover with Carnatyon silke
By the Lady Gresham in golde
By the Lady Cromwell Sir Henryes wife in golde
By the Lady Ratclyf a vale of white worke with spangles and a small bone lace of Siluer a sute of ruffes being of Chaungeable silke with a small bone lace of golde
By the Lady Throgmorton a large bag to put a pillowe in of murre Satten allover enbrawderid with golde siluer and silke of sondry collors with iiij Tassells of grene silke and golde and a Cusshen clothe of net worke florisshed over with flowers of golde siluer and silke of sondry collors lyned with white Satten
By the Lady Cromwell Lorde Cromwells wife iij sutes of Ruffes of white cutworke edged with a passamayne of white
By the Lady Wilforde thre peces of lawne wroughte with white and florisshed with golde
By the Lady Marbery a paire of Sleaves of Orenge collor Satten
By the Lady Crofte a petticote of Carnation Satten enbrawderid with flowers of silke of sondry collors
By the Lady Sowche thre peces of cutworke florisshed with golde

By the Lady *Marvey*, a paire of sleaves of oringe-colour satten.
Delivered to the forsaid *Rauf Hope*.
By the Lady *Crofts*, a peticote of carnation satten, enbrawderid with flowers of silke of sondry collours.
Delivered to the same *Rauf Hope*.
By the Lady *Souche*, thre peces of superior cut-worke, florisshd with golde.
Delivered to Mrs. *Skydmore*.

Knights.

By Sir *Frauncis Knowles*, Treasorour of our Householde, 3 angells	10	0	0
By Sir *James Crofts*, Comptrolor of the same, in di. sovereignes	10	0	0

Delivered to the forsaid *Henry Sackford*.
By Sir *Chrystopher Hatton*, Vice-chamberlen, a carkanet and a border of golde; the same carkanet contayning seven redd roses of golde, in every of them very smale diamondes, and in the topp a garnet and eight troches of meane pearles, four in every troche, and fourteen perles pendante, being lose; and the said border containing twenty-four redd roses of golde garnished with a very smale diamonde, in every of them a garnet and perle pendaunte, garnished with very small seed perle, and seven open pendants of golde; every one of them garnished with very small dyamondes, three meane perles, and thedges garnished with a very small seed perle.
Delivered to the Lady *Haward*.
By Sir *Frauncis Waulsingham*, Pryncipall Secretary, a night-gowne of tawney satten, allover enbraderid, faced with satten like heare collour.
Delivered to the forsaid *Rauf Hope*.
By Mr. *Thomas Wilson*, Esquire, also Secretary, a cup of agath, with a cover and garnisshment of golde enamuled, the same agath crased in dyvers places, per oz. 17 oz. qrt.
Delivered to Mr. *Asteley*, Mr. Threausorour of the Juells.

By Sir *Rauf Sadler*, Chauncellor of the Duchey	15	0	0
By Sir *Waulter Mildmay*, Chauncellor of the Exchequer, in angells	10	0	0
By Sir *William Cordell*, Master of the Rolles, in golde	10	0	0

Delivered to the forsaid *Henry Sackford*.
By Sir *Henry Sydney*, Lorde Deputie of Irelande, a feyer juell of golde, with a Dyana, fully garnisshed wythe dyamonds, one biggar than the rest, three rubyes, two pearles, and a pearle pendante; the backsyde a ship.
Delivered to the Lady *Hawarde*.

By Sir *William Damsell*, Recevor of the Courte of Wardes	10	0	0
By Sir *Owine Hopton*, Livetenant of the Tower	10	0	0

Delivered to the forsaid *Henry Sackford*.
By Sir *Thomas Hennaige*, Treasoror of the Chamber, a proper ringe of golde ennamulled in the top thereof, an white rubye without a foyle, with a grahounde in it.
By Sir *Edwarde Horsey*, Captayne of thile of Wight, a touthe picke of golde, the top beinge garneshed with a faire emeraude, a dyamond, and ruby, and other smale dyamonds and rubies, with two perles pendaunt.
Delivered to the Lady *Hawarde*.
By Sir *Guilbarte Dethicke*, alias *Garter*, Principall Kinge at Armes, a booke at armes.

By Sir *Christopher Haydon*, in golde	10	0	0
By Sir *Henry Cromwell*, in golde	10	0	0

Delivered to the foresaid *Henry Sackford*.
By Sir *Gawine Carowe*, a smoke of cameryke, wrought with blake worke, and edged with bone lace of golde.
Delivered to Mrs. *Skydmore*.

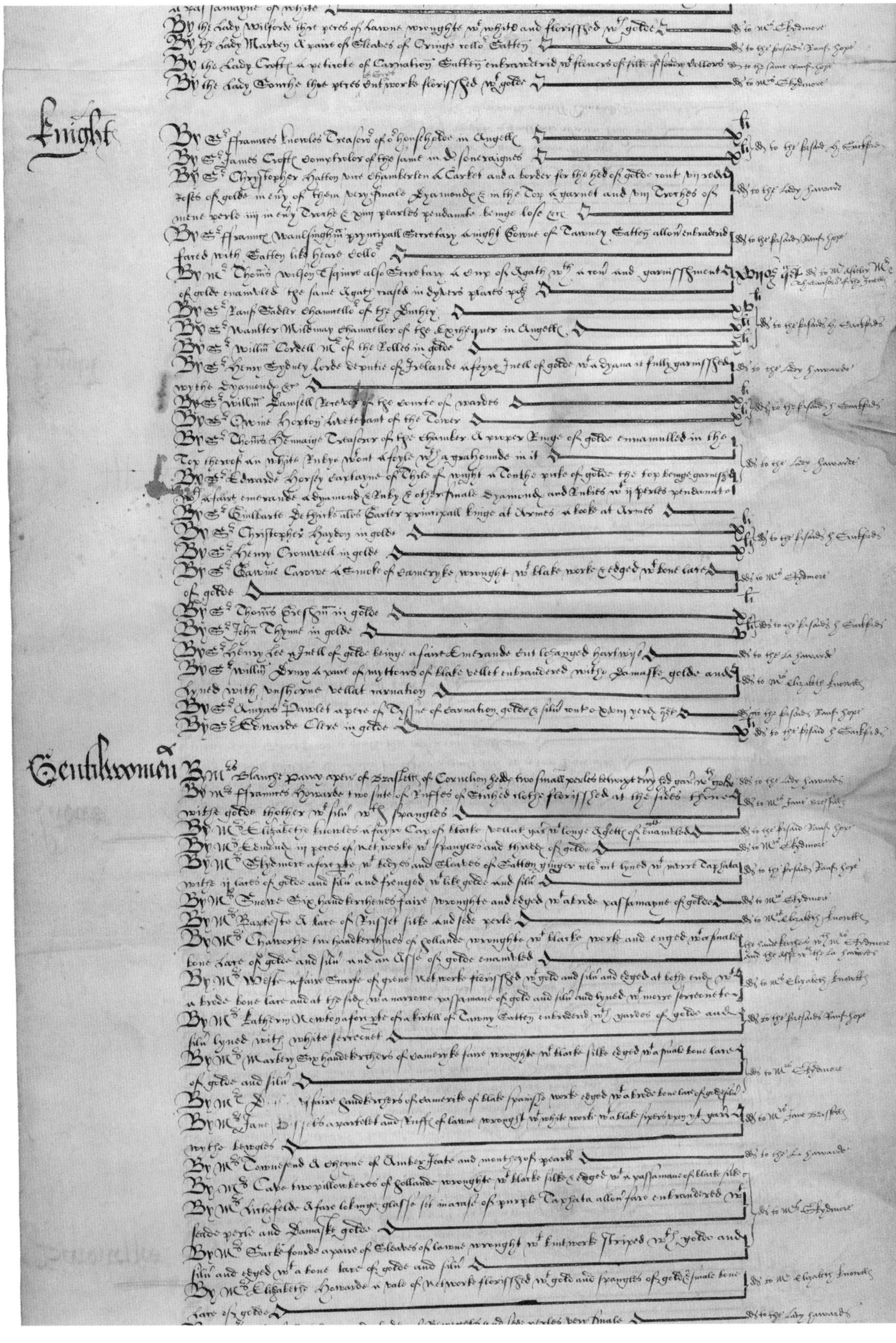

By the Lady Wilforde that peice of lawne wrought with white and florisshed with golde
By the Lady Marbery a paire of sleaves of Cipres rolle sattin
By the Lady Crofte a peticote of Carnation sattin enbrawdred with flowers of silk of sondry collors
By the Lady Sowthe that peice owt worke florisshed with golde

Knight

By Sir ffrauncis knowles Treasorer of our houshold in Angells
By Sir James Crofte Comptroler of the same in dimi sovraignes
By Sir Christopher Hatton vice Chamberlen a Carkenet and a border for the hed of golde
By Sir ffrauncis Walsingham principall Secretary a nyght Cowle of Tawny sattin allover enbrawdred
By Mr Thomas Wilson Esquire also Secretary a Cup of Agath with a cover and garnisshment of golde enamuled
By Sir Rauf Sadler Chauncellor of the Duchy
By Sir Walter Mildmay Chauncellor of the Exchequer in Angells
By Sir William Cordell Mr of the Rolles in golde
By Sir Henry Sydney lorde deputie of Irelande a feyre Juell of golde with a Dyana
By Sir William Damsell Receiver of the courte of wardes
By Sir Owen Hopton Lieutenant of the Tower
By Sir Thomas Henneage Treasorer of the chamber a pece of golde enamuled
By Sir Edwarde Horsy Captayne of the Ile of wight
By Sir Gilbarte Dethicke alias Garter principall kinge at Armes a booke at Armes
By Sir Christopher Haydon in golde
By Sir Henry Cromwell in golde
By Sir Gawine Carowe a Smock of Camryke wrought with blake worke and edged with bone lace of golde
By Sir Thomas Gresham in golde
By Sir John Thynne in golde
By Sir Henry Lee a Juell of golde
By Sir William Drury a paire of mytteyns of blake vellet enbrawdered with Damaske golde and lyned with unshorne vellat carnation
By Sir Amyas Pawlet a pece of Tyssue of carnation golde and silver
By Sir Edwarde Clere in golde

Gentilwomen

By Mrs Blaunche Parry a pece of Brasilett
By Mrs ffrauncis Howarde two sute of Ruffes of Cambrike
By Mrs Elizabeth knowles a fayre Cap of blake vellat
By Mrs Edmund
By Mrs Skydmore
By Mrs Snowe Six handkerchers faire wroughte and edged with a brode passamaynt of golde
By Mrs Barteley a lace of Russet silk and sede perle
By Mrs Chaworth Six handkerchers of hollande wroughte with blake worke
By Mrs Weste a faire Scarfe of grene Networke florisshed with golde and silver
By Mrs Katheryn Newton a fore parte of a kirtill of Tawny sattin
By Mrs Marbery Six handkerchers of Cameryke faire wroughte with blake silke
By Mrs Jane Bisshop a partelet and Ruffe of lawne wrought with white worke
By Mrs Townesend a Cheyne of Amber
By Mrs Cave two pillowberes of hollande wroughte with blake silke
By Mrs Litchefelde a fare lokinge glasse set in a case of purple Taffata
By Mrs Sackforde a paire of sleaves of lawne wrought with knitworke striped with golde and silver
By Mrs Elizabeth Howarde a vale of Networke florisshed with golde and spangells of golde

By Sir *Thomas Gresham*, in golde	10	0	0
By Sir *John Thynne*, in golde	5	0	0

Delivered to the foresaid *Henry Sackford.*

By Sir *Henry Lee*, a juell of golde, being a faire emeraude, cut lozanged hartwise.

Delivered to the Lady *Hawarde.*

By Sir *William Drury*, a paire of myttows of blake vellet enbraudered with damaske golde, and lyned with unshorne vellat carnation.

Delivered to Mrs. *Elizabeth Knowlls.*

By Sir *Amyas Pawlet*, a pece of tyssue of carnation golde and siluer, cont' 18 yedrs qr.

Delivered to the foresaid *Rauf Hope.*

By Sir *Edwarde Clere*, in golde.

Delivered to the foresaid *Henry Sackford.*

Gentilwomen.

By Mrs. *Blanche Parry*, a peir of brasletts of Cornelion hedds two small perles betwixt every hed, gar' with golde.

Delivered to the Lady *Haward.*

By Mrs. *Fraunces Howarde*, two sute of ruffes of stitched clothe florisshed at the sides, thone withe golde, thother with siluer with spangles.

Delivered to Mrs. *Jane Bressills.*

By Mrs. *Elizabethe Knowles*, a fayre cap of black vellat, gar' ith longe agetts golde enamuled.

Delivered to the foresaid *Rauf Hope.*

By Mrs. *Edmonds*, three peces of networke with spangles and threds of golde.

Delivered to Mrs. *Skydmore.*

By Mrs. *Skydmore*, a foreparte with bodyes and sleaves of satten, ginger colour, cut, lyned with murre taphata, with two laces of golde and siluer, and frenged with like golde and siluer.

Delivered to the foresaid *Rauf Hope.*

By Mrs. *Snowe*, six handkercheues, faire wroughte and edged, with a passamayne of golde.

Delivered to Mrs. *Skydmore.*

By Mrs. *Bapteste*, a lace of russet silke and sede perle.

Delivered to Mrs. *Elizabeth Knowlls.*

By Mrs. *Chaworthe*, two handkerchives of Hollande, wroughte with blacke worke, and edged with a smale bone lace of golde and siluer; and an asse of golde enamuled.

The handekerchers with Mrs. *Skydmore*; and the asse with the Lady *Haward.*

By Mrs. *Weste*, a faire scarfe of grene networke florisshed with golde and siluer, and edged at bothe ends with a brode bone lace, and at the side with a narrowe passamane of golde and siluer, and lyned with murre serceonete.

Delivered to Mrs. *Elizabeth Knowlls.*

By Mrs. *Katherin Newton*, a forepart of a kirtill of tawny satten, enbroderid with gardes of golde and siluer, lyned with white sercenet.

Delivered to the foresaid *Rauf Hope.*

By Mrs. *Marbery*, six handekerchers of cameryke faire wrought with blacke silke, edged with a smale bone lace of golde and siluer.

By Mrs. *Digby*, six faire handkerchers of camerike of blake Spanish worke, edged with a brode bone lace of golde and siluer.

Delivered to Mrs. *Skydmore.*

By Mrs. *Bissels*, a partelet and ruffs of lawne wrought with white worke, with a blake sipers upon yt, gar' wythe bewgles.

Delivered to Mrs. *Jane Brissetts.*

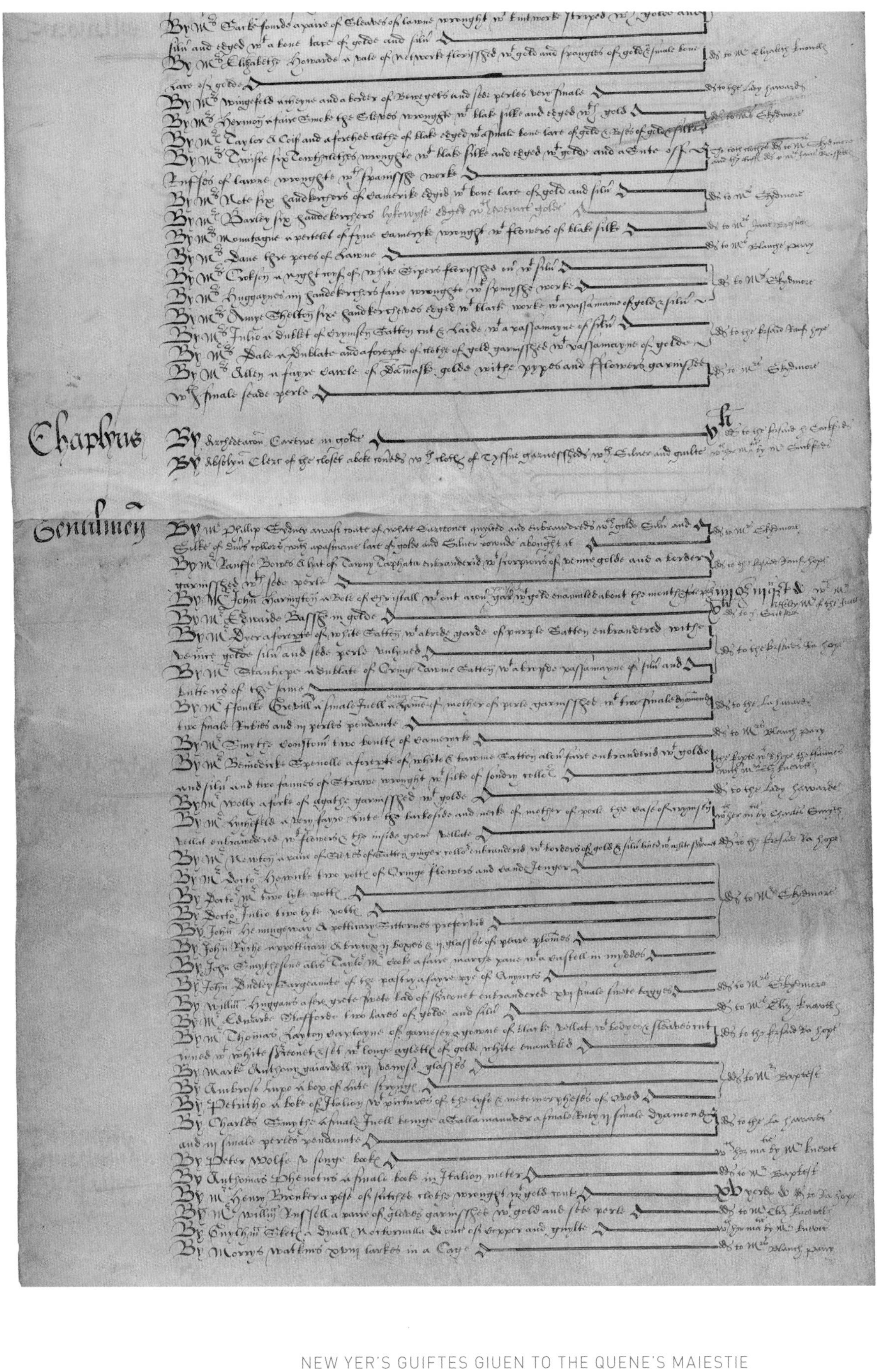

By Mrs. *Townesend*, a cheyne of ambey, jeate, and mouther of pearll.
Delivered to the Lady *Hawarde*.
By Mrs. *Cave*, two pillowberes of Hollande, wroughte with blacke silke, and edged with a passamane of blacke silke.
By Mrs. *Lichefelde*, a fare lokinge glasse set in a case of purple taphata, allou' fare enbrawdered with seade perle and damaske golde.
By Mrs. *Sackefourde*, a paire of sleaves of lawne wrought with knit worke, striped with golde and siluer, and edged wtih a bone lace of golde and siluer.
Delivered to Mrs. *Skydmore*.
By Mrs. *Elizabeth Howarde*, a vale of networke florisshed with gold and spangles of gold, and smale bone lace of golde.
Delivered to Mrs. *Elizabeth Knowlls*.
By Mrs. *Wingefeld*, a chaine and a border of bewegels and seed perles very smale.
Delivered to the Lady *Haward*.
By Mrs. *Hermon*, a faire smoke, the sleves wroughte with blake silke, and edged with gold.
By Mrs. *Taylor*, a coif and forehed clothe of blake, edged with a smale bone lace of gold, and roses of gold and silke.
Delivered to Mrs. *Skydmore*.
By Mrs. *Twiste*, six towthclothes wroughte with blake silke, and edged with golde; and a sute of ruffes of lawne, wroughte with Spanisshe worke.
The toth clothes delivered to Mrs. *Skydmore*; and the ruffes delivered to Mrs. *Jane Brissetts*.
By Mrs. *Note*, sixe handkerchers of camerike, edged with bone lace of gold and siluer.
By Mrs. *Barley*, six handekerchers, lykewyse edged with Venice golde.
Delivered to Mrs. *Skydmore*.
By Mrs. *Mountague*, a pertelet of fyne cameryke, wroughte with flowers of blake silke.
Delivered by Mrs. *Jane Bressett*.
By Mrs. *Dane*, thre peces of lawne.
Delivered to Mrs. *Blanche Parry*.
By Mrs. *Crokson*, a night coyf of white Cipers florisshed ouer with siluer.
By Mrs. *Huggaynes*, four handekerchers faire wroughte with Spanyshe worke.
By Mrs. *Amye Shelton*, sixe handkercheves edged with black worke with a passamaine of golde and siluer.
Delivered to Mrs. *Skydmore*.
By Mrs. *Julio*, a dublet of crymsen satten, cut and laide with a passamayne of siluer.
By Mrs. *Dale*, a dublate and foreparte of clothe of gold, garnisshed with a passamayne of golde.
Delivered to the forsaid *Rauf Hope*.
By Mrs. *Allen*, a fayre cawle of damaske golde, with pypes and flowers garnished with a smale seade perle.
Delivered to Mrs. *Skydmore*.

Chaplyns.

By Archedeacon *Carewe*, in golde £10.
Delivered to the forsaid *Henry Sackford*.
By *Absolyn*, Clerc of the Closet, a boke couered with cloth of tyssue, garnesshed with siluer and guilte.
With her Majestie, by Mr. *Sackford*.

Summa totalis of all the money giuen to her Maiestie and deliuered in man and fourme aboue declared
Elizabeth R

GENTILMEN.

By Mr. *Philip Sydney*, a wastcoate of white sarceonet, quylted and enbrawdred with golde, siluer, and silke of diuers collors, with a pasmane lace of golde and siluer rownde abought it.

Delivered to Mrs. *Skydmore*.

By Mr. *Rauffe Bowes*, a hat of tawny taphata, enbrauderid with scorpions of Venice golde, and a border garnisshed with sede perle.

Delivered to the forsaid *Rauf Hope*.

By Mr. *John Harington*, a bole of christall without a couer, grasd, garnisshed with gold enamuled about the mouth and fote, per oz. 4 oz. 3 qr. di.

With Mr. *Asteley*, Master of the Juells.

By Mr. *Edward Basshe*, in golde £10.

Delivered to *Henry Sackford*.

By Mr. *Dyer*, a foreparte of white satten, with a brode garde of purple satten, enbraudered withe Venice golde, silluer, and sede perle, unlyned.

By Mr. *Stanhope*, a dublate of oringe tawnie satten with a brode passamayne of siluer and buttons of the same.

Delivered to the foresaid *Rauf Hope*.

By Mr. *Foulke Grevill*, a smale juell, being a lambe of mother-of-perle, garnished with two smale dyamonds, two smale rubies, and three perles pendante.

Delivered to the Lady *Hawarde*.

By Mr. *Smythe Coustom'*, two boults of camerycke.

Delivered to Mrs. *Blanch Pary*.

By Mr. *Beinedicke Spenolle*, a foreparte of white and tawnie satten, al ouer faire, enbrauderid with golde and siluer; and two fannes of strawe, wrought with silke of sondry collours.

The foreparte with *Rauf Hope*; the fannes with Mrs. *Elizabeth Knowll*.

By Mr. *Wolly*, a forke of agathe garnisshed with golde.

Delivered to the Lady *Hawarde*.

By Mr. *Lychfeld*, a very fayre lute, the backeside and necke of mother-of-perle, the case of crymsen vellat, enbrawedered with flowers, and the inside grene vellate.

With her Majestie, by *Charles Smyth*.

By Mr. *Newton*, a paire of sleves of satten, ginger collour, enbrauderid with borders of gold and siluer, lined with white sarceonet.

Delivered to the foresaid *Rauf Hope*.

By Mr. Doctor *Hewicke*, two potts of oringe flowers, and cande jenger.

By Doctor *Mr.* two lyke potts.

By Doctor *Julio*, two lyke potts.

By *John Hemnigeway*, Apotticary, sittornes preservid.

By *John Ryche*, Apotticary, abrycos two boxes, and two glasses of peare pomes.

Delivered to Mrs. *Skydmore*.

By *John Smythesone*, alias *Taylor*, Master Cooke, a fayre march pane with a cattell in myddes.

By *John Dudley*, Sargeaunte of the Pastry, a fayre pye of quynces.

By *William Huggans*, a fere grete bad of sarceonet, enbraudered, sixteen smale swete bagges.

Delivered to Mrs. *Skydmore*.

By Mr. *Edwarde Stafforde*, two laces of golde and siluer.

Delivered to Mrs. *Elizabeth Knowlls*.

By Mr. *Thomas Layton*, Captayne of Garnesey, a gowne of blacke vellat, with bodyes and sleaves cut, lyned with white sarceonet, and sett with longe agletts of golde white enamuled.

Delivered to the forsaid *Rauf Hope*.

By *Marke Anthony Gaiardell*, four Venyse glasses.

By *Ambrose Lupo*, a box of lute-strynge.
By *Petricho*, a boke of Italian, with pictures of the lyfe and metomerpheses of Oved.
Delivered to Mr. *Baptest*.
By *Charles Smythe*, a small juell, being a salamaunder, a smale ruby, two smale dyamonds, and three smale perles pendaunte.
Delivered to the Lady *Haward*.
By *Peter Wolfe*, five songe books.
With her Majestie, by Mr. *Knevet*.
By *Anthonias Phenotus*, a smale booke in Italian meter.
Delivered to Mr. *Baptest*.
By Mr. *Henry Bronker*, a pese of stitched clothe wrought with gold cont' fifteen yerds di.
Delivered to *Rauf Hope*.
By Mr. *William Russell*, a paire of gloves, garnished with gold and sede perle.
Delivered to Mrs. *Elizabeth Knowlls*.
By *Guylham Sketh*, a dyall noctornalla, di. onc' of copper, and guylte.
With her Majestie, by Mrs. *Knevet*.
By *Morrys Watkins*, eighteen larkes in a cage.
Delivered to Mrs. *Blanch Parry*.

Summa totalis of all the money giuen to her Maiestie, and deliuered in man' and fourme aboue declared	497	13	4

List No. 039

FATHER'S OBJECTIONS

CHARLES DARWIN
1831

In August 1831, having recently graduated from the University of Cambridge and shortly to join the church, twenty-two-year-old Charles Darwin was invited to join a two-year expedition to South America and beyond aboard the HMS *Beagle*, in the role of Captain's Companion. That voyage, which would end up taking five years, became his life's most important journey. For it was on that voyage, while studying the fossils and wildlife en route, that Darwin truly became a scientist, resulting first in the publication of his *Journal of Researches* (1838; now generally known as *The Voyage of the Beagle*) and helping to inspire the thinking that would inform his groundbreaking book on evolution, *On the Origin of Species* (1859). Before he could even set foot on the ship, however, his father supplied him with a list of objections to the trip. Seen here are those objections written in Darwin's hand in a letter to his Uncle Josiah, who succeeded in bringing Darwin's father around.

(1) Disreputable to my character as a Clergyman hereafter

(2) A wild scheme

(3) That they must have offered to many others before me, the place of Naturalist

(4) And from its not being accepted there must be some serious objection to the vessel or expedition

(5) That I should never settle down to a steady life hereafter

(6) That my accommodations would be most uncomfortable

(7) That you should consider it as again changing my profession

(8) That it would be a useless undertaking

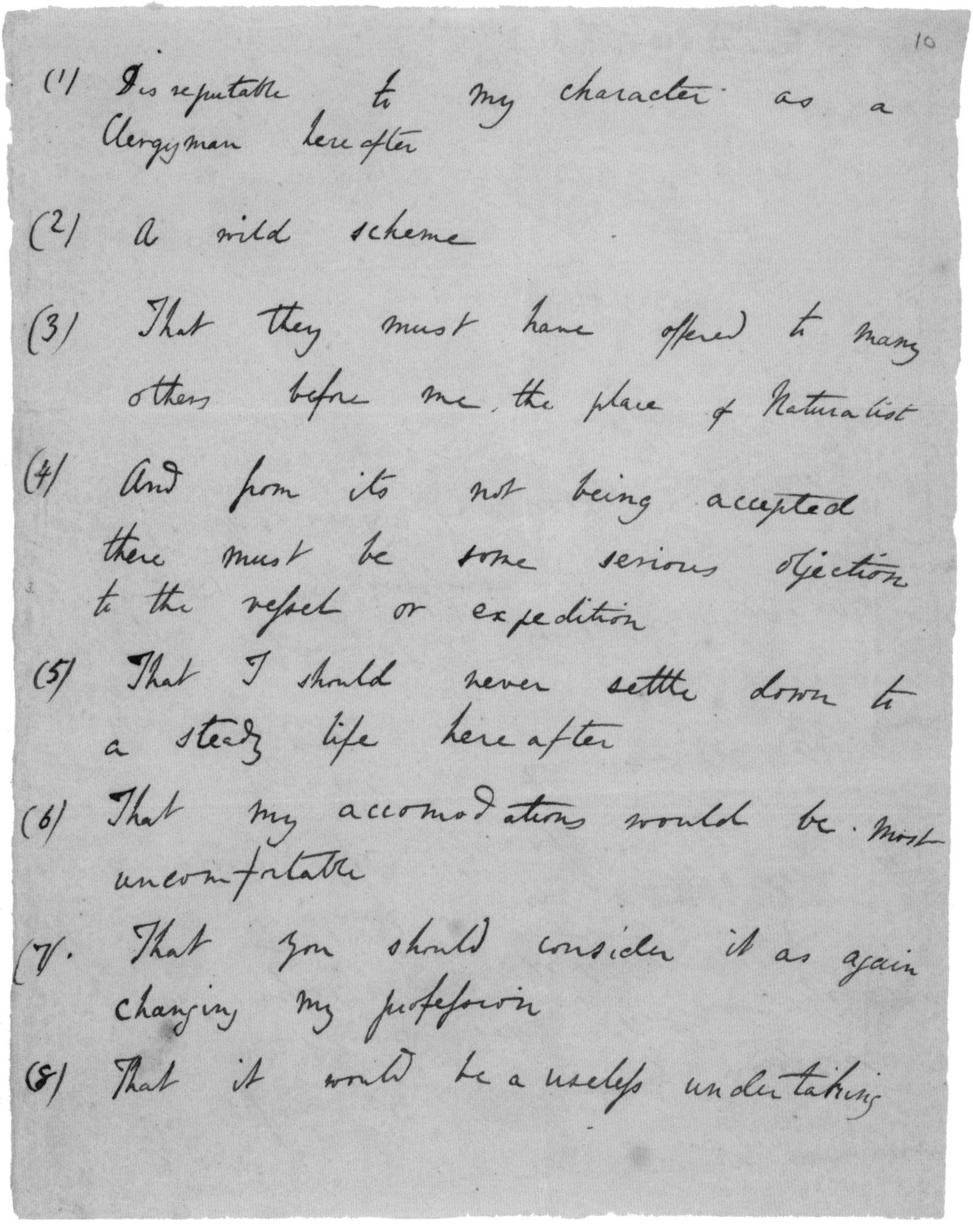

10

(1) Disreputable to my character as a Clergyman hereafter

(2) A wild scheme.

(3) That they must have offered to many others before me, the place of Naturalist

(4) And from its not being accepted there must be some serious objection to the vessel or expedition

(5) That I should never settle down to a steady life hereafter

(6) That my accomodations would be most uncomfortable

(7. That you should consider it as again changing my profession

(8) That it would be a useless undertaking

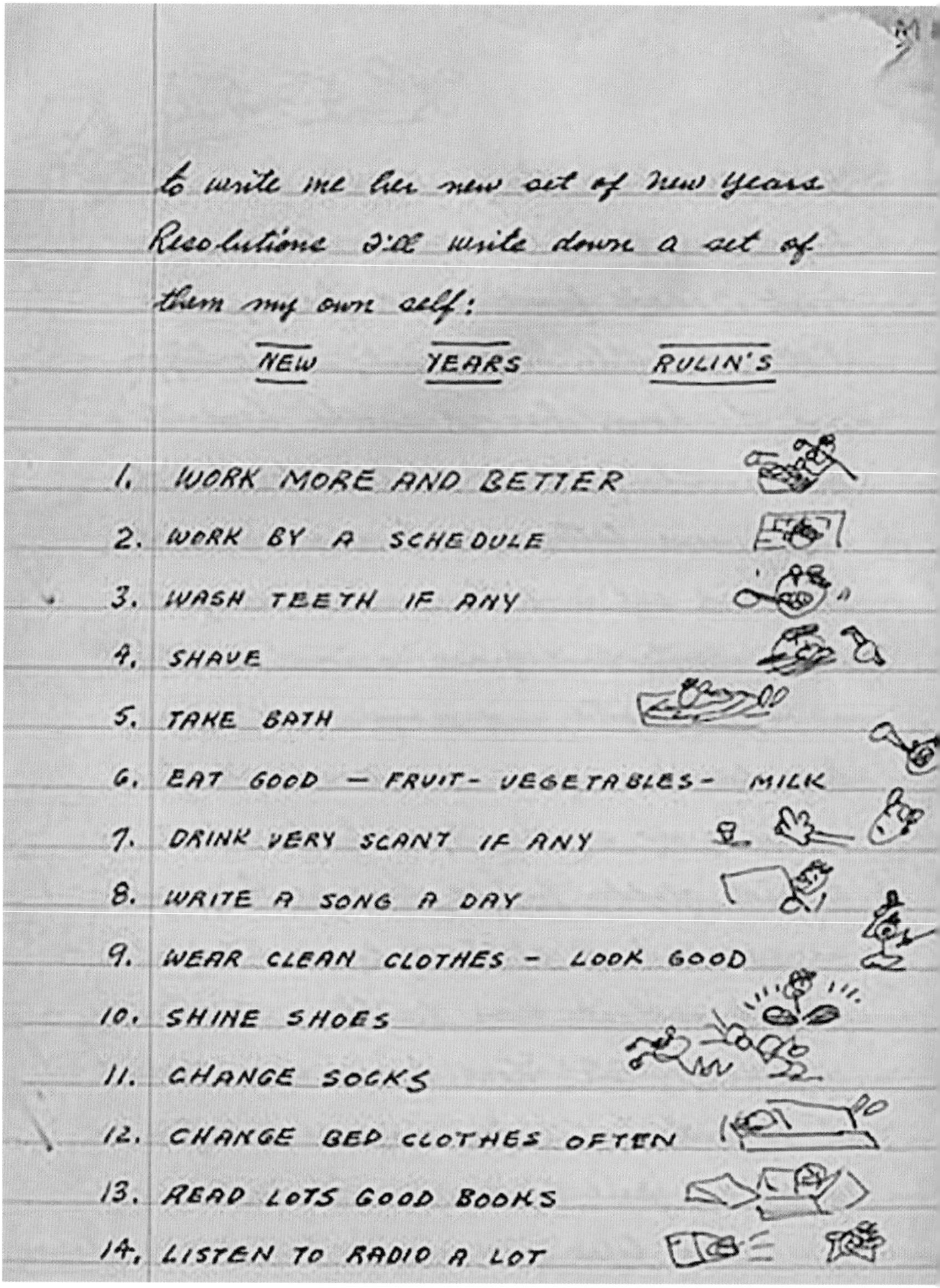

to write me her new set of New Years
Resolutions I'll write down a set of
them my own self:

NEW YEARS RULIN'S

1. WORK MORE AND BETTER
2. WORK BY A SCHEDULE
3. WASH TEETH IF ANY
4. SHAVE
5. TAKE BATH
6. EAT GOOD — FRUIT — VEGETABLES — MILK
7. DRINK VERY SCANT IF ANY
8. WRITE A SONG A DAY
9. WEAR CLEAN CLOTHES — LOOK GOOD
10. SHINE SHOES
11. CHANGE SOCKS
12. CHANGE BED CLOTHES OFTEN
13. READ LOTS GOOD BOOKS
14. LISTEN TO RADIO A LOT

NEW YEAR'S RULIN'S

WOODY GUTHRIE
1941

The hugely influential American folk singer Woody Guthrie (1912–1967) recorded more than four hundred songs during his all too brief career, the most famous being 1944's "This Land Is Your Land." A couple of years earlier, with 1942 soon to begin, Guthrie wrote and illustrated this charming list of New Year's "Rulin's" in his journal.

15. LEARN PEOPLE BETTER
16. KEEP RANCHO CLEAN
17. DONT GET LONESOME
18. STAY GLAD
19. KEEP HOPING MACHINE RUNNING
20. DREAM GOOD
21. BANK ALL EXTRA MONEY
22. SAVE DOUGH
23. HAVE COMPANY BUT DONT WASTE TIME
24. SEND MARY AND KIDS MONEY
25. PLAY AND SING GOOD
26. DANCE BETTER
27. HELP WIN WAR — BEAT FASCISM
28. LOVE MAMA
29. LOVE PAPA
30. LOVE PETE
31. LOVE EVERYBODY
32. MAKE UP YOUR MIND
33. WAKE UP AND FIGHT

List No. 041

MUST MAKE EFFORT TO DO

MARILYN MONROE
1955

As 1955 came to a close, Marilyn Monroe wrote this motivational set of New Year's resolutions in one of her address books—a list that, if followed, would hopefully lead to another twelve months as successful as the last. The year 1955 had seen the release of *The Seven Year Itch,* featuring the iconic shot of the twenty-nine-year-old Monroe standing over a grate, her white skirt billowing. She also started dating playwright Arthur Miller and was accepted as a student with Lee Strasberg of the renowned Actors Studio in New York. Judging by this list, Monroe was determined to make the most of her opportunities. The new year would bring marriage to Miller and her acclaimed role in *Bus Stop;* and Paula Strasberg, Lee's wife, became her acting coach. But 1956 also brought a miscarriage and the troubled shooting of her movie with Laurence Olivier, *The Prince and the Showgirl.*

Must make effort to do

Must have the discipline to do the following—

z – go to class—my own always—without fail

x – go as often as possible to observe Strasberg's other private classes

g – never miss my actors studio sessions

v – work whenever possible—on class assignments—and always keep working on the acting exercises.

u – start attending Clurman lectures—also Lee Strasberg's directors' lectures at theater wing—enquire about both

l – keep looking around me—only much more so—observing—but not only myself but others and everything—take things (it) for what they (it's) are worth.

y – must make strong effort to work on current problems and phobias that out of my past has arisen—making much much much more more more more more effort in my analysis. And be there always on time—no excuses for being ever late.

w – if possible take at least one class at university—in literature—

o – follow RCA thing through.

p – try to find someone to take dancing from—body work (creative)

t – take care of my instrument—personally & bodily (exercise)

try to enjoy myself when I can—I'll be miserable enough as it is.

RULES OF PALSHIP

NOËL COWARD
August 1915

In August 1915, at just sixteen years of age and in an effort to minimize arguments in what was an incredibly close and sometimes turbulent friendship, future playwright Noël Coward and his best friend, fellow actor Esmé Wynne, drew up an endearing list of sixteen "Rules of Palship," to be signed and followed by both parties. The list proved successful; the pair remained friends for some years.

RULES OF PALSHIP BETWEEN ESMÉ WYNNE AND NOËL COWARD

(1). We must not tease each other and if we begin we must stop directly we are asked.

(2). We must take it in turns to go and see one another and if one goes twice running to the other's house, the other must do the same afterwards.

(3). We must *never* split on one another even if the PALSHIP is dissolved and we must hold all confidences sacred.

(4). We must share all profits in any transaction made together, however slight the help of the other may be. Profits are excluded from any expenses incurred during the said transaction.

(5). In case of serious quarrel a week or a fortnight may be taken to think things over before abolishing the PALSHIP.

(6). If one hits the other either in anger or fun, he must allow the other to hit back. Any other offence must be paid for.

(7). We must stick up for each other against anyone or anything, and stand by each other in all danger.

(8). We must tell each other all secrets concerned with ourselves, others confidences may be held sacred even from one another.

(9). We must not talk RELIGION unless it is enevitable.

(10). When writing to mutual friends we must tell each other, we must also tell each other what we have said in the letter.

(11). We must swear by "HONOUR AS A PAL" and hold it THE most sacred of bonds in the world.

(12). We must tell each other what we think about the other's appearance or behaviour.

(13). We must go straight to one another in case of mischief being made and believe NOTHING unless it comes from the other's own lips.

(14). NO ONE not even our Parents may keep us from one another.

(15). If any other rules are formed or thought of they must be added (with the consent of both) at the end of this document.

(16). NO OTHER PERSON may be admitted into our PALSHIP or SECRETS.

SIGNATURE OF BOTH

(Signed)

Dated August the 11th 1915.

List No. 043

A LITTLE BILL OF FARE

MARK TWAIN
1870s

As he journeyed around Europe in the late 1870s writing *A Tramp Abroad* (1880), American author Mark Twain grew increasingly tired of an abundance of what he described as "fair-to-middling" food. As he explained in his travelogue:

"The number of dishes is sufficient; but then it is such a monotonous variety of unstriking dishes . . . Three or four months of this weary sameness will kill the robustest appetite."

As the end of his trip neared, Twain began to prepare for his return to the United States by compiling the following—an enormous list of the foods he had longed for the most, all of which were to be prepared and consumed when he arrived home.

It has now been many months, at the present writing, since I have had a nourishing meal, but I shall soon have one—a modest, private affair, all to myself. I have selected a few dishes, and made out a little bill of fare, which will go home in the steamer that precedes me, and be hot when I arrive—as follows:

Radishes. Baked apples, with cream

Fried oysters; stewed oysters. Frogs.

American coffee, with real cream.

American butter.

Fried chicken, Southern style.

Porter-house steak.

Saratoga potatoes.

Broiled chicken, American style.

Hot biscuits, Southern style.

Hot wheat-bread, Southern style.

Hot buckwheat cakes.

American toast. Clear maple syrup.

Virginia bacon, broiled.

Blue points, on the half shell.

Cherry-stone clams.

San Francisco mussels, steamed.

Oyster soup. Clam Soup.

Philadelphia Terapin soup.

Oysters roasted in shell, Northern style.

Soft-shell crabs. Connecticut shad.

Baltimore perch.

Brook trout, from Sierra Nevadas.

Lake trout, from Tahoe.

Sheep-head and croakers, from New Orleans.

Black bass from the Mississippi.

American roast beef.

Roast turkey, Thanksgiving style.

Cranberry sauce. Celery.

2120

✓ Radishes.
Baked apples, ~~[illegible]~~ with cream.
Fried oysters; stewed oysters. Frogs.
American coffee, with real cream.
American butter, ~~fresh & genuine~~.
Fried chicken, southern style.
Porter-house steak, ~~with mushrooms~~.
Saratoga potatoes.
Broiled chicken, American style.
Hot biscuits, Southern style.
Hot wheat-bread, Southern style. Hot light rolls.
Hot buckwheat cakes.
American ~~[illegible]~~ toast.
Clear maple syrup.
Virginia bacon, broiled.
~~[illegible]~~
Blue-points, on the half shell.
Cherry-stone clams.
San Francisco mussels, ~~[illegible]~~ steamed.
Oyster soup. Clam soup.
~~Shell~~ oysters roasted in the shell—northern style.
Philadelphia terrapin soup.
(Soft-shell ~~crabs~~.
Connecticut shad.
Baltimore perch.
Brook trout, from Sierra Nevadas.
Lake trout, from Tahoe.
Sheep-head & croakers, from New Orleans.
Black bass from the Mississippi.

Roast wild turkey. Woodcock.

Canvas-back-duck, from Baltimore.

Prairie liens, from Illinois.

Missouri partridges, broiled.

'Possum. Coon.

Boston bacon and beans.

Bacon and greens, Southern style.

Hominy. Boiled onions. Turnips.

Pumpkin. Squash. Asparagus.

Butter beans. Sweet potatoes.

Lettuce. Succotash. String beans.

Mashed potatoes. Catsup.

Boiled potatoes, in their skins.

New potatoes, minus the skins.

Early rose potatoes, roasted in the ashes, Southern style, served hot.

Sliced tomatoes, with sugar or vinegar. Stewed tomatoes.

Green corn, cut from the ear and served with butter and pepper.

Green corn, on the ear.

Hot corn-pone, with chitlings, Southern style.

Hot hoe-cake, Southern style.

Hot egg-bread, Southern style.

Hot light-bread, Southern style.

Buttermilk. Iced sweet milk.

Apple dumplings, with real cream.

Apple pie. Apple fritters.

Apple puffs, Southern style.

Peach cobbler, Southern style

Peach pie. American mince pie.

Pumpkin pie. Squash pie.

All sorts of American pastry.

Fresh American fruits of all sorts, including strawberries which are not to be doled out as if they were jewelry, but in a more liberal way.

Ice-water—not prepared in the ineffectual goblet, but in the sincere and capable refrigerator.

List No. 044

NEWTON'S SINS

SIR ISAAC NEWTON
1662

Sir Isaac Newton remains one of the most influential scientists in human history. In 1668, he built the world's first successful reflecting telescope. In 1687, he published *Philosophiae Naturalis Principia Mathematica*, a hugely important book in which he laid out the laws of motion and universal gravitation. For many years, he was a fellow at the University of Cambridge, and at that time Cambridge fellows were also obliged to become ordained Anglican priests. Although a Christian, Newton steadfastly refused, finally receiving dispensation from King Charles II himself. As a nineteen-year-old, his theological reflections had taken a different slant. In 1964, three centuries after Newton made his mark on the world, a page in one of his notebooks, penned cryptically in 1662, was finally decoded; on it, addressed to God, was a list of sins the young Newton had committed.

Before Whitsunday 1662.

1. Using the word (God) openly
2. Eating an apple at Thy house
3. Making a feather while on Thy day
4. Denying that I made it.
5. Making a mousetrap on Thy day
6. Contriving of the chimes on Thy day
7. Squirting water on Thy day
8. Making pies on Sunday night
9. Swimming in a kimnel on Thy day
10. Putting a pin in Iohn Keys hat on Thy day to pick him.
11. Carelessly hearing and committing many sermons
12. Refusing to go to the close at my mothers command.
13. Threatning my father and mother Smith to burne them and the house over them
14. Wishing death and hoping it to some
15. Striking many
16. Having uncleane thoughts words and actions and dreamese.
17. Stealing cherry cobs from Eduard Storer
18. Denying that I did so
19. Denying a crossbow to my mother and grandmother though I knew of it
20. Setting my heart on money learning pleasure more than Thee
21. A relapse
22. A relapse
23. A breaking again of my covenant renued in the Lords Supper.
24. Punching my sister
25. Robbing my mothers box of plums and sugar
26. Calling Derothy Rose a jade
27. Glutiny in my sickness.
28. Peevishness with my mother.
29. With my sister.
30. Falling out with the servants
31. Divers commissions of alle my duties
32. Idle discourse on Thy day and at other times
33. Not turning nearer to Thee for my affections
34. Not living according to my belief
35. Not loving Thee for Thy self.
36. Not loving Thee for Thy goodness to us
37. Not desiring Thy ordinances
38. Not long for Thee in [illegible]
39. Fearing man above Thee
40. Using unlawful means to bring us out of distresses
41. Caring for worldly things more than God
42. Not craving a blessing from God on our honest endeavors.
43. Missing chapel.
44. Beating Arthur Storer.

45. Peevishness at Master Clarks for a piece of bread and butter.
46. Striving to cheat with a brass halfe crowne.
47. Twisting a cord on Sunday morning
48. Reading the history of the Cn champions on Sunday

Since Whitsunday 1662

1. Glutony
2. Glutony
3. Using Wilfords towel to spare my own
4. Negligence at the chapel.
5. Sermons at Saint Marys (4)
6. Lying about a louse
7. Denying my chamberfellow of the knowledge of him that took him for a [illegible] sot.
8. Neglecting [illegible] to pray 3
9. Helping Pettit to make his water watch at 12 of the clock on Saturday night

[illegible] [illegible] 1662.

[illegible] 1	[illegible] 19
[illegible] 2	[illegible] 20
[illegible] 3	[illegible] 21
[illegible] 4	[illegible] 22
[illegible] 5	[illegible] 23
[illegible] 6	[illegible] 24
[illegible] 7	[illegible] 25
[illegible] 8	[illegible] 26
[illegible] 9	[illegible] 27
[illegible] 10	[illegible] 28
[illegible] 11	[illegible] 29
[illegible] 12	[illegible] 30
[illegible] 13	[illegible] 31
[illegible] 14	[illegible] 32
[illegible] 15	[illegible] 33.
[illegible] 16	[illegible] 34
[illegible] 17	[illegible] 35
[illegible] 18	[illegible] 36
	[illegible] 37
	[illegible] 38
	[illegible] 39

List No. 045

THE PILLOW BOOK

SEI SHŌNAGON
Circa 996 AD

Born circa 966 AD, Sei Shōnagon was a Japanese court lady responsible for writing *The Pillow Book*, a wonderful collection of hundreds of observational notes that paint a vivid, amusing, and often touching picture of life in eleventh-century Japan. Much of the book is written in list form, with headings such as "Pleasing things," "Infuriating things," "Things it's frustrating and embarrassing to witness," as well as the things seen here.

Rare Things

A son-in-law who's praised by his wife's father. Likewise, a wife who's loved by her mother-in-law.

A pair of silver tweezers that can actually pull out hairs properly.

A retainer who doesn't speak ill of his master.

A person who is without a single quirk. Someone who's superior in both appearance and character, and who's remained utterly blameless throughout his long dealings with the world.

You never find an instance of two people living together who continue to be overawed by each other's excellence and always treat each other with scrupulous care and respect, so such a relationship is obviously a great rarity.

Copying out a tale or a volume of poems without smearing any ink on the book you're copying from. If you're copying it from some beautiful bound book, you try to take immense care, but somehow you always manage to get ink on it.

Two women, let alone a man and a woman, who vow themselves to each other forever, and actually manage to remain on good terms to the end.

Things that should be small

Thread for sewing something in a hurry. The hair of women in the lower classes. The voice of someone's daughter. Lampstands.

Things now useless that recall a glorious past

A fine embroidery-edged mat that's become threadbare.

A screen painted in the Chinese style, that's now turned dark and discolored and developed a scarred surface.

A painter with poor eyesight.

A switch of false hair seven or eight feet long, that's now fading and taking on a reddish tinge.

Grape-colored fabric when the ash dye has turned.

A man who was a great lover in his day but is now old and decrepit.

A tasteful house whose garden trees have been destroyed by fire. The pond is still there, but it's now uncared for and thick with pond weed.

Repulsive things

The back of a piece of sewing. Hairless baby mice tumbled out of their nest. The seams of a leather robe before the lining's been added. The inside of a cat's ear. A rather dirty place in darkness.

夏は夜。
月のころはさらなり。
やみもなほ、
蛍の多く飛びちがひたる。
また、ただ一つ二つなど、
ほのかにうち光りて行くもをかし。
雨など降るもをかし。

List No. 046

ELOQUENT SILENCE

WALT WHITMAN
1865

As the nation reeled following the assassination of Abraham Lincoln on April 14, 1865, *Leaves of Grass* poet Walt Whitman began work on an elegy to mark the death of the US president, whom Whitman greatly admired. As he prepared to write the mourning poem that would come to be published later that year as *When Lilacs Last in the Dooryard Bloom'd*, Whitman drew up a list of words related to such loss.

sorrow (saxon)
grieve
sad
mourn (sax)
" ing
" ful
melancholy
dismal
heavy-hearted
tears
black
sobs -ing
sighing
funeral rites
wailing
lamenting
mute grief
eloquent silence
bewail
bemoan
deplore
regret deeply
loud lament
pitiful
loud weeping
violent lamentation

anguish
wept sore
depression
pain of mind
passionate regret
afflicted with grief
cast down
downcast
gloomy
serious
sympathy
moving compassion
tenderness
tender-hearted
full of pity
obscurity
partial or total darkness
(as the gloom of a forest—gloom of midnight)
cloudy
cloudiness
" of mind
mind sunk in gloom
soul " " "

dejection
dejected

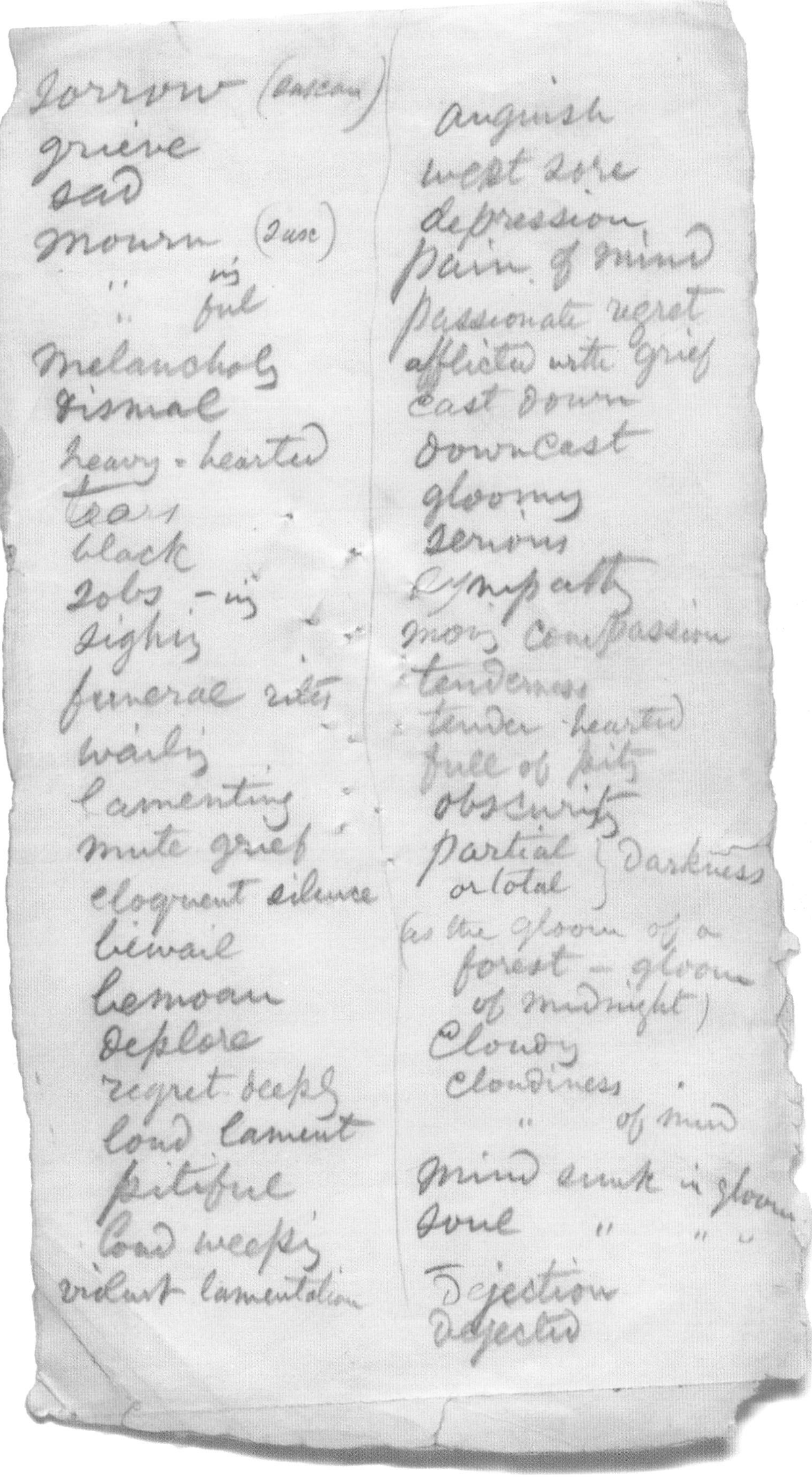
Sorrow ([illegible])
grieve
sad
mourn (2 use)
" ing
" ful
melancholy
dismal
heavy-hearted
~~tears~~
black
sobs -ing
sighing
funeral rites
wailing
lamenting
mute grief
eloquent silence
bewail
bemoan
deplore
regret deeply
loud lament
pitiful
loud weeping
violent lamentation

anguish
wept sore
depression
pain of mind
passionate regret
afflicted with grief
cast down
downcast
gloomy
serious
sympathy
moving compassion
tenderness
tender-hearted
full of pity
obscurity
partial or total } Darkness
(as the gloom of a forest – gloom of midnight)
Cloudy
Cloudiness
" of mind
mind sunk in gloom
soul " "
Dejection
dejected

[shades?] of night
heavy
dull—sombre
sombre shades
" ness
affliction
oppress—oppressi~~o~~ve
" ion
prostration
humble—humility
suffering—silent suffering
burdensome
Distress—distressing
Calamity
Extreme anguish (either of mind or body)
Misery
torture
harrassed
weighed down
trouble
deep affliction
plaintive
Calamity
disaster
something that strikes down—~~as by Almighty~~

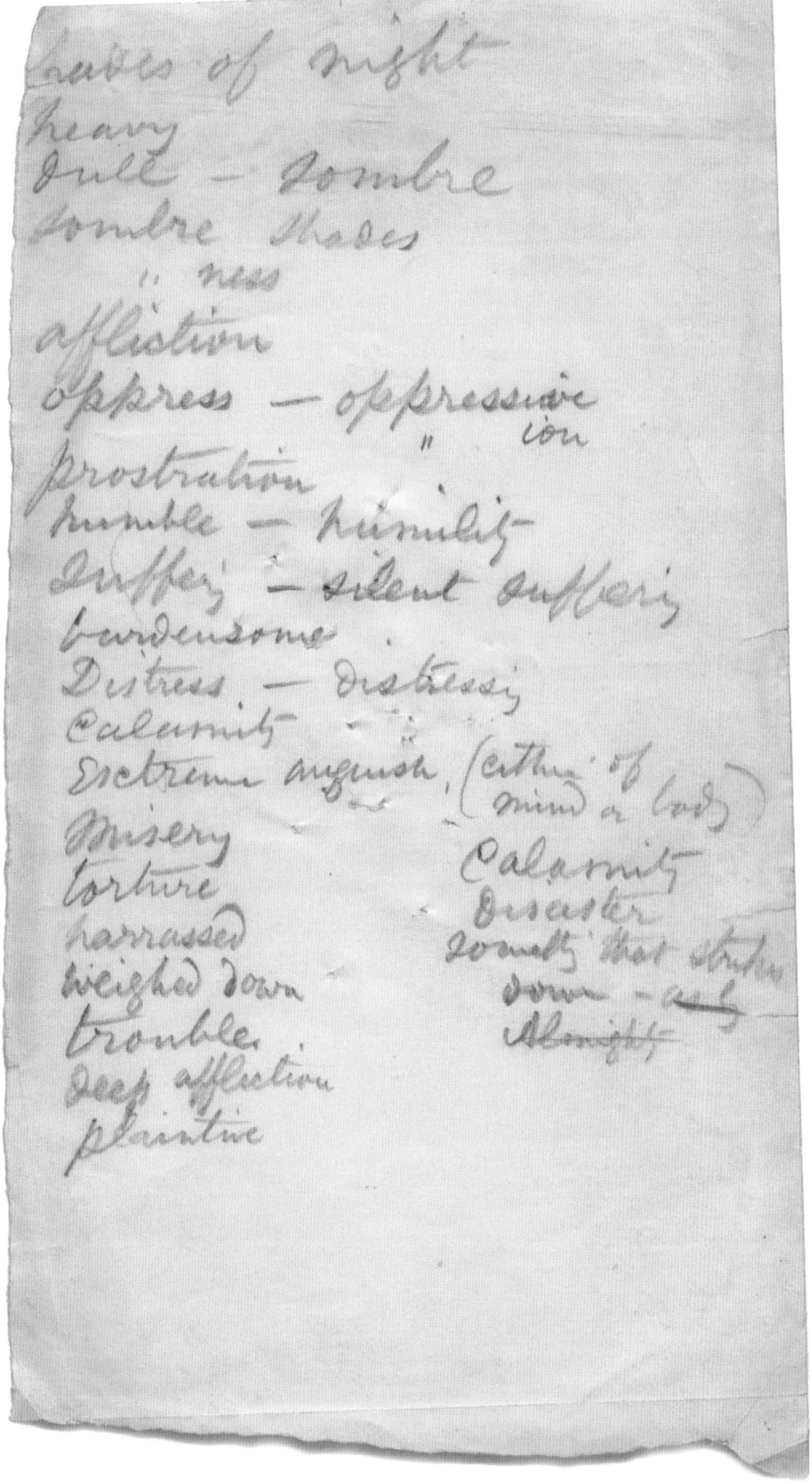

Shades of night
heavy
Dull — sombre
Sombre shades
" ness
affliction
oppress — oppressive
" ion
prostration
humble — humility
Suffering — silent suffering
burdensome
Distress — distressing
Calamity
Extreme anguish (either of mind or body)
Misery
torture
harrassed
weighed down
trouble
Deep affliction
plaintive

Calamity
Disaster
something that strikes
~~down — as by~~
~~Almighty~~

List No. 047

ADVICE TO YOUNG LADIES

THE LADIES' POCKET MAGAZINE
1830

Established toward the end of the Georgian era in 1824, *The Ladies' Pocket Magazine* was one of the few publications catering to women of that time and was filled with stories, readers' letters, etiquette guides, and fashion. In the first issue of 1830, sandwiched between a piece called "Effects of Beauty" and another titled "The Ladies' Toilet," was printed this list of "advice to young ladies."

ADVICE TO YOUNG LADIES.

If you have blue eyes, you need not languish.

If black eyes, you need not leer.

If you have pretty feet, there is no occasion to wear short petticoats.

If you are doubtful as to that point, there can be no harm in letting them be long.

If you have good teeth, do not laugh for the purpose of shewing them.

If you have bad ones, do not laugh less than the occasion may justify.

If you have pretty hands and arms, there can be no objection to your playing on the harp, if you play well.

If they are disposed to be clumsy, work tapestry.

If you have a bad voice, rather speak in a low tone.

If you dance well, dance but seldom.

If you dance ill, never dance at all.

If you sing well, make no previous excuses.

If you sing indifferently, hesitate not a moment when you are asked, for few people are judges of singing, but every one is sensible of a desire to please.

If you would preserve beauty, rise early.

If you would preserve esteem, be gentle.

If you would obtain power, be condescending.

If you would live happily, endeavour to promote the happiness of others.

THE LADIES' POCKET MAGAZINE
1824

List No. 048

TEN FAVORITE AMERICAN NOVELS

NORMAN MAILER
1988

In January 1988, Pulitzer Prize-winning American author Norman Mailer (1923–2007) was asked by editors of *The Reader's Catalog*—this was a curated directory of approximately 40,000 books that you might find in a local bookshop, any or all of which could be delivered to your door—to choose ten of his favorite novels for inclusion in the next edition. He responded with this list, noting,

"With the exception of *Huckleberry Finn*, which I reread recently, the other nine books were devoured in my freshman year at Harvard, and gave me the desire, which has never gone completely away, to be a writer, an American writer."

Ten Favorite American Novels

U.S.A. John Dos Passos

Huckleberry Finn Mark Twain

Studs Lonigan James T. Farrell

Look Homeward, Angel Thomas Wolfe

The Grapes of Wrath John Steinbeck

The Great Gatsby F. Scott Fitzgerald

The Sun Also Rises Ernest Hemingway

Appointment in Samarra John O'Hara

The Postman Always Rings Twice James M. Cain

Moby-Dick Herman Melville

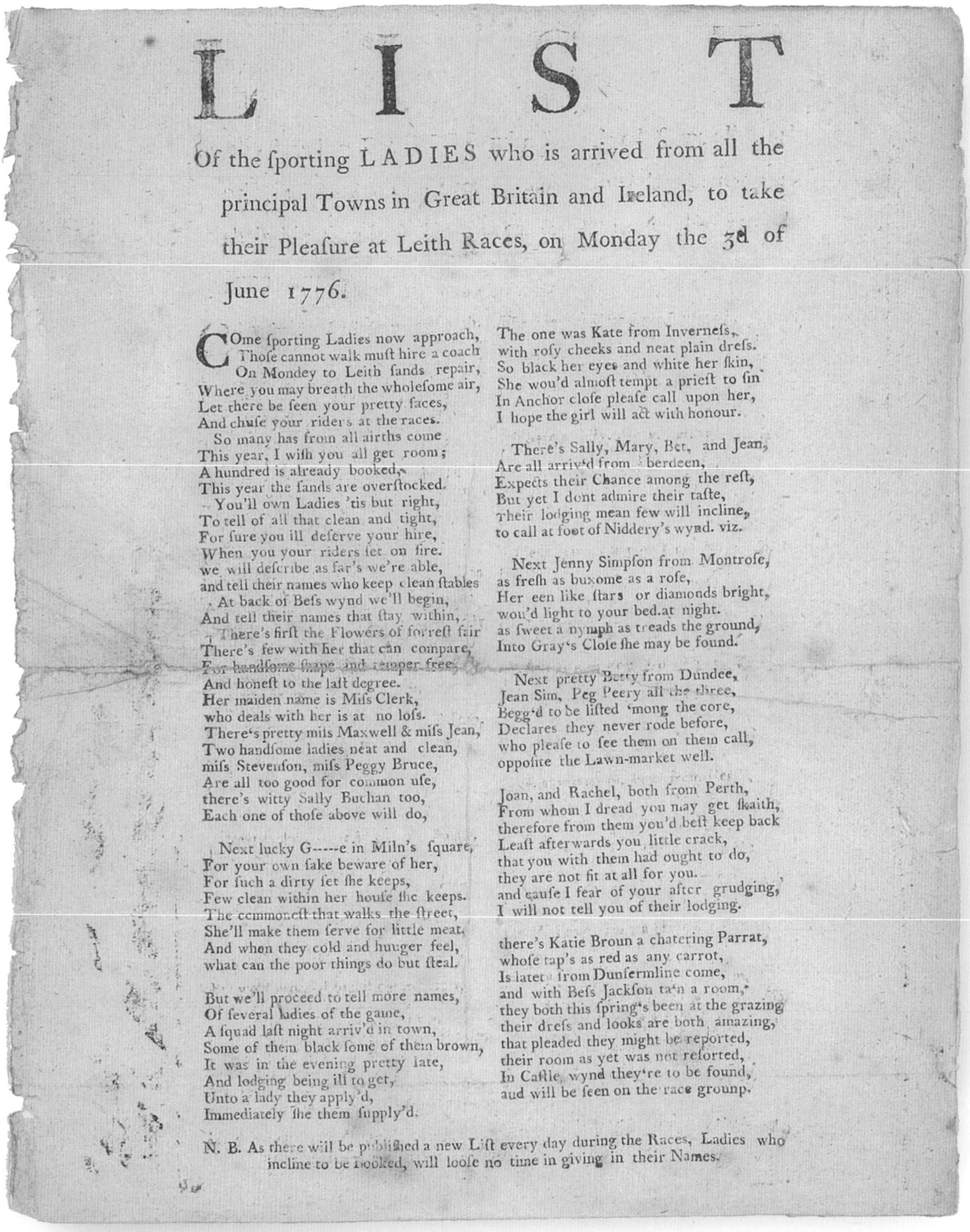

LIST

Of the ſporting LADIES who is arrived from all the principal Towns in Great Britain and Ireland, to take their Pleaſure at Leith Races, on Monday the 3d of June 1776.

COme ſporting Ladies now approach,
Thoſe cannot walk muſt hire a coach
On Mondey to Leith ſands repair,
Where you may breath the wholeſome air,
Let there be ſeen your pretty faces,
And chuſe your riders at the races.
So many has from all airths come
This year, I wiſh you all get room;
A hundred is already booked,
This year the ſands are overſtocked.
You'll own Ladies 'tis but right,
To tell of all that clean and tight,
For ſure you ill deſerve your hire,
When you your riders ſet on fire.
we will deſcribe as far's we're able,
and tell their names who keep clean ſtables
At back of Beſs wynd we'll begin,
And tell their names that ſtay within,
There's firſt the Flowers of forreſt fair
There's few with her that can compare,
For handſome ſhape and temper free,
And honeſt to the laſt degree.
Her maiden name is Miſs Clerk,
who deals with her is at no loſs.
There's pretty miſs Maxwell & miſs Jean,
Two handſome ladies neat and clean,
miſs Stevenſon, miſs Peggy Bruce,
Are all too good for common uſe,
there's witty Sally Buchan too,
Each one of thoſe above will do,

Next lucky G-----e in Miln's ſquare,
For your own ſake beware of her,
For ſuch a dirty ſet ſhe keeps,
Few clean within her houſe ſhe keeps.
The commoneſt that walks the ſtreet,
She'll make them ſerve for little meat,
And when they cold and hunger feel,
what can the poor things do but ſteal.

But we'll proceed to tell more names,
Of ſeveral ladies of the game,
A ſquad laſt night arriv'd in town,
Some of them black ſome of them brown,
It was in the evening pretty late,
And lodging being ill to get,
Unto a lady they apply'd,
Immediately ſhe them ſupply'd.

The one was Kate from Inverneſs,
with roſy cheeks and neat plain dreſs.
So black her eyes and white her ſkin,
She wou'd almoſt tempt a prieſt to ſin
In Anchor cloſe pleaſe call upon her,
I hope the girl will act with honour.

There's Sally, Mary, Bet, and Jean,
Are all arriv'd from Aberdeen,
Expects their Chance among the reſt,
But yet I dont admire their taſte,
Their lodging mean few will incline,
to call at foot of Niddery's wynd. viz.

Next Jenny Simpſon from Montroſe,
as freſh as buxome as a roſe,
Her een like ſtars or diamonds bright,
wou'd light to your bed at night.
as ſweet a nymph as treads the ground,
Into Gray's Cloſe ſhe may be found.

Next pretty Betty from Dundee,
Jean Sim, Peg Peery all the three,
Begg'd to be liſted 'mong the core,
Declares they never rode before,
who pleaſe to ſee them on them call,
oppoſite the Lawn-market well.

Joan, and Rachel, both from Perth,
From whom I dread you may get ſkaith,
therefore from them you'd beſt keep back
Leaſt afterwards you little crack,
that you with them had ought to do,
they are not fit at all for you.
and cauſe I fear of your after grudging,
I will not tell you of their lodging.

there's Katie Broun a chatering Parrat,
whoſe tap's as red as any carrot,
Is latel from Dunſermline come,
and with Beſs Jackſon ta'n a room,
they both this ſpring's been at the grazing
their dreſs and looks are both amazing,
that pleaded they might be reported,
their room as yet was not reſorted,
In Caſtle wynd they're to be found,
aud will be ſeen on the race groun.

N. B. As there will be publiſhed a new Liſt every day during the Races, Ladies who incline to be booked, will looſe no time in giving in their Names.

LIST OF THE SPORTING LADIES

AUTHOR UNKNOWN

1776

Prostitution was rampant in eighteenth-century Great Britain and a widely acknowledged activity. So widely acknowledged, in fact, that local guides were often printed in an effort to promote (and sometimes warn against) various ladies working around town. This particular example was published in 1776 in honor of Scotland's Leith Races, a hugely popular horse-racing event run on the sands of Leith, near Edinburgh, for four or five days every summer. It lists, in verse, those women who were available on June 3, although as noted at the foot of this anonymously authored list, new editions would be circulated for every day of the races.

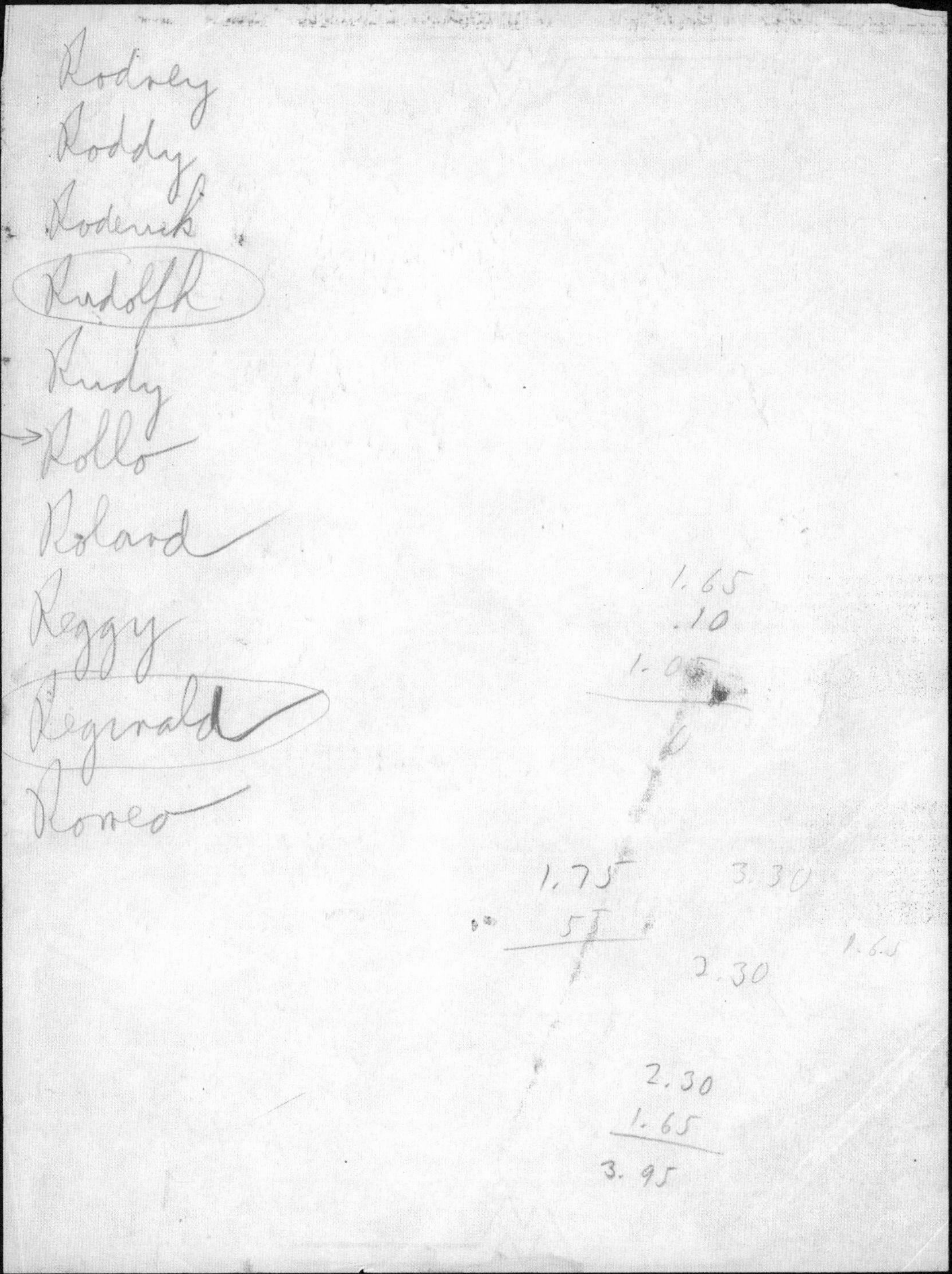

REGINALD THE RED-NOSED REINDEER

ROBERT MAY

1939

Thirty-five-year-old Robert May was working as an advertising copywriter for Montgomery Ward department store when, in early 1939, his boss tasked him with writing a "cheery" book to give to the store's customers that holiday season. The one he came up with months later was *Rudolph the Red-Nosed Reindeer*. It was subsequently handed out, for free, to 2.5 million shoppers in the first year alone. Luckily for May, his boss transferred all rights to him in 1946. Here's a snapshot of how different our Christmas cheer might have been—an early list of names being considered for the reindeer, penned in May's hand. Early favorites were Rollo, Reginald, and the eventual winner.

List No. 051

LEONARDO'S TO-DO LIST

LEONARDO DA VINCI
1510

Leonardo da Vinci was one of history's great polymaths—a genius who excelled as a sculptor, painter, engineer, inventor, musician, mathematician, cartographer, writer, architect, scientist, and geologist. He was also an expert anatomist, and around 1510 he traveled to the University of Pavia's medical school to dissect and then draw some corpses. Sometime before he left, on a page of his notebook thick with notes and sketches of the brain, nerves, and veins, Leonardo wrote a list, of things to do and things to take.

Have Avicenna translated. "On the Utilities."

Spectacles with case, firestick, fork, bistoury, charcoal, boards, sheets of paper, chalk, white, wax, forceps, pane of glass, fine-tooth bone saw, scalpel, inkhorn, pen-knife. Zerbi, and Angnolo Benedetti. Get hold of a skull. Nutmeg.

Observe the holes in the substance of the brain, where there are more or less of them.

Describe the tongue of the woodpecker and the jaw of a crocodile.

Give the measurement of the dead using his finger.

The book "On Mechanical Science" precedes that "On the Utilities." Get your books on anatomy bound. Boots, stockings, comb, towel, shirts, shoe-laces, shoes, pen-knife, pens, a skin for the chest, gloves, wrapping paper, charcoal.

Mental matters that have not passed through the *senso comune* ['common sense' – a place in the centre of the human head, according to Leonardo da Vinci, where all five of one's senses meet, to be judged—S.U.] are vain and they beget nothing but the prejudiced truth. And because such discourses arise from poverty of wit, such reasoners are always poor, and if they are born rich they will die poor in old age because it seems that Nature revenges herself on those who want to work miracles, so that they have less than quieter men. And those who want to grow rich in a day live for a long time in great poverty, as happens, and will happen to eternity—the alchemists, searchers after the creation of gold and silver, and those engineers who want dead water to give itself moving life with perpetual motion, and the supreme fool, the necromancer and enchanter.

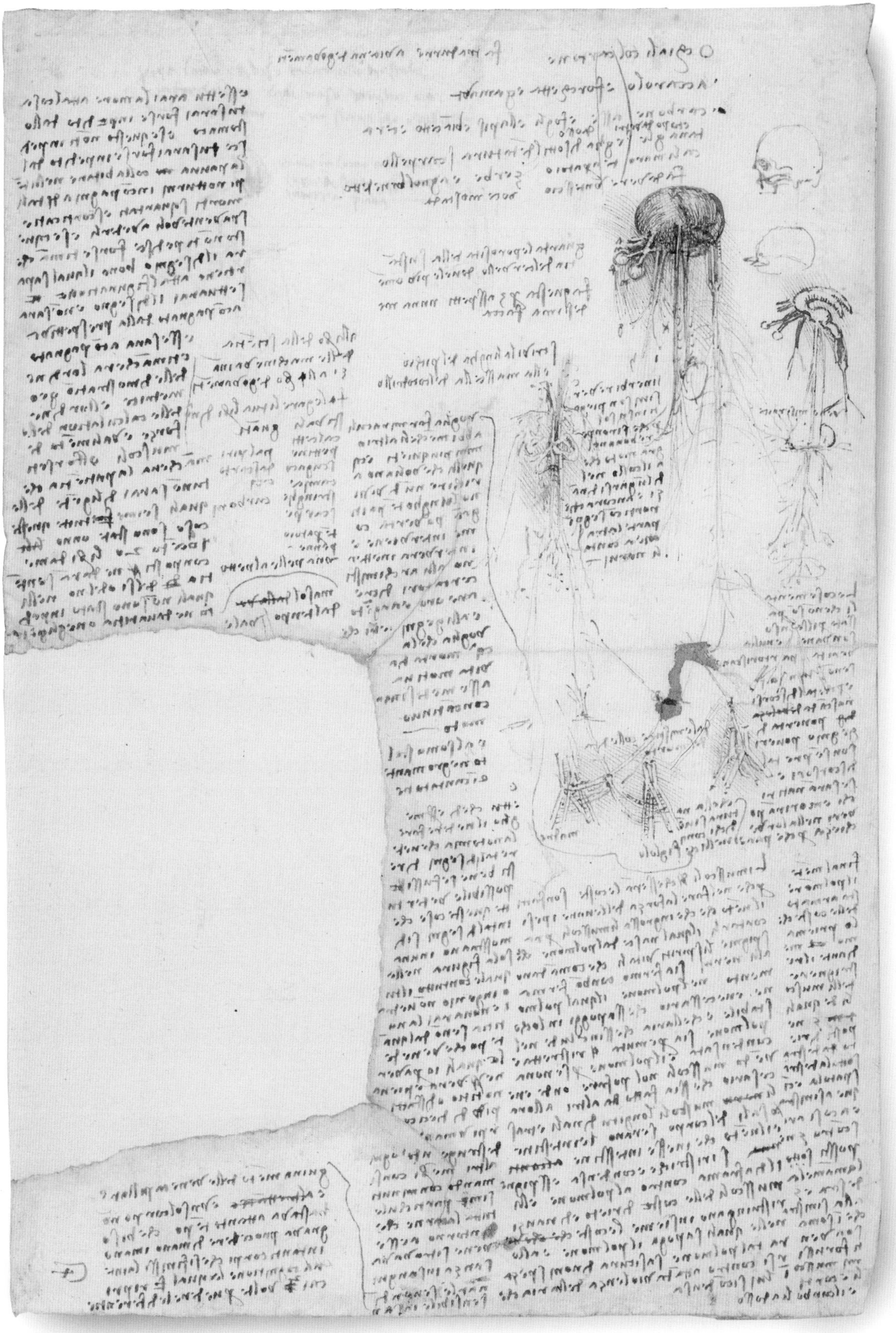

How My Life Has Changed
Hilary North

I can no longer flirt with Lou.
I can no longer dance with Mayra.
I can no longer eat brownies with Suzanne Y.
I can no longer meet the deadline with Mark.
I can no longer talk to George about his daughter.
I can no longer drink coffee with Rich.
I can no longer make a good impression on Chris.
I can no longer smile at Paul.
I can no longer hold the door open for Tony.
I can no longer confide in Lisa.
I can no longer complain about Gary.
I can no longer work on a project with Donna R.
I can no longer get to know Yolanda.
I can no longer call the client with Nick.
I can no longer contribute to the book drive organized by Karen.
I can no longer hang out with Millie.
I can no longer give career advice to Suzanne P.
I can no longer laugh with Donna G.
I can no longer watch Mary Ellen cut through the bull shit.
I can no longer drink beer with Paul.
I can no longer have a meeting with Dave W.
I can no longer leave a message with Andrea.
I can no longer gossip with Anna.
I can no longer run into Dave P. at the vending machine.
I can no longer call Steve about my computer.
I can no longer compliment Lorenzo.
I can no longer hear Herman's voice.
I can no longer trade voice mails with Norman.
I can no longer ride the elevator with Barbara.
I can no longer be happy about Jennifer's pregnancy.
I can no longer walk with Adam.
I can no longer say hello to Steven every morning.
I can no longer see the incredible view from the 103rd Floor of the South Tower.
I can no longer take my life for granted.

HOW MY LIFE HAS CHANGED

HILARY NORTH
2001

On the morning of September 11, 2001, Hilary North decided to stop en route to her job at the insurance brokers Aon in order to vote in the New York mayoral primaries, making her late for work. Had she turned up on time, it's almost certain that she would have perished along with 176 of her coworkers, for her office was situated on the 103rd floor of the World Trade Center's South Tower, approximately twenty floors above the entry point of the second hijacked jet airliner. Hilary North wrote this list shortly after the tragedy. A recording of it being read by her is featured in the Sonic Memorial Project, an audio archive of reactions to the event from all over the world.

OUTFIT FOR AN EXCURSION

HENRY DAVID THOREAU
1857

In 1854 Henry David Thoreau published *Walden*, his firsthand account of a two-year stay in a cabin he built in the woodland of Massachusetts in the mid-1840s, in an experiment in simple living, independence, and survival. After that he made three trips to Maine, inspiring the essays that would be published as *The Maine Woods* (1864). The last of these was a twelve-day jaunt that occurred in 1857 with a companion, an Indian guide, and a "little canoe, so neat and strong." He later described his packing list—which, as it happens, is not so simple—for such a trip.

The following will be a good outfit for one who wishes to make an excursion of *twelve* days into the Maine woods in July, with a companion, and one Indian for the same purposes that I did.

Wear, — a check shirt, stout old shoes, thick socks, a neck ribbon, thick waistcoat, thick pants, old Kossuth hat, a linen sack.

Carry, — in an India-rubber knapsack, with a large flap, two shirts (check), one pair thick socks, one pair drawers, one flannel shirt, two pocket-handkerchiefs, a light India-rubber coat or a thick woollen one, two bosoms and collars to go and come with, one napkin, pins, needles, thread, one blanket, best gray, seven feet long.

Tent, — six by seven feet, and four feet high in middle, will do; veil and gloves and insect-wash, or, better, mosquito-bars to cover all at night; best pocket-map, and perhaps description of the route; compass; plant-book and red blotting-paper; paper and stamps, botany, small pocket spy-glass for birds, pocket microscope, tape-measure, insect-boxes.

Axe, full size if possible, jackknife, fish-lines, two only apiece, with a few hooks and corks ready, and with pork for bait in a packet, rigged; matches (some also in a small vial in the waist-coat pocket); soap, two pieces; large knife and iron spoon (for all); three or four old newspapers, much twine, and several rags for dishcloths; twenty feet of strong cord, four-quart tin pail for kettle, two tin dippers, three tin plates, a fry-pan.

Provisions. — Soft hardbread, twenty-eight pounds; pork, sixteen pounds; sugar, twelve pounds; one pound black tea or three pounds coffee, one box or a pint of salt, one quart Indian meal, to fry fish in; six lemons, good to correct the pork and warm water; perhaps two or three pounds of rice, for variety. You will probably get some berries, fish, &c., beside.

A gun is not worth the carriage, unless you go as hunters. The pork should be in an open keg, sawed to fit; the sugar, tea or coffee, meal, salt, &c., should be put in separate water-tight India-rubber bags, tied with a leather string; and all the provisions, and part of the rest of the baggage, put into two large India-rubber bags, which have been proved to be water-tight and durable. Expense of preceding outfit is twenty-four dollars.

An Indian may be hired for about one dollar and fifty cents per day, and perhaps fifty cents a week for his canoe (this depends on the demand). The canoe should be a strong and tight one. This expense will be nineteen dollars.

Such an excursion need not cost more than twenty-five dollars apiece, starting at the foot of Moosehead, if you already possess or can borrow a reasonable part of the outfit. If you take an Indian and canoe at Oldtown, it will cost seven or eight dollars more to transport them to the lake.

List No. 054

BELIEF & TECHNIQUE FOR MODERN PROSE

JACK KEROUAC
1958

In 1958, a year after the publication of his magnum opus—the sprawling, rambling *On the Road*—American beat poet and novelist Jack Kerouac sent a letter to friend and publisher Donald Allen that included this "list of essentials" for writers of modern prose, written in his own inimitable style. The next year, with Kerouac's blessing, it was printed in *Evergreen Review*, the literary magazine then edited by Allen.

*****BELIEF & TECHNIQUE FOR MODERN PROSE*****

List of Essentials
****

1. Scribbled secret notebooks, and wild typewritten pages, for yr own joy
2. Submissive to everything, open, listening
3. Try never get drunk outside yr own house
4. Be in love with yr life
5. Something that you feel will find its own form
6. Be crazy dumbsaint of the mind
7. Blow as deep as you want to blow
8. Write what you want bottomless from bottom of the mind
9. The unspeakable visions of the individual
10. No time for poetry but exactly what is
11. Visionary tics shivering in the chest
12. In tranced fixation dreaming upon object before you
13. Remove literary, grammatical and syntactical inhibition
14. Like Proust be an old teahead of time
15. Telling the true story of the world in interior monolog
16. The jewel center of interest is the eye within the eye
17. Write in recollection and amazement for yourself
18. Work from pithy middle eye out, swimming in language sea
19. Accept loss forever
20. Believe in the holy contour of life
21. Struggle to sketch the flow that already exists intact in mind
22. Dont think of words when you stop but to see picture better
23. Keep track of every day the date emblazoned in yr morning
24. No fear or shame in the dignity of yr experience, language & knowledge
25. Write for the world to read and see yr exact pictures of it
26. Bookmovie is the movie in words, the visual American form
27. In praise of Character in the Bleak inhuman Loneliness
28. Composing wild, undisciplined, pure, coming in from under, crazier the better
29. You're a Genius all the time
30. Writer-Director of Earthly movies Sponsored & Angeled in Heaven

List No. 055

BACK TO SCHOOL COMMANDMENTS

SYLVIA PLATH
January 1953

In December 1952, at twenty years of age, future Pulitzer Prize-winning poet and author Sylvia Plath broke her leg while skiing in New York—an accident that resulted in a brief stay in the hospital and, most frustratingly, a cast on her leg for two months. As she prepared to return to her junior year at Smith College, downbeat yet eager to get back to classes and see her new love interest, Myron Lotz, who was attending Yale, she wrote two lists: first, a three-point reminder to appear calm in front of Myron; and second, a set of "Back to School Commandments" to keep her focused. Among her to-dos were interactions with her English and German professors, Robert Gorham Davis and Marie Schnieders, respectively; and also completing work on her (successful) application to be a guest editor the forthcoming summer at *Mademoiselle* magazine.

1 I will not overwhelm him by breathless over-enthusiasm.
2 I will not throw myself at him physically.
3 I will be moderate, yet intense, and interested.

Back to School Commandments

1 Keep a CHEERFUL FRONT continuously.
2 Science — don't get upset. You have to get an A so you have to learn this. You can: You proved it by getting 2 good test marks.
3 Unit — Don't panic. Ask for an extension if you need it. Write allegory paper this weekend. You were in infirmary a week if he needs excuses.
4 Davis — ask for extension if you need it. You've done enough words theoretically anyway. Do paper for him in exam period.
5 See Schnieders. Be calm, even if it is a matter of life & death.
6 Get Mlle written.
7 DO EXERCISES
8 Get a lot of sleep: afternoon naps if necessary
9 Remember: 5 months is not eternity. 2 months is not eternity. Even if it looks that way now.
10 Attitude is everything: so KEEP CHEERFUL, even if you fail your science, your unit, get a hateful silence from Myron, no dates, no praise, no love, nothing. There is a certain clinical satisfaction in seeing just how bad things can get.

P.S. Remember—you're a hell of a lot better off than 9/10 of the world anyway!

Love,
Syl

List No. 056

WHEN I COME TO BE OLD

JONATHAN SWIFT
1699

Irish author and cleric Jonathan Swift is best known for *Gulliver's Travels*, a biting satirical novel first published in 1726 that went on to sell millions of copies. It was only after Swift's death, in 1745, that a list of resolutions was found among his personal papers, written in 1699 when he was thirty-two and comprising advice directed at his future self. He never did marry a young woman, or any woman, for that matter—although the nature of his relationships with Esther Johnson, fourteen years his junior, and Esther Vanhomrigh, about twenty years his junior, who appear in his writings as "Stella" and "Vanessa," continues to be the subject of scholarly debate.

When I come to be old. 1699.

Not to marry a young Woman.
Not to keep young Company unless they reely desire it.
Not to be peevish or morose, or suspicious.
Not to scorn present Ways, or Wits, or Fashions, or Men, or War, &c.
Not to be fond of Children, ~~or let them come near me hardly~~.
Not to tell the same Story over and over to the same People.
Not to be covetous.
Not to neglect decency, or cleenlyness, for fear of falling into Nastyness.
Not to be over severe with young People, but give Allowances for their youthfull follyes, and Weeknesses.
Not to be influenced by, or give ear to knavish tatling Servants, or others.
Not to be too free of advise nor trouble any but those that desire it.
To desire some good Friends to inform me wch of these Resolutions I break, or neglect, & wherein; and reform accordingly.
Not to talk much, nor of my self.
Not to boast of my former beauty, or strength, or favor with Ladyes, &c.
Not to hearken to Flatteryes, nor conceive I can be beloved by a young woman, et eos qui hereditatem captant, odisse ac vitare [and to hate and avoid those who try to gain an inheritance].
Not to be positive or opinionative.
Not to sett up for observing all these Rules; for fear I should observe none.

1699

When I come to be old

Not to marry a young Woman.

Not to keep young Company unless they realy desire it.

Not to be peevish or morose, or suspicious.

Not to scorn present Ways, or Wits, or Fashions, or Men, or War, &c.

Not to be fond of Children, ~~or let them come near me hardly~~

Not to tell the same story over & over to the same People.

Not to be covetous.

Not to neglect decency, or cleenlyness, for fear of falling into Nastyness.

Not to be over severe with young People, but give Allowances for their youthfull follyes, and weeknesses.

Not to be influenced by, or give ear to knavish tatling servants, or others.

Not to be too free of advise, nor trouble any but those that desire it.

To ~~keep~~ desire some good Friends to inform me wch of these Resolutions I break, or neglect, & wherein; and reform accordingly.

Not to talk much, nor of my self.

Not to boast of my former beauty, or strength, or favor with Ladyes, &c.

Not to hearken to Flatteryes, nor conceive I can be beloved by a young woman. et eos qui hereditatem captant ~~[illegible]~~ odisse ac vitare.

Not to be positive or opiniatre.

Not to sett up for observing all these Rules; for fear I should observe none.

Houdini's

SCENE AND PROP. LIST

Open and close in full stage. (Palace.)

Time of act—About 25 minutes.

As I leave stage soaking wet in bathing suit, require two dressing rooms nearest stage (6 in company). Couch in dressing room.

Require a small trap in center of stage, not less than 8 inches square (8x8 inches) two feet in rear of front cloth.

Must have use of Fire Hose to reach from side of stage, about 3 feet past center of stage. Hose is used in view of audience.

Please see to it that the water in Hose is run off. It must be clear, so that audience can see through same.

100 gallons of Boiling water (must be boiling).

We carry four brass tubs to hold this water, which must be filled ready on stage **before** each performance.

Prepare a chute, or get-away, for 250 gallons of water, from the small 8x8-inch trap to most convenient spot underneath stage. The outlet in our Water Cloth is 6 inches in Diameter .

Our Water Carpet must be flied after each show back of stage, for which we require a strong batten.

Two small occasional tables (gold if possible, and 4 gold chairs) and 18 Bent-wood Chairs.

A run or stair case, so that committee from audience can come over footlights onto stage.

A small, clean looking (mahogany colored if possible) step ladder about 3 feet 6 inches high.

Two 20 feet and two 16 feet lengths of Lumber 4 inches by 2 inches (4x2 inches), or battens would do, which must be 4 inches wide.

PLEASE DO NOT PURCHASE ANYTHING AT MY EXPENSE

HOUDINI'S SCENE AND PROP. LIST

HARRY HOUDINI

Circa 1900

The great Harry Houdini was a master escapologist who wowed audiences by somehow escaping from a wide range of breathtaking predicaments. In 1912 he unveiled to the public what would be his most famous act, called "Houdini Upside Down!," in which he would hang, head first and underwater, in a device named the Chinese Water Torture Cell and then break free against all odds. Houdini performed the trick for fourteen years, until his death at age fifty-two in 1926. Before each and every show, this list was supplied to the venue.

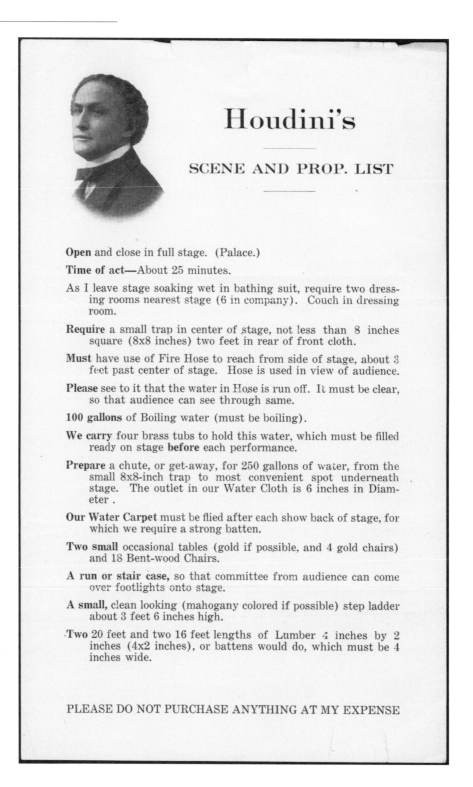

REASONS FOR ADMISSION

WEST VIRGINIA HOSPITAL FOR THE INSANE

1864–1889

In 1858, construction work began on what would eventually become the West Virginia Hospital for the Insane, a 250-capacity psychiatric hospital located on 269 acres in the city of Weston, West Virginia, the main building of which is now a National Historic Landmark. Progress on the hospital was slow due to a pause brought on by the Civil War. However, six years later, its doors finally opened and the first patients were admitted for care. The list seen here, published the year before the hospital closed its doors in 1994, details the official "reasons for admission" of patients between 1864 and 1889, as recorded in its logbook.

REASONS FOR ADMISSION
WEST VIRGINIA HOSPITAL FOR THE INSANE (WESTON)
OCTOBER 22, 1864 to DECEMBER 12, 1889

Amenorrhea

Asthma

Bad company

Bad habits & political Excitement

Bad whiskey

Bite of rattle snake

Bloody flux

Brain fever

Business nerves

Carbonic acid gas

Carbuncle

Cerebral softening

Cold

Congestion of brain

Constitutional

Death of sons in war

Decoyed into the army

Deranged masturbation

Desertion by husband

Diphtheria

Disappointed affection

Disappointed love

Disappointment

Dissipation of nerves

Dissolute habits

Dog bite

Domestic affliction

Domestic Trouble

Doubt about his mothers Ancestors

Dropsy

Effusion on the brain

Egotism

Epileptic fits

Excessive sexual abuse

Excitement as officer

Explosion of a shell nearby

Exposure and hereditary

Exposure and quackery

Exposure in Army

Fall from horse

False confinement

Feebleness of intellect

Fell from horse in war

Female disease

Fever and loss of law suit

Fever and Nerved

Fever and Jealousy

Fighting fire

Fits and desertion of husband

Gastritis

Gathering in the head

Greediness

Grief

Gunshot wound

Hard study

Hereditary predisposition

Hysteria

Ill treatment by husband

Imaginary female trouble

Immoral life

Imprisonment

Indigestion

Intemperance

Intemperance & business Trouble

Interference

Jealousy and religion

Kick of horse

Kicked in the head by a horse

Laziness
Liver and social disease
Loss of arm
Marriage of son
Masturbation & syphilis
Masturbation for 30 years
Medicine to prevent conception
Menstrual deranged
Mental excitement
Milk fever
Moral sanity
Novel reading
Nymphomania
Opium habit
Over action of the mind
Over heat
Over study of religion
Over taxing mental powers
Parents were cousins
Pecuniary losses
Periodical fits, tobacco & Masturbation
Political excitement
Politics
Puerperal
Religious enthusiasm
Religious Excitement
Remorse
Rumor of husband murder
Salvation Army
Scarlatina

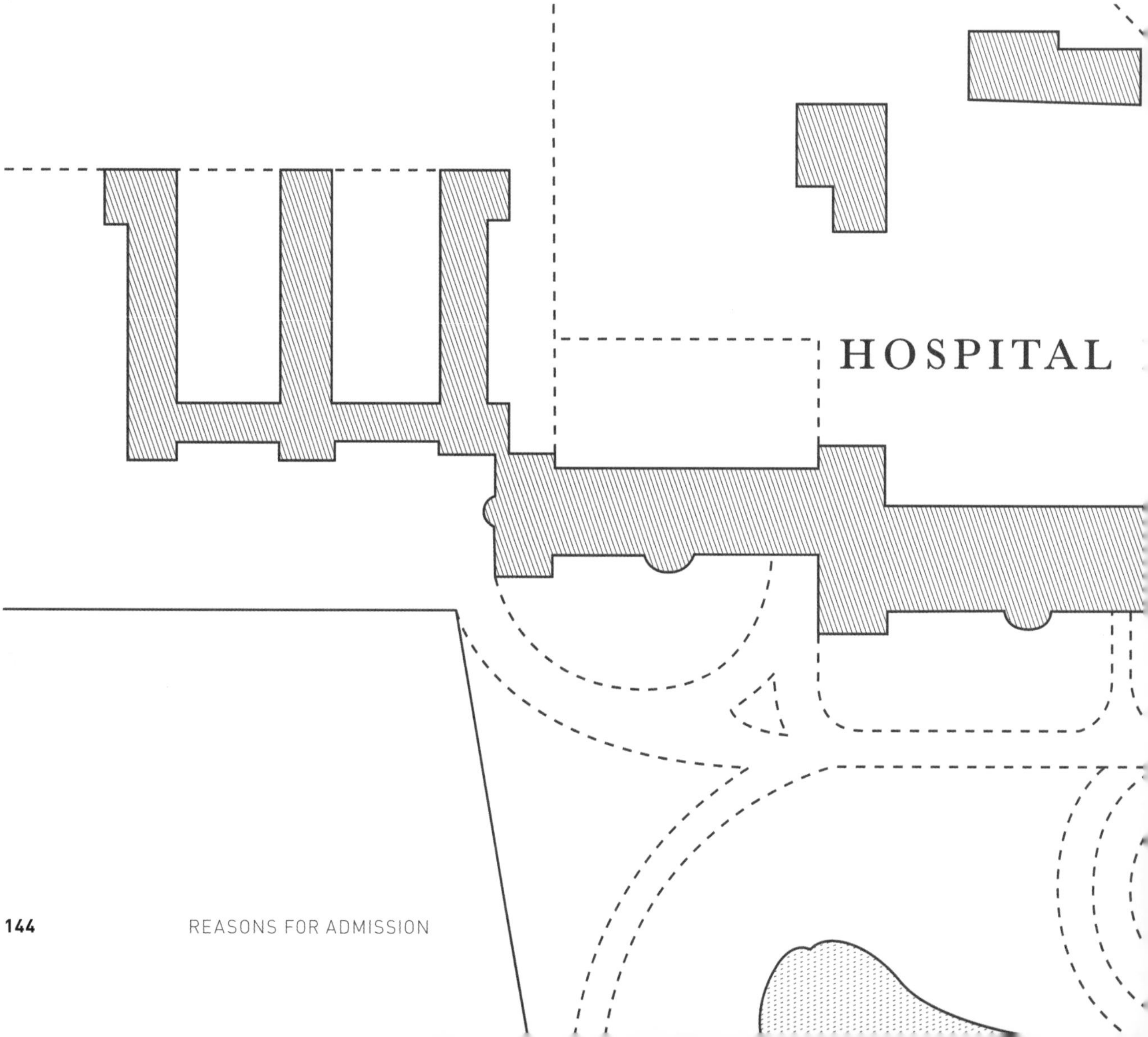

Seduction

Seduction & disappointment

Self Abuse

Severe labor

Sexual abuse and stimulants

Sexual derangement

Shooting of daughter

Small pox

Snuff eating for 2 years

Softening of the brain

Spinal irritation

Sun stroke

Superstition

Suppressed masturbation

Suppression of menses

The War

Time of life

Trouble

Uterine derangement

Venereal Excesses

Vicious vices in early life

Women

Women trouble

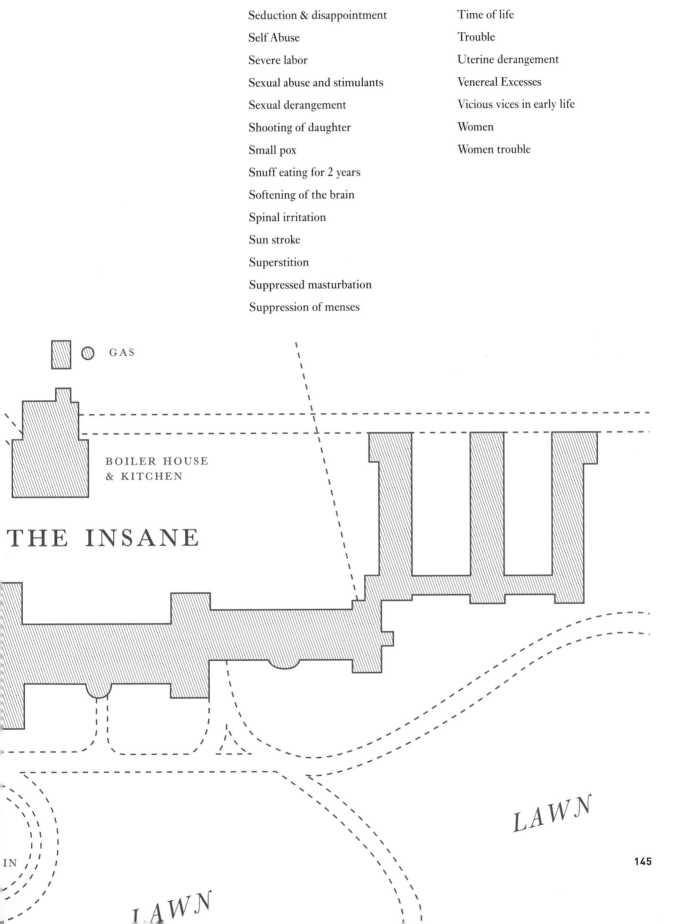

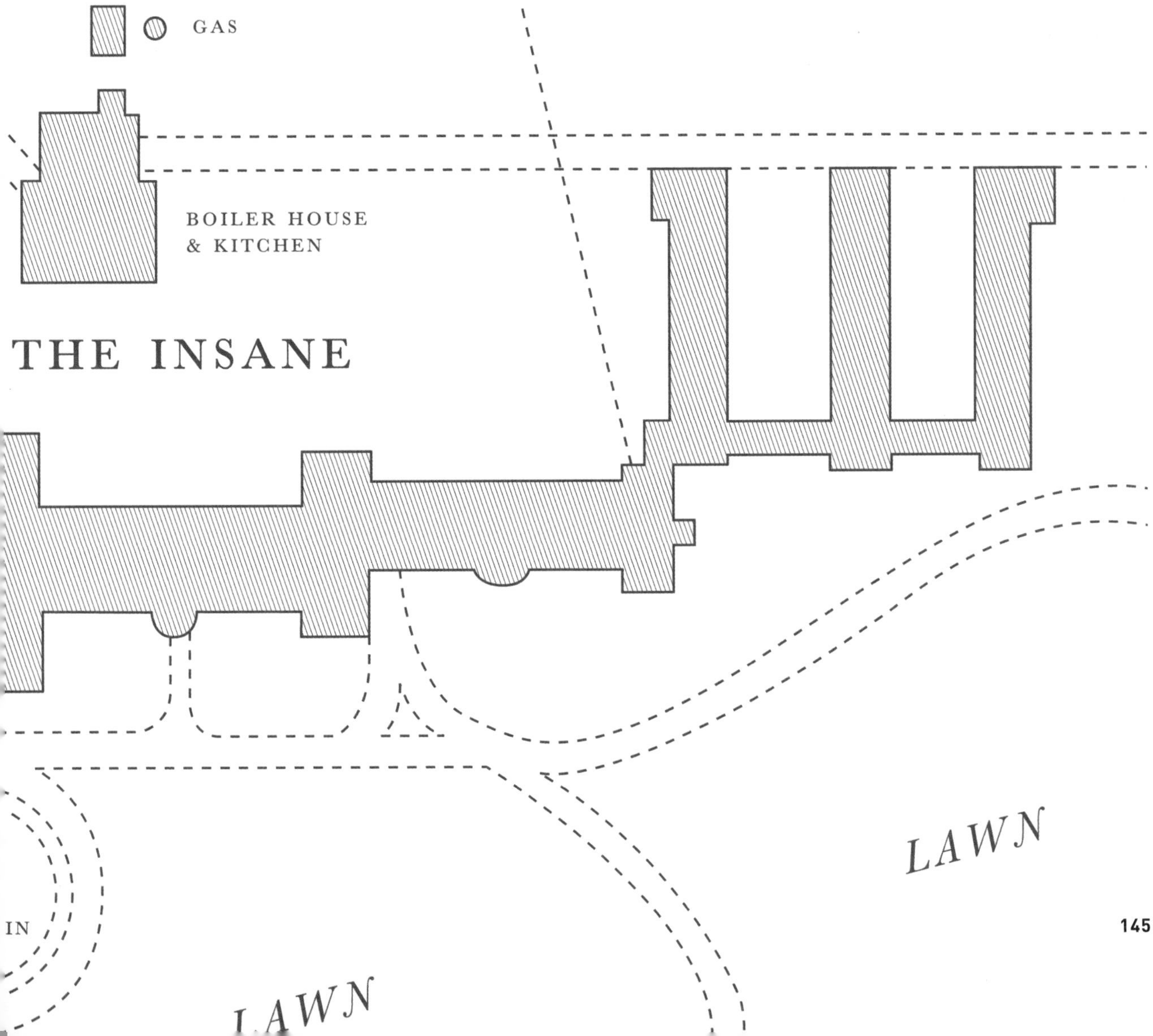

THE EIGHT KINDES OF DRUNKENNES

THOMAS NASHE
1592

Born in 1567, Thomas Nashe was a popular Elizabethan satirist who made his name writing plays, poetry, novels, and pamphlets—small, cheaply produced books that were largely seen as disposable, and which were all the rage in London in the late 1600s among the reading public. One of Nashe's most popular pamphlets was *Pierce Penniless, His Supplication to the Divell*, a quite cutting look at modern society from which this entertaining list, "The Eight Kindes of Drunkennes," is taken.

THE EIGHT KINDES OF DRUNKENNES

The first is ape drunke; and he leapes, and singes, and hollowes, and daunceth for the heauens: the second is lion drunke; and he flings the pots about the house, calls his hostesse whore, breakes the glasse windowes with his dagger, and is apt to quarrell with anie man that speaks to him: the third is swine drunke; heauie, lumpish, and sleepie, and cries for a little more drinke, and a fewe more cloathes: the fourth is sheepe drunke; wise in his conceipt, when he cannot bring foorth a right word: the fifth is mawdlen drunke; when a fellowe will weepe for kindnes in the midst of ale, and kisse you, saying, "By God, captaine, I loue thee. Goe thy wayes; thou dost not thinke so often of me as I doo of thee; I would (if it pleased God) I could not loue thee as well as I doo;" and then he puts his finger in his eye, and cryes: the sixt is Martin drunke; when a man is drunke, and drinkes himselfe sober ere he stirre: the seuenth is goate drunke; when, in his drunkennes, he hath no minde but on lecherie: the eighth is fox drunke—when he is craftie drunke, as manie of the Dutchmen bee, that will neuer bargaine but when they are drunke.

Ape Drunke

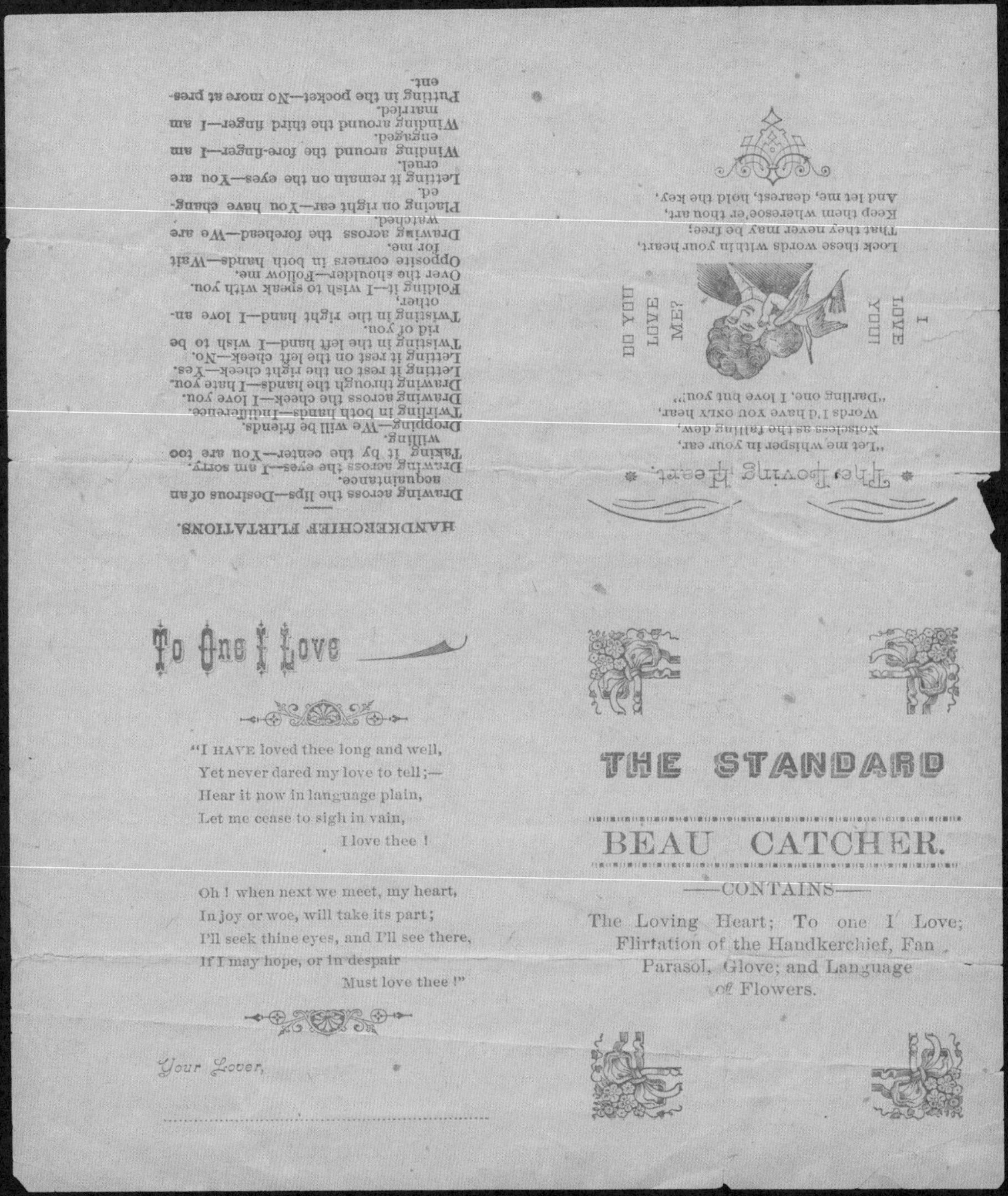

HANDKERCHIEF FLIRTATIONS.
Drawing across the lips—Desirous of an acquaintance.
Drawing across the eyes—I am sorry.
Taking it by the center—You are too willing.
Dropping—We will be friends.
Twirling in both hands—Indifference.
Drawing across the cheek—I love you.
Drawing through the hands—I hate you.
Letting it rest on the right cheek—Yes.
Letting it rest on the left cheek—No.
Twisting in the left hand—I wish to be rid of you.
Twisting in the right hand—I love another.
Folding it—I wish to speak with you.
Over the shoulder—Follow me.
Opposite corners in both hands—Wait for me.
Drawing across the forehead—We are watched.
Placing on right ear—You have changed.
Letting it remain on the eyes—You are cruel.
Winding around the fore-finger—I am engaged.
Winding around the third finger—I am married.
Putting in the pocket—No more at present.
The Loving Heart.
"Let me whisper in your ear,
Noiseless as the falling dew,
Words I'd have YOU ONLY hear,
"Darling one, I love but you!"
I LOVE YOU!
DO YOU LOVE ME?
Lock these words within your heart,
That they never may be free;
Keep them wheresoe'er thou art,
And let me, dearest, hold the key,
To One I Love
"I HAVE loved thee long and well,
Yet never dared my love to tell;—
Hear it now in language plain,
Let me cease to sigh in vain,
I love thee!
Oh! when next we meet, my heart,
In joy or woe, will take its part;
I'll seek thine eyes, and I'll see there,
If I may hope, or in despair
Must love thee!"
Your Lover,
THE STANDARD
BEAU CATCHER.
—CONTAINS—
The Loving Heart; To one I Love; Flirtation of the Handkerchief, Fan, Parasol, Glove; and Language of Flowers.

THE STANDARD BEAU CATCHER

AUTHOR UNKNOWN

Late 1800s

A pamphlet published around 1890, The Standard Beau Catcher was a flirtation guide for the discerning Victorian lady. In it could be found a number of lists, most of them revealing the hidden meanings behind various movements made by those holding gloves, fans, parasols, and handkerchiefs—a secret code of accessories. Also included was a brief guide to the "Language of Flowers."

PARASOL FLIRTATIONS.

Carrying it elevated in left hand,	Desiring acquaintance.
Carrying it elevated in right hand,	You are too willing.
Carrying it closed in left hand,	Meet on the first crossing.
Carrying it closed in right hand by side,	Follow me.
Carrying it in front of you.	No more at present.
Carrying it over the right shoulder,	You can speak to me.
Carrying it over the left shoulder,	You are too cruel.

Closing it,—I wish to speak to you.
Dropping it.—I love you.
End of tip to lips,—Do you lôve me?
Folding it up,—Get rid of your company.
Letting it rest on right cheek,—Yes.
Letting it rest on left cheek.—No.

Striking it on the hand,	I am very much displeased.
Swinging by handle on left side,	I am engaged.
Swinging by handle on right side,	I am married.
Tapping the chin gently,	I am in love with another.
Twirling it around,	Be careful, we are watched.
Using it as a fan.	Introduce me to your company.

With handle to lips,—Kiss me.

LANGUAGE OF FLOWERS.

Arbor Vitæ,—Unchanging Friendship.
Apple Blossom,—My Preference.
Alyssum,—Worth above Beauty.
Aspen Tree,—Sorrow.
Blue Canterberry Bell,—Fidelity.
China Pink,—Hate.
Coreopsis,—Love at first sight.
Dead Leaves,—Heavy Heart.
Forget-me-not,—True Love.
Geranium,—Lost Hope.
Hazel,—Let us bury the Hatchet.
Hawthorne,—Hope.
Heliotrope,—You are Loved.
Ivy,—Frienship.
Lily of the Valley,—Happy again.
Linden Tree,—Marriage.
Marigold,—I'm Jealous.
Myrtle,—Unalloyed Affection.
Pansy,—Think of Me.
Pea,—Meet me by Moonlight.
Peach Blossom,—My heart is thine.
Phlox,—Our Souls are United.
Pink, red,—Woman's Love.
Rose,—Perfect Beauty.
Rose Bud,—My Heart knows no Love.
Rose Geranium,—You are preferred.
Sweet William,—Let this be our last.
Tulip,—Declare your Love.
Wall Flower,—You will find me true.
Yellow Lily,—You are a Coquette.

FAN FLIRTATIONS.

Carrying in right hand—You are too willing.
Carrying in right hand, in front of face—Follow me.
Carrying in left hand—Desirous of ar acquaintance.
Closing it—I wish to speak with you.
Drawing across the forehead—We are watched.
Drawing across the cheek—I love you.
Drawing across the eyes—I am sorry.
Drawing through the hand—I hate you.
Dropping—We will be friends.
Fanning fast—I am engaged.
Fanning slow—I am married.
Letting it rest on the right cheek—Yes.
Letting it rest on the left cheek—No.
Open and shut—You are cruel.
Open wide—Wait for me.
Shut—I have changed.
Placing on right ear—You have changed.
Twirling in left hand—I wish to get rid of you.
Twirling in right hand—I love another.
With handle to lips—Kiss me.

GLOVE FLIRTATIONS.

Biting the tips—I wish to be rid of you.
Clenching them, rolled in right hand—No.
Drawing half way on left hand—Indifference.
Dropping both of them—I love you.
Dropping one of them—Yes.
Folding up carefully—Get rid of your company.
Holding with tips downward—I wish to be acquainted.
Holding loose in right hand—Be contented.
Holding loose in left hand—I am satisfied.
Left hand, naked thumb exposed—Do you love me?
Putting them away—I am vexed.
Right hand, naked thumb exposed—Kiss me.
Smoothing out gently—I wish I were with you.
Striking over the hand—I am displeased.
Striking over the shoulder—Follow me.
Tapping the chin—I love another.
Tossing them up gently—I am engaged.
Turning them inside out—I hate you.
Twirling around the fingers—Be careful, we are watched.
Using them as a fan—Introduce me your company.

YOU'VE GOT TO DIG IT TO DIG IT, YOU DIG?

THELONIOUS MONK
1960

Through a musical career spanning more than three decades, legendary jazz pianist and composer Thelonious Monk (1917–1982) has an influence that can still be heard. A pioneer of bebop in the 1940s, he created such standards as "Round Midnight" and the Blue Note classic "Straight, No Chaser."

In 1960, a couple of years before the release of his most successful album, *Monk's Dream*, he relayed a typically colorful selection of suggestions for music and life to his friend and onetime band member, saxophonist Steve Lacy, who transcribed his words into the list of advice seen here.

T.MONK'S ADVICE (1960)

JUST BECAUSE YOU'RE NOT A DRUMMER, DOESN'T MEAN THAT YOU DON'T HAVE TO KEEP TIME.

PAT YOUR FOOT + SING THE MELODY IN YOUR HEAD, WHEN YOU PLAY.

STOP PLAYING ALL (THAT BULLSHIT) THOSE WEIRD NOTES, PLAY THE MELODY!

MAKE THE DRUMMER SOUND GOOD.

DISCRIMINATION IS IMPORTANT.

YOU'VE GOT TO DIG IT TO DIG IT, YOU DIG?

ALL REET!

ALWAYS KNOW . . . (MONK)

IT MUST BE ALWAYS NIGHT, OTHERWISE THEY WOULDN'T NEED THE LIGHTS.

LET'S LIFT THE BAND STAND!!

I WANT TO AVOID THE HECKLERS.

DON'T PLAY THE PIANO PART, I'M PLAYING THAT. DON'T LISTEN TO ME. I'M SUPPOSED TO BE ACCOMPANYING YOU!

THE INSIDE OF THE TUNE (THE BRIDGE) IS THE PART THAT MAKES THE OUTSIDE SOUND GOOD.

DON'T PLAY EVERYTHING (OR EVERY TIME); LET SOME THINGS GO BY. SOME MUSIC JUST IMAGINED. WHAT YOU DON'T PLAY CAN BE MORE IMPORTANT THAN WHAT YOU DO.

ALWAYS LEAVE THEM WANTING MORE.

A NOTE CAN BE SMALL AS A PIN OR AS BIG AS THE WORLD, IT DEPENDS ON YOUR IMAGINATION.

STAY IN SHAPE! SOMETIMES A MUSICIAN WAITS FOR A GIG, + WHEN IT COMES, HE'S OUT OF SHAPE + CAN'T MAKE IT.

WHEN YOU'RE SWINGING, SWING SOME MORE! (WHAT SHOULD WE WEAR TONIGHT? SHARP AS POSSIBLE!)

DON'T SOUND ANYBODY FOR A GIG, JUST BE ON THE SCENE. THOSE PIECES WERE WRITTEN SO AS TO HAVE SOMETHING TO PLAY, + TO GET CATS INTERESTED ENOUGH TO COME TO REHEARSAL.

YOU'VE GOT IT! IF YOU DON'T WANT TO PLAY, TELL A JOKE OR DANCE, BUT IN ANY CASE, YOU GOT IT! (TO A DRUMMER WHO DIDN'T WANT TO SOLO).

WHATEVER YOU THINK CAN'T BE DONE, SOMEBODY WILL COME ALONG + DO IT. A GENIUS IS THE ONE MOST LIKE HIMSELF.

THEY TRIED TO GET ME TO HATE WHITE PEOPLE, BUT SOMEONE WOULD ALWAYS COME ALONG + SPOIL IT.

1. MONK'S ADVICE (1960)

JUST BECAUSE YOU'RE NOT A DRUMMER, DOESN'T MEAN THAT YOU DON'T HAVE TO KEEP TIME.

PAT YOUR FOOT + SING THE MELODY IN YOUR HEAD, WHEN YOU PLAY.

STOP PLAYING ALL THAT BULLSHIT / THOSE WIERD NOTES, PLAY THE MELODY!

MAKE THE DRUMMER SOUND GOOD.

DISCRIMINATION IS IMPORTANT.

YOU'VE GOT TO DIG IT TO DIG IT, YOU DIG?

ALL REET!

ALWAYS KNOW . . . (MONK)

IT MUST BE ALWAYS NIGHT, OTHERWISE THEY WOULDN'T NEED THE LIGHTS.

LET'S LIFT THE BANDSTAND!! (I WANT TO)

AVOID THE HECKLERS.

DON'T PLAY THE PIANO PART, I'M PLAYING THAT. DON'T LISTEN TO ME, I'M SUPPOSED TO BE ACCOMPANING YOU!

THE INSIDE OF THE TUNE (THE BRIDGE) IS THE PART THAT MAKES THE OUTSIDE SOUND GOOD.

DON'T PLAY EVERYTHING (OR EVERYTIME); LET SOME THINGS GO BY. SOME MUSIC JUST IMAGINED. WHAT YOU DON'T PLAY CAN BE MORE IMPORTANT THAN WHAT YOU DO PLAY.

A NOTE CAN BE SMALL AS A PIN OR AS BIG AS THE WORLD, IT DEPENDS ON YOUR IMAGINATION.

STAY IN SHAPE! SOMETIMES A MUSICIAN WAITS FOR A GIG, + WHEN IT COMES, HE'S OUT OF SHAPE + CAN'T MAKE IT.

WHEN YOU'RE SWINGING, SWING SOME MORE! (WHAT SHOULD WE WEAR TONIGHT? SHARP AS POSSIBLE!)

ALWAYS LEAVE THEM WANTING MORE.

DON'T SOUND ANYBODY FOR A GIG, JUST BE ON THE SCENE.

THOSE PIECES WERE WRITTEN SO AS TO HAVE SOMETHING TO PLAY, + TO GET CATS INTERESTED ENOUGH TO COME TO REHEARSAL!

YOU'VE GOT IT! IF YOU DON'T WANT TO PLAY, TELL A JOKE OR DANCE, BUT IN ANY CASE, YOU GOT IT! (TO A DRUMMER WHO DIDN'T WANT TO SOLO).

WHATEVER YOU THINK CAN'T BE DONE, SOMEBODY WILL COME ALONG + DO IT. A GENIUS IS THE ONE MOST LIKE HIMSELF.

THEY TRIED TO GET ME TO HATE WHITE PEOPLE, BUT SOMEONE WOULD ALWAYS COME ALONG + SPOIL IT.

List No. 062

GALILEO'S SHOPPING LIST

GALILEO GALILEI
1609

In August 1609, Galileo Galilei presented his latest telescope to the public: an instrument built using pre-made spectacle lenses that boasted an approximate magnification of 8x. Although it was effective, Galileo was determined to improve its power. However, the only way to do so would be to make his own lenses. The shopping list seen here, written by Galileo on the back of a letter dated November 23, 1609, in preparation for a trip to Venice from Padua, where he was teaching at the university, shows (among other items, including things for his companion, Marina, and their son, Vincenzo) the equipment needed for such an endeavor. In January 1610, he wrote a letter in which he announced the discovery of Jupiter's moons, spotted thanks to the 20x magnification improvements in his new telescope.

Scarfarotti e cappelletto per Vinc.o.
La cassa delle robe di Mar[in]a.
Lente, ceci bianchi, risi, uva passa, farro.
Zucchero, pepe, garofani, cannella, spezie, confetture.
Sapone, aranci.
Pettine d'avorio n.° 2.
Malvagia da i S.i Sagredi.
Palle d'artiglieria n.° 2.
Canna d'organo di stagno.
Vetri todeschi spianati.
Spianar cristallo di monte.
Pezzi di specchio.
Tripolo, ~~spantia~~
Lo specchiaro all'insegna del Re.
In calle delle aqque si fanno sgubie.
Trattare in materia di scodelle di ferro, o di gettarle in pietre, o vero come le palle d'artiglieria.
Privilegio per il vocabolario.
Ferro da spianare.
Pece greca.
Feltro, specchio per fregare.
Follo.
Pareggiarsi col S. Mannucci, et rendergli l'Edilio.

[TRANSLATION]

Shoes and hat for Vincenzo.
The case of wares for Marina.
Lentils, white chickpeas, rice, raisins, spelt.
Sugar, pepper, cloves, cinnamon, spices, jams.
Soaps, oranges.
Two ivory combs.
Malvasia by Lords Sagredo.
Two artillery balls.
Organ pipe of tin.
German lenses, polished.
Have rock crystal polished.
Pieces of mirror.
Tripolitan, ~~'spantia'~~
The mirror-maker under the insignia of the Kmg.
Small iron tuning chisels made in the *Calle delle Acque*.
To haggle about iron bowls, or to make them out of stone, or like the artillery balls.
Privilege for the vocabulary.
Iron plane.
Greek pitch.
Felt, mirror to rub.
Wool.
Pay debts to Mr. Mannucci and give him back the Edilio [a first edition—S.U.].

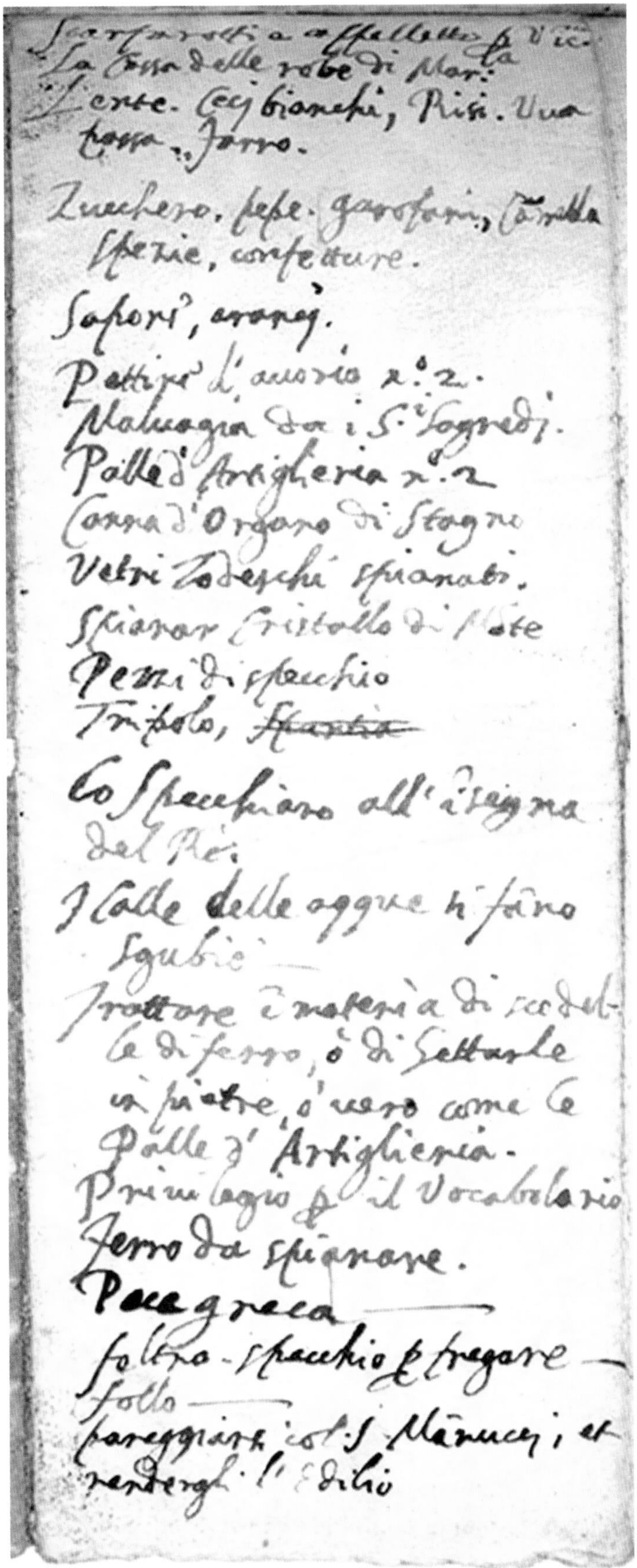
[illegible] a [illegible] p Vic.
La [illegible] delle robe di Mar:la
Lente. Ceci bianchi, Risi. Uva passa. Farro.

Zucchero, pepe. garofani, Cannella Spezie, confetture.

Sapori, aranci.

Pettini d'avorio n.° 2.
Malvagia dai S.ri Sagredi.
Palle d'Artiglieria n.° 2
Canna d'Organo di Stagno
Vetri Todeschi spianati.
Spianar Cristallo di Monte
Pezzi di specchio
Tripolo, ~~[illegible]~~

Lo Specchiaro all'insegna del Rè.

Palle delle acque si fanno sgubbie

Trattare in materia di saldarle di ferro, ò di gettarle in pietre, ovvero come le Palle d'Artiglieria.
Privilegio p il Vocabolario
Ferro da spianare.
Pece greca
feltro - specchio p fregare
follo
pareggiare col S. Manucci, et rendergli l'Edilio

List No. 063

IMMACULATE HEART COLLEGE ART DEPARTMENT RULES

CORITA KENT
Circa 1967

For 30 years, until she left the order of the Immaculate Heart of Mary in 1968, Sister Mary Corita headed the art department at Immaculate Heart College in Los Angeles, which quickly became known for its forward-thinking art classes. Later known as Corita Kent, she was influential in the Pop Art movement thanks to her unique and bold screen printing. She was also good friends with such cultural luminaries as Alfred Hitchcock, Saul Bass, and John Cage. During her time teaching at the college, she wrote a list of rules for the department.

IMMACULATE HEART COLLEGE ART DEPARTMENT RULES

RULE ONE: Find a place you trust and then try trusting it for a while.

RULE TWO: General duties of a student: pull everything out of your teacher. Pull everything out of your fellow students.

RULE THREE: General duties of a teacher: pull everything out of your students.

RULE FOUR: Consider everything an experiment.

RULE FIVE: Be self disciplined. This means finding someone wise or smart and choosing to follow them. To be disciplined is to follow in a good way. To be self disciplined is to follow in a better way.

RULE SIX: Nothing is a mistake. There's no win and no fail. There's only make.

RULE SEVEN: The only rule is work. If you work it will lead to something. It's the people who do all of the work all the time who eventually catch on to things.

RULE EIGHT: Don't try to create and analyze at the same time. They're different processes.

RULE NINE: Be happy whenever you can manage it. Enjoy yourself. It's lighter than you think.

RULE TEN: "We're breaking all the rules. Even our own rules. And how do we do that? By leaving plenty of room for x quantities." John Cage

HELPFUL HINTS: Always be around. Come or go to everything. Always go to classes. Read anything you can get your hands on. Look at movies carefully, often. Save everything—it might come in handy later.

List No. 064

HARRY S. TRUMAN'S LOVE LIST

HARRY S. TRUMAN
June 28, 1957

The thirty-third US president, Harry Truman, was married to his wife, Bess, for fifty-three years, having first met her in Sunday school when he was a young boy. Every year, on their anniversary, he would write her a letter. However, on their thirty-eighth he gave her something a little different: a list of each of their preceding anniversaries and a (very) brief summary of that year. Here's a little glossary:

1922 Broke because the men's furnishings store he co-owned in Kansas City closed as a result of the tumbling agriculture economy.

1923 Eastern Judge was Truman's first political campaign, for the eastern district of Jackson county, outside Kansas City.

1924 Daughter Mary Margaret, known as Margaret and Margie.

1925 Defeated by the Republican Henry Rummel, and took odd jobs.

1926 Not entirely out of a job: among other pursuits he sold memberships in the Kansas City Automobile Club, garnering $5000 in commission.

1927 Truman would spend eight years as presiding judge in Kansas City, to widespread approval.

1928 Himself a gifted pianist, Truman gave Margaret a baby grand piano. Al Smith was the governor of New York, whom Truman supported.

1932 New road system for Jackson County, which Truman had been instrumental in instigating.

1933 Employment Director for Kansas City, whose work program then has been credited as an inspiration for the WPA.

1934 Those buildings were the Jackson County Courthouses.

1935 US Senator for Missouri. Gunston Hall was Margaret's new school.

1936 Democrats convened in Philadelphia and renominated FDR as their presidential candidate.

1939 The Wheeler-Truman Bill (the Transportation Act of 1940).

1940 Truman "fought" Maurice Milligan and Lloyd Stark for a Senate seat.

1941 Senate Special Committee to Investigate the National Defense Program (AKA the Truman Committee). Margaret begins singing lessons.

1944 Truman was reluctant to have his name put forward for the vice-presidency and he had agreed to nominate another potential candidate, Jimmy Byrnes. Truman told a reporter, "Hell, I don't want to be President."

1945 Three months serving as VP, then commander-in-chief following the death of President Roosevelt

1948 A long, stressful campaign that covered 21,928 miles.

1950 Truman ordered US forces to defend South Korea from North Korea. Fighting ended in 1953.

1955 On June 20, Truman had an emergency gallbladder operation.

1957 Jobes served with Truman during World War II.

June 28, 1920	One happy year.
June 28, 1921	Going very well.
June 28, 1922	Broke and in a bad way.
June 28, 1923	Eastern Judge. Eating.
June 28, 1924	Daughter 4 mo. old.
June 28, 1925	Out of a job.
June 28, 1926	Still out of a job.
June 28, 1927	Presiding Judge—eating again.
June 28, 1928	All going well. Piano. Al Smith.
June 28, 1929	Panic, in October.
June 28, 1930	Depression. Still going.
June 28, 1931	Six year old daughter.
June 28, 1932	Roads finished.
June 28, 1933	Employment Director.
June 28, 1934	Buildings finished. Ran for the Senate.
June 28, 1935	U.S. Senator Gunston.
June 28, 1936	Resolutions Philadelphia. Roosevelt reelected.
June 28, 1937	Great time in Washington.
June 28, 1938	Very happy time. Margie 14.
June 28, 1939	Named legislation.
June 28, 1940	Senate fight coming.
June 28, 1941	Special Senate Committee. Margie wants to sing.
June 28, 1942	Also a happy time.
June 28, 1943	Lots of work.
June 28, 1944	Talk of V.P. Bad business.
June 28, 1945	V.P. & President. War end.
June 28, 1946	Margie graduate & singer. 80th Congress.
June 28, 1947	Marshall Plan & Greece & Turkey. A grand time 28th Anniversary.
June 28, 1948	A terrible campaign. Happy day.
June 28, 1949	President again. Another happy day.
June 28, 1950	Korea—a terrible time.
June 28, 1951	Key West—a very happy day.
June 28, 1952	All happy. Finish, Jan. 20, 1953.
June 28, 1953	Back home. Lots of *Roses*.
June 28, 1954	A happy 35th.
June 28, 1955	All cut up but still happy.
June 28, 1956	A great day—more elation.
June 28, 1957	Well here we are again, as Harry Jobes would say.

Only 37 to go for the diamond jubilee!

HARRY S. TRUMAN
FEDERAL RESERVE BANK BUILDING
KANSAS CITY 6, MISSOURI

June 28, 1920 One happy year.
June 28, 1921 Going very well.
June 28, 1922 Broke and in a bad way.
June 28, 1923 Eastern Judge. Eating
June 28, 1924 Daughter 4 mo. old.
June 28, 1925 Out of a job.
June 28, 1926 Still out of a job.
June 28, 1927 Presiding Judge - eating again
June 28, 1928 All going well. Piano.
June 28, 1929 Panic, in October. (Al Smith)
June 28, 1930 Depression. Still going.
June 28, 1931 Six year old daughter
June 28, 1932 Roads finished
June 28, 1933 Employment Director.
June 28, 1934 Buildings finished.
Ran for the Senate
June 28, 1935 U.S. Senator, Washington.
June 28, 1936 Resolutions Philadelphia.
Roosevelt reelected.

HARRY S. TRUMAN
FEDERAL RESERVE BANK BUILDING
KANSAS CITY 6, MISSOURI

June 28, 1937 Grand time in Washington.
June 28, 1938 Very happy time. Margie 14.
June 28, 1939 Named legislation.
June 28, 1940 Senate fight comming.
June 28, 1941 Special Senate Committee
Margie wants to sing.
June 28, 1942 Also a happy time
June 28, 1943 Lots of work.
June 28, 1944 Talk of V.P. Bad business
June 28, 1945 V.P. & President. War End
June 28, 1946 Margie graduate & singer
80th Congress.
June 28, 1947 Marshall Plan & Greece & Turkey
A grand time 28th anna
June 28, 1948 A terrible campaign. Happy day.
June 28, 1949 President again. Another happy day.
June 28, 1950 Korea - a terrible time.
June 28, 1951 Key West - a very happy day.
June 28, 1952 All happy. Finish Jan 20, 1953
June 28, 1953 Back home. Lots of Rokes.
June 28, 1954 A happy 35th

HARRY S. TRUMAN
FEDERAL RESERVE BANK BUILDING
KANSAS CITY 6, MISSOURI

June 28, 1955 All cut up but still happy.
June 28, 1956 A great day - more election.
June 28, 1957 Well here we are again
as ~~Harry~~ Jokes would say.

Only 37 to go for the
diamond jubilee!

H. S. T.

MAKE YOUR HOTEL

List No. 065

HOW TO WRITE

DAVID OGILVY
September 7, 1982

British-born David Ogilvy was one of the original "ad men." His name, and that of his agency, have been mentioned more than once in the television show *Mad Men,* and for good reason. In 1948, he started what would eventually be known as Ogilvy & Mather, the Manhattan-based advertising agency that has since been responsible for some of the world's most iconic ad campaigns. In 1963 Ogilvy wrote *Confessions of an Advertising Man,* a bestselling book that is to this day considered essential reading for all who enter the industry, and around the same time *Time* magazine called him "the most sought-after wizard in today's advertising industry."

On September 7, 1982, Ogilvy sent an internal memo, titled "How to Write," to all employees at Ogilvy & Mather, and it consisted of this list of advice.

The better you write, the higher you go in Ogilvy & Mather. People who *think* well, *write* well.

Woolly minded people write woolly memos, woolly letters and woolly speeches.

Good writing is not a natural gift. You have to *learn* to write well. Here are 10 hints:

(1) Read the Roman-Raphaelson book on writing. [*Writing that Works.*] Read it three times.

(2) Write the way you talk. Naturally.

(3) Use short words, short sentences and short paragraphs.

(4) Never use jargon words like *reconceptualize*, *demassification*, *attitudinally*, *judgmentally*. They are hallmarks of a pretentious ass.

(5) Never write more than two pages on any subject.

(6) Check your quotations.

(7) Never send a letter or a memo on the day you write it. Read it aloud the next morning—and then edit it.

(8) If it is something important, get a colleague to improve it.

(9) Before you send your letter or your memo, make sure it is crystal clear what you want the recipient to do.

(10) If you want ACTION, *don't write*. Go and *tell* the guy what you want.

REJECTING *WITTGENSTEIN'S MISTRESS*

DAVID MARKSON
Date Unknown

Wittgenstein's Mistress by David Markson (1927–2010) is not your average novel. Written largely in single-sentence paragraphs, it tells the story of a woman who is convinced that she is alone in this world; that is, that no other human being exists. When published in 1988, it received strong reviews and is now considered to be Markson's masterpiece. In 1999, fellow American novelist David Foster Wallace called it "pretty much the high point of experimental fiction in this country."

Despite the praise garnered after publication, it hadn't all been smooth sailing. The list you see here, handwritten by the book's exasperated author, details each and every one of the fifty-four rejections he (and his agent and ex-wife, Elaine) received, citing editor and publisher, over the course of four-plus years before *Wittgenstein's Mistress* eventually found a home at Dalkey Archive Press, where Steven Moore was its editor.

1 – Asher – Harper & Row – No

2 – Cannon – Dutton? – No

3 – Talese – HM Co – No –

4 – Silberman – Summit – Brilliant / Classy – No

5 – Strachan – FSG – Too Brilliant / not know who – No

6 – Sifton – Viking – Admin, not love – rhythm – No

7 – Knopf – Lish want – cannot get through – No (Lee Goerner said no)

8 – Entrekin – S&S – nice letter – No

9 – Phillips – Little Brown – not "love" enough – No

10 – Sale – Putnam – not sort of voice can get into – No

11 – Landis – Morrow – No –

12 – Ann Patty – Poseidon – No

13 – Tom Engelhart – Pantheon – No

14 – Freedgood – Random – Admire writing – not love – No

15 – Stewart – Atheneum – Doesn't thicken – No

16 – Peter Davison – Atlantic Monthly Press – Brilliant – Hummed – No

17 – Tom Wallace – Norton – No

18 – Barbara Grossman – Crown – Brilliant – 25yrs ahead of its time – No

19 – Godine – No

20 – Catherine Court – Penguin – Didn't understand – No

21 – Lish – Knopf – asked for it back – No

22 – Fred Jordan – Grove – No

23 – Irene Skolnick – HBJ – she love – cldn't get 2nd reader – No

24 – Karen Brazillar – Persea – Brilliant – Can't do – No

25 – Bob Wyatt – Ballantine – No

26 Shoemaker – North Point – Brilliant creative No

27 – Roger Angell – NY'er – No concessions – Hard to stay with – No

28 – Pantheon – 2nd Ed (via Lish) – Brilliant – No

29 – Fran McCullough – Dial – No

30 – St. Martins – Brilliant – Beattie 100% Right – No

31 – Delacorte – No

32 – Braziller – No

33 – Sam Vaughan – Doubleday – No

34 – Vanguard – No

35 – Donald I. Fine – No

36 – Congdon – Congdon & Weed – No

37 – Cork Smith – Ticknor & Fields – No

38 – Fisketjon – Random House – No

39 – Raebuth – Horizon 5/7/84 – spoke 3/85 – personal problems – can't do but wld – maybe later

40 – Carrol – Carroll & Geoff – No

41 – Lish – Knopf – Had asked – No

42 – Scribner's – No

43 – Pushcart Press – No

44 – McPherson & Co – No

45 – Putnam – 2nd Ed. Stacy Kramer – No

46 – New Directions – Abish & Laughlin – rejection slip – No – told Walter never read it

47 – Juri Jurevis – SoHo Press – No

48 – Overlook – No

49 – Weidenfield & Nicholson – No

50 Sun & moon – No

51 Algonquin – No

52 Delphinium Press – Joe Papaleo – Brilliant – spectacular – No

53 William Abraham – No

54 Thunder's Mouth – No

SUBMISSIONS — "WITTGENSTEIN'S MISTRESS" (as "Keeper of the Ghosts")

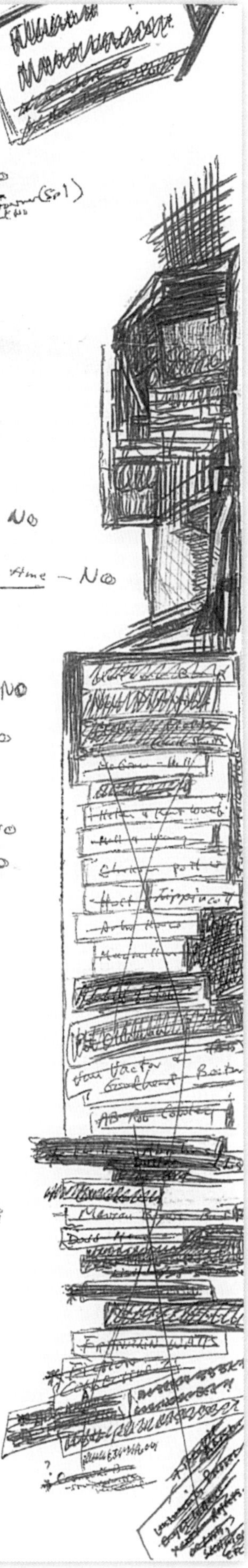

(1) – Asher – Harper & Row — NO
(2) – Cannon – Dutton — NO —
(3) – Talese – HM Co — NO
(4) – Silberman – Summit — Brilliant / Classy NO
(5) – Strachan – FSG – Too Brilliant / not know who – NO
(6) – Sifton – Viking — Admire, not love — rhythms – NO
~~(7) Knopf – Lish Wait~~ – cannot get through – NO (The Gunner (Sol) Can't Do)
(8) – Entekon – S&S — Nice letter — NO
(9) – Phillips – Little Brown – not "love" enough – NO
(10) – Sale – Putnam – not sort of voice can get into – NO
(11) – Landis – Morrow — No –

(12) – Ann Patty – Poseidon – NO [redacted]
(13) – Tom Englehart – Pantheon – NO –
(14) – Freedgood – Random – Admire writing – not love – NO
(15) – Stewart – Atheneum – Doesn't thicken – NO
(16) – Peter Davison – Atlantic Monthly Press – Brilliant – Unusual – NO
(17) – Tom Wallace – Norton – NO
(18) Barbara Grossman – Crown – Brilliant – 25 yrs ahead of its time – NO
(19) – Godine – NO
(20) – Catherine Court – Penguin – Didn't Understand – NO
← (21) Lish – Knopf [redacted] asked for it back – NO
(22) – Fred Jordan – Grove – NO
(23) – Irene Skolnick – HBJ – She love – Couldn't get 2nd reader – NO
(24) – Karen Braziller – Persea – Brilliant – Can't do – NO
(25) – Bob Wyatt – Ballantine – NO
(26) Schumacher – North Point – Brilliant writing [redacted] NO
(27) – Roger Angell – NY'er – No concessions – Hard to stay with – NO
(28) – Pantheon – 2nd Ed (via Lish) – Brilliant – NO
(29) – Fran McCullough – Dial – NO
(30) – St. Martins – Brilliant – Beattie 100% Right – NO
(31) – Delacorte – NO
(32) – Braziller – NO
(33) – Sam Vaughan – Doubleday – NO
(34) – Vanguard – NO
(35) – Donald I. Fine – NO
(36) – Congdon – Congdon & Weed – NO
(37) – Cork Smith – Ticknor & Fields – NO
(38) – Fisketjon – Random House – NO
(39) – Raeburn – Horizon 5/7/84 – Spoke 3/85 – personal problems – Can't Do But told – Maybe later (Grant)
(40) – Carroll – Carroll & Graf – NO – [redacted]
(41) – Lish – Knopf – Had asked – NO – [redacted]
(42) – Scribner's – NO
(43) – Pushcart Press – NO
(44) – McPherson & Co – NO
(45) – Putnam – 2nd Ed. Stacey Kramer – NO
(46) – New Directions – Abish to Laughlin – ~~NO~~ Rejection Slip – NO – Told Walter wasn't read it.
(47) – Jon Jurevics – ~~[illegible]~~ → SOHO Press – NO
(48) – Overlook – [redacted] (NO)
(49) – Weidenfeld & Nicholson – (NO)
(50) SunMoon – (NO)
(51) Algonquin – (NO)
(52) Delphinium Press – Joe Papaleo – Brilliant – Spectacular (NO)
(53) William Abrahams – (NO)
(54) Thunder's Mouth (NO)

LOVECRAFT'S WEIRD IDEAS

H. P. LOVECRAFT
Circa 1919–1934

In a letter dated January 1920, revered horror author H. P. Lovecraft (1890–1937) revealed to his friend and frequent correspondent Reinhardt Kleiner that he had recently begun compiling a list of "ideas and images for subsequent use in fiction." He went on, "For the first time in my life, I am keeping a 'commonplace book'—if that term can be applied to a repository of gruesome and fantastick thoughts." Fourteen years later he handed the now sprawling list to a curious friend with an explanatory note that read:

"This book consists of ideas, images, & quotations hastily jotted down for possible future use in weird fiction. Very few are actually developed plots—for the most part they are merely suggestions or random impressions designed to set the memory or imagination working. Their sources are various—dreams, things read, casual incidents, idle conceptions, & so on."

(In brackets below, Lovecraft noted references to books and stories the ideas were explored in.)

1 *Demophon* shivered when the sun shone upon him. (Lover of darkness = ignorance.)

2 Inhabitants of *Zinge*, over whom the star Canopus rises every night, are always gay and without sorrow.

3 The shores of Attica respond in song to the waves of the Aegean.

4 Horror Story—Man dreams of falling—found on floor mangled as tho' from falling from a vast height.

5 Narrator walks along unfamiliar country road,—comes to strange region of the unreal.

6 In Ld Dunsany's "Idle Days on the Yann": The inhabitants of the antient Astahahn, on the Yann, do all things according to antient ceremony. Nothing new is found. "Here we have fetter'd and manacled Time, who wou'd otherwise slay the Gods."

7 *Horror Story:* The sculptured hand—or other artificial hand—which strangles its creator.

8 Hor. Sto.: Man makes appt. with old enemy. Dies—body keeps appt.

9 Dr. Eben Spencer plot.

10 Dream of flying over city. [Celephaïs]

11 Odd nocturnal ritual. Beasts dance and march to musick.

12 Happenings in interval between preliminary sound and striking of clock—ending: "It was the tones of the clock striking three".

13 House and garden—old—associations. Scene takes on strange aspect.

14 Hideous sound in the dark.

15 Bridge and slimy black waters. [Fungi—The Canal.]

16 The walking dead—seemingly alive, but—

17 Doors found mysteriously open and shut &c.—excite terror.

18 Calamander-wood—a very valuable cabinet wood of Ceylon and S. India, resembling rosewood.

19 Revise 1907 tale—painting of ultimate horror.

20 Man journeys into the past—or imaginative realm—leaving bodily shell behind.

21 A very ancient colossus in a very ancient desert. Face gone—no man hath seen it.

22 Mermaid Legend—*Encyc. Britt.* XVI—40.

23 The man who would not sleep—dares not sleep—takes drugs to keep himself awake. Finally falls asleep—and *something* happens— Motto from Baudelaire p. 214. [Hypnos]

24 Dunsany—"Go-By Street": Man stumbles on dream world—returns to earth—seeks to go back—succeeds, but finds dream world ancient and decayed as though by thousands of years.

[1919]

25 Man visits museum of antiquities—asks that it accept a bas-relief *he has* just made—*old* and learned curator laughs and says he cannot accept anything so modern. Man says that 'dreams are older than brooding Egypt or the contemplative Sphinx or garden-girdled Babylonia' and that he had fashioned the sculpture in his dreams. Curator bids him shew his product, and when he does so curator shews horror, asks who the man may be. He tells modern name. "No—*before that*" says curator. Man does not remember except in dreams. Then curator offers high price, but man fears he means to destroy sculpture. Asks fabulous price—curator will consult directors.

Add good development and describe nature of bas-relief. [Cthulhu]

26 Dream of ancient castle stairs—sleeping guards—narrow window—battle on plain between men of England and men of

yellow tabards with red dragons. Leader of English challenges leader of foe to single combat. They fight. Foe unhelmeted, *but there is no head revealed.* Whole army of foe fades into mist, and watcher finds himself to be the English knight on the plain, mounted. Looks at castle, and sees a peculiar concentration of fantastic clouds over the highest battlements.

27 *Life and Death:* Death—its desolation and horror—bleak spaces—sea-bottom—dead cities. But Life—the greater horror! Vast unheard-of reptiles and leviathans—hideous beasts of prehistoric jungle—rank slimy vegetation—evil instincts of primal man—Life is more horrible than death.

28 *The Cats of Ulthar:* The cat is the soul of antique AEgyptus and bearer of tales from forgotten cities of Meroë and Ophir. He is the kin of the jungle's lords, and heir to the secrets of hoary and sinister Africa. The Sphinx is his cousin, and he speaks her language; but he is more ancient than the Sphinx, and remembers that which she hath forgotten. [used]

29 Dream of Seekonk—ebbing tide—bolt from sky—exodus from Providence—fall of Congregational dome.

30 Strange visit to a place at night—moonlight—castle of great magnificence &c. Daylight shews either abandonment or unrecognisable ruins—perhaps of vast antiquity.

31 Prehistoric man preserved in Siberian ice. (See Winchell—*Walks and Talks in the Geological Field*—p. 156 et seq.)

32 As dinosaurs were once surpassed by mammals, so will man-mammal be surpassed by insect or bird—fall of man before the new race.

33 Determinism and prophecy.

34 Moving away from earth more swiftly than light—past gradually unfolded—horrible revelation.

35 Special beings with special senses from remote universes. Advent of an external universe to view.

36 Disintegration of all matter to electrons and finally empty space assured, just as devolution of energy to radiant heat is known. Case of *acceleration*—man passes into space.

37 Peculiar odour of a book of childhood induces repetition of childhood fancy.

38 Drowning sensations—undersea—cities—ships—souls of the dead. Drowning is a horrible death.

39 *Sounds*—possibly musical—heard in the night from other worlds or realms of being.

40 Warning that certain ground is sacred or accursed; that a house or city must not be built upon it—or must be abandoned or destroyed if built, under penalty of catastrophe.

41 The Italians call *Fear* La figlia della Morte—the daughter of Death.

42 Fear of *mirrors*—memory of dream in which scene is altered and climax is hideous surprise at seeing oneself in the water or a mirror. (Identity?) [Outsider?]

43 Monsters born living—burrow underground and multiply, forming race of unsuspected daemons.

44 Castle by pool or river—reflection fixed thro' centuries—castle destroyed, reflection lives to avenge destroyers weirdly.

45 Race of immortal Pharaohs dwelling beneath pyramids in vast subterranean halls down black staircases.

46 Hawthorne—unwritten plot: Visitor from tomb—stranger at some publick concourse followed at midnight to graveyard where he descends into the earth.

47 From "Arabia" *Encyc. Britan.* II—255: Prehistoric fabulous tribes of Ad in the south, Thamood in the north, and Tasm and Jadis in the centre of the peninsula. "Very gorgeous are the descriptions given of Irem, the City of Pillars (as the Koran styles it) supposed to have been erected by Shedad, the latest despot of Ad, in the regions of Hadramaut, and which yet, after the annihilation of its tenants, remains entire, so Arabs say, invisible to ordinary eyes, but occasionally, and at rare intervals, revealed to some heaven-favoured traveller." Rock excavations in N. W. Hejaz ascribed to Thamood tribe.

48 Cities wiped out by supernatural wrath.

49 AZATHOTH—hideous name.

50 *Phleg'*e-thon—a river of liquid fire in Hades.

51 Enchanted garden where moon casts shadow of object or ghost invisible to the human eye.

52 Calling on the dead—voice or familiar sound in adjacent room.

53 Hand of dead man writes.

54 Transposition of identity.

55 Man followed by invisible *thing*.

56 Book or MS. too horrible to read—warned against reading it—someone reads and is found dead. Haverhill incident.

57 Sailing or rowing on lake in moonlight—sailing into invisibility.

58 A queer village—in a valley, reached by a long road and visible from the crest of the hill from which that road descends—or close to a dense and antique forest.

59 Man in strange subterranean chamber—seeks to force door of bronze—overwhelmed by influx of waters.

60 Fisherman casts his net into the sea by moonlight—what he finds.

61 A terrible pilgrimage to seek the nighted throne of the far daemon-sultan *Azathoth*.

62 Live man buried in bridge masonry according to superstition—or black cat.

63 Sinister names—Nasht—Kaman-Thah.

64 Identity—reconstruction of personality—man makes duplicate of himself.

65 Riley's fear of undertakers—door locked on inside after death.

66 Catacombs discovered beneath a city (in America?).

67 An impression—city in peril—dead city—equestrian statue—men in closed room—clattering of hooves heard from outside—marvel disclosed on looking out—*doubtful* ending.

68 Murder discovered—body located—by psychological detective who pretends he has made walls of room transparent. Works on fear of murderer.

69 Man with unnatural face—oddity of speaking—found to be a *mask*—Revelation.

70 *Tone of extreme phantasy:* Man transformed to island or mountain.

71 Man has sold his soul to devil—returns to family from trip—life afterward—fear—culminating horror—novel length.

72 Hallowe'en incident—mirror in cellar—face seen therein—death (claw-mark?).

73 Rats multiply and exterminate first a single city and then all mankind. Increased size and intelligence.

74 Italian revenge—killing self in cell with enemy—under castle. [used by FBL, Jr.]

75 Black Mass under antique church.

76 Ancient cathedral—hideous gargoyle—man seeks to rob—found dead—gargoyle's jaw bloody.

77 Unspeakable dance of the gargoyles—in morning several gargoyles on old cathedral found transposed.

78 Wandering thro' labyrinth of narrow slum streets—come on distant light—unheard-of rites of swarming beggars—like Court of Miracles in *Notre Dame de Paris*.

79 Horrible secret in crypt of ancient castle—discovered by dweller.

80 Shapeless living *thing* forming nucleus of ancient building.

81 Marblehead—dream—burying hill—evening—unreality. [Festival?]

82 Power of wizard to influence dreams of others.

[1920]

83 Quotation: ". . .a defunct nightmare, which had perished in the midst of its wickedness, and left its flabby corpse on the breast of the tormented one, to be gotten rid of as it might."—Hawthorne

84 Hideous cracked discords of bass musick from (ruin'd) organ in (abandon'd) abbey or cathedral. [Red Hook]

85 "For has not Nature, too, her grotesques—the rent rock, the distorting lights of evening on lonely roads, the unveiled structure of man in the embryo, or the skeleton?" Pater—*Renaissance* (da Vinci).

86 To find something horrible in a (perhaps familiar) book, and not to be able to find it again.

87 *Borellus* says, "that the Essential Salts of animals may be so prepared and preserved, that an ingenious man may have the whole ark of Noah in his own Study, and raise the fine shape of an animal out of its ashes at his pleasure; and that by the like method from the Essential Salts of humane dust, a Philosopher may, without any criminal necromancy, call up the shape of any dead ancestor from the dust whereinto his body has been incinerated." [Charles Dexter Ward]

88 Lonely philosopher fond of cat. Hypnotises it—as it were—by repeatedly talking to it and looking at it. After his death the cat evinces signs of possessing his personality. N. B. He has trained cat, and leaves it to a friend, with instructions as to fitting a pen to its right fore paw by means of a harness. Later writes with deceased's own handwriting.

89 Lone lagoons and swamps of Louisiana—death daemon—ancient house and gardens—moss-grown trees—festoons of Spanish moss.

[1922?]

90 *Anencephalous* or brainless monster who survives and attains prodigious size.

91 Lost winter day—slept over—20 yrs. later. Sleep in chair

on summer night—false dawn—old scenery and sensations—cold—old persons now dead—horror—frozen?

[1922?]

92 Man's body dies—but corpse retains life. Stalks about—tries to conceal odour of decay—detained somewhere—hideous climax. [Cool Air]

93 A place one has been—a beautiful view of a village or farm-dotted valley in the sunset—which one cannot find again or locate in memory.

94 Change comes over the sun—shews objects in strange form, perhaps restoring landscape of the past.

95 Horrible Colonial farmhouse and overgrown garden on city hillside—overtaken by growth. Verse "The House" as basis of story. [Shunned House]

96 Unknown fires seen across the hills at night.

97 Blind fear of a certain woodland hollow where streams writhe among crooked roots, and where on a buried altar terrible sacrifices have occur'd—Phosphorescence of dead trees. Ground bubbles.

98 Hideous old house on steep city hillside—Bowen St.—beckons in the night—black windows—horror unnam'd—cold touch and voice—the welcome of the dead.

[1923]

99 Salem story—the cottage of an aged witch—wherein after her death are found sundry terrible things.

100 Subterranean region beneath placid New England village, inhabited by (living or extinct) creatures of prehistoric antiquity and strangeness.

101 Hideous secret society—widespread—horrible rites in caverns under familiar scenes—one's own neighbour may belong.

102 Corpse in room performs some act—prompted by discussion in its presence. Tears up or hides will, etc.

103 Sealed room—or at least no lamp allowed there. Shadow on wall.

104 Old sea-tavern now far inland from made land. Strange occurrences—sound of lapping of waves—

105 Vampire *visits* man in ancestral abode—is his own father.

106 A *thing* that sat on a sleeper's chest. Gone in morning, but something left behind.

[1923]

107 Wall paper cracks off in sinister shape—man dies of fright. [Rats in Walls]

108 Educated mulatto seeks to displace personality of white man and occupy his body.

109 Ancient negro voodoo wizard in cabin in swamp—possesses white man.

110 Antediluvian—Cyclopean ruins on lonely Pacific island. Centre of earthwide subterranean witch cult.

111 Ancient ruin in Alabama swamp—voodoo.

112 Man lives near graveyard—how does he live? Eats no food.

113 Biological-hereditary memories of other worlds and universes. Butler—*God Known and Unk*. p. 59. [Belknap]

114 Death lights dancing over a salt marsh.

115 Ancient castle within sound of weird waterfall—sound ceases for a time under strange conditions.

116 Prowling at night around an unlighted castle amidst strange scenery.

117 A secret living thing kept and fed in an old house.

[1924]

118 Something seen at oriel window of forbidden room in ancient manor house.

119 Art note—fantastick daemons of Salvator Rosa or Fuseli (trunk-proboscis).

120 Talking bird of great longevity—tells secret long afterward.

121 Photius tells of a (lost) writer named Damascius, who wrote *Incredible Fictions*, *Tales of Daemons*, *Marvellous Stories of Appearances from the Dead*.

122 Horrible things whispered in the lines of Gauthier de Metz (13th cen.) *Image du Monde*.

123 Dried-up man living for centuries in cataleptic state in ancient tomb.

124 Hideous secret assemblage at night in antique alley—disperse furtively one by one—one seen to drop something—a human hand—

125 Man abandon'd by ship—swimming in sea—pickt up hours later with strange story of undersea region he has visited—mad??

126 Castaways on island eat unknown vegetation and become strangely transformed.

127 Ancient and unknown ruins—strange and immortal bird who *speaks* in a language horrifying and revelatory to the explorers.

128 Individual, by some strange process, retraces the path of evolution and becomes amphibious. ⍰ Dr. insists that the particular amphibian from which *man* descends is not like any known to palaeontology. To prove it, indulges in (or relates) strange experiment.

[1925]

129 *Marble Faun* p. 346—strange and prehistorick Italian city of stone.

130 N. E. region call'd "Witches' Hollow"—along course of a river. Rumours of witches' sabbaths and Indian powwows on a broad mound rising out of the level where some old hemlocks and beeches formed a dark grove or daemon-temple. Legends hard to account for. Holmes—*Guardian Angel.*

131 Phosphorescence of decaying wood—call'd in New England "fox-fire".

132 Mad artist in ancient sinister house draws *things*. What were his models? Glimpse. [Pickman's Model]

133 Man has miniature shapeless Siamese twin—exhib. in circus—twin surgically detached—disappears—does hideous things with malign life of his own. [HSW—Cassius]

134 Witches' Hollow novel? Man hired as teacher in private school misses road on first trip—encounters dark hollow with unnaturally swollen trees and small cottage (light in window?). Reaches school and hears that boys are forbidden to visit hollow. One boy is strange—teacher sees him visit hollow—odd doings—mysterious disappearance or hideous fate.

135 Hideous world superimposed on visible world—gate through—power guides narrator to ancient and forbidden book with directions for access.

136 A secret language spoken by a very few old men in a wild country leads to hidden marvels and terrors still surviving.

137 Strange man seen in lonely mountain place talking with great winged thing which flies away as others approach.

138 Someone or something cries in fright at sight of the rising moon, as if it were something strange.

139 DELRIO asks "An sint unquam daemones incubi et succubae, et an ex tali congressu proles nasci queat?" [Red Hook] ['Have there ever been demons, incubi, or succubae, and from such a union can offspring be born?'—S.U.]

140 Explorer enters strange land where some atmospheric quality darkens the sky to virtual blackness—marvels therein.

[1926]

141 Footnote by Haggard or Lang in *The World's Desire:* "Probably the mysterious and indecipherable ancient books, which were occasionally excavated in old Egypt, were written in this dead language of a more ancient and now forgotten people. Such was the book discovered at Coptos, in the ancient sanctuary there, by a priest of the Goddess. 'The whole earth was dark, but the moon shone all about the Book.' A scribe of the period of the Ramessids mentions another in indecipherable ancient writing. 'Thou tellest me thou understandest no word of it, good or bad. There is, as it were, a wall about it that none may climb. Thou art instructed, yet thou knowest it not; this makes me afraid.' Birch *Zeitschrift*, 1871 pp. 61–64. *Papyrus Anastasi* I, pl. X, l. 8, pl. X l. 4. Maspero, *Hist. Anc.*, pp. 66–67."

142 Members of witch-cult were buried face downward. Man investigates ancestor in family tomb and finds disquieting condition.

143 Strange well in Arkham country—water gives out (or was never struck —hole kept tightly covered by a stone ever since dug)—no bottom—shunned and feared—what lay beneath (either unholy temple or other very ancient thing, or great cave-world). [Fungi—The Well]

144 Hideous book glimpsed in ancient shop—never seen again.

145 Horrible boarding house—closed door never opened.

146 Ancient lamp found in tomb—when filled and used, its light reveals strange world. [Fungi]

147 Any very ancient, unknown, or prehistoric object—its power of suggestion—forbidden memories.

148 Vampire *dog*.

149 Evil alley or enclosed court in ancient city—Union or Milligan Pl. [Fungi]

150 Visit to someone in wild and remote house—ride from station through the night—into the haunted hills—house by forest or water—terrible things live there.

151 Man forced to take shelter in strange house. Host has thick beard and dark glasses. Retires. In night guest rises and sees host's clothes about—also *mask* which was the apparent face of *whatever* the host was. Flight.

152 Autonomic nervous system and subconscious mind *do not reside in the head*. Have mad physician decapitate a man but keep him alive and subconsciously controlled. Avoid copying tale by W. C. Morrow.

[1928]

153 Black cat on hill near dark gulf of ancient inn yard. Mew hoarsely—invites artist to nighted mysteries beyond. Finally dies at advanced age. Haunts dreams of artist—lures him to follow—strange outcome (never wakes up? or makes bizarre discovery of an elder world outside 3-dimensioned space?). [used by Dwyer] [The author Bernard Austin Dwyer, Lovecraft's friend and frequent correspondent.—S.U.]

154 Trophonius—cave of. Vide Class. Dict. and *Atlantic* article.

155 Steepled town seen from afar at sunset—*does not light up at night*. Sail has been seen putting out to sea. [Fungi]

156 Adventures of a disembodied spirit—thro' dim, half-familiar cities and over strange moors—thro' space and time—other planets and universes in the end.

157 Vague lights, geometrical figures, &c., seen on retina when eyes are closed. Caus'd by rays from *other dimensions* acting on optick nerve? From *other planets?* Connected with a life or phase of being in which person could live if he only knew how to get there? *Man afraid to shut eyes*—he has been somewhere on a terrible pilgrimage and this fearsome seeing faculty remains.

158 Man has terrible wizard friend who gains influence over him. Kills him in defence of his soul—walls body up in ancient cellar—BUT—the dead wizard (who has said strange things about soul lingering in body) *changes bodies with him* . . . leaving him a conscious corpse in cellar. [Thing on Doorstep]

159 Certain kind of deep-toned stately music of the style of the 1870's or 1880's recalls certain visions of that period—gas-litten parlours of the dead, moonlight on old floors, decaying business streets with gas lamps, &c.—under terrible circumstances.

160 Book which induces sleep on reading—cannot be read—determined man reads it—goes mad—precautions taken by aged initiate who knows—protection (as of author and translator) by incantation.

161 Time and space—past event—150 years ago—unexplained. Modern period—person intensely homesick for past says or does something which is psychically transmitted back and *actually causes* the past event.

162 Ultimate horror—grandfather returns from strange trip—mystery in house—wind and darkness—grandf. and mother engulfed—questions forbidden—somnolence—investigation—cataclysm—screams overheard—

163 Man whose money was *obscurely* made loses it. Tells his family he must go *again* to THE PLACE (horrible and sinister and extra-dimensional) where he got his gold. Hints of possible pursuers—or of his possible non-return. He goes—record of what happens to him—or what happens at his home when he returns. Perhaps connect with preceding topic. Give fantastic, quasi-Dunsanian treatment.

164 Man observed in a publick place with features (or ring or jewel) identified with those of man long (perhaps generations) buried.

165 Terrible trip to an ancient and forgotten tomb.

166 Hideous family living in shadow in ancient castle by edge of wood near black cliffs and monstrous waterfall.

167 Boy rear'd in atmosphere of considerable mystery. Believes father dead. Suddenly is told that father is about to return. Strange preparations—consequences.

168 Lonely bleak islands off N. E. coast. Horrors they harbour—outpost of cosmic influences.

169 What hatches from primordial egg.

170 Strange man in shadowy quarter of ancient city possesses something of immemorial archaic horror.

171 Hideous old book discovered—directions for shocking evocation.

[1930]

172 Pre-human idol found in desert.

173 Idol in museum *moves* in a certain way.

174 Migration of Lemmings—Atlantis.

175 Little green Celtic figures dug up in an ancient Irish bog.

176 Man blindfolded and taken in closed cab or car to some very ancient and secret place.

177 The *dreams* of one man actually *create* a strange half-mad world of quasi-material substance in *another dimension*. *Another*

man, also a dreamer, blunders into this world in a dream. What he finds. Intelligence of denizens. Their dependence on the first dreamer. What happens at his death.

178 A very ancient tomb in the deep woods near where a 17th century Virginia manor-house used to be. The undecayed, bloated thing found within.

179 Appearance of an ancient god in a lonely and archaic place—prob. temple ruin. Atmosphere of beauty rather than horror. Subtle handling—presence revealed by faint sound or shadow. Landscape changes? Seen by child? Impossible to reach or identify locale again?

180 A general house of horror—nameless crime—sounds—later tenants—(Flammarion) (novel length?).

181 Inhabitant of another world—face masked, perhaps with human skin or surgically alter'd to human shape, but body alien beneath robes. Having reached earth, tries to mix with mankind. Hideous revelation. [Suggested by CAS] [CAS was Clark Ashton Smith, poet, artist, and friend of Lovecraft. —S.U.]

182 In ancient buried city a man finds a mouldering prehistoric document *in English and in his own handwriting*, telling an incredible tale. Voyage from present into past implied. Possible actualisation of this.

183 Reference in Egyptian papyrus to a secret of secrets under tomb of high-priest Ka-Nefer. Tomb finally found and identified—trap door in stone floor—staircase, and the illimitable black abyss.

184 Expedition lost in Antarctic or other weird place. Skeletons and effects found years later. Camera films used but undeveloped. Finders develop—and find strange horror.

185 Scene of an urban horror—Sous le Cap or Champlain Sts.—Quebec—rugged cliff-face—moss, mildew, dampness—houses half-burrowing into cliff.

186 Thing from sea—in dark house, man finds doorknobs &c. *wet* as from touch of *something*. He has been a sea-captain, and once found a strange temple on a volcanically risen island.

[1931]

187 Dream of awaking in vast hall of strange architecture, with sheet-covered forms on slabs—in positions similar to one's own. Suggestions of disturbingly non-human outlines under sheets. One of the objects moves and throws off sheet—non-terrestrial being revealed. Sugg. that *oneself* is also such a being—mind has become transferred to body on other planet.

188 Desert of rock—prehistoric door in cliff, in the valley around which lie the bones of uncounted billions of animals both modern and prehistoric—some of them puzzlingly gnawed.

189 Ancient necropolis—bronze door in hillside which opens as the moonlight strikes it—focussed by ancient lens in pylon opposite?

[1932]

190 Primal mummy in museum—awakes and changes place with visitor.

191 An odd wound appears on a man's hand suddenly and without apparent cause. Spreads. Consequences.

[1933]

192 Thibetan ROLANG—Sorcerer (or NGAGSPA) reanimates a corpse by holding it in a dark room—lying on it mouth to mouth and repeating a magic formula with all else banished from his mind. Corpse slowly comes to life and stands up. Tries to escape—leaps, bounds, and struggles—but sorcerer holds it. Continues with magic formula. Corpse sticks out tongue and sorcerer bites it off. Corpse then collapses. Tongue becomes a valuable magic talisman. If corpse escapes—hideous results and death to sorcerer.

193 Strange book of horror discovered in ancient library. Paragraphs of terrible significance copies. Later unable to find and verify text. Perhaps discover body or image or charm under floor, in secret cupboard, or elsewhere. Idea that book was merely hypnotic delusion induced by dead brain or ancient magic.

194 Man enters (supposedly) own house in pitch dark. Feels way to room and shuts door behind him. Strange horrors—or turns on lights and finds alien place or presence. Or finds past restored or future indicated.

195 Pane of peculiar-looking glass from a ruined monastery reputed to have harboured devil-worship set up in modern house at edge of wild country. Landscape looks vaguely and unplaceably *wrong* through it. It has some unknown time-distorting quality, and comes from a primal, lost civilisation. Finally, hideous things in other world seen through it.

196 Daemons, when desiring an human form for evil purposes, take to themselves the bodies of hanged men.

197 Loss of memory and entry into a cloudy world of strange sights and experiences after shock, accident, reading of strange book, participation in strange rite, draught of strange brew, &c. Things seen have vague and disquieting familiarity. Emergence. Inability to retrace course.

[1934]

198 Distant tower visible from hillside window. Bats cluster thickly around it at night. Observer fascinated. One night wakes to find self on unknown black circular staircase. In tower? Hideous goal.

199 Black winged thing flies into one's house at night. Cannot be found or identified—but subtle developments ensue.

200 Invisible Thing felt—or seen to make prints—on mountain top or other height, inaccessible place.

201 Planets form'd of invisible matter.

202 A monstrous derelict—found and boarded by a castaway or shipwreck survivor.

203 A return to a place under dreamlike, horrible, and only dimly comprehended circumstances. Death and decay reigning—town fails to light up at night—Revelation.

204 Disturbing conviction that all life is only a deceptive dream with some dismal or sinister horror lurking behind.

205 Person gazes out window and finds city and world dark and dead (or oddly changed) outside.

206 Trying to identify and visit the distant scenes dimly seen from one's window—bizarre consequences.

207 Something snatched away from one in the dark—in a lonely, ancient, and generally shunned place.

208 (Dream of) some vehicle—railway train, coach, &c.—which is boarded in a stupor or fever, and which is a fragment of some past or ultra-dimensional world—taking the passenger out of reality—into vague, age-crumbled regions or unbelievable gulfs of marvel.

209 Special Correspondence of *N. Y. Times*—March 3, 1935: "Halifax, N. S.—Etched deeply into the face of an island which rises from the Atlantic surges off the S. coast of Nova Scotia 20 m. from Halifax is the strangest rock phenomenon which Canada boasts. Storm, sea, and frost have graven into the solid cliff of what has come to be known as Virgin's Island an almost perfect outline of the Madonna with the Christ Child in her arms.

"The island has sheer and wave-bound sides, is a danger to ships, and is absolutely uninhabited. *So far as is known, no human being has ever set foot on its shores.*"

210 An ancient house with blackened pictures on the walls—so obscured that their subjects cannot be deciphered. Cleaning—and revelation. Cf. Hawthorne—"Edw. Rand. Port.

211 Begin story with presence of narrator—inexplicable to himself—in utterly alien and terrifying scenes (dream?).

212 Strange human being (or beings) living in some ancient house or ruins far from populous district (either old N. E. or far exotic land). Suspicion (based on shape and habits) that it is not *all* human.

213 Ancient winter woods—moss—great boles—twisted branches—dark—ribbed roots—always dripping. . . .

214 Talking rock of Africa—immemorially ancient oracle in desolate jungle ruins that *speaks* with a voice out of the aeons.

215 Man with lost memory in strange, imperfectly comprehended environment. Fears to regain memory—a *glimpse*. . . .

216 Man idly shapes a queer image—some power impels him to make it queerer than he understands. Throws it away in disgust—but something is abroad in the night.

217 Ancient (Roman? prehistoric?) stone bridge washed away by a (sudden and curious?) storm. *Something* liberated which had been sealed up in the masonry of years ago. Things happen.

218 Mirage in *time*—image of long-vanish'd pre-human city.

219 Fog or smoke—assumes shaped under incantations.

220 Bell of some ancient church or castle rung by some unknown hand—a thing . . . or an invisible Presence.

221 Insects or other entities from space attack and penetrate a man's head and cause him to *remember* alien and exotic things—possible displacement of personality.

222 Quoted as motto by John Buchan: "The effect of night, of any flowing water, of lighted cities, of the peep of day, of ships, of the open ocean, calls up in the mind an army of anonymous desires and pleasures. Something, we feel, should happen; we know not what, yet we proceed in quest of it."—*R. L. Stevenson.*

List No. 068

FUMBLERULES OF GRAMMAR

WILLIAM SAFIRE
Late 1979

New York Times political columnist and presidential speechwriter William Safire (1929–2009) compiled a list of thirty-six "Fumblerules of Grammar"—rules of writing, all humorously self-contradictory—and published them in his popular *New York Times Magazine* column, "On Language," on November 4, 1979. Ten years later, he devoted a book to the same subject. Those original thirty-six "fumblerules" can be seen below, along with another eighteen that later featured in Safire's book *Fumblerules: A Lighthearted Guide to Grammar and Good Usage*.

1. Remember to never split an infinitive.
2. A preposition is something never to end a sentence with.
3. The passive voice should never be used.
4. Avoid run-on sentences they are hard to read.
5. Don't use no double negatives.
6. Use the semicolon properly, always use it where it is appropriate; and never where it isn't.
7. Reserve the apostrophe for it's proper use and omit it when its not needed.
8. Do not put statements in the negative form.
9. Verbs has to agree with their subjects.
10. No sentence fragments.
11. Proofread carefully to see if you any words out.
12. Avoid commas, that are not necessary.
13. If you reread your work, you will find on rereading that a great deal of repetition can be avoided by rereading and editing.
14. A writer must not shift your point of view.
15. Eschew dialect, irregardless.
16. And don't start a sentence with a conjunction.
17. Don't overuse exclamation marks!!!
18. Place pronouns as close as possible, especially in long sentences, as of 10 or more words, to their antecedents.
19. Hyphenate between sy-llables and avoid un-necessary hyphens.
20. Write all adverbial forms correct.
21. Don't use contractions in formal writing.
22. Writing carefully, dangling participles must be avoided.
23. It is incumbent on us to avoid archaisms.
24. If any word is improper at the end of a sentence, a linking verb is.
25. Steer clear of incorrect forms of verbs that have snuck in the language.
26. Take the bull by the hand and avoid mixing metaphors.
27. Avoid trendy locutions that sound flaky.
28. Never, ever use repetitive redundancies.
29. Everyone should be careful to use a singular pronoun with singular nouns in their writing.
30. If I've told you once, I've told you a thousand times, resist hyperbole.
31. Also, avoid awkward or affected alliteration.
32. Don't string too many prepositional phrases together unless you are walking through the valley of the shadow of death.

1049
prestress
example

33. Always pick on the correct idiom.
34. “Avoid overuse of ‘quotation “marks.”’”
35. The adverb always follows the verb.
36. Last but not least, avoid clichés like the plague; seek viable alternatives.
37. Never use a long word when a diminutive one will do.
38. Employ the vernacular.
39. Eschew ampersands & abbreviations, etc.
40. Parenthetical remarks (however relevant) are unnecessary.
41. Contractions aren’t necessary.
42. Foreign words and phrases are not apropos.
43. One should never generalize.
44. Eliminate quotations. As Ralph Waldo Emerson said, “I hate quotations. Tell me what you know.”
45. Comparisons are as bad as clichés.
46. Don’t be redundant; don’t use more words than necessary; it’s highly superfluous.
47. Be more or less specific.
48. Understatement is always best.
49. One-word sentences? Eliminate.
50. Analogies in writing are like feathers on a snake.
51. Go around the barn at high noon to avoid colloquialisms.
52. Who needs rhetorical questions?
53. Exaggeration is a billion times worse than understatement.
54. capitalize every sentence and remember always end it with a point

CHRISTOPHER HITCHENS'S COMMANDMENTS

CHRISTOPHER HITCHENS
2010

Divisive journalist, author, and critic Christopher Hitchens (1949–2011) was seldom anything but outspoken, especially when discussing religion. It was a subject particularly close to his heart, debated regularly and with passion. In the April 2010 issue of *Vanity Fair*, in a column titled "The New Commandments," Hitchens argued that, far from being writ in stone, the Ten Commandments should be considered "a work in progress." His piece ended with this list of suggested replacements.

Do not condemn people on the basis of their ethnicity or *color*.

Do not ever use people as private property.

Despise those who use violence or the threat of it in sexual relations.

Hide your face and weep if you dare to harm a child.

Do not condemn people for their inborn *nature*—why would God create so many homosexuals only in order to torture and destroy them?

Be aware that you too are an animal and dependent on the web of nature, and think and act accordingly.

Do not imagine that you can escape judgment if you rob people with a false prospectus rather than with a knife.

Turn off that fucking cell phone—you can have no idea how *un*important your call is to us.

Denounce all jihadists and crusaders for what they are: psychopathic criminals with ugly delusions.

Be willing to renounce any god or any religion if any holy commandments should contradict any of the above.

List No. 070

OLYMPIC VICTOR LIST

AUTHOR UNKNOWN
Third Century AD

In 1897, in the Egyptian city of Oxyrhynchus, this fragment of papyrus bearing Greek script was found by archaeologists who concluded that it dates back to the middle of the third century AD. Due to its condition, a complete transcript is impossible; however, what we do know is this: written on it is a list of winners—known as a "victor list"—at various Ancient Olympic Games, beginning, top-left, with the Seventy-fifth Games in 480 BC and ending, bottom-right, with the Eighty-third in 448 BC. Winners include Damagetos of Rhodes (boxing), Astylos of Croton (stadion run), and Leontiscus of Messana (wrestling); and, for each year, thirteen events are listed in the following order.

στάδιον	*stadion run (192.27 meter sprint)*
δίαυλος	*2 stadia run*
δόλιχος	*dolichos (2000 meter run)*
πένταθλον	*Pentathlon*
πάλη	*Wrestling*
πύξ	*Boxing*
παγκράτιον	*pancration (combined wrestling and boxing)*
παίδων στάδ	*boys' stadio*
παίδων πάλη	*boys' wrestling*
παίδων πύξ	*boys' boxing*
όπλίτης	*hoplite (running in armor)*
τέθριππον	*four horse chariot race*
κέλης	*horse riding*

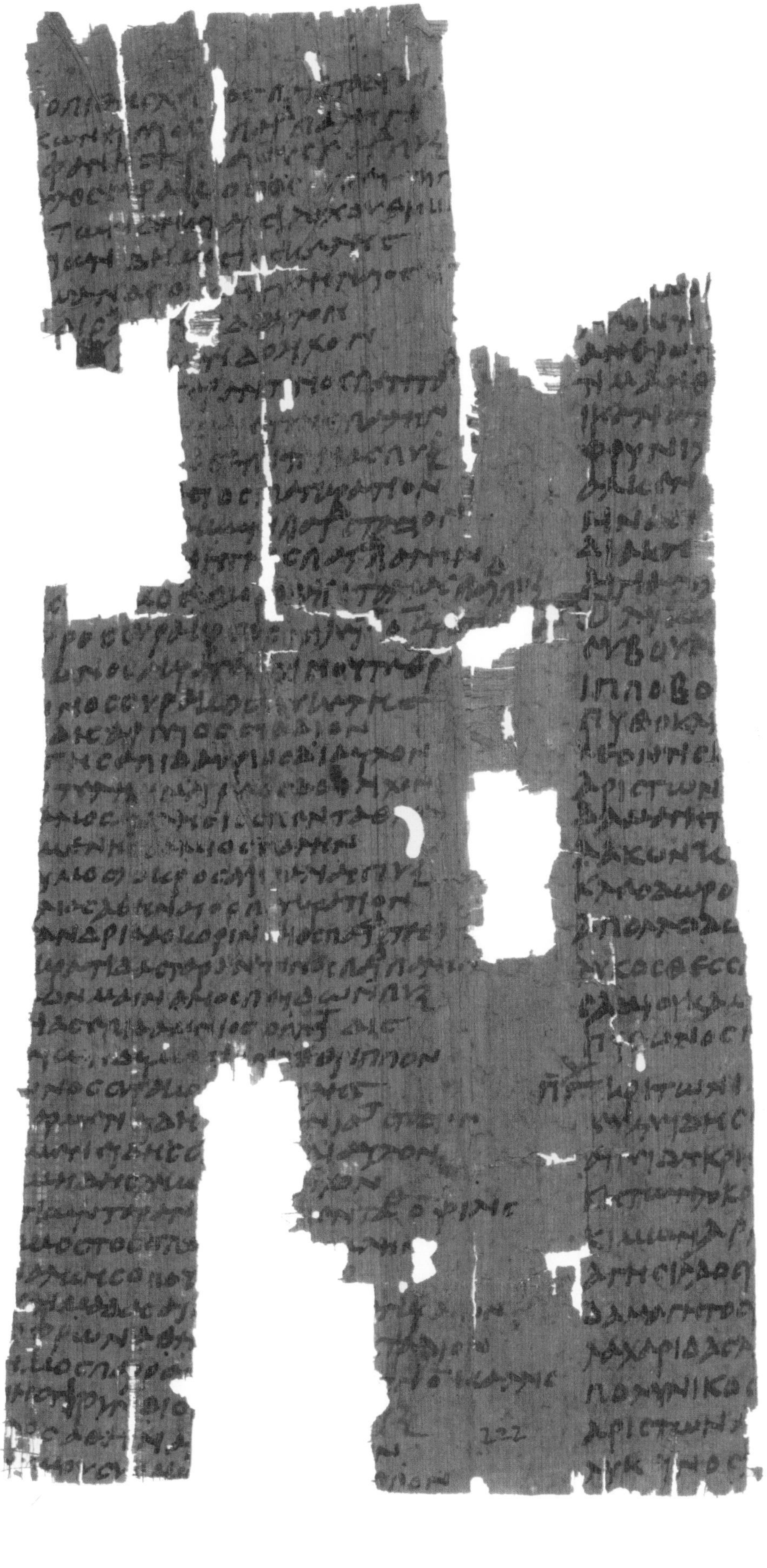

HOW TO ATTAIN SMARTNESS

EDNA WOOLMAN CHASE
1954

In 1914, having steadily worked her way up from the mail room, Edna Woolman Chase (1877–1975) became editor in chief of *Vogue* magazine, a role she held until her retirement thirty-eight years later. Two years after stepping down, Chase wrote her autobiography, *Always in Vogue*, in which she presented a list of advice for ladies on "how to attain smartness."

Perhaps this is as good a place as any to set down, as concisely as I can, [the] code on how to attain smartness that, over a long life and through years of dealing with a capricious art, I have found to be the most serviceable. Much of it is obvious, but every season new, young eyes become style-conscious and I believe it bears repetition.

Point #1: Study yourself with the unblinking eye of your meanest enemy. Could that throat, so like a swan to your lover, perhaps be considered a long, skinny neck, thrust forward at a cranelike angle, by one who cares for you less? Or could that short neck and submissive little chin, which make you so cuddlesome, could they, with the years, develop into a thick, indeterminate oneness, with that middle-aged hump at the back? Are your legs or upper arms too thin or too fat? Do you have pretty hands and nails, so that you can permit yourself eye-attracting gestures and jewelry, or are they large and capable, profiting from a decent anonymity? And your hair? Is it sexy or serviceable? This questionnaire could go on indeterminately, but its point, I think, is clear. Your person is the material you have to work with.

Study yourself with dispassionate eyes *and* in a three-ply mirror. It is a grueling ordeal, but it pays off. Remember your enemy, the rival who sees you always in 3-D. Make sure you are at least as well informed as she.

Point #2: This does not have to do with clothes; it does have to do with good grooming, a vital part of fashion, and I think it is valid. Set your dressing table in front of a window, so that the uncompromising light of day will fall evenly upon your face when you are making up. If, because of architectural reasons, this is impossible, place it so the light, day or artificial, comes equally from both sides. This will help you to achieve a well-blended make-up and to do your hair becomingly. Also always have your hand mirror within reach, that you may see yourself from the side and back as well as from the front.

Point #3: Choose for yourself clothes that play up your good points and subdue your bad. Have you pretty legs, but a thick middle? Perhaps your hips depress you, but from the waist up you are a Tanagra figurine? Or have you the lean, lithe flanks of a Diana yet are overly emphasized above? For this silhouette the French have an apt expression: "*Beaucoup de monde au balçon*"— a lot of people in the balcony. These are the assets and defects you must be aware of.

Know thyself and dress accordingly is the great fashion edict. Certain cliche warnings on the whole are probably sound; if you are partridge-plump a print of cabbage roses may not be for you. On the other hand, if you are small and slim the dictum that you should wear only "dainty" jewelry is groundless. If you yearn for chunks, go ahead. A massive bracelet makes a slender wrist more fragile. There are times when the truly chic woman achieves style and individuality through breaking with tradition, but remember! Revolution takes experience. It can take money as well, which brings us to . . .

Point #4: In fashion do *not* have the courage of your mistakes. Since you are human you will make them, yet if you want a reputation for elegance hide them. They are expensive, yes, which is one reason you should read *Vogue*, so that you will make fewer of them, but you must be brave. If you've pulled a fearful boner, if the dress or hat so beguiling in the shop is a dud in the home, pitch it out. Give it to some dear relation or send it to the thrift shop: don't wear it. To be considered well dressed, you must be it continuously. Not in fits and starts.

Point #5: Select clothes appropriate to the life you lead. The wildly inappropriate

garment is usually the mistake of youth, before the discipline of taste and budget has had the time to sink in. Although the temptation may be strong, even in maturity, to purchase the dress that would be knockout for a unique occasion and completely out of key the rest of the time, unless you're rich, don't succumb. Compromise. Obviously, if you sense that a certain ravishing garment will cause him to pop the question don't be a fool. Buy it.

Point #6: The allotment of budget. There are certain articles in one's wardrobe on which one not only may, but should, splurge. Within reason, of course. Remember this is a Quaker speaking. A good cashmere sweater will last for years. Your winter coat should be the very best you can afford. It is meant to survive several seasons, keep you warm, and be worn every day. The same is true of your tailored suit. It should be of good fabric and well cut. Also your street shoes should be the best. Smart, comfortable, and with a medium heel. For walking the city streets they should not have open toes and heels. This misbegotten fashion I have already dwelt on at length. Keep your shoes in good repair; you prolong their life indefinitely.

Economize on evening slippers. They are fragile and unless you are a debutante the wear you exact from them will probably be limited. If you are a debutante you will want several pairs, but they need not be expensive.

Point #7: Don't buy too much. There is nothing to sap the morale and dull the appearance like a closet full of half-worn, no-longer-at-their-peak clothes. With the exception of the aforementioned staples — coats, suits, and street shoes, which should last several seasons — buy only what you need at the time, make it serve you well, and get rid of it.

Point #8: In your wardrobe consider color carefully. If you use restraint you will find it makes both for elegance and economy. This does not mean you have to be drab and monotonous; if your clothes are interchangeable, shoes and accessories doing duty with several dresses and suits instead of only one, you will achieve greater variety at less cost. Don't get a blue hat and a red bag and a brown coat and black shoes, each good in itself but as incompatible as whisky and wine. Plan your wardrobe as a whole. Don't just buy it, compose it.

Point #9: Consider color; don't get set in concrete as to what colors you can and cannot wear. To be adamant on the subject of black or brown, shrimp pink or almond green is nonsense. Quite possibly with the right shades of rouges, lipstick, and powder we can wear them. Another thing to remember is that as we grow older we can frequently change our color spectrum with flattering results.

Point #10:

A: Dress your age. A hat that really belongs above a mature, thoughtful face is far more flattering, and incidentally in better taste, than a cute pixie cap. Clothes that are too young paradoxically make their wearer look older. Remember that the interesting men of the world *like women who appear youthful but who are not pathetic carbon copies of the girls they were*. On the other hand, clothes that are too sophisticated do not imbue the youthful wearer with the femme fatale look she longs to achieve, but tend, on the contrary, to give her a comically childlike appearance.

B: As you grow older, cover up. Aging flesh is not appealing. Whether a Bikini bathing suit on a charming young body is modest or immodest is a matter of the current mode or local morals or good taste; it has nothing to do with aestheticism, but too much revelation of a figure that is too thin, too fat, or too old can be lamentable.

For the older woman, misty tulle scarves in the evening or little jackets or stoles are pleasant bits of decorative fancy.

Point #11

A: Stand up when you buy a hat. This may sound daft, but it is rooted in wisdom. Few ladies, we trust, are so foolish as to buy a hat without viewing it from the profile and three-quarter angles as well as from the front, but many a lady fails to realize that her hat must be integrated with the rest of her, that it must be in proportion to her entire body. If you see what you secretly feel to be an enchanting reflection in the milliner's mirror, restrain yourself yet a moment. Stand up, move a few feet away, and view yourself in the altogether. Are you small, so that under a wide brim you look strangely like a gnome under a toadstool? Are you tall, so that too small a hat is reminiscent of a thimble on a broomstick? What looks enchanting in one dimension, sitting down, may be a different story in the round and long.

B: Just as you should stand up when you buy a hat so should you sit down when you buy a dress. It may be all good when you are erect, but how does it sit? Is it so full that it lies in puddles on the floor? Does the wrap-around skirt fall open? Is it so tight that it rides above your knees? Sit down in it in front of the mirror, and then walk, enough to make sure it doesn't bind. There is nothing more aggravating than a too narrow skirt on one who likes to stride freely.

Point #12: Pare down the nonessentials. This does not mean eschew jewels and flowers, scarves and bows and hair ornaments; it does mean to use them with discretion, to integrate them into your costume so that they are a deliberate accent, the perfect finishing touch. The observer, and you, should feel that with whatever you have chosen you are complete. Without it there would be something lacking. This system is infinitely more satisfactory than tossing gewgaws on yourself because they happen to be kicking around the bureau drawer.

Point #13: Let us now suppose your wardrobe is admirably chosen from every point of view and that even if you are wealthy you have adopted as your own a slogan I coined for *Vogue* long ago: "More Taste than Money." It is still so much our philosophy of good dressing that annually we bring out a "More Taste than Money" issue, proving our premise in page after page of fashions that are admirable rather than costly.

The same point of view has resulted in our more recent and very popular "Young Nillionaire" feature. Taste is better than money at any age, but if one has youth, a good figure, and is well informed on fashion, thanks to the ready-to-wear industry and *Vogue*'s guidance, one can be well dressed on surprisingly little outlay.

Yet even when every article is chosen with foresight and taste there is still one great fashion law to bear in mind. As in cooking or bartending, so in good dressing: the mixture is the secret. Never be guilty of wearing fancy shoes with a sports costume, an elaborate hat with a simple tailored suit. Do not wear long earrings for traveling or carry a businesslike leather bag with a filmy summer frock. Ask yourself always, Am I harmoniously put together, am I appropriately clad for the deed at hand, and am I free of nonessentials? If you can truthfully answer yes, you are a well-dressed woman.

CONTEMPT FOR:

WALKER EVANS AND JAMES AGEE
December 26, 1937

In 1936, famed photographer Walker Evans collaborated with writer and close friend James Agee to produce what would eventually become, five years later, *Let Us Now Praise Famous Men*, a powerful, well-received book that documents the lives of three farming families in Depression-era America. Their original intention had been to write and shoot an article for *Fortune* magazine. But, in 1937, *Fortune* rejected their hard work. With nothing to show for the past year's commitment but an unwanted article, Evans and Agee were left feeling tired and angry. On December 26 they each sat down and wrote lists of the things they hated the most.

James Agee's list

Contempt or hatred for:
The Anglo Saxon tristesse
the Anglo Saxon optimism
Anglo Saxon men in relation to their women
Anglo Saxon women
English girls
female athletes
intellectual women
most women who say fuck, shit, fart, etc
most women who do not
all women who like dirty jokes
most women who do not
the liking for dirty jokes
limited editions, especially when signed
literary pornography
handsome volumes
slim volumes
zest
gusto
Rabelaisianism
book reviewers
sex education
literature
moving picture versions of Shakespeare, famous novels, and the lives of famous people
famous people
fame
English slang
the Americanisms of Englishmen
the Anglicisms of Americans
the Anglicisms of Englishmen
the professional American
"smart" women
"smart" people
those who live in the Barbizon Plaza
doctors
plays about doctors
The Group Theater
Orson Welles's lighting
Archibald MacLeish's courage
whatever was responsible for my maternal grandmother, for Mrs. Saunders, for my mother, for my stepfather, for my sister's trouble, for sexual pain, for the pain of sexual love.
every conception of motherhoods functions
those who bring forth, and up, children
those who despise them
those who say that things are slowly working themselves out towards the best
everything about William Shakespeare expect William Shakespeare and his own writing
" " Christ except himself as I presume him, Dostoevsky, Blake, Kafka.
those who say, 'if only everyone would love one another'
the Van Gogh show at the Museum of Modern Art

the Surrealist show at same
those who saw these shows
everything about Salvador Dali except a few of his paintings
Tchelitchev
Julien Levy
Film Groups, Guilds, Societés, etc.,
theaters which show the best foreign films
the word film
the word shot
the words cinema, swing, stuff, reactionary, swell, modest, contact, sexual intercourse, coitus, classical historical objective, act of kind, conventional, unconventional, poet, art, cultivated, mind, integrity, love, God, cozy, cunning, sweet, etc etc; such as, angle.
Walter Winchell
Bohemians
Lucius Beebe
pedantic wit
those who use no effort not to have their lives and thinking governed by their feelings
those who are not sceptical of their own premises
all self-confessed mystics and mahatmas who permit even one disciple
sensitive young men
unconsciousness of the self-betrayal of spoken language
peasant art in other than peasant contexts
old furniture
period interiors
the distortions which every falsehood imposes on every truth
most whose feelings get hurt
those who carry off unpleasant incidents with laughter
pipes and pipe smokers
the libraries of clergy men
Alice in Wonderland
dog-lovers
the words pooch and mutt
the words prostie, bordello, etc.
the elaborate oaths of prep school boys
dictionaries of slang
the New Republic
Josef Stalin
Leon Trotsky
Karl Marx
Jane Austen
Paul Rotha
all books on movies
women through whose crotch you can see daylight when their knees are together
any creased droop under the breast
social crediters
American children who speak French
Every confusion of friendship and business
the face of Max Eastman
Walt Disney's human beings
most of the public of Disney and of Clair [René Clair—S.U.]
publishers
journalists who like their jobs
" who say they don't but do

12 26 37 NYC

contempt for:

men who try to fascinate women with their minds;

gourmets, liberals, cultivated women;

writers;

successful artists who use the left to buttress their standing;

the sex life of America;

limited editions, "atmosphere", Bennington College, politics;

men of my generation who became photographers during the depression;

journalism, new dealers, readers of the New Yorker;

the corner of Madison Avenue and 56th Street;

the public;

Richard Wagner, radio announcers;

hobbies and hobbyists;

the soul of Josef von Sternberg;

the gay seventies, eighties, nineties, or hundreds;

art in America, the artist of America, the art lovers of America, the art patrons of America, the art museums of America, the art directors of America, the wivwes and mistresses and paramours of the artists of America; the etchings and the christmas cards and the woodcuts and the paintings and the letters and the memoirs and the talk and the beards or the cleanshaven faces of the artists of America;

for college bred intellectual communists with private incomes;

for safe experimentation in living or in expression;

for merrie England;

for critics;

for passing away, passing on, going on, leaving us; instead of dying;

for school spirit, Christmas spirit, gallant spirit, and whatever is meant by The American Spirit;

The Bohemian Dinner.

The ride down town.
The Washington Square district.
The "bohemian" restaurant.
The descending steps.
The narrow hall-way.
The semi darkness.
The checking the hat.
The head waiter.
The effusive greeting.
The corner table.
The candle light.
The brick walls.
The "artistic atmosphere".
The man who plays the piano.
The wailing sounds.
The boy fiddler.
The doleful discords.
The other diners.
The curious types.
The long hair.
The low collar.
The flowing tie.
The loose clothes.
The appearance of food.
The groan.
The messy waiter.
The thumb in the soup.
The grated cheese.
The twisted bread.
The veal paté.
The minced macaroni.
The cayenne pepper.
The coughing fit.
The chemical wine.
The garlic salad.
The rum omelette.
The black coffee.
The bénedictine.
The Russian cigarette.
The "boatman's song".
The mock applause.
The 'tempermental' selection.
The drowsy feeling.
The snooze.
The sudden awakening.
The appearance of the check.
The dropped jaw.
The emptied pockets.
The last penny.
The bolt for the door.
The hat.
The street.
The lack of car fare.
The long walk up town.
The limping home.
The Bed.

THE BOHEMIAN DINNER

CHARLES GREEN SHAW
Circa 1930

Born in New York in 1892, Charles Green Shaw was an abstract painter whose artworks are still celebrated in a number of prestigious art museums. He was also, at various points in his life, a writer, poet, illustrator, and journalist. Most interestingly, however, for the purposes of this book at least, Shaw was an avid list maker. The delightful example seen here, in which he describes a recent visit to a "bohemian" restaurant in Manhattan in list form, is typically entertaining.

List No. 074

10 COMPOSERS I LIKE BEST

LUCAS AMORY

January 2011

On January 21, 2011, the chief music critic at *The New York Times*, Anthony Tommasini, concluded a two-week project in which he discussed the world's finest composers by unveiling a list he had personally compiled of "the top 10 classical music composers in history." As can be expected, much discussion was generated by his list, but it was a written response from schoolboy Lucas Amory, son of noted violists Misha Amory and Hsin-Yun Huang, that really stood out.

The Top 10 Composers chosen by Anthony Tommasini

1. Bach
2. Beethoven
3. Mozart
4. Schubert
5. Debussy
6. Stravinsky
7. Brahms
8. Verdi
9. Wagner
10. Bartok

Hi Mr Tommasini,

I read about you in the newspaper. Like you, I adore music. So I've written two lists: The 10 Greatist Composers and: The Ones I Like Best. Lets start with 10 Greatist:

1, 2, 3: You're right about those: Bach, Beethoven, and Mozart.
4: I disagree about that; I'd go with Haydn. Haydn is as good as Mozart, but goes with 4.
4A: If I hurt your feelings I'm sorry.
5: This one my dad chose for me: Schubert. I gotta say, I'll have to agree. I don't know why, but I'll do it.
6: This is hard. I'll go with Brahms. He was supposed to be lower but when I learned he burned his music. . .
7: Tchaikovsky. Most definaly. He was an awesome composer.
8, 9: Chopin is 8. Schumanns nine.
10: Lizst?

TURN OVER FOR THE TEN COMPOSERS I LIKE BEST

Zwei Seiten: Letzte Aufzeichnungen zur „Kunst der Fuge“.

Ist in der Ausgabe von B. W. 25[1] in vorliegender Notirung nicht mitgetheilt.

1. Even though my favorite piece is Tchaikovskys Violin Concerto, someone else is beside him: Schumann. Schumann wins.

[drawing]

1A: Uh-huh you get the picture
2: Tchaikovsky.
3: Rachmaninoff.
4: Lizst
5: Chopin
6: Schubert
7: You won't believe it: Paganini
8: Rossini
9: Prokoviev
10: Grieg

Well, thats about it.

Sincerly,

Lucas Amory

P.S. I go to Lucy Moses School. I'm 8 years old.

Nr. 33b. B. W. 25¹. In doppelt langen Notenwerthen: Seite 73 Takt 4 — Seite 74 Takt 28. Blatt 139.

List No. 075

THURBER'S RULES

JAMES THURBER
1949

As a successfully published and much-loved author, cartoonist, and satirist whose work regularly found a home on the pages of the *New Yorker*, James Thurber (1894–1961) was often the recipient of unsolicited manuscripts from aspiring writers. So much so, in fact, that in his 1949 book, *Thurber Country*, he printed the following list with an introduction that read, "I have established a few standing rules of my own about humor, after receiving dozens of humorous essays and stories from strangers over a period of twenty years."

1. The reader should be able to find out what the story is about.

2. Some inkling of the general idea should be apparent in the first five hundred words.

3. If the writer has decided to change the name of his protagonist from Ketcham to McTavish, Ketcham should not keep bobbing up in the last five pages. A good way to eliminate this confusion is to read the piece over before sending it out, and remove Ketcham completely. He is a nuisance.

4. The word "I'll" should not be divided so that the "I" is on one line and "'ll" on the next. The reader's attention, after the breaking up of "I'll," can never be successfully recaptured.

5. It also never recovers from such names as Ann S. Thetic, Maud Lynn, Sally Forth, Bertha Twins, and the like.

6. Avoid comic stories about plumbers who are mistaken for surgeons, sheriffs who are terrified by gunfire, psychiatrists who are driven crazy by women patients, doctors who faint at the sight of blood, adolescent girls who know more about sex than their fathers do, and midgets who turn out to be the parents of a two-hundred-pound wrestler.

I have a special wariness of people who write opening sentences with nothing in mind, and then try to create a story around them. These sentences, usually easy to detect, go like this: "Mrs. Ponsonby had never put the dog in the oven before," "'I have a wine tree, if you would care to see it,' said Mr. Dillingworth," and "Jackson decided suddenly, for no reason, really, to buy his wife a tricycle." I have never traced the fortunes of such characters in the stories I receive beyond the opening sentence, but, like you, I have a fair notion of what happens, or doesn't happen, in "The Barking Oven," "The Burgundy Tree," and "A Tricycle for Mama."

THE GODFATHER

FRANCIS FORD COPPOLA
Circa 1970

Few movies in the history of cinema have garnered as much praise as *The Godfather*, Francis Ford Coppola's sublimely directed crime saga set in 1940s New York. So many aspects of the film seem perfect, including an impressive roster of acting talent that includes Marlon Brando, Al Pacino, James Caan, and Robert Duvall. It could, however, have been so different. Here, from one of Coppola's notepads, is a list of potential cast members, written before production began.

CAST

Don Corleone:	MarlonBrando
John Marley	Laurence Olivier
Carlo Ponti*	*Frank Dekova
Michael Corleone:	*Al Pacino
	*Scott Marlowe
Robert di Niro	Mike Margota
Art Genovese	(Richard Romanos)
Dustin Hoffman	Jimmy Caan
Mike Parks	~~Martin Sheen~~
SONNY CORLEONE:	
	*Jimmy Caan
Tony Lo Bianco	Carmine Caridi
~~Peter Falk~~	*Scott Marlowe
Al Letteiri	*Don Gordon
	*(Tony Zerbe)
	*Lou Antonio
	(Paul Banteo)
	Robert Viharo
	(Rudy Solari)
	John Saxon
	John Brascia
	Johnny Sette (7)
	Adam Roake
Harry Guardino	Ben Gazzara
TOM HAGEN:	Ben Piazza
	*Robert Duvall
	Tony Zerbe
	*Peter Donat

List No. 077

MYSTERIES OF OPIUM REVEAL'D

DR. JOHN JONES
1700

Written by English physician Dr. John Jones and published in 1700, *Mysteries of Opium Reveal'd* was possibly the first treatise to tackle the subject of opium at a time when, despite its numerous dangerous side effects, the drug was freely available and used by many to treat and cure all manner of ailments. Much of Jones's book takes the form of lists, two of which are seen here: "The Effects of Opium taken in an Excessive Quantity" and "The seeming Contradictions in the Effects of Opium."

The Effects of Opium taken in an Excessive Quantity.

1. A Heat at Stomach.
2. A sense of Weight at Stomach (sometimes.)
3. Gaity of Humour at first.
4. Sardonick Laughter afterward.
5. Laxity, and Debility of all Parts.
6. Alienation of the Mind.
7. Loss of Memory.
8. Darkness of the Eyes.
9. Laxity of the Cornea.
10. Appearance of divers Colours.
11. Deadness of the Eyes to the View.
12. Faltring of the Tongue.
13. A Sopor.
14. A slow, and wide Pulse.
15. A high Color.
16. Looseness of the Jaw, and Lips.
17. Intumescence of the Lips.
18. Difficulty of Breathing.
19. Fury, and Madness.
20. Venereal Fury.
21. Priapisms.
22. Violent Itchings.
23. Nausea's.
24. Swimmings in the Head.
25. Vertigo's.
26. Vomitings.
27. Hiccoughs.
28. A turbulent Pulse.
29. Convulsions, and Cold Sweats.
30. Faintings and Leipothymies.
31. Cold Breath.
32. Death.

Such as escape it generally have,

33. Plentiful Purging.
34. Sweats that smell of the Opium.
35. Violent Itchings in the Skin.

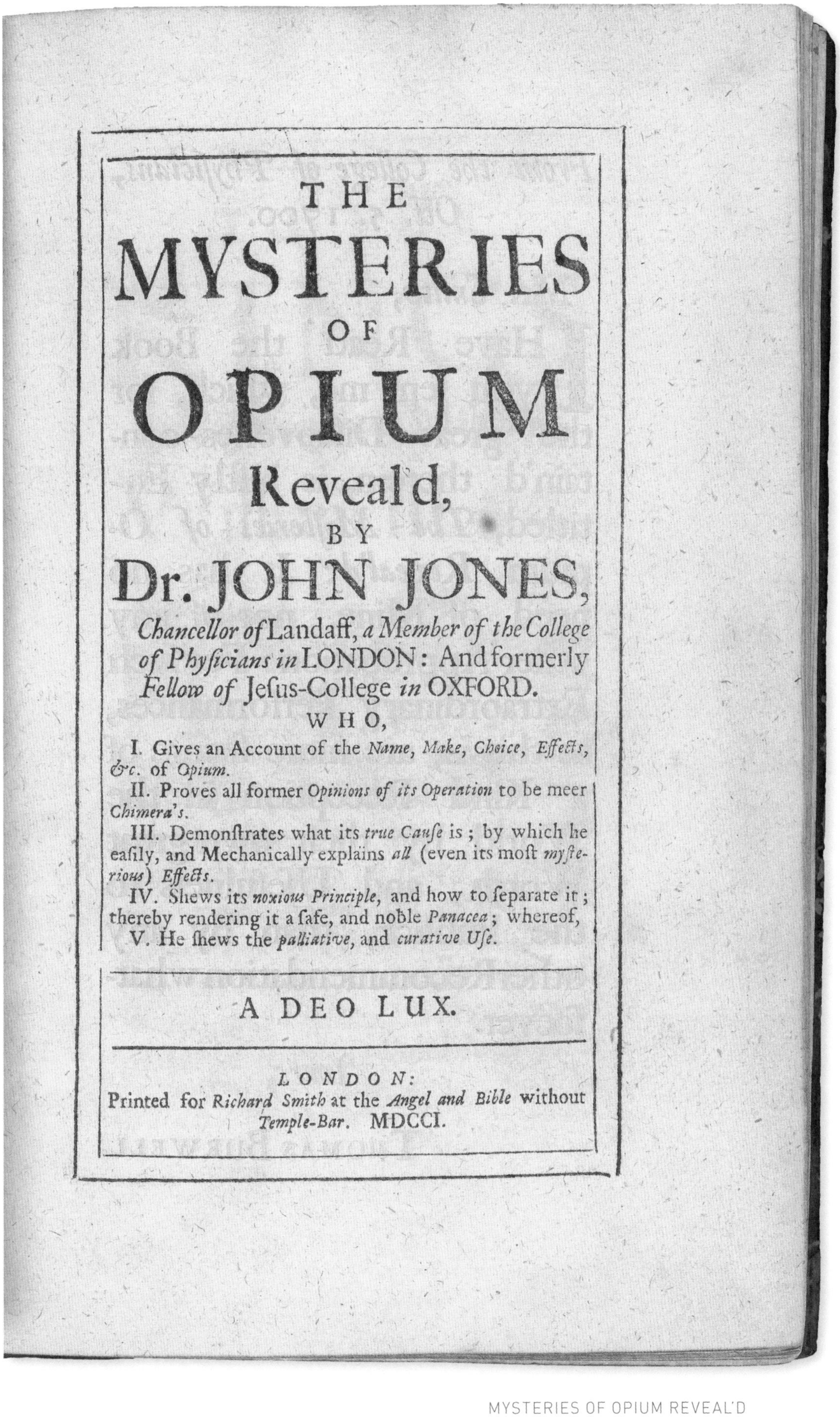

THE

MYSTERIES

OF

OPIUM

Reveal'd,

BY

Dr. JOHN JONES,

Chancellor of Landaff, *a Member of the College of Phyſicians in* LONDON: And formerly *Fellow of* Jeſus-College *in* OXFORD.

WHO,

I. Gives an Account of the *Name, Make, Choice, Effects, &c.* of *Opium.*

II. Proves all former *Opinions of its Operation* to be meer *Chimera's.*

III. Demonſtrates what its *true Cauſe* is; by which he eaſily, and Mechanically explains *all* (even its moſt *myſterious*) *Effects.*

IV. Shews its *noxious Principle,* and how to ſeparate it; thereby rendering it a ſafe, and noble *Panacea*; whereof,

V. He ſhews the *palliative,* and *curative Uſe.*

A DEO LUX.

LONDON:
Printed for *Richard Smith* at the *Angel and Bible* without *Temple-Bar.* MDCCI.

The seeming Contradictions in the Effects of Opium.

1. It causes Sleeping, and Watching.
2. It causes, and prevents Sweat.
3. It relaxes, and stops Loosenesses.
4. It stops Fluxes, and causes that of Sweat, &c.
5. It stupifies the Sense of Feeling, yet irritates by that Sense to Venery.
6. It causes Stupidity, and Promptitude in Business; Cloudiness, and Serenity of Mind.
7. It excites the Spirits, and quiets them.
8. It is very hot, yet cools in Fevers.
9. It is hot, and bitter; yet lessens Appetite, even in Cold Stomachs.
10. It stops, and promotes Urine.
11. It relaxes, and weakens; yet enables us to undergo Labours, Journeys, &c.
12. It causes, and prevents Abortions.
13. It stops Vomiting above all things; yet causes most violent, tedious, and dangerous Vomitings.
14. It stops Purging in a most eminent manner; yet sometimes causes it.
15. It is very acrimonious, yet (as all say) obtunds Acrimony; however, it allays Pain proceeding from Acrimony.
16. It causes a furious Madness; yet composes the Spirits above all things.
17. It causes Dropsies; yet sometimes cures them (as Willis says.)
18. It causes Palsies; yet have I known it to cure a Palsie.
19. It causes Driness in the Mouth; yet takes off Thirst in Fevers.
20. It cures, and causes a Hiccough.
21. It stanches Blood; yet causes the Blood to come outward, (as appears by the Efflorescence, or Redness of the Skin that it causes) yet moves the Menses and Lochia.
22. We have many Instances of it promoting, and hindering Critical Motions.
23. It raises very weak People, (when nothing besides will do it) yet it kills other weak People.
24. It causes, and cures Convulsions.
25. It causes Relaxation, and Contraction of the same Parts.
26. It Relaxes; yet causes Rigidity, Tension, and Erection of the Penis, Priapisms, &c.

List No. 078

AVAILABLE NAMES

CHARLES DICKENS
1855–1865

Over the course of his illustrious career, Charles Dickens created hundreds of characters to inhabit his many novels, short stories, and plays. Understandably, thinking of names for these characters, and indeed titles for the works, was quite a task, and so Dickens kept lists of such things to be considered for future use. Those seen here were recorded in a single notebook that he called *Memoranda* and kept from 1855 until 1865; it also contained story ideas, snippets of dialogue, and general jottings of ideas.

AVAILABLE NAMES

Titles for books

THE LUMBER ROOM.
SOMEBODY'S LUGGAGE.
TO BE LEFT TILL CALLED FOR.
SOMETHING WANTED.
EXTREMES MEET.
NOBODY'S FAULT.
THE GRINDSTONE.
ROKESMITH'S FORGE.
OUR MUTUAL FRIEND.
THE CINDER HEAP.
TWO GENERATIONS.
BROKEN CROCKERY.
DUST.
THE HOME DEPARTMENT.
THE YOUNG PERSON.
NOW OR NEVER.
MY NEIGHBOURS.
THE CHILDREN OF THE FATHERS.
NO THOROUGHFARE.

Girls from Privy Council Education lists.

LELIA.
MENELLA.
RUBINA.
IRIS.
REBECCA.
ETTY.
REBINAH.
SEBA.
PERSIA.
ARAMANDA.
DORIS.
BALZINA.
PLEASANT.
GENTILLA.

Boys from Privy Council Education lists.

DOCTOR.
HOMER.
ODEN.
BRADLEY.
ZERUBBABEL.
MAXIMILIAN.
URBIN.
SAMILIAS.
PICKLES.
ORANGE.
FEATHER.

Girls and Boys from Ditto.

AMANDA, ETHLYNIDA; BOETIUS, BOLTIUS.

More Boys.

ROBERT LADLE.
JOLY STICK.
BILL MARIGOLD.
STEPHEN MARQUICK.
JONATHAN KNOTWELL.
PHILIP BROWNDRESS.
HENRY GHOST.
GEORGE MUZZLE.
WALTER ASHES.
ZEPHANIAH FERRY (or FURY).
WILLIAM WHY.
ROBERT GOSPEL.
THOMAS FATHERLY.
ROBIN SCRUBBAN.

More Girls.

SARAH GOLDSACKS.
ROSETTA DUST.
SUSAN GOLORING.
CATHERINE TWO.
MATILDA RAINBIRD.
MIRIAM DENIAL.
SOPHIA DOOMSDAY.
ALICE THORNEYWORE.
SALLY GIMBLET.
VERITY MAWKYARD.
BIRDIE NASH.
AMBROSINA EVENTS.
APAULINA VERNON.
NELTIE ASHFORD.

[Untitled list]

TOWNDLING.
MOOD.
GUFF.
TREBLE.
CHILBY.
SPESSIFER.
WODDER.
WHELPFORD.
FENNERCK.
GANNERSON.
CHINKERBLE.
BINTREY.
FLEDSON.
HIRLL.
BRAYLE.
MULLENDER.
TRESLINGHAM.
BRANKLE.
SITTERN.
DOSTONE.
CAY-LON.
SNOWELL.
LOTTRUM.
LAMMLE.
FROSER.
HOLBLACK.
MULLEY.
REDWORTH.
REDFOOT.
TARBOX (B).
TINKLING.
DUDDLE.
JEBUS.
POWDERHILL.
GRIMMER.
SKUSE.
TITCOOMBE.
CRABBLE.
SWANNOCK.
TUZZEN.
TWEMLOW.
SQUAB.
JACKMAN.
SUGG.

BREMMIDGE.
SILAS BLODGET.
MELVIN BEAL.
BUTTRICK.
EDSON.
SANLORN.
LIGHTWORD.
TITBULL.
BANGHAM.
KYLE—NYLE.
PEMBLE.
MAXEY.
ROKESMITH.
CHIVERY.
SLYANT.
QUEEDY.
BESSELTHUR.
MUSTY.
GROUT.
TERTIUS JOBBER.
AMON HEADSTON.
STRAYSHOTT.
HIGDEN.
MORFIT.
GOLDSTRAW.
BARREL.
INGE.
JUMP.
JIGGINS.
BONES.
COY.
DAWN.
TATKIN.
DROWVEY.
PUDSEY.
WABBLER.
PEEX—SPEEX.
GANNAWAY.
MRS. FLINKS.
FLINX.
JEE.
HARDEN.
MERDLE.
MURDEN.

TOPWASH.
PORDAGE.
DORRET—DORRIT.
CARTON.
MINIFIE.
SLINGO.
JOAD.
KINCH.
MAG.
CHELLYSON.
BLENNAM—CL.
BARDOCK.
SNIGSWORTH.
SWENTON.
CASBY—BEACH.
LOWLEIGH—LOWELY.
PIGRIN.
YERBURY.
PLORNISH.
MAROON.
BANDY-NANDY.
STONEBURY.
MAGWITCH.
MEAGLES.
PANCKS.
HAGGAGE.
PROVIS.
STILTINGTON.
PEDSEY.
DUNCALF.
TRICKLEBANK.
SAPSEA.
READYHUFF.
DUFTY.
FOGGY.
TWINN.
BROWNSWORD.
PEARTREE.
SUDDS.
SILVERMAN.
KIMBER.
LAUGHLEY.
LESSOCK.
TIPPINS.

MINNITT.
RADLOWE.
PRATCHET.
MAWDETT.
WOZENHAM.
STILTWALK.
STILTINGSTALK.
STILTSTALKING.
RAVENDER.
PODSNAP.
CLARRIKER.
COMPERY.
STRIVER—STRYVER.
PUMBLECHOOK.
WANGLER.
BOFFIN.
BANTINCK.
DIBTON.
WILFER.
GLIBBERY.
MULVEY.
HORLICK.
DOOLGE.
GANNERY.
GARGERY.
WILLSHARD.
RIDERHOOD.
PRATTERSTONE.
CHINKIBLE.
WOPSELL.
WOPSLE.
WHELPINGTON.
WHELPFORD.
GAYVERY.
WEGG.
HUBBLE.
URRY.
KIBBLE.
SKIFFINS.
WODDER.
ETSER.
AKERSHEM.

List No. 079

LIVE AS WELL AS YOU DARE

SYDNEY SMITH
February 16, 1820

On learning that his good friend Lady Georgiana Morpeth was suffering from a bout of depression during the winter of 1820, noted English essayist and clergyman Sydney Smith (1771–1845) sent her a precious letter filled with sound advice, to be followed in an effort to overcome "low spirits." Smith presented his wise words in the form of a list.

Foston, Feb. 16th, 1820

Dear Georgiana,

Nobody has suffered more from low spirits than I have—so I feel for you. Here are my prescriptions.

1st Live as well as you dare.

2nd Go into the shower-bath with a small quantity of water at a temperature low enough to give you a slight sensation of cold.

3rd Amusing books.

4th Short views of human life—not further than dinner or tea.

5th Be as busy as you can.

6th See as much as you can of those friends who respect and like you.

7th And of those acquaintances who amuse you.

8th Make no secret of low spirits to your friends, but talk of them freely—they are always worse for dignified concealment.

9th Attend to the effects tea and coffee produce upon you.

10th Compare your lot with that of other people.

11th Don't expect too much from human life—a sorry business at the best.

12th Avoid poetry, dramatic representations (except comedy), music, serious novels, melancholy sentimental people, and every thing likely to excite feeling or emotion not ending in active benevolence.

13th Do good, and endeavour to please everybody of every degree.

14th Be as much as you can in the open air without fatigue.

15th Make the room where you commonly sit, gay and pleasant.

16th Struggle by little and little against idleness.

17th Don't be too severe upon yourself, or underrate yourself, but do yourself justice.

18th Keep good blazing fires.

19th Be firm and constant in the exercise of rational religion.

20th Believe me, dear Georgiana, your devoted servant, Sydney Smith

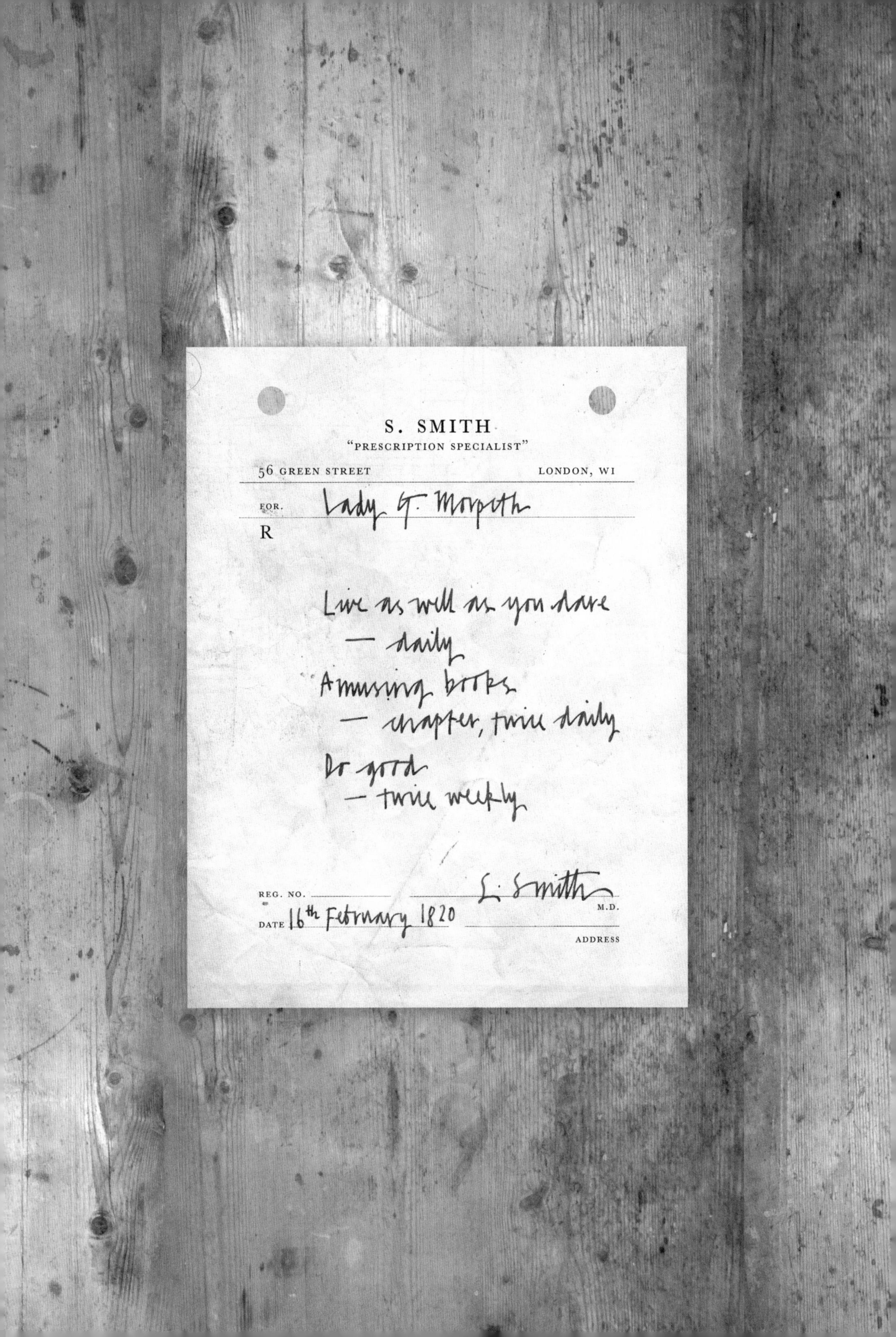
S. SMITH
"PRESCRIPTION SPECIALIST"

56 GREEN STREET LONDON, WI

FOR. Lady G. Morpeth

R

Live as well as you dare
— daily
Amusing books
— chapter, twice daily
Do good
— twice weekly

REG. NO. S. Smith
M.D.

DATE 16th February 1820

ADDRESS

List No. 080

A LOVE LIST

EERO SAARINEN

1954

Finnish-American architect and industrial designer Eero Saarinen (1910–1961), responsible for iconic buildings, chairs, and other designs, is perhaps most famed for the Gateway Arch in St. Louis, Missouri, the seemingly gravity-defying steel archway, which is the largest of its kind on earth. In 1954, Saarinen married art critic Aline Bernstein Louchheim; soon after the wedding, he wrote her a list.

I — FIRST I RECOGNIZED THAT YOU WERE VERY CLEVER

II — THAT YOU WERE VERY HANSOME

III — THAT YOU WERE PERCEPTIVE

IV — THAT YOU WERE ENTHUSIASIC.

V — THAT YOU WERE GENEROUS.

VI — THAT YOU WERE BEAUTIFUL

VII — THAT YOU WERE TERRIBLY WELL ORGANIZED

VIII — THAT YOU WERE FANTASTICALLY EFFICIENT

IX — THAT YOU DRESS VERY VERY WELL

IIIA — THAT YOU HAVE A MARVELOUS SENSE OF HUMOR

X — THAT YOU HAVE A VERY VERY BEATIFUL BODY.

XI — THAT YOU ARE UNBELIEVABLY GENEROUS TO ME.

XII — THAT THE MORE ONE DIGS THE FOUNDATIONS THE MORE AND MORE ONE FINDS THE SOLIDEST OF GRANIT FOR YOU AND I TO BUILD A LIFE TOGETHER UPON (I KNOW THIS IS NOT A GOOD SENTENCE)

I - FIRST I RECOGNIZED THAT YOU WERE
VERY CLEVER

II - THAT YOU WERE VERY HANSOME

III - THAT YOU WERE PERCEPTIVE

IV - THAT YOU WERE ENTHUSIASIC.

V - THAT YOU WERE GENEROUS.

VI - THAT YOU WERE BEAUTIFUL

VII - THAT YOU WERE TERRIBLY WELL ORGANIZED

VIII - THAT YOU WERE FANTASTICALLY EFFICENT

IX - THAT ~~YOU~~ YOU ~~~~ DRESS VERY VERY WELL

III A - THAT YOU HAVE A MARVELOUS SENSE
OF HUMOR

X THAT YOU HAVE A VERY VERY BEATIFUL
BODY.

XI THAT YOU ARE UNBELIEVABLY GENEROUS
TO ME.

XII THAT THE MORE ONE DIGS THE
FOUNDATIONS THE MORE AND MORE
ONE FINDS THE SOLIDEST OF
GRANIT FOR YOU AND I TO BUILD
A LIFE TOGETHER UPON

← I KNOW THIS IS NOT
A GOOD SENTENCE

List No. 081

COCKTAIL!

F. SCOTT FITZGERALD
January 1926

F. Scott Fitzgerald (1896–1940) is one of the most famous novelists of the twentieth century, the author of such classics as *The Great Gatsby* and *Tender Is the Night*. He was also notorious for his excessive drinking during the Roaring Twenties and spent much of the decade filled to the brim with alcohol, ultimately to the detriment of his health. It seems quite apt, then, to find, in a letter written to publisher Blanche W. Knopf, a list in which he conjugates the verb "to cocktail."

Present	I cocktail Thou cocktail It cocktails	We cocktail You cocktail They cocktail
Imperfect	I was cocktailing	
Perfect (pastdefinate)	I cocktailed	
Past perfect	I have cocktailed	
Conditional	I might have cocktailed	
Pluperfect	I had cocktailed	
Subjunctive	I would have cocktailed	
Voluntary Sub.	I should have cocktailed	
Preterite	I did cocktail	
Imperative	Cocktail!	
Interrogative	Cocktailest thou? (Dos't Cocktail?) (or Wilt Cocktail?)	
Subjunctive Conditional	I would have had to have cocktailed	
Conditional Subjunctive	I might have had to have cocktailed	
Participle	Cocktailing	

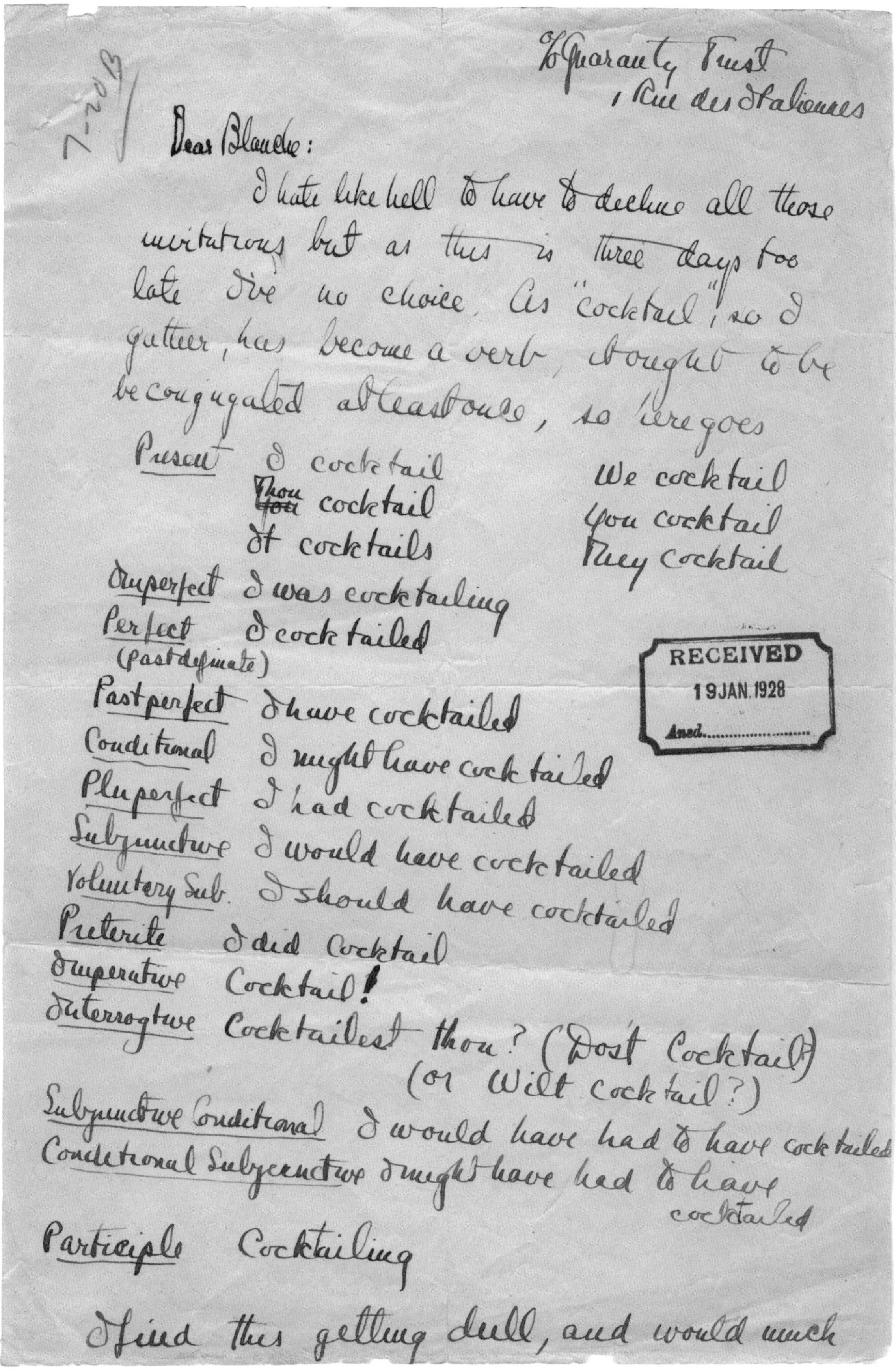

% Guaranty Trust
, Rue des Italiennes

7-20B

Dear Blanche:

I hate like hell to have to decline all those invitations but as this is three days too late I've no choice. As "cocktail," so I gather, has become a verb, it ought to be be conjugated at least once, so here goes

Present I cocktail — We cocktail
~~You~~ Thou cocktail — You cocktail
It cocktails — They cocktail
Imperfect I was cocktailing
Perfect (past definite) I cocktailed
Pastperfect I have cocktailed
Conditional I might have cocktailed
Pluperfect I had cocktailed
Subjunctive I would have cocktailed
Voluntary Sub. I should have cocktailed
Preterite I did cocktail
Imperative Cocktail!
Interrogtive Cocktailest thou? (Dost cocktail?)
(or Wilt cocktail?)
Subjunctive Conditional I would have had to have cocktailed
Conditional Subjunctive I might have had to have cocktailed
Participle Cocktailing

I find this getting dull, and would much

RECEIVED
19 JAN. 1928
Ansd. ....

List No. 082

HENRY MILLER'S ELEVEN COMMANDMENTS

HENRY MILLER
Circa 1932

The American author Henry Miller (1891–1980) was a breaker of literary rules and, in turn, of social laws, an innovator whose now classic novels were originally banned in the United States and other countries for obscenity. Not until the 1960s was his first published novel, the hugely influential *Tropic of Cancer,* freely sold in the US and UK. But Miller had rules of his own. In the early 1930s, as he was writing what would become *Tropic of Cancer*, he wrote a list of eleven commandments, to be followed by himself.

COMMANDMENTS

1. Work on one thing at a time until finished.

2. Start no more new books, add no more new material to "Black Spring."

3. Don't be nervous. Work calmly, joyously, recklessly on whatever is in hand.

4. Work according to Program and not according to mood. Stop at the appointed time!

5. When you can't *create* you can *work*.

6. Cement a little every day, rather than add new fertilizers.

7. Keep human! See people, go places, drink if you feel like it.

8. Don't be a draught-horse! Work with pleasure only.

9. Discard the Program when you feel like it—but go back to it next day. *Concentrate. Narrow down. Exclude.*

10. Forget the books you want to write. Think only of the book you *are* writing.

11. Write first and always. Painting, music, friends, cinema, all these come afterwards.

BRAINES.

A.T. (PRACTITIONER IN PHISICKE AND CHIRURGERIE.)
1596

From the concisely titled self-help medical book, *A Rich Store-house or Treasury for the Diseased. Wherein, are many approved Medicines for diuers and sundry Diseases, which haue been long hidden, and not come to light before this time. Now set foorth for the great benefit and comfort of the poorer sort of people that are not of abillitie to go to the Physitions*, comes two lists: the first, of things that were then, in 1596, considered "good" for the brain; the second, of things thought to be "ill" for the brain.

Braines.

A Rule to knowe what thinges are good and holosome for the Braine.

To smell to Camamill or Muske, + To eate Sage, but not ouermuch, + To drinke Wine measurablie, + To keepe the Head warme, + To washe your Hands often, + To walke measurablie, + To sleepe measurablie, + To heare litle noise or Musicke or singers, + To eate Mustarde & Pepper, + To smell the sauoue of Red-roses, & to washe the Temples of your Head often with Rose-Water.

These Thinges are ill for the Braine.

All maner of Braines, + Gluttony, + Drunkennes, + Late Suppers, + To sleepe much after meate, + Anger, + Heauines of minde, + To stand much bare-headed, + Corrupt Aires, + To eate ouermuch or hastely, + Ouermuch heate in Trauaylinge or Labouringe, + Ouermuch Watching, + Ouermuch Colde, + Ouermuch Bathing, + Milke, + Cheese, + Garlicke, + Oynions + Ouermuch Knocking or Noise, & to smell a white Rose.

Cap. 144.

¶ A Rule to knowe what thinges are good and holosome for the Braine.

++ To smell to Camamill or Muske, + To eate Sage, but not ouermuch, + To drinke Wine measurablie, + To keepe the Head warme, + To washe your Hands often, + To walke measurablie, + To sleepe measurablie, + To heare litle noise of Musicke or singers, + To eate Mustarde & Pepper, + To smell the sauour of Red-roses, & to washe the Temples of your Heade often with Rose-Water. +

Cap. 145.

¶ These Thinges are ill for the Braine.

+ All maner of Braines, + Gluttony, + Drunkennes, + Late Suppers, + To sleepe much after meate, + Anger, + Heauines of minde, + To stande much bare-headed, + Corrupt Aires, + To eate ouermuch or hastely, + Ouermuch heate in Trauaylinge or Labouringe, + Ouermuch Watching, + Ouermuch Colde, + Ouermuch Bathing, + Milke, + Cheese, + Garlicke, + Oynions + Ouermuch Knocking or Noise, & to smell to a white + Rose. +

List No. 084

SIMPLE RULES FOR LIFE IN LONDON

RUDYARD KIPLING
June 9, 1908

Nobel Prize winner Rudyard Kipling (1865–1936) is probably now most famous for *The Jungle Book* (1894), a collection of stories that has since been enjoyed in various forms by many millions of people, but which was just one of countless poems, tales, and essays he penned. On June 9, 1908, he wrote a particularly important piece: a letter to his younger daughter, twelve-year-old Elsie, who was soon to be traveling to London, many miles away, in which this list of "rules for Life in London" was included.

Dear Bird,

. . .

I send you a few simple rules for Life in London.

1. Wash early and often with soap and hot water.

2. Do not roll on the grass of the parks. It will come off black on your dress.

3. Never eat penny buns, oysters, periwinkles or peppermints on the top of a bus. It annoys the passengers.

4. Be kind to policemen. You never know when you may be taken up.

5. Never stop a motor bus with your foot. It is not a croquet ball.

6. Do not attempt to take pictures off the wall of the National Gallery, or to remove cases of butterflies from the National History Museum. You will be noticed if you do.

7. Avoid late hours, pickled salmon, public meetings, crowded crossings, gutters, water-carts and over-eating.

Ever your

Daddo

THE FAKE BOOKS OF CHARLES DICKENS

CHARLES DICKENS
October 1851

In 1851, Charles Dickens and his family moved to Tavistock House, the London home in which he would go on to write *A Tale of Two Cities*, *Bleak House*, and *Little Dorrit*. His new abode was close to perfect, but there was one small dilemma: Dickens didn't have in his possession enough books to fill its many bookshelves. Rather than purchase more reading material, Dickens's creative solution was to fill the gaps with fake books, the witty titles of which he had invented and then supplied, by letter, to a local bookbinder named Thomas Robert Eeles. The list read as follows.

History of a Short Chancery Suit
Catalogue of Statues of the Duke of Wellington
Five Minutes in China. 3 vols.
Forty Winks at the Pyramids. 2 vols.
Abernethy on the Constitution. 2 vols.
Mr. Green's Overland Mail. 2 vols.
Captain Cook's Life of Savage. 2 vols.
A Carpenter's Bench of Bishops. 2 vols.
Toots' Universal Letter-Writer. 2 vols.
Orson's Art of Etiquette.
Downeaster's Complete Calculator.
History of the Middling Ages. 6 vols.
Jonah's Account of the Whale.
Captain Parry's Virtues of Cold Tar.
Kant's Ancient Humbugs. 10 vols.
Bowwowdom. A Poem.
The Quarrelly Review. 4 vols.
The Gunpowder Magazine. 4 vols.
Steele. By the Author of "Ion."
The Art of Cutting the Teeth.
Matthew's Nursery Songs. 2 vols.
Paxton's Bloomers. 5 vols.
On the Use of Mercury by the Ancient Poets.
Drowsy's Recollections of Nothing. 3 vols.
Heavyside's Conversations with Nobody. 3 vols.
Commonplace Book of the Oldest Inhabitant. 2 vols.
Growler's Gruffiology, with Appendix. 4 vols.
The Books of Moses and Sons. 2 vols.
Burke (of Edinburgh) on the Sublime and Beautiful. 2 vols.
Teazer's Commentaries.
King Henry the Eighth's Evidences of Christianity. 5 vols.
Miss Biffin on Deportment.
Morrison's Pills Progress. 2 vols.
Lady Godiva on the Horse.
Munchausen's Modern Miracles. 4 vols.
Richardson's Show of Dramatic Literature. 12 vols.
Hansard's Guide to Refreshing Sleep. As many volumes as possible.

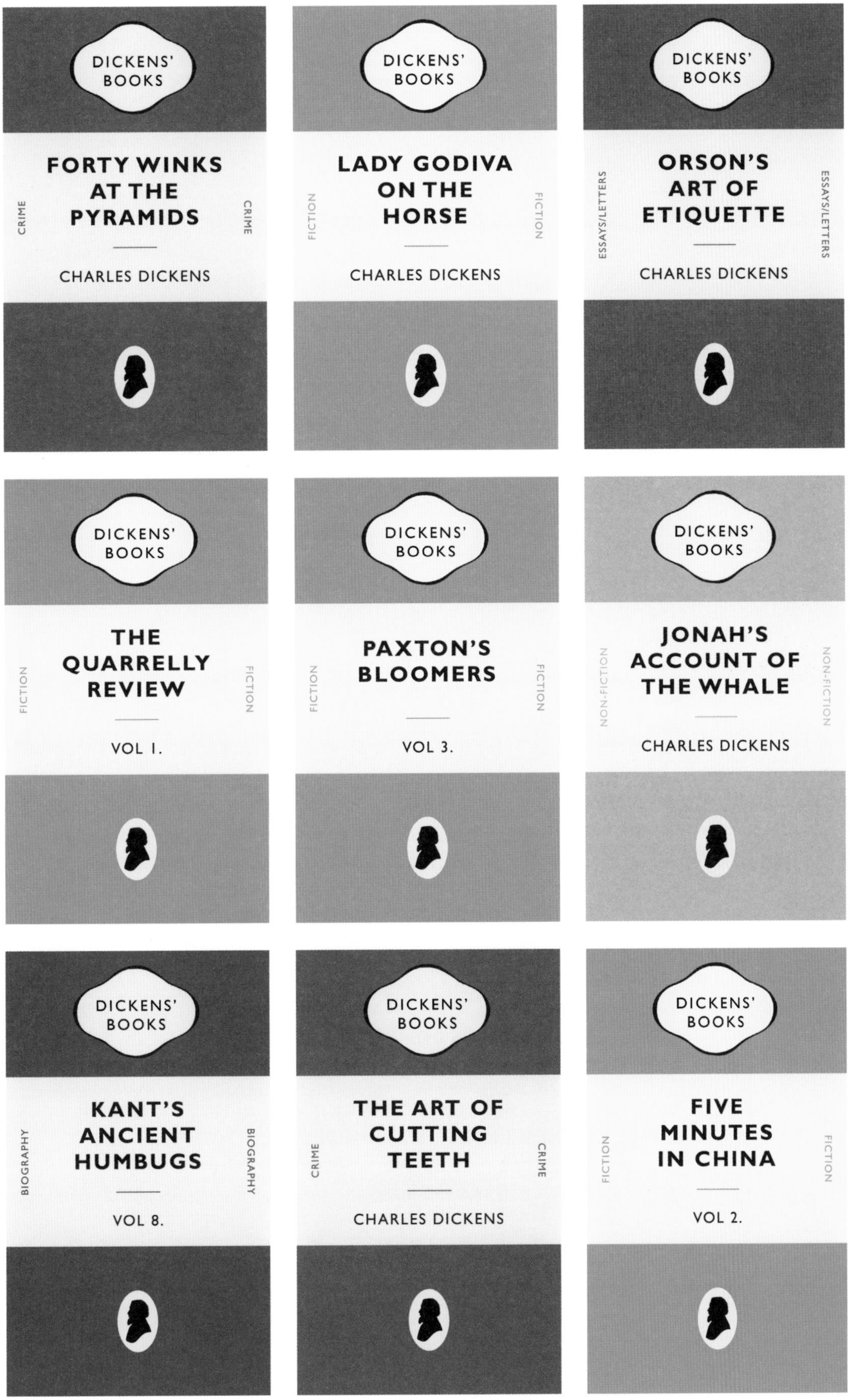
DICKENS' BOOKS
CRIME
FORTY WINKS AT THE PYRAMIDS
CRIME
CHARLES DICKENS
DICKENS' BOOKS
FICTION
LADY GODIVA ON THE HORSE
FICTION
CHARLES DICKENS
DICKENS' BOOKS
ESSAYS/LETTERS
ORSON'S ART OF ETIQUETTE
ESSAYS/LETTERS
CHARLES DICKENS
DICKENS' BOOKS
FICTION
THE QUARRELLY REVIEW
FICTION
VOL 1.
DICKENS' BOOKS
FICTION
PAXTON'S BLOOMERS
FICTION
VOL 3.
DICKENS' BOOKS
NON-FICTION
JONAH'S ACCOUNT OF THE WHALE
NON-FICTION
CHARLES DICKENS
DICKENS' BOOKS
BIOGRAPHY
KANT'S ANCIENT HUMBUGS
BIOGRAPHY
VOL 8.
DICKENS' BOOKS
CRIME
THE ART OF CUTTING TEETH
CRIME
CHARLES DICKENS
DICKENS' BOOKS
FICTION
FIVE MINUTES IN CHINA
FICTION
VOL 2.

THE DON'TS AND BE CAREFULS

MOTION PICTURE PRODUCERS AND DISTRIBUTORS OF AMERICA
1927

In an effort to clean up Hollywood's increasingly controversial output and help the studios avoid further clashes with the country's regional censorship boards, in 1927 the Motion Picture Producers and Distributors of America produced and published "The Don'ts and Be Carefuls." The list consisted of eleven things to be completely avoided in future movies (the "Don'ts"), and twenty-five things that required careful consideration before inclusion (the "Be Carefuls"). Much to their annoyance, the list was unenforceable, and so largely ignored. In 1930 it was ditched in favor of the Motion Picture Production Code, which in turn gave way to the MPAA film rating system we now know.

"The Don'ts and Be Carefuls"

Motion Picture Producers and Distributors of America, 1927

Resolved, That those things which are included in the following list shall not appear in pictures produced by the members of this Association, irrespective of the manner in which they are treated.

1. Pointed profanity — by either title or lip — this includes the words "God," "Lord," "Jesus," "Christ" (unless they be used reverently in connection with proper religious ceremonies), "hell," "damn," "Gawd," and every other profane and vulgar expression however it may be spelled;
2. Any licentious or suggestive nudity — in fact or in silhouette; and any lecherous or licentious notice thereof by other characters in the picture;
3. The illegal traffic in drugs;
4. Any inference of sex perversion;
5. White slavery;
6. Miscegenation (sex relationships between the white and black races);
7. Sex hygiene and venereal diseases;
8. Scenes of actual childbirth — in fact or in silhouette;
9. Children's sex organs;
10. Ridicule of the clergy;
11. Willful offense to any nation, race or creed;

And be it further resolved, That special care be exercised in the manner in which the following subjects are treated, to the end that vulgarity and suggestiveness be eliminated and that good taste may be emphasized:

1. The use of the flag;
2. International relations (avoiding picturizing in an unfavorable light another country's religion, history, institutions, prominent people, and citizenry);
3. Arson;
4. The use of firearms;
5. Theft, robbery, safe-cracking, and dynamiting of trains, mines, building, etc. (having in mind the effect which a too-detailed description of these may have upon the moron);
6. Brutality and possible gruesomeness;
7. Techniques of committing murder by whatever method;
8. Methods of smuggling;
9. Third-degree methods;
10. Actual hangings or electrocutions as legal punishment for crime;
11. Sympathy for criminals;
12. Attitude toward public characters and institutions;
13. Sedition;
14. Apparent cruelty to children and animals;
15. Branding of people or animals;

16. The sale of women, or of a woman selling her virtue;
17. Rape or attempted rape;
18. First-night scenes;
19. Man and woman in bed together;
20. Deliberate seduction of girls;
21. The institution of marriage;
22. Surgical operations;
23. The use of drugs;
24. Titles or scenes having to do with law enforcement or law-enforcing officers;
25. Excessive or lustful kissing, particularly when one character or the other is a "heavy."

MARRY/NOT MARRY

CHARLES DARWIN
July 1838

In July 1838, twenty-one years before his groundbreaking book *On the Origin of Species* was published, twenty-nine-year-old naturalist Charles Darwin found himself facing a difficult decision: whether or not to propose to the love of his life, Emma Wedgwood. This was his handwritten solution—a list of gems of pros and cons of marriage. Indeed, the pros were too numerous to ignore, and six months later Charles Darwin and Emma Wedgwood were wed. The couple remained married until Darwin's death in 1882. They had ten children.

This is the Question

Marry

Children — (if it Please God) — Constant companion, (& friend in old age) who will feel interested in one, — object to be beloved & played with. — better than a dog anyhow. — Home, & someone to take care of house — Charms of music & female chit-chat. — These things good for one's health. — Forced to visit & receive relations but terrible loss of time. —

W My God, it is intolerable to think of spending ones whole life, like a neuter bee, working, working, & nothing after all. — No, no won't do. — Imagine living all one's day solitarily in smoky dirty London House. — Only picture to yourself a nice soft wife on a sofa with good fire, & books & music perhaps — Compare this vision with the dingy reality of Grt. Marlbro' St.

Not Marry

No children, (no second life), no one to care for one in old age.— What is the use of working 'in' without sympathy from near & dear friends — who are near & dear friends to the old, except relatives

Freedom to go where one liked — choice of Society & little of it. — Conversation of clever men at clubs — Not forced to visit relatives, & to bend in every trifle. — to have the expense & anxiety of children — perhaps quarelling — Loss of time. — cannot read in the Evenings — fatness & idleness — Anxiety & responsibility — less money for books &c — if many children forced to gain one's bread. — (But then it is very bad for ones health to work too much)

Perhaps my wife wont like London; then the sentence is banishment & degradation into indolent, idle fool —

Marry, Marry, Marry Q.E.D.

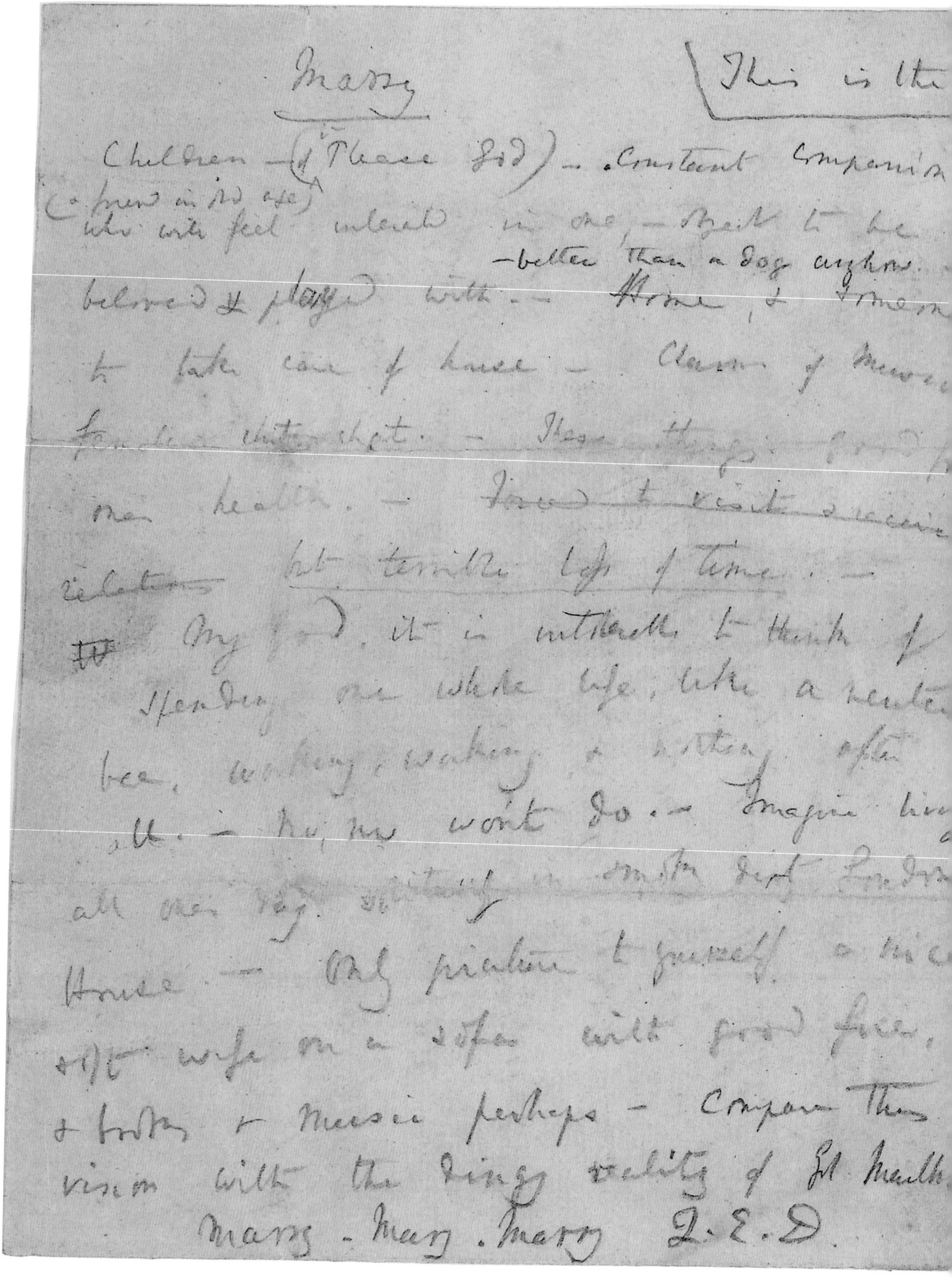
Marry
This is the
Children — (if it Please God) — Constant companion
(& friend in old age) who will feel interested in one, — object to be
— better than a dog anyhow.
beloved & played with. — Home, & someone
to take care of house — Charms of music
& female chit-chat. — These things good for
one's health. — ~~Forced to visit & receive~~
~~relations~~ but terrible loss of time. —
My God, it is intolerable to think of
spending one's whole life, like a neuter
bee, working, working, & nothing after
all. — No, no won't do. — Imagine living
all one's day solitarily in smoky dirty London
House. — Only picture to yourself a nice
soft wife on a sofa with good fire,
& books & music perhaps — Compare this
vision with the dingy reality of Grt. Marlbro'
Marry — Mary — Marry Q.E.D.

…ation) Not Marry

o children, (no second life) no one to care for one in old age.— what is the use of working …t without sympathy from near & dear friends— …ho are near & dear friends to the old, except …elatives Freedom to go where one liked— choice of Society & little of it.— Conversation of clever men at clubs— Not forced to visit relatives, & to bend in every trifle— to have the expense & anxiety of children— perhaps quarelling— Loss of time.— cannot read in the Evenings— fatness & idleness— Anxiety & responsibility— less money for books &c— if many children forced to gain one's bread.— (But then it is very bad for ones health to work too much)

Perhaps my wife wont like London; then the sentence is banishment & degradation with indolent, idle fool—

VONNEGUT'S COMMITMENTS

KURT VONNEGUT
January 26, 1947

By January 1947, less than two years after escaping captivity during World War II and a few years before his writing career took off, Kurt Vonnegut had been married to his first wife, Jane, for sixteen months. She was also pregnant with their first child, a situation that prompted Vonnegut to produce a contract in which was listed a number of commitments for him to adhere to—essentially an amusingly worded promise to take care of certain household chores. Kurt and Jane went on to have three children; they also adopted three of his sister's children following her and her husband's deaths in 1957.

I, Kurt Vonnegut, Jr., that is, do hereby swear that I will be faithful to the commitments hereunder listed:

I. With the agreement that my wife will not nag, heckle, and otherwise disturb me, on the subject, I promise to scrub the bathroom and kitchen floors once a week, on a day and hour of my own choosing. Not only that, but I will do a good and thorough job, and by that she means that I will get *under* the bathtub, *behind* the toilet, *under* the sink, *under* the icebox, *into* the corners; and I will pick up and put in some other location whatever movable objects happen to be on said floors at the time so as to get under them too, and not just around them. Furthermore, while I am undertaking these tasks I will refrain from indulging in such remarks as "Shit," "Goddamn sonofabitch," and similar vulgarities, as such language is nervewracking to have around the house when nothing more drastic is taking place than the facing of Necessity. *If I do not live up to this agreement*, my wife is to feel free to nag, heckle and otherwise disturb me until I am driven to scrub the floors anyway—*no matter how busy I am.*

II. I furthermore swear that I will observe the following minor amenities:

a. I will hang up my clothes and put my shoes in the closet when I am not wearing them;

b. I will not track dirt into the house needlessly, by such means as not wiping my feet on the mat outside, and by wearing my bedroom slippers to take out the garbage, and other things;

c. I will throw such things as used up match folders, empty cigarette packages, the piece of cardboard that comes in shirt collars, etc, into a wastebasket instead of leaving them around on chairs or the floor;

d. After shaving I will put my shaving equipment back in the medicine closet;

e. In case I should be the direct cause of a ring around the bathtub after taking a bath, I will, with the aid of Swift's Cleanser and a brush, *not* my washcloth, remove said ring;

f. With the agreement that my wife collects the laundry, places it in a laundry bag, and leaves the laundry bag in plain sight in the hall, I will take said laundry to the Laundry not more than three days after said laundry has made its appearance in the hall; I will furthermore bring the *clean* laundry back from the Laundry within two weeks after I have taken it, dirty that is;

g. When smoking I will make every effort to keep the ashtray which I am using at the time upon a surface that does not slant, sag, slope, dip, wrinkle, or give way upon the slightest provocation; such surfaces may be understood to include stacks of books precariously mounted on the edge of a chair, the arms of the chair that has arms, and my own knees;

h. I will not put out cigarettes upon the sides of, or throw ashes into either the red leather waste-basket, or the stamp waste-basket which my loving wife made me for Christmas, 1945, as such practise noticeably impairs the beauty, and ultimate practicability of said waste-baskets;

i. In the event that my wife makes a request of me, and that request cannot be regarded as other than reasonable and wholly within the province of a man's work (when his wife is pregnant, that is), I will comply with said request within three days after my wife has presented it: It is understood that my wife will make no reference to the subject, other than saying thank you, of course, *within these three days*; if, however, I fail to comply with said request after a more substantial length of time has elapsed, my wife shall be completely justified in nagging heckling and otherwise disturbing me, until I am driven to do that which I should have done;

j. An exception to the above three-day time limit is the taking out of the garbage, which, as any fool knows, had better not wait that long; I will take out the garbage within three *hours* after the need for disposal has been pointed out to me by my wife. It would be nice, however, if, upon observing the need for disposal with my own two eyes, I should perform this particular task upon my own initiative, and thus not make it necessary for my wife to bring up a subject that is moderately distasteful to her;

k. It is understood that, should I find these commitments in any way unreasonable or too binding upon my freedom, I will take steps to amend them by counter-proposals, constitutionally presented and politely discussed, instead of unlawfully terminating my obligations with a simple burst of obscenity, or something like that, and the subsequent persistent neglect of said obligations;

l. The terms of this contract are understood to be binding up until that time after the arrival of our child, (to be specified by the doctor,) when my wife will once again be in full possession of all her faculties, and able to undertake more arduous pursuits than are now advisable.

SIGNATURE

KURT VONNEGUT

List No. 089

A DECALOGUE OF CANONS FOR OBSERVATION IN PRACTICAL LIFE

THOMAS JEFFERSON
1825

In 1825, the year before his death, Thomas Jefferson, a Founding Father of the United States of America, was asked by a new father to supply some words of wisdom to his young son, Thomas Jefferson Smith, who had recently been named after the United States' third president. Jefferson graciously responded with a handwritten letter, at the end of which was a ten-point list of advice for the youngster.

A Decalogue of Canons for observation in practical life.

1. Never put off till tomorrow what you can do to-day.
2. Never trouble another for what you can do yourself.
3. Never spend your money before you have it.
4. Never buy a what you do not want, because it is cheap; it will be dear to you.
5. Pride costs us more than hunger, thirst and cold.
6. We never repent of having eaten too little.
7. Nothing is troublesome that we do willingly.
8. How much pain have cost us the evils which have never happened!
9. Take things always by their smooth handle.
10. When angry, count ten, before you speak; if very angry, an hundred.

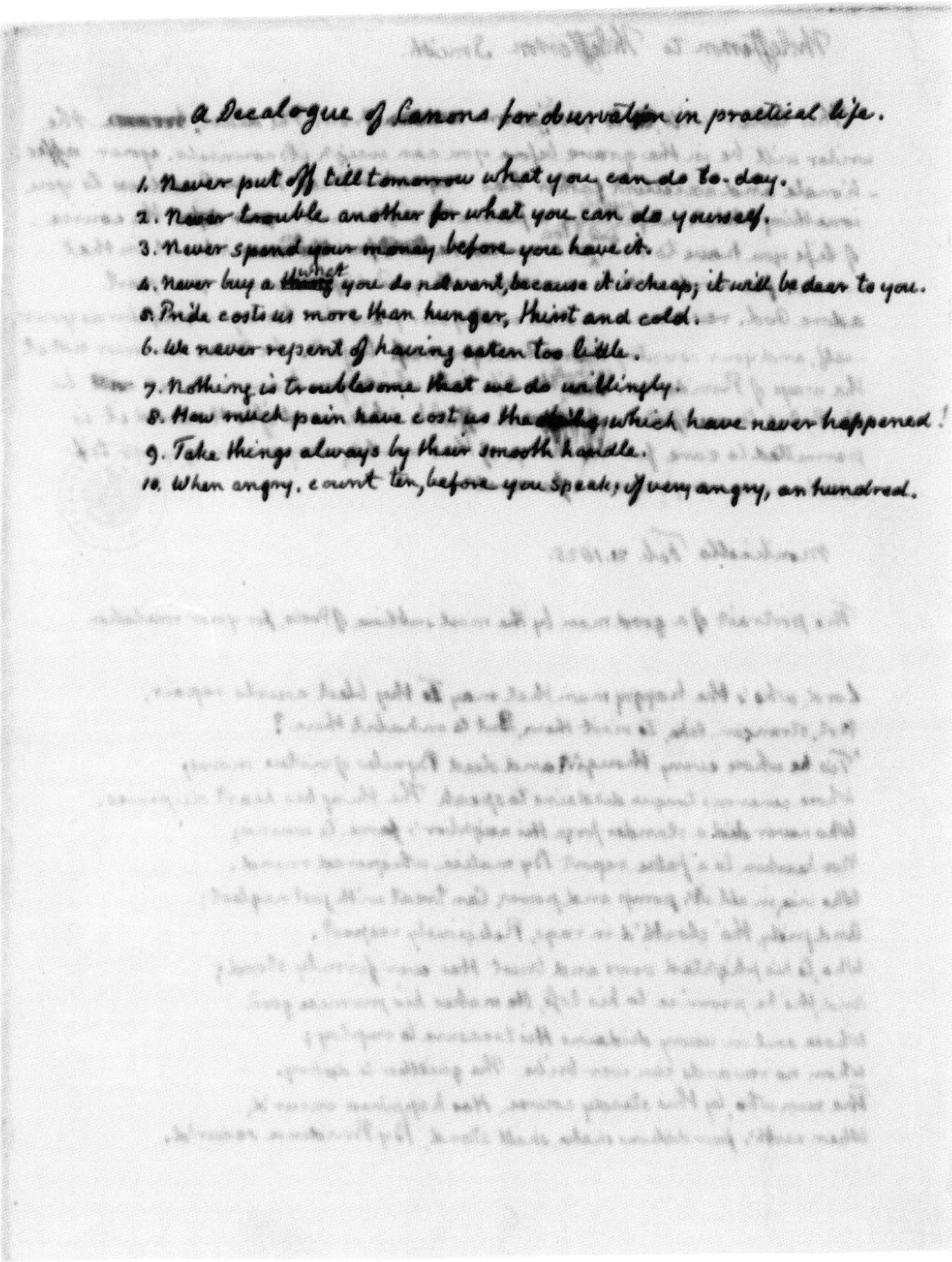

A Decalogue of Canons for observation in practical life.

1. Never put off till tomorrow what you can do to-day.
2. Never trouble another for what you can do yourself.
3. Never spend your money before you have it.
4. Never buy a ~~thing~~ what you do not want, because it is cheap; it will be dear to you.
5. Pride costs us more than hunger, thirst and cold.
6. We never repent of having eaten too little.
7. Nothing is troublesome that we do willingly.
8. How much pain have cost us the evils which have never happened!
9. Take things always by their smooth handle.
10. When angry, count ten, before you speak; if very angry, an hundred.

TEN COMMANDMENTS OF GUITAR PLAYING

CAPTAIN BEEFHEART
Late 1970s

Captain Beefheart (1941–2010), who in later life would be collected as an artist, was a musician and singer whose innovative work and subsequent influence belies the relatively little commercial success it enjoyed at the time. His 1969 masterwork, *Trout Mask Replica*, sits firmly in numerous "greatest albums" lists. In 1976, Moris Tepper joined Beefheart's Magic Band to play guitar, which he did until Beefheart's retirement in 1982. It was during this period that Tepper was handed the "Ten Commandments of Guitar Playing,"as written by Beefheart himself.

1. Listen to the birds.
   That's where all the music comes from. Birds know everything about how it should sound and where that sound should come from. And watch hummingbirds. They fly really fast, but a lot of times they aren't going anywhere.

2. Your guitar is not really a guitar.
   Your guitar is a divining rod. Use it to find spirits in the other world and bring them over. A guitar is also a fishing rod. If you're good, you'll land a big one.

3. Practice in front of a bush.
   Wait until the moon is out, then go outside, eat a multi-grained bread and play your guitar to a bush. If the bush doesn't shake, eat another piece of bread.

4. Walk with the devil.
   Old Delta blues players referred to guitar amplifiers as the "devil box." And they were right. You have to be an equal opportunity employer in terms of who you're bringing over from the other side. Electricity attracts devils and demons. Other instruments attract other spirits. An acoustic guitar attracts Casper. A mandolin attracts Wendy. But an electric guitar attracts Beelzebub.

5. If you're guilty of thinking, you're out.
   If your brain is part of the process, you're missing it. You should play like a drowning man, struggling to reach shore. If you can trap that feeling, then you have something that is fur bearing.

6. Never point your guitar at anyone.
   Your instrument has more clout than lightning. Just hit a big chord then run outside to hear it. But make sure you are not standing in an open field.

7. Always carry a church key.
   That's your key-man clause. Like One String Sam. He's one. He was a Detroit street musician who played in the fifties on a homemade instrument. His song "I Need a Hundred Dollars" is warm pie. Another key to the church is Hubert Sumlin, Howlin' Wolf's guitar player. He just stands there like the Statue of Liberty—making you want to look up her dress the whole time to see how he's doing it.

8. Don't wipe the sweat off your instrument.
   You need that stink on there. Then you have to get that stink onto your music.

9. Keep your guitar in a dark place.
   When you're not playing your guitar, cover it and keep it in a dark place. If you don't play your guitar for more than a day, be sure you put a saucer of water in with it.

10. You gotta have a hood for your engine.
    Keep that hat on. A hat is a pressure cooker. If you have a roof on your house, the hot air can't escape. Even a lima bean has to have a piece of wet paper around it to make it grow.

List No. 091

THINGS DOING AND TO BE DONE

THOMAS EDISON
January 3, 1888

Born in 1847, Thomas Edison remains to this day one of the most prolific inventors in history with an impressive 1,093 patents to his name in the United States alone. Some of his biggest breakthroughs included the invention of the phonograph, the development of the first practical incandescent light bulb, and the design of the Kinetograph, an early motion picture camera. It is therefore no surprise to learn that Edison relied on to-do lists that could make the busiest of us feel comparatively slothful. He kicked off 1888 with these five pages of things 'doing and to be done.'

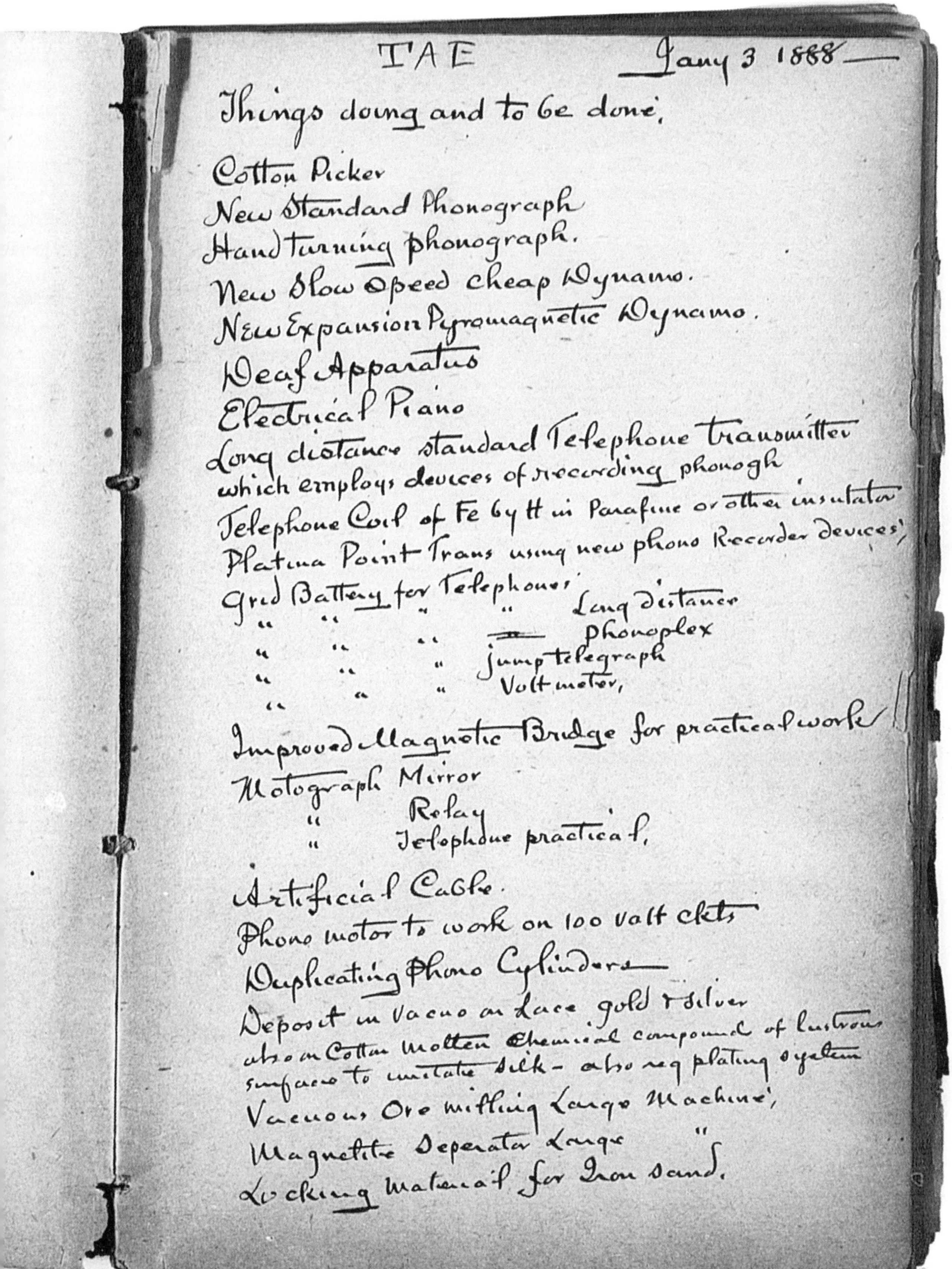

TAE Jany 3 1888

Things doing and to be done.

Cotton Picker
New Standard Phonograph
Hand turning phonograph.
New Slow Speed cheap Dynamo.
New Expansion Pyromagnetic Dynamo.
Deaf Apparatus
Electrical Piano
Long distance standard Telephone transmitter
which employs devices of recording phonogh
Telephone Coil of Fe by H in Parafine or other insulator
Platina Point Trans using new phono Recorder devices;
Grid Battery for Telephones
" " " " Long distance
" " " — phonoplex
" " " jump telegraph
" " " Volt meter,
"

Improved Magnetic Bridge for practical work
Motograph Mirror
" Relay
" Telephone practical,

Artificial Cable.
Phono motor to work on 100 Volt ckts
Duplicating Phono Cylinders
Deposit in Vacuo on Lace gold & silver
also on Cotton Molten Chemical compound of lustrous
surfaces to imitate silk — also reg plating system
Vacuous Ore milling Large Machine,
Magnetite Seperator Large "
Locking Material for Iron sand.

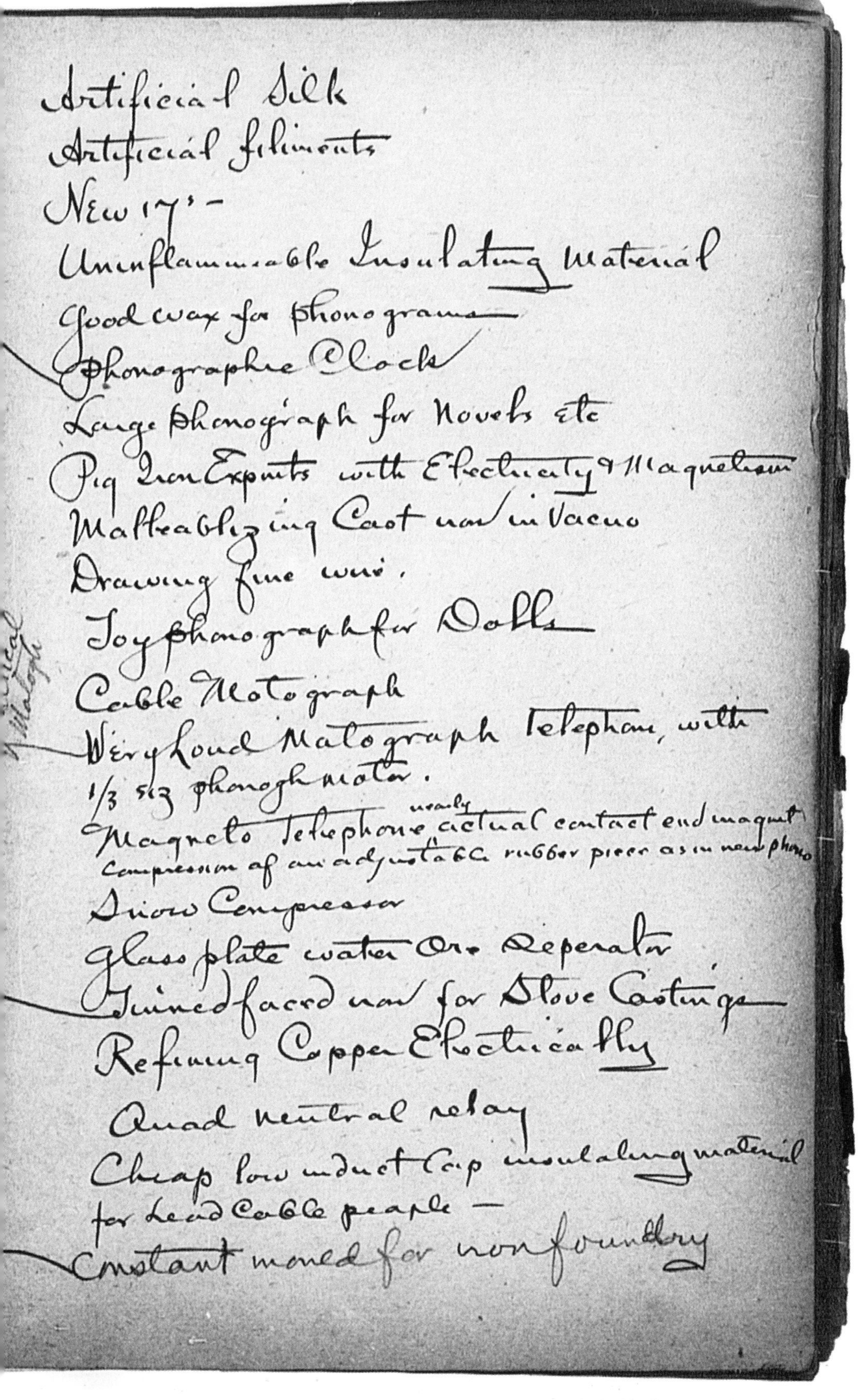
Artificial Silk
Artificial filiments
New 17' -
Uninflammable Insulating Material
Good wax for phonograms
Phonographic Clock
Large Phonograph for Novels etc
Pig Iron Expmts with Electricity & Magnetism
Malleablizing Cast iron in Vacuo
Drawing fine wire.
Toy Phonograph for Dolls
Cable Motograph
Very Loud Motograph Telephone, with
1/3 size phonogh motor.
Magneto Telephone nearly actual contact end magnet
compression of an adjustable rubber piece as in new phono
Snow Compressor
Glass plate water Ore Seperator
Tinned faced iron for Stove Castings
Refining Copper Electrically
Quad neutral relay
Cheap low induct Cap insulating material
for Lead Cable people —
Constant mould for iron foundry

200 Volt 20 cp lamp
Cheap pressure Indicator
Recording Volt Indicator
Box balancing System
Alternating Machine & Transformer
Silver Surface Switches
Vulcanizing the 7c African Rubber adulterant.
Platinum wire Ice cutting Machine,
Silver wire wood cutting system
Silvering or Coppering bolting Cloth in Vac for durability
S Motor altered over with new devices for C speed
Expansion Mirror Plat-Irid- wire in Vacuo
Photoghg through Opaque Screens;
Photoghg by causing heat at the Critical points -
Boron fil.
Hg out of lamp
Phonoplex Repeater
Squirting glass sheet tube Etc Nickel Moulds
Artificial Mother Pearl.
Red lead pencils equal to Graphite
India Ink
Tracing Cloth
Ink for Blind

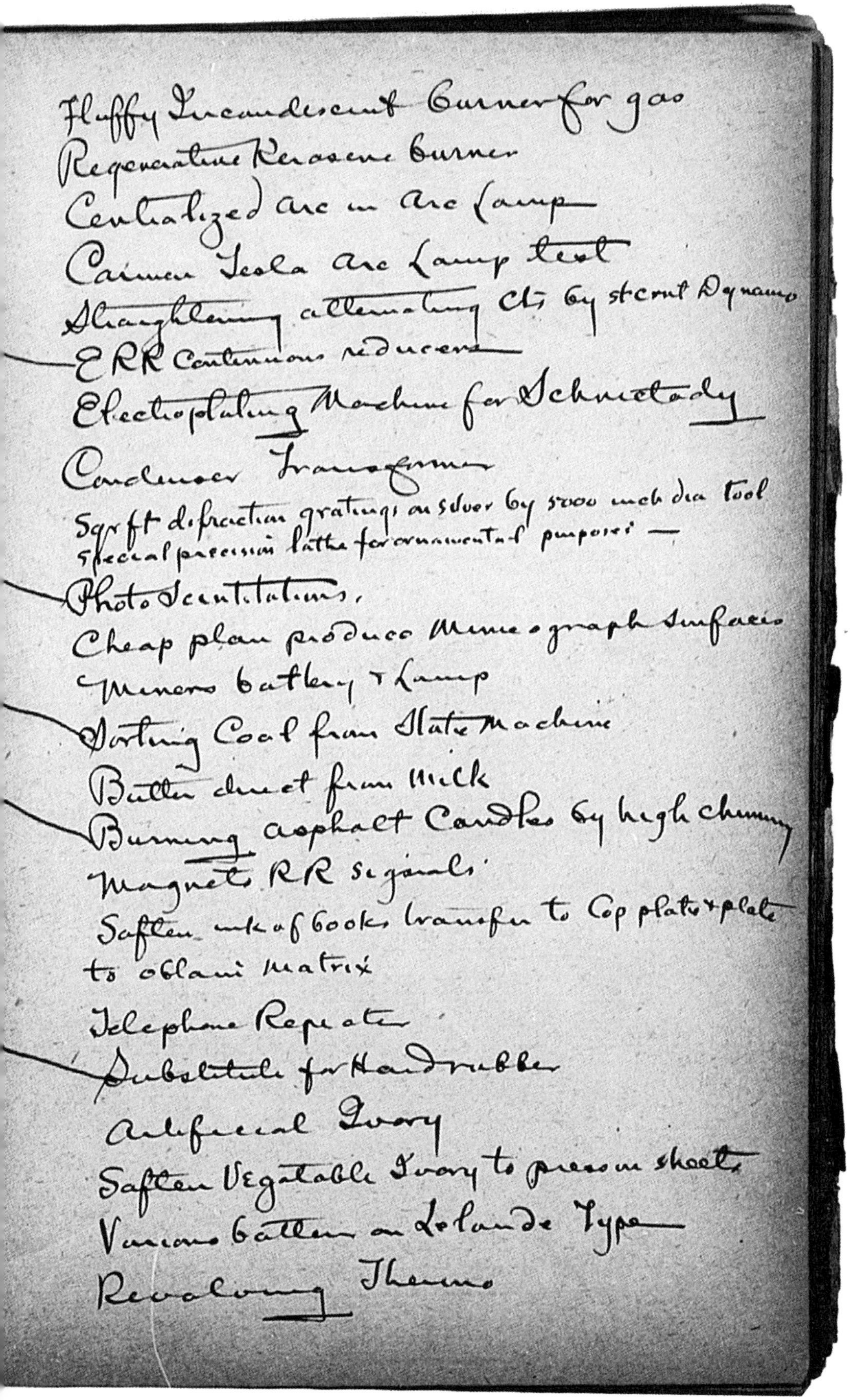
Fluffy Incandescent Burner for gas
Regenerative Kerosene burner
Centralized arc in arc lamp
Carmen Tesla arc lamp test
Straightening alternating Cts by st cont Dynamo
ERR Continuous reducers
Electroplating Machine for Schenectady
Condenser Transformer
Sq ft difraction gratings on silver by 5000 inch dia tool
special precision lathe for ornamental purposes —
Photo Scintillations.
Cheap plan produce Mimeograph surfaces
Miners battery & lamp
Sorting Coal from Slate Machine
Butter direct from Milk
Burning asphalt Candles by high chimney
Magnetic RR signals
Soften ink of books transfer to Cop plate & plate to obtain matrix
Telephone Repeater
Substitute for Hard rubber
Artificial Ivory
Soften Vegetable Ivory to press in sheets
Various batteries on Lalande Type
Revolving Thermo

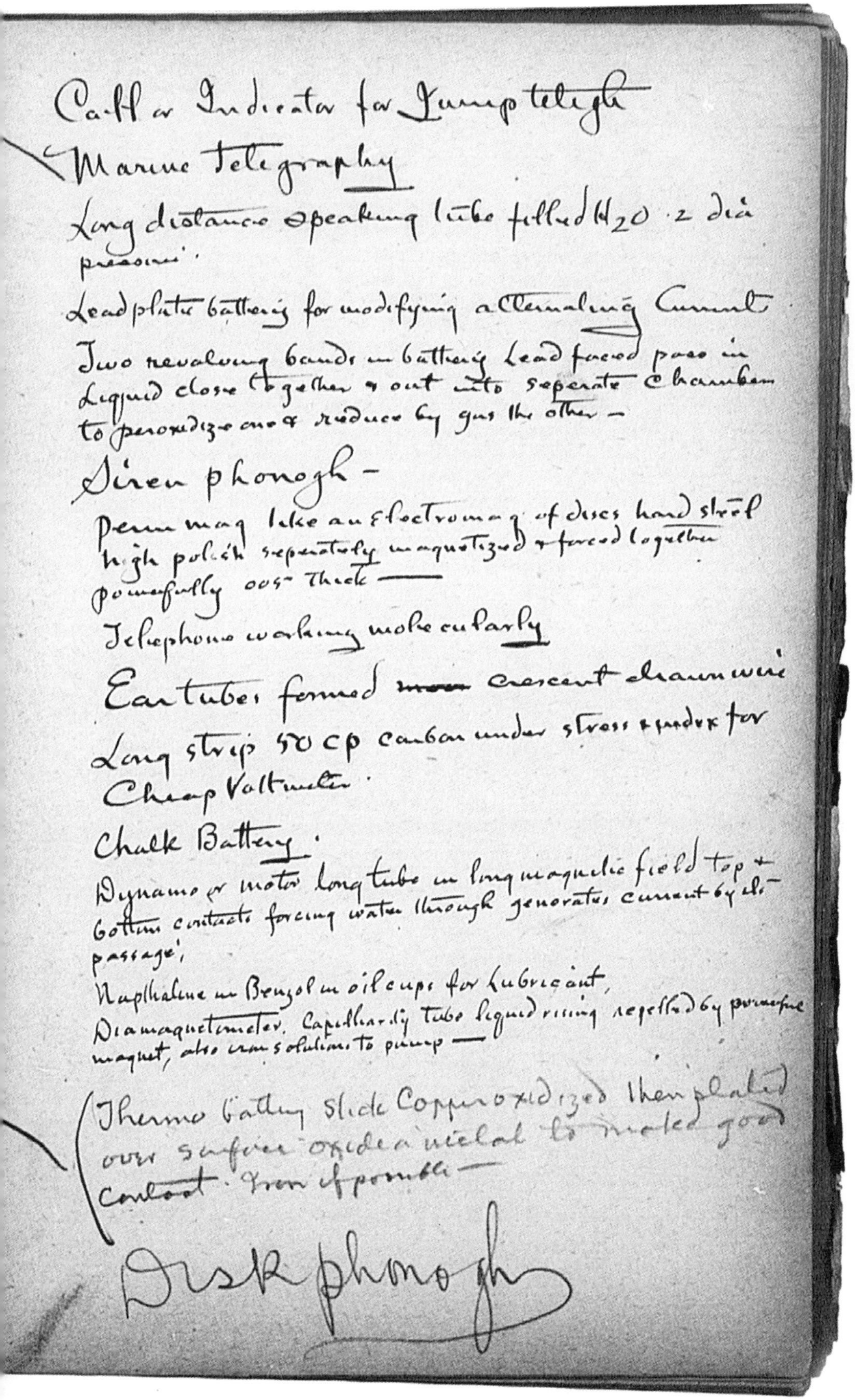

Call or Indicator for Jump telegh

Marine Telegraphy

Long distance speaking tube filled H_2O 2 dia pressure.

Lead plate battery for modifying alternating Current

Two revolving bands in battery Lead faced pass in liquid close together & out into seperate chambers to peroxidize one & reduce by gas the other —

Siren phonogh —

Perm mag like an Electromag of discs hard steel high polish seperately magnetized & forced together powerfully .005" thick —

Telephone working molecularly

Ear tubes formed ~~mou~~ crescent drawn wire

Long strip 50 cp carbon under stress & index for Cheap Voltmeter.

Chalk Battery.

Dynamo or motor long tube in long magnetic field top & bottom contacts forcing water through generates current by its passage;

Napthaline in Benzol in oil cups for Lubricant,

Diamagnetometer. Capillarity tube liquid rising repelled by powerful magnet, also iron solutions to pump —

Thermo battery slide Copper oxidized then plated over surface oxide a metal to make good contact. Iron if possible —

Disk phonogh

List No. 092

11 RULES FOR BOX-OFFICE APPEAL

PRESTON STURGES
1941

In 1940, American filmmaker and father of the screwball comedy Preston Sturges (1898–1959) made his directorial debut with *The Great McGinty*, a political satire that was warmly received by critics. One of the movie's original writer-directors, Sturges also won the first-ever Original Screenplay Academy Award® for it. In 1941, with his Hollywood star well on the rise, Sturges drew up a list of "eleven rules for box-office appeal."

1. A pretty girl is better than an ugly one.
2. A leg is better than an arm.
3. A bedroom is better than a living room.
4. An arrival is better than a departure.
5. A birth is better than a death.
6. A chase is better than a chat.
7. A dog is better than a landscape.
8. A kitten is better than a dog.
9. A baby is better than a kitten.
10. A kiss is better than a baby.
11. A pratfall is better than anything.

List No. 093

DEGREES OF VAGABOND

THOMAS HARMAN
1566

In 1566, Thomas Harman published *A Caveat or Warning for Common Cursitors, Vulgarly called Vagabonds*, a book that aimed to shine a light on what he believed to be the devious rogues of society. As well as retelling stories of thievery, detailing the techniques of such criminals, and providing a dictionary of rogues' secret language ("Thieves' Cant"), each of the book's first twenty-three chapters was named after a different class of vagabond, as identified by Harman. Those chapter titles soon became the following popular list, as described eleven years later in William Harrison's *Description of England* (who added the explanations in square brackets seen here).

The several disorders and degrees amongst our idle vagabonds:

1. Rufflers [thieving beggars, apprentice uprightmen]
2. Uprightmen [leaders of robber bands]
3. Hookers or anglers [thieves who steal through open windows with hooks]
4. Rogues [rank-and-file vagabonds]
5. Wild rogues [those born of rogues]
6. Priggers of prancers [horse thieves]
7. Palliards [male and female beggars, traveling in pairs]
8. Fraters [sham proctors, pretending to beg for hospitals, etc.]
9. Abrams [feined lunatics]
10. Fresh-water mariners or whipjacks [beggars pretending shipwreck]
11. Dummerers [sham deaf-mutes]
12. Drunken tinkers [thieves using the trade as a cover]
13. Swadders or peddlers [thieves pretending to be peddlers]
14. Jarkmen [forgers of licenses] or patricoes [hedge priests].

Of womenkind

1. Demanders for glimmer or fire [female beggars pretending loss from fire]
2. Bawdy baskets [female peddlars]
3. Morts [prostitutes and thieves]
4. Autem [married] morts
5. Walking [unmarried] morts
6. Doxies [prostitutes who begin with uprightmen]
7. Dells [young girls, incipient doxies]
8. Kinchin morts [female beggar children]
9. Kinchin coes [male beggar children].

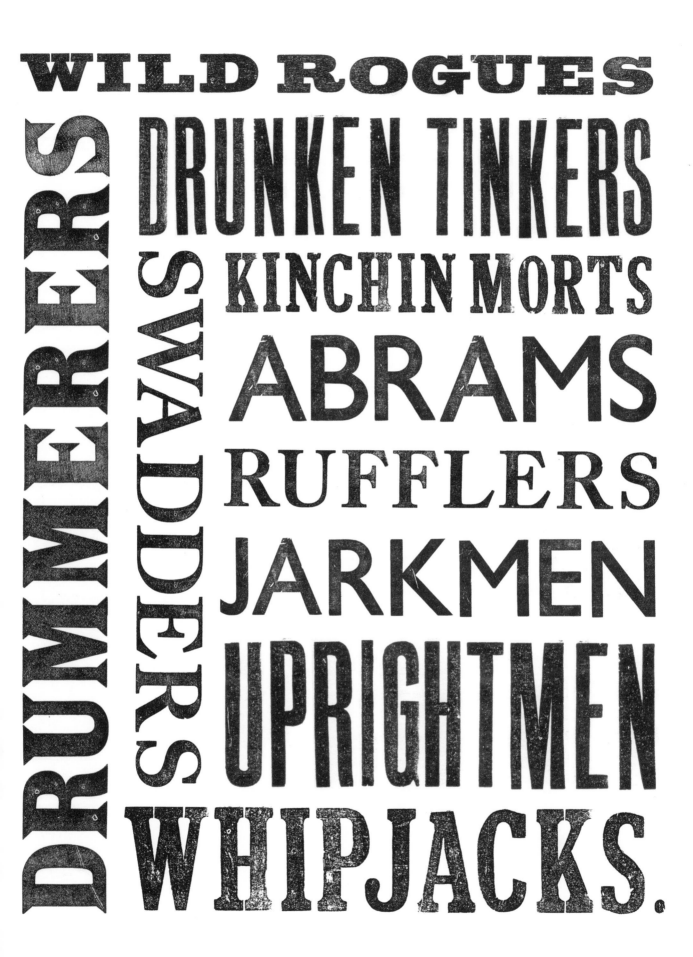

WILD ROGUES

DRUMMERERS

DRUNKEN TINKERS

SWADDERS

KINCHIN MORTS

ABRAMS

RUFFLERS

JARKMEN

UPRIGHTMEN

WHIPJACKS.

List No. 094

VERTIGO

PARAMOUNT

October 24, 1957

As production on the movie adaptation of the novel *D'entre les morts* progressed during 1957, a tug-of-war developed behind the scenes between its director, Alfred Hitchcock, and studio, Paramount—all because of its title. Hitchcock wanted *Vertigo*, and nothing else. The studio repeatedly shot it down and offered a selection of alternatives that included *Tonight Is Ours* and *The Mad Carlotta*. Still Hitchcock refused to budge. Finally, on October 24, 1957, Paramount executive Sam Frey tried one last time to change Hitchcock's mind and sent him this list of suggestions.

Yet again, Hitchcock stood firm. Paramount threw in the towel.

Afraid to Love
Alone in the Dark
The Apparition
Behind the Mask
Carlotta
Checkmate
Conscience
Cry from the Rooftop
The Dark Tower
Deceit
Deceitful
Deception
Don't Leave Me
Dream Without Ending
The Face
Variations
Footsteps
For the Last Time
The Hidden life
In the Shadows
The Investigator
A Life Is Forever
The Lure
Malice
The Mask and the Face
The Mask Illusion
My Madeleine
~~A Matter of Fact~~
Never Leave Me
Night Shade
Nothing Is Forever
Now and Forever
Past, Present and Future
The Phantom
The Second Chance
The Shadow
Shadow and Substance
Shadow on the Stairs Shock
Steps on the Stairs Terror
To Live Again
Tonight Is Ours
Too Late My Love
Two Kinds of Women
The Unknown
Wanted
Without A Trace
The Witness

PARAMOUNT PRESENTS
JAMES STEWART
KIM NOVAK
IN ALFRED HITCHCOCK'S
MASTERPIECE
'VERTIGO'
CO STARRING
BARBARA BEL GEDDES
WITH
TOM HELMORE HENRY JONES
DIRECTED BY
ALFRED HITCHCOCK
SCREENPLAY BY
ALEC COPPEL & SAMUEL TAYLOR
TECHNICOLOR®
VISTAVISION®
BASED UPON THE NOVEL 'D'ENTRE LES MORTS' BY PIERRE BOILEAU AND THOMAS NARCEJAC MUSIC BY BERNARD HERRMANN
Copyright 1958 Paramount Pictures Corporation. Country of Origin U.S.A.
58/7 68
58/241

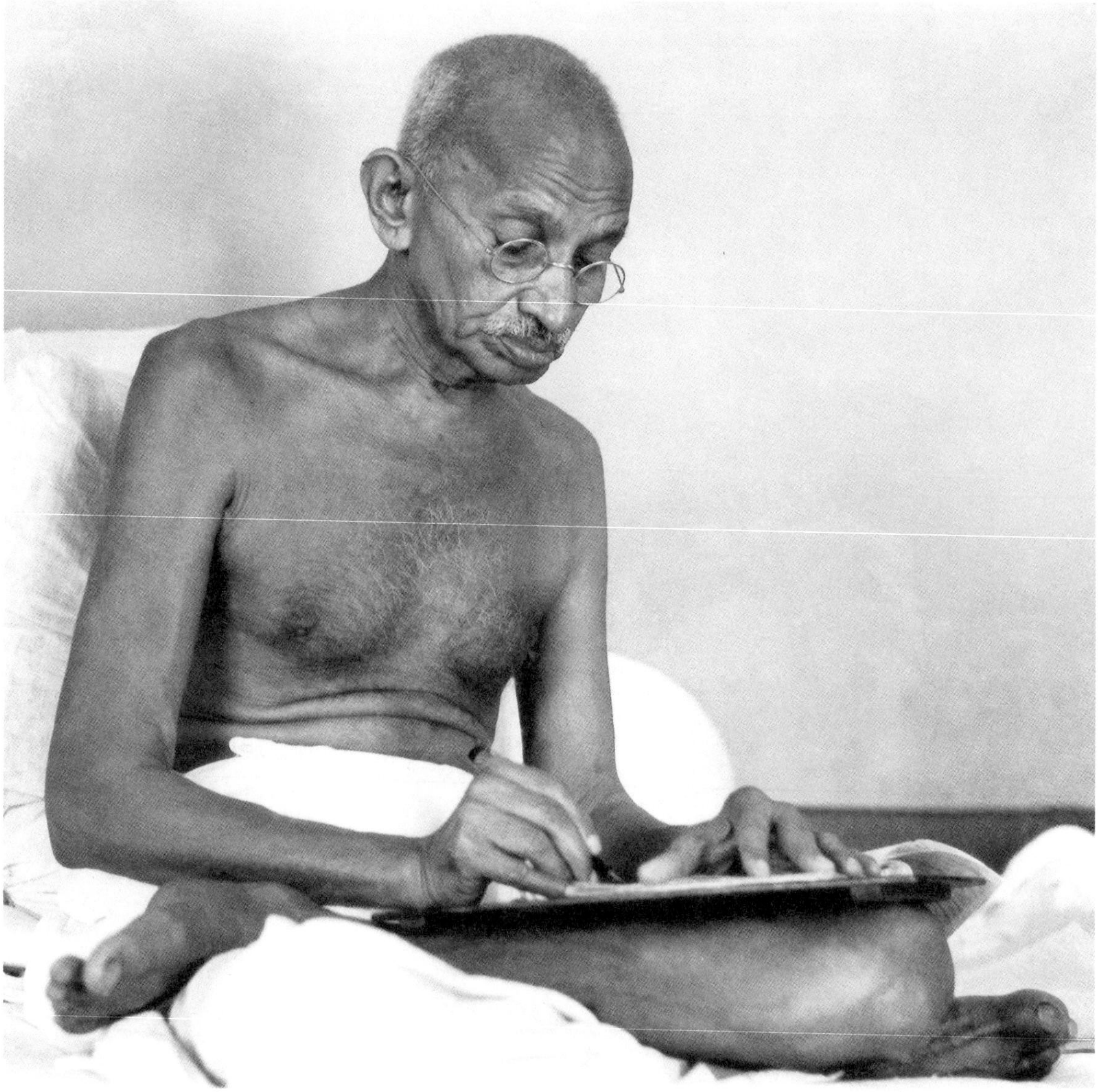

SEVEN SOCIAL SINS

MOHANDAS GANDHI
October 1947

In October 1947, Mohandas Gandhi handed a piece of paper to his visiting thirteen-year-old grandson, Arun Gandhi, upon which was written a list—one that he said contained "the seven blunders that human society commits, and that cause all the violence." The next day, Arun returned home to South Africa with the list, never to see his grandfather again. Gandhi was assassinated three months later. The very same list was originally published by Gandhi in his journal, *Young India*, in 1925, where it was titled "Seven Social Sins."

Wealth without work.

Pleasure without conscience.

Knowledge without character.

Commerce without morality.

Science without humanity.

Worship without sacrifice.

Politics without principles.

BODY PARTS FOR WHICH I AM GRATEFUL

TINA FEY
2011

American comedian Tina Fey first made a name for herself as a writer and performer on *Saturday Night Live*, a stint that began in the mid-1990s. However, it was for her television show *30 Rock*, which she created in 2006, that she won the affections of millions and numerous awards. These two lists—one of women's supposed deficiencies, the other of the body parts for which she is grateful—were written by Fey and printed in her 2011 memoir, *Bossypants*.

At any given moment on planet Earth, a woman is buying a product to correct one of the following "deficiencies":

- big pores
- oily T-zone
- cankles
- fivehead
- lunch lady arms
- nipples too big
- nipples too small
- breasts too big
- breasts too small
- one breast bigger than the other
- one breast smaller than the other (How are those two different things? I don't know.)
- nasal labial folds
- "no arch in my eyebrows!"
- FUPA (a delightfully crude acronym for a protruding lower belly)
- muffin top
- spider veins
- saddlebags
- crotch biscuits (that's what I call the wobbly triangles on one's inner thighs)
- thin lashes
- bony knees
- low hairline
- calves too big
- "no calves!"
- "green undertones in my skin"
- and my personal favorite, "bad nail beds"

If you don't have a good body, you'd better starve the body you have down to a neutral shape, then bolt on some breast implants, replace your teeth, dye your skin orange, inject your lips, sew on some hair, and call yourself the Playmate of the Year.

How do we survive this? How do we teach our daughters and our gay sons that they are good enough the way they are?

We have to lead by example. Instead of trying to fit an impossible ideal, I took a personal inventory of all my healthy body parts for which I am grateful:

- Straight Greek eyebrows. They start at the hairline at my temple and, left unchecked, will grow straight across my face and onto yours.
- A heart-shaped ass. Unfortunately, it's a right-side-up heart; the point is at the bottom.
- Droopy brown eyes designed to confuse predators into thinking I'm just on the verge of sleep and they should come back tomorrow to eat me.
- Permanently rounded shoulders from years of working at a computer.
- A rounded belly that is pushed out by my rounded posture no matter how many sit-ups I do. Which is mostly none.

• A small high waist.
• A wad of lower-back fat that never went away after I lost my "baby weight." One day in the next ten years, this back roll will meet up with my front pouch, forever obscuring my small high waist, and I will officially be my mother.
• Wide-set knockers that aren't so big but can be hoisted up once or twice a year for parades.
• Good strong legs with big gym teacher calves that I got from walking pigeon-toed my whole life.
• Wide German hips that look like somebody wrapped Pillsbury dough around a case of soda.
• My father's feet. Flat. Bony. Pale. I don't know how he even gets around, because his feet are in my shoes.

I would not trade any of these features for anybody else's. I wouldn't trade the small thin-lipped mouth that makes me resemble my nephew. I wouldn't even trade the acne scar on my right cheek, because that recurring zit spent more time with me in college than any boy ever did.

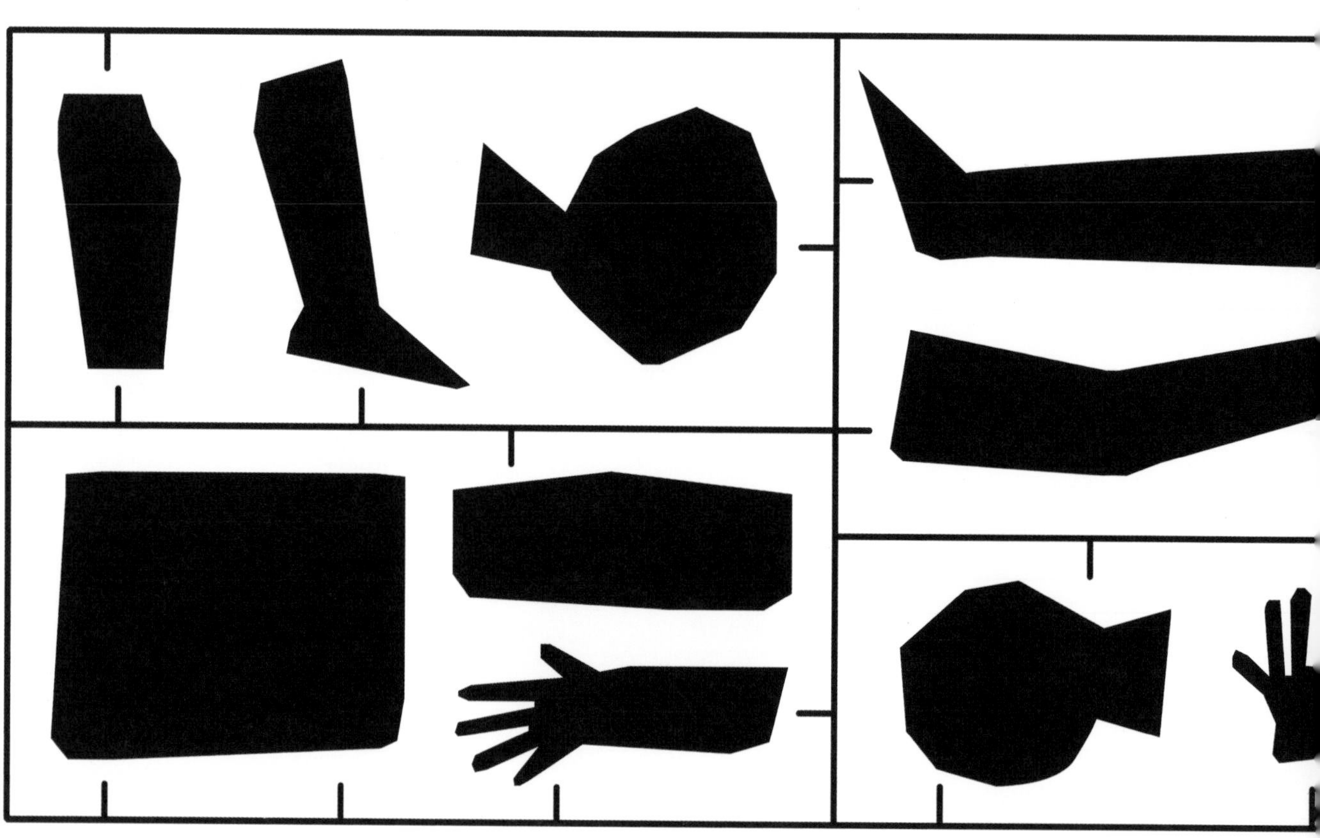

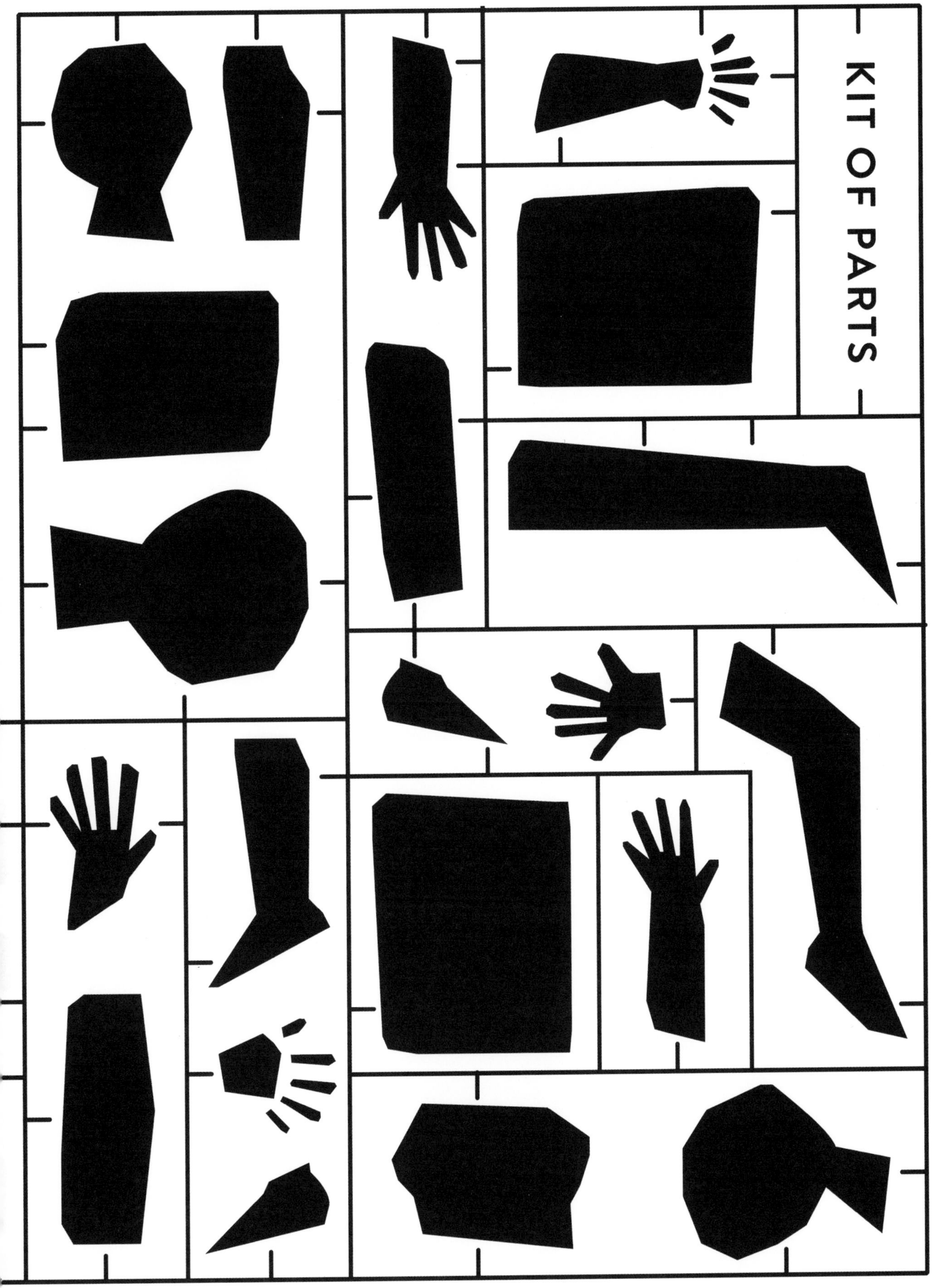
KIT OF PARTS

List No. 097

MICHELANGELO'S SHOPPING LIST

MICHELANGELO
1518

Having been commissioned by Pope Leo X to design and craft the façade of Basilica of San Lorenzo in Florence, the Italian artist known to most as Michelangelo spent his time traveling to and from Pietrasanta to quarry marble for the ultimately unrealized project. During this period, on the back of a letter dated March 18, 1518, he wrote a list of foods. This list is believed by some to be a three-meal shopping list, charmingly illustrated for the benefit of his illiterate servant; others imagine it to be simply a recollection of meals gone by; on the other hand, it could, of course, just be a doodle from the mind of a hungry artist. We will never know for certain.

pani dua
un bochal di vino
una aringa
tortegli

---

una insalata
quatro pani
un bochal di tondo
un quartuccio di bruscho
un piatello di spinaci
quatro alice
tortelli

---

sei pani
dua minestre di finochio
una aringa
un bochal di tondo

[TRANSLATION]

two bread rolls
a jug of wine
a herring
tortelli

---

a salad
four bread rolls
a jug of full-bodied wine
a quarter of dry wine
a dish of spinach
four anchovies
tortelli

---

six bread rolls
two dishes of fennel
a herring
a jug of full-bodied wine

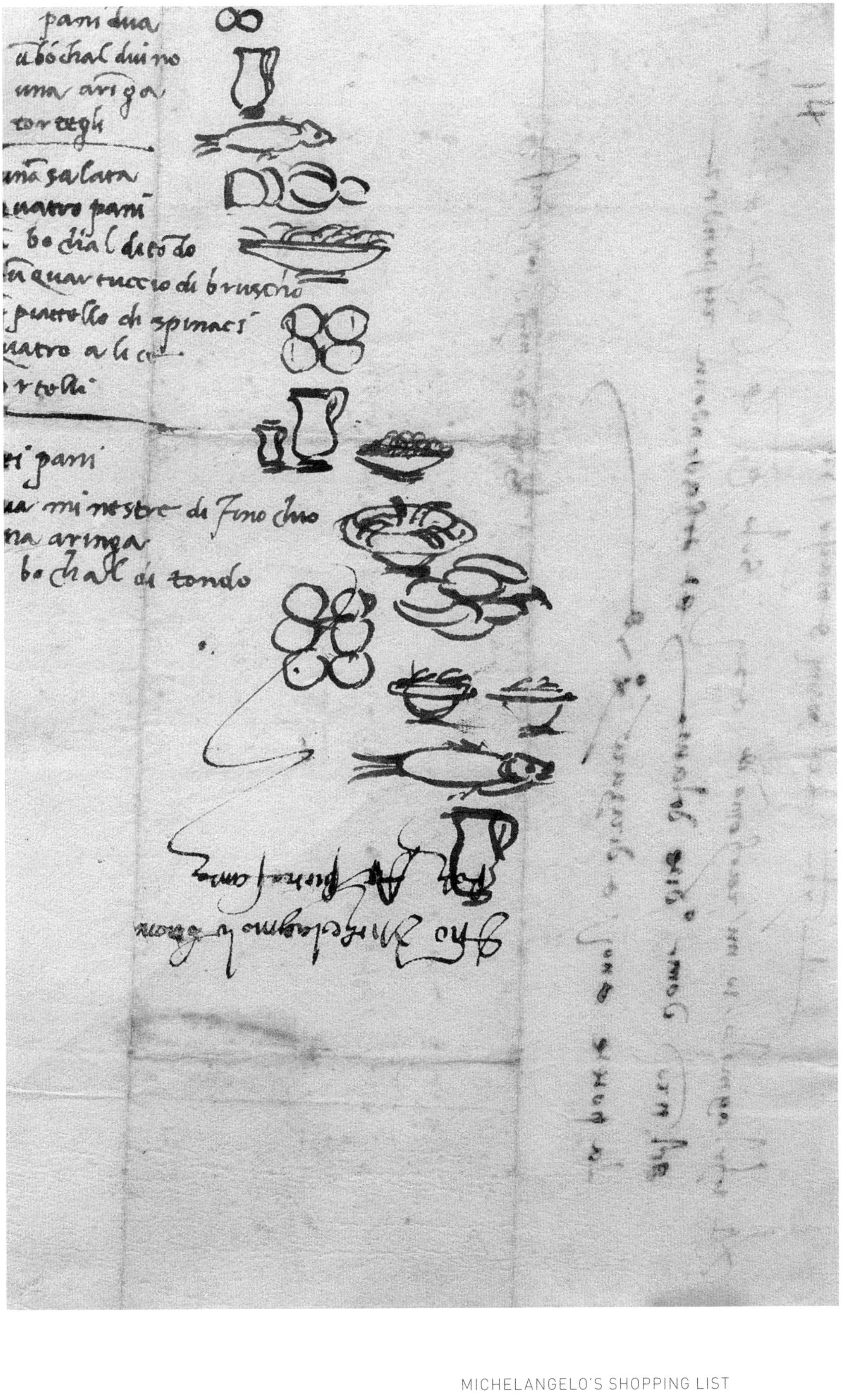
pani dua
una ariga
una salata
quatro pani
un quartuccio di bruscho
piattello di spinaci
quatro alici
pani
minestre di finochio
aringa
bochal di tondo

List No. 098

SIMILES AND COMPARISONS

RAYMOND CHANDLER
Date Unknown

The American detective fiction writer Raymond Chandler (1888–1959) laced such much-loved novels as *The Big Sleep* (1939) and *Farewell, My Lovely* (1940) with memorable turns of phrase, snappy one-liners, and lyrical similes. Chandler prepared for those similes by keeping lists of them in his notebooks, ready to be plucked out for future use. Here's just one example.

As noiseless as a finger in a glove

Lower than a badger's balls (!!) (Vulgar—belly)

As systematic as a madam counting the take

About as French as a doughnut (i.e. not French at all)

His face was long enough to wrap twice around his neck

As much sex appeal as a turtle

A nose like a straphanger's elbow

As clean as an angel's neck

Smart as a hole through nothing

A face like a collapsed lung

So tight his head squeaks when he takes his hat off

As cold as a nun's breeches

High enough to have snow on him

As shiny as a clubwoman's nose

He sipped like a hummingbird drinking dew from a curled leaf

As gaudy as a chiropractor's chart

A mouth like wilted lettuce

His smile was wide, about three quarters of an inch

A thready smile

As cold as Finnegan's feet

As rare as a fat postman (Cissy)

The triangular eye of a squirrel

Longer than a round trip to Siam

As cute as a washtub

Lonely as a caboose of a fifty car freight

A great long gallows of a man with a ravaged face and a haggard eye

A sea sick albatross

SCOTT'S TURKEY RECIPES

F. SCOTT FITZGERALD
Date Unknown

When he wasn't writing such classics as *The Great Gatsby* and *Tender Is the Night*, American novelist F. Scott Fitzgerald could often be found filling his many notebooks with anecdotes, jokes, lyrics, observations on life, and ideas for future books. Indeed, judging from those notebooks which were posthumously published, it seems that from 1932 until his death eight years later, Fitzgerald was keen to document as much of his thought process as possible. As can be seen here, he also wrote a number of lists, this particular example being a tongue-in-cheek rundown of thirteen ways to use leftover turkey.

TURKEY REMAINS AND HOW TO INTER THEM WITH NUMEROUS SCARCE RECIPES

At this post holiday season, the refrigerators of the nation are overstuffed with large masses of turkey, the sight of which is calculated to give an adult an attack of dizziness. It seems, therefore, an appropriate time to give the owners the benefit of my experience as an old gourmet, in using this surplus material. Some of the recipes have been in the family for generations. (This usually occurs when rigor mortis sets in.) They were collected over years, from old cook books, yellowed diaries of the Pilgrim Fathers, mail order catalogues, golf-bats and trash cans. Not one but has been tried and proven—there are headstones all over America to testify to the fact.

Very well then: here goes:

1. *Turkey Cocktail:* To one large turkey add one gallon of vermouth and a demijohn of angostura bitters. Shake.

2. *Turkey à la Française:* Take a large ripe turkey, prepare as for basting and stuff with old watches and chains and monkey meat. Proceed as with cottage pudding.

3. *Turkey and Water:* Take one turkey and one pan of water. Heat the latter to the boiling point and then put in the refrigerator. When it has jelled, drown the turkey in it. Eat. In preparing this recipe it is best to have a few ham sandwiches around in case things go wrong.

4. *Turkey Mongole:* Take three butts of salami and a large turkey skeleton, from which the feathers and natural stuffing have been removed. Lay them out on the table and call up some Mongole in the neighborhood to tell you how to proceed from there.

5. *Turkey Mousse:* Seed a large prone turkey, being careful to remove the bones, flesh, fins, gravy, etc. Blow up with a bicycle pump. Mount in becoming style and hang in the front hall.

6. *Stolen Turkey:* Walk quickly from the market, and, if accosted, remark with a laugh that it had just flown into your arms and you hadn't noticed it. Then drop the turkey with the white of one egg—well, anyhow, beat it.

7. *Turkey à la Crême:* Prepare the crême a day in advance. Deluge the turkey with it and cook for six days over a blast furnace. Wrap in fly paper and serve.

8. *Turkey Hash:* This is the delight of all connoisseurs of the holiday beast, but few understand how really to prepare it. Like a lobster, it must be plunged alive into boiling water, until it becomes bright red or purple or something, and then before the color fades, placed quickly in a washing machine and allowed to stew in its own gore as it is whirled around. Only then is it ready for hash. To hash, take a large sharp tool like a nail-file or, if none is handy, a bayonet will serve the purpose—and then get at it! Hash it well! Bind the remains with dental floss and serve.

9. *Feathered Turkey:* To prepare this, a turkey is necessary and a one pounder cannon to compel anyone to eat it. Broil the feathers and stuff with sage-brush, old clothes, almost anything you can dig up. Then sit down and simmer. The feathers are to be eaten like artichokes (and this is not to be confused with the old Roman custom of tickling the throat.)

10. *Turkey à la Maryland:* Take a plump turkey to a barber's and have him shaved, or if a female bird, given a facial and a water wave. Then, before killing him, stuff with old newspapers and put him to roost. He can then be served hot or raw, usually with a thick gravy of mineral oil and rubbing alcohol. (Note: This recipe was given me by an old black mammy.)

11. *Turkey Remnant:* This is one of the most useful recipes for, though not, "chic," it tells us what to do with the turkey after the holiday, and how to extract the most value from it. Take the remnants, or, if they have been consumed, take the various plates on which the turkey or its parts have rested and stew them for two hours in milk of magnesia. Stuff with moth-balls.

12. *Turkey with Whiskey Sauce:* This recipe is for a party of four. Obtain a gallon of whiskey, and allow it to age for several hours. Then serve, allowing one quart for each guest. The next day the turkey should be added, little by little, constantly stirring and basting.

13. *For Weddings or Funerals:* Obtain a gross of small white boxes such as are used for bride's cake. Cut the turkey into small squares, roast, stuff, kill, boil, bake and allow to skewer. Now we are ready to begin. Fill each box with a quantity of soup stock and pile in a handy place. As the liquid elapses, the prepared turkey is added until the guests arrive. The boxes delicately tied with white ribbons are then placed in the handbags of the ladies, or in the men's side pockets.

There I guess that's enough turkey talk. I hope I'll never see or hear of another until—well, until next year.

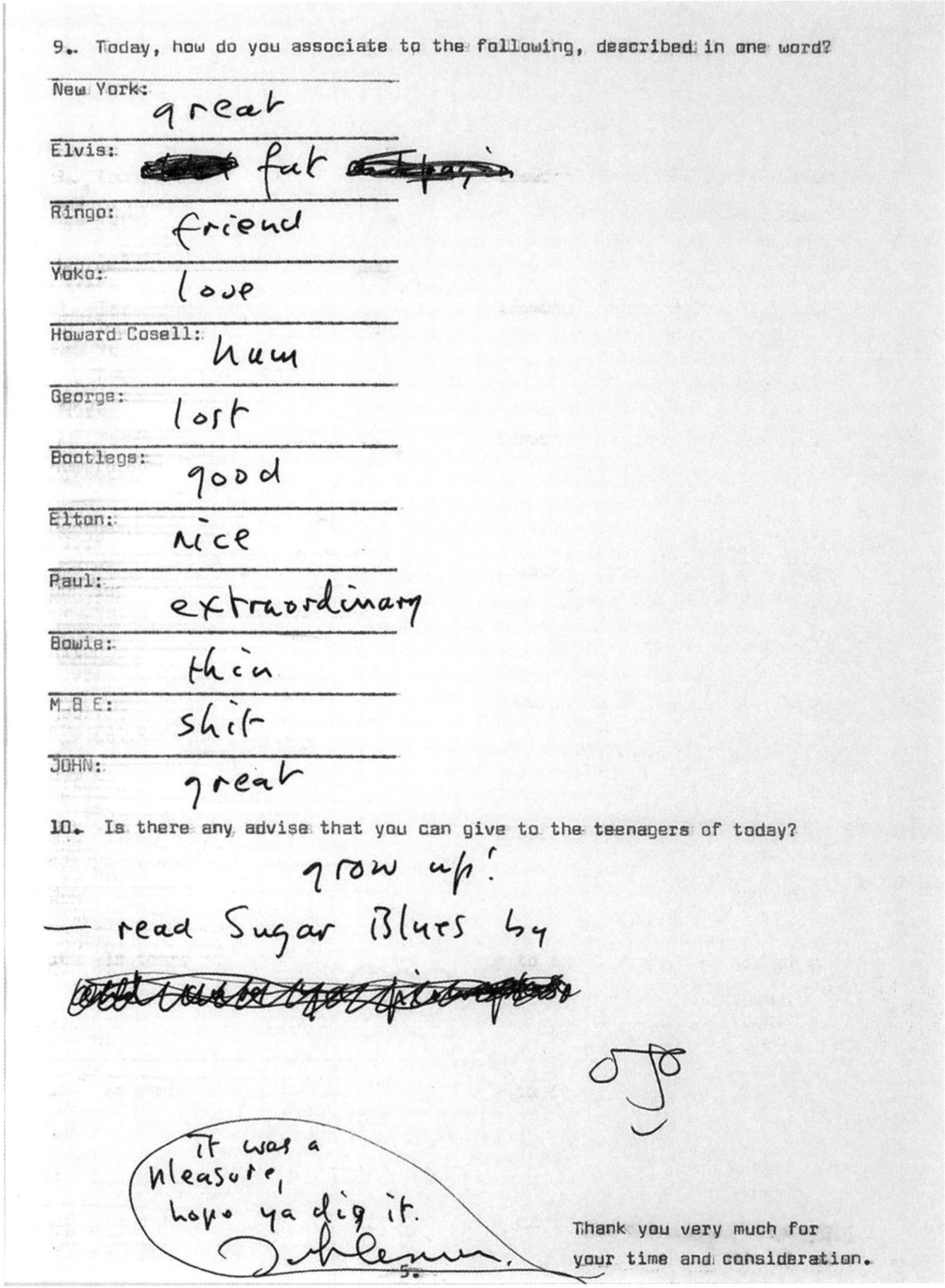

9. Today, how do you associate to the following, described in one word?

New York: great

Elvis: [illegible] fat [illegible]

Ringo: friend

Yoko: love

Howard Cosell: ham

George: lost

Bootlegs: good

Elton: nice

Paul: extraordinary

Bowie: thin

M.B.E: shit

JOHN: great

10. Is there any advise that you can give to the teenagers of today?

grow up!

— read Sugar Blues by

[illegible]

It was a pleasure, hope ya dig it.

John Lennon

Thank you very much for your time and consideration.

5.

ELVIS: FAT

JOHN LENNON
1976

In 1976, a young man named Stuart took a chance and sent six pages of interview questions to one of the most famous people on the planet, John Lennon. Much to his surprise, a reply soon arrived. Here we have Question 9, in which Stuart offered a list of ten things and asked Lennon to describe each with a single word. Four years later, it was Howard "Ham" Cosell, listed here, who would announce the death of John Lennon to millions of US television viewers during a *Monday Night Football* game.

BOOKS YOU OUGHT TO READ

ERNEST HEMINGWAY
1934

In the spring of 1934, a twenty-two-year-old aspiring novelist named Arnold Samuelson hitch-hiked from Minnesota to Key West, Florida, to meet his idol, Ernest Hemingway. Hoping at best to spend ten minutes in the company of the "greatest writer alive," Samuelson found himself taken under the author's wing, and he spent the best part of the next year as Hemingway's deck-hand aboard his boat, *Pilar*. Their very first day together, Hemingway offered an early piece of advice to his young visitor: upon learning that he had yet to read *War and Peace*, Hemingway said, "That's a damned good book. You ought to read it. We'll go up to my workshop, and I'll make out a list you ought to read."

Stephen Crane —
The Blue Hotel
The Open Boat.
Madame Bovary — Gustave Flaubert
Dubliners — James Joyce —
The Red and The Black — By Stendhal —
(OF Human Bondage — Somerset Maugham) —
Anna Karenina — Tolstoy —
War and Peace — Tolstoy —
Buddenbrooks — Thomas Mann —
Hail and Farewell — George Moore —
Brothers Karamazov — Doestoevsky —
Oxford Book of English Verse —
The Enormous Room — EE Cummings.
Wuthering Heights — Emily Bronte
Far Away and Long Ago — W.H. Hudson —
The American — Henry James.

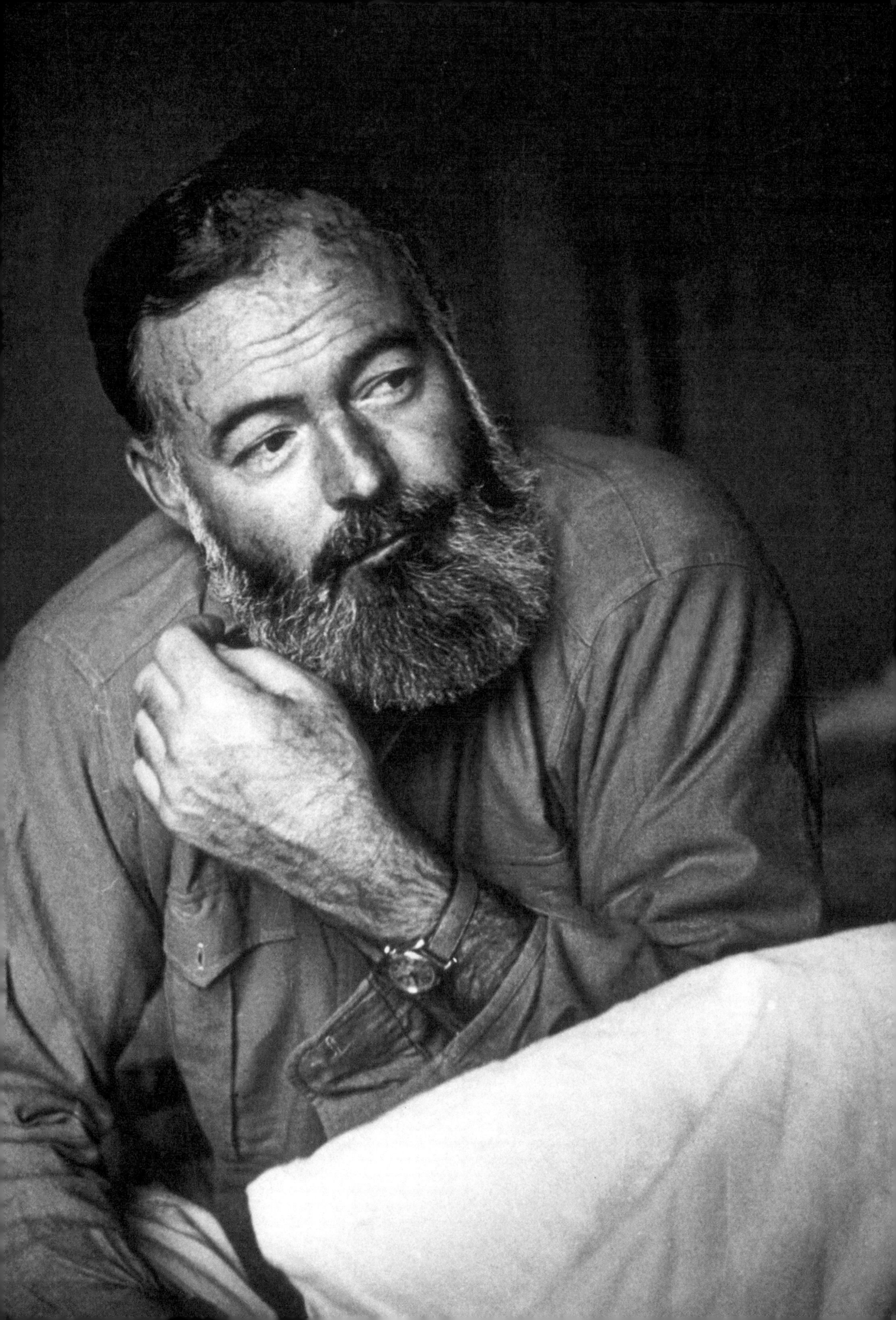

Basket. Ball.

The ball to be an ordinary Association foot ball.

1. The ball may be thrown in any direction with one or both hands.

2. The ball may be batted in any direction with one or both hands (never with the fist).

3. A player cannot run with the ball, the player must throw it from the spot on which he catches it, allowance to be made for a man who catches the ball when running at a good speed.

4. The ball must be held in or between the hands, the arms or body must not be used for holding it.

5. No shouldering, holding, pushing, tripping or striking, in any way the person of an opponent shall be allowed. The first infringement of this rule by any person shall count as a foul, the second shall disqualify him until the next goal is made, or if there was evident intent to injure the person, for the whole of the game, no substitute allowed.

6. A foul is striking at the ball with the fist, violation of rules 3 and 4, and such as described in rule 5.

7. If either side makes three consecutive fouls it shall count a goal for the opponents (consecutive means without the opponents in the meantime making a foul).

8. A goal shall be made when the ball is thrown or batted from the grounds into the basket and stays there, providing those defending the goal do not touch or disturbe the goal. If the ball rests on the edge and the opponent moves the basket it shall count as a

BASKET. BALL.

JAMES NAISMITH

December 6, 1891

In December 1891, having been asked to invent a new indoor game for his students during the winter months, a teacher named James Naismith, who hailed from Canada, wrote this thirteen-point list of rules and attached it to the wall of a gym at the YMCA Training School in Springfield, Massachusetts. The game he had just invented was basketball. And today, more than a century later, the Basketball Hall of Fame, named after James Naismith, is in Springfield, Massachusetts. Over the years, Naismith's list has evolved to include rules for such things as dribbling and dunking. The official rules of basketball, as approved by the FIBA, are now eighty pages long. The original draft of this list was sold by Sotheby's auction house in 2012 for $4.3 million.

goal.

9. When the ball goes out of bounds it shall be thrown into the field, and played by the person first touching it. In case of a dispute the umpire shall throw it straight into the field. The thrower in is allowed five seconds, if he holds it longer it shall go to the opponent. If any side presists in delaying the game, the umpire shall call a foul on them.

10. The umpire shall be judge of the men, and shall note the fouls, and notify the referee when three consecutive fouls have been made. He shall have power to disqualify men according to Rule 5.

11. The referee shall be judge of the ball and shall decide when the ball is in play, in bounds, and to which side it belongs, and shall keep the time. He shall decide when a goal has been made, and keep account of the goals with any other duties that are usually performed by a referee.

12. The time shall be two fifteen minutes halves, with five minutes rest between.

13. The side making the most goals in that time shall be declared the winners. In case of a draw the game may, by agreement of the captains, be continued until another goal is made.

First draft of Basket Ball rules.
Hung in the gym that the boys might
learn the rules - Dec. 1891 James Naismith
6-28-31.

List No. 103

DON'TS FOR WOMEN RIDERS

UNIQUE CYCLING CLUB OF CHICAGO

June 21, 1895

In June 1895, the New Jersey's *Newark Sunday Advocate* ran an alarming story, syndicated from *New York World*, about a recent gathering of the Unique Cycling Club of Chicago—an event that saw two lady riders publicly shamed for having the audacity to turn up wearing short skirts over their bloomers. Bloomers, yes; but short skirts over them, no. The story can be seen here, as can a list that followed the piece. (The "century" referred to below was a one-hundred-mile bike ride that was to be completed within twelve hours.) Published in an effort to better educate female cyclists following their sartorial fiasco, it was titled "Don'ts for Women Riders."

BLOOMERS IN CHICAGO.

How the Unique Club Disciplined Two Members Who Appeared In Skirts.

The Unique Cycling club of Chicago is all that its name implies. One of its laws is that on all runs bloomers or knickerbockers shall be worn, and two members who disobeyed this rule recently met with a punishment that they will not forget soon. Union park was the rendezvous for the last run, and 50 members turned out. The president. Mrs. Langdon, and the captain, Miss Bunker, observed two women wearing short skirts over their bloomers.

"Take the skirts off," ordered Captain Bunker.

"Indeed we won't," was the reply.

A crowd of 200 had collected to see the start. The president and the captain held a consultation, and then, taking several strong armed members with them, fell on the skirt wearers and stripped them down to their bloomers.

"It was done in all seriousness," said Mrs. Langdon. "The club's rules are made to be kept and not to be broken. Why did we take off the skirts in public? For no other reason but to make examples of the offenders. They publicly defied our rules and were punished accordingly."—American Wheelman

DON'TS FOR WOMEN RIDERS.

Don't be a fright
Don't faint on the road.
Don't wear a man's cap.
Don't wear tight garters.
Don't forget your toolbag
Don't attempt a "century."
Don't coast. It is dangerous.
Don't criticise people's "legs."
Don't boast of your long rides
Don't wear loud hued leggings
Don't cultivate a "bicycle face."
Don't refuse assistance up a hill.
Don't wear clothes that don't fit.
Don't "talk bicycle" at the table.
Don't neglect a "light's out" cry.
Don't wear jewelry while on a tour.
Don't race. Leave that to the scorchers.

Don't imagine everybody is looking at you.

Don't go to church in your bicycle costume.

Don't wear laced boots. They are tiresome.

Don't keep your mouth open on dirty roads.

Don't converse while in a scorching position.

Don't go out after dark without a male escort.

Don't contest the right of way with cable cars.

Don't wear a garden party hat with bloomers.

Don't wear white kid gloves. Silk is the thing.

Don't chew gum. Exercise your jaws in private.

Don't tempt fate by riding too near the curbstone.

Don't ask, "What do you think of my bloomers?"

Don't use bicycle slang. Leave that to the boys.

Don't discuss bloomers with every man you know.

Don't think you look as pretty as every fashion plate.

Don't go out without a needle, thread and thimble.

Don't allow your dear little Fido to accompany you.

Don't scratch a match on the seat of your bloomers.

Don't try to have every article of your attire "match"

Don't let your golden hair be hanging down your back.

Don't appear in public until you have learned to ride well.

Don't try to ride in your brother's clothes "to see how it feels."

Don't overdo things. Let cycling be a recreation, not a labor.

Don't ignore the laws of the road because you are a woman.

Don't throw your legs over the handle bar and coast down hill.

Don't scream if you meet a cow. If she sees you first, she will run.

Don't cultivate everything that is up to date because you ride a wheel.

Don't emulate your brother's attitude if he rides parallel with the ground.

Don't undertake a long ride if you are not confident of performing it easily.

Don't appear to be up on "records" and "record smashing." That is sporty.—New York World.

FRANKLIN'S THIRTEEN VIRTUES

BENJAMIN FRANKLIN
1726

Benjamin Franklin (1706–1790) was a high achiever, to say the least. At various stages of his life he was a scientist, musician, printer, journalist, author, businessman, politician, and signatory to the Constitution of the United States. Such a diverse range of roles, somehow all mastered by one man! All of which certainly makes his attitude to life and work worth studying by those attempting to better themselves. And the list seen here makes a perfect start. Here is his set of thirteen virtues to live by, written by the twenty-year-old Franklin in 1726 in an attempt to "live without committing any fault at any time." And follow them he did (if not always successfully), until his death at age eighty-four, all the while keeping a book filled with charts to track his progress.

1. TEMPERANCE. Eat not to dullness; drink not to elevation.
2. SILENCE. Speak not but what may benefit others or yourself; avoid trifling conversation.
3. ORDER. Let all your things have their places; let each part of your business have its time.
4. RESOLUTION. Resolve to perform what you ought; perform without fail what you resolve.
5. FRUGALITY. Make no expense but to do good to others or yourself; i.e., waste nothing.
6. INDUSTRY. Lose no time; be always employ'd in something useful; cut off all unnecessary actions.
7. SINCERITY. Use no hurtful deceit; think innocently and justly, and, if you speak, speak accordingly.
8. JUSTICE. Wrong none by doing injuries, or omitting the benefits that are your duty.
9. MODERATION. Avoid extreams; forbear resenting injuries so much as you think they deserve.
10. CLEANLINESS. Tolerate no uncleanliness in body, cloaths, or habitation.
11. TRANQUILLITY. Be not disturbed at trifles, or at accidents common or unavoidable.
12. CHASTITY. Rarely use venery but for health or offspring, never to dulness, weakness, or the injury of your own or another's peace or reputation.
13. HUMILITY. Imitate Jesus and Socrates.

TEMPERANCE.

Eat not to dulness: drink not to elevation.

	Sun.	M.	T.	W.	Th.	F.	S.
Temp.							
Sil.							
Ord.	*	*		*		*	
Res.	*	*	*		*	*	*
Fru.		*				*	
Ind.		*				*	
Sinc.			*				
Jus.							
Mod.							
Clea.							
Tran.							
Chas.							
Hum.							

List No. 105

RESCUE ETIQUETTE

MARK TWAIN
Date Unknown

In 1962, fifty-two years after the death of Mark Twain, a collection of his previously unseen writing was published in the form of a book titled *Letters from the Earth.* Included in that book, along with numerous pieces on such subjects as religion and morality, is an extract from Twain's "unfinished burlesque of books on etiquette," which presents this listing, in order of importance, of twenty-seven types of people and furniture to be rescued from boardinghouse fires.

In assisting at a fire in a boarding house, the true gentleman will always save the young ladies first—making no distinction in favor of personal attractions, or social eminence, or pecuniary predominance—but taking them as they come, and firing them out with as much celerity as shall be consistent with decorum. There are exceptions, of course, to all rules; the exceptions to this one are:

Partiality, in the matter of rescue, to be shown to:

1. Fiancées.
2. Persons toward whom the operator feels a tender sentiment, but has not yet declared himself.
3. Sisters.
4. Stepsisters.
5. Nieces.
6. First cousins.
7. Cripples.
8. Second cousins.
9. Invalids.
10. Young-lady relations by marriage.
11. Third cousins, and young-lady friends of the family.
12. The Unclassified.

Other material in boarding house is to be rescued in the following order:

13. Babies.
14. Children under 10 years of age.
15. Young widows.
16. Young married females.
17. Elderly married ditto.
18. Elderly widows.
19. Clergymen.
20. Boarders in general.
21. Female domestics.
22. Male ditto.
23. Landlady.
24. Landlord.
25. Firemen.
26. Furniture.
27. Mothers-in-law.

List No. 106

MY FAVORITE BOOKS

EDITH WHARTON
1909

Novelist Edith Wharton was born in 1862 in New York and lived in New England for much of her early life, working as a writer and garden and interior designer. It wasn't until 1920, when she had settled in France, that she wrote *The Age of Innocence*, her twelfth novel and the one that would see her awarded a Pulitzer Prize for Fiction—the first ever awarded to a woman. She was also nominated for a Nobel Prize in Literature on three occasions. In 1909, she wrote a list of her favorite books.

My Favorite Books, 1909

Faust; Goethe
Shakespeare
Divina Commedia; Dante Alighieri
Seneca the Younger
Giacomo Leopardi, John Keats
Blaise Pascal: *Pensées & Provinciales*
Schopenhauer
Origin of Species; Charles Darwin
Walt Whitman; *The Leaves of Grass*
Nietzsche: *Jenseits v. gut u Böse* (Beyond Good and Evil); *Genealogie der Moral* (On the Genealogy of Morality); *Wille zur Macht* (The Will to Power)
Lettres de Flaubert
Goethe's Conversations with Eckermann
Le Rouge et la noir; Stendhal
La Chartreuse de Parme; Stendhal
Mme Bovary; Gustave Flaubert
The Egoist; George Meredith
Anna Karenina; Leo Tolstoy
Harry Richmond; George Meredith
The Portrait of a Lady; Henry James
Adolphe; Benjamin Constant
Manon Lescaut; Abbé Prévost
Tyndall's Essays

List No. 107

CELESTIAL EMPORIUM OF BENEVOLENT KNOWLEDGE

JORGE LUIS BORGES
1942

In 1942, Argentine writer Jorge Luis Borges penned *El idioma analítico de John Wilkins* (The Analytical Language of John Wilkins), an essay in which he discussed the difficulties associated with man's repeated attempts to classify all that existed. Borges did this, primarily, by focusing on a universal language proposed by seventeenth-century philosopher John Wilkins. Wilkins's concept divided the contents of the universe into forty *genera*, each of which gave an object its first two letters; those categories were then split into 241 *differences*, which offered another letter; and those differences were then divided into 2,030 *species* to add the final fourth letter. So, for example, in Wilkins's language, *salmon* would become *Zana*, as follows: *Za* would identify "fish" (the genus); *Zan* would identify "squamous river fish" (the difference); and *Zana* would identify "largest red-fleshed kind" (the species).

Unimpressed, Borges ridiculed the idea, comparing the system's "ambiguities, redundancies, and deficiencies" to a taxonomy of the animal kingdom found in *Celestial Emporium of Benevolent Knowledge*, an ancient Chinese encyclopedia. Unbeknownst to the countless people who went on to be influenced by *Celestial Emporium of Benevolent Knowledge*, this delightful text didn't actually exist outside of Borges's imagination. Here's a list of how the *Emporium* went about its classifications.

Those that belong to the emperor

Embalmed ones

Those that are trained

Suckling pigs

Mermaids (or Sirens)

Fabulous ones

Stray dogs

Those that are included in this classification

Those that tremble as if they were mad

Innumerable ones

Those drawn with a very fine camel hair brush

Et cetera

Those that have just broken the flower vase

Those that, at a distance, resemble flies

List No. 108

A LIBERAL DECALOGUE

BERTRAND RUSSELL
December 16, 1951

Bertrand Russell (1872–1970) was a distinguished British philosopher, responsible for, among other writings, *On Denoting*, a seminal essay described by fellow philosopher Frank P. Ramsey as "that paradigm of philosophy." He was also, at various points in his lifetime, a mathematician, social critic, and teacher. In 1951 he wrote a piece on liberalism in the *New York Times Magazine*, at the end of which was this set of commandments to be passed on by teachers. It was later reprinted in his autobiography, under the title "A Liberal Decalogue."

Perhaps the essence of the Liberal outlook could be summed up in a new decalogue, not intended to replace the old one but only to supplement it. The Ten Commandments that, as a teacher, I should wish to promulgate, might be set forth as follows:

1. Do not feel absolutely certain of anything.

2. Do not think it worth while to proceed by concealing evidence, for the evidence is sure to come to light.

3. Never try to discourage thinking for you are sure to succeed.

4. When you meet with opposition, even if it should be from your husband or your children, endeavour to overcome it by argument and not by authority, for a victory dependent upon authority is unreal and illusory.

5. Have no respect for the authority of others, for there are always contrary authorities to be found.

6. Do not use power to suppress opinions you think pernicious, for if you do the opinions will suppress you.

7. Do not fear to be eccentric in opinion, for every opinion now accepted was once eccentric.

8. Find more pleasure in intelligent dissent than in passive agreement, for, if you value intelligence as you should, the former implies a deeper agreement than the latter.

9. Be scrupulously truthful, even if the truth is inconvenient, for it is more inconvenient when you try to conceal it.

10. Do not feel envious of the happiness of those who live in a fool's paradise, for only a fool will think that it is happiness.

List No. 109

HENSLOWE'S INVENTORY

PHILIP HENSLOWE
March 10, 1598

Born in the 1550s, Philip Henslowe was a famous theater owner whose establishments, particularly the Rose, were in direct competition with the Globe Theater, co-owned by William Shakespeare and where his plays were performed. Among the playwrights whose work Henslowe championed were Ben Johnson and Christopher Marlowe. Between 1592 and 1603, Henslowe kept a record of his financial dealings, box office takings, etc., in what is now known as *Henslowe's Diary*—a historically invaluable document that throws light on the theater industry of that period as no other. Featured in that diary is this wonderful Elizabethan inventory of props relating to the Admiral's Men, Henslowe's resident performing company for many years.

The inventory taken of all the properties for my Lord Admiral's Men on the 10th of March 1598

Item: 1 rock, 1 cage, 1 tomb, 1 Hell mouth.
Item: 1 tomb of Guido, 1 tomb of Dido, 1 bedstead.
Item: 8 lances, 1 pair of stairs for *Phaeton*.
Item: 2 steeples, and 1 chime of bells, and 1 beacon.
Item: 1 hecfor for the play of Phaeton, the limbs dead.
Item: 1 globe, and 1 golden scepter; 3 clubs.
Item: 2 marchpanes, and the city of Rome.
Item: 1 golden fleece; 2 rackets; 1 bay tree.
Item: 1 wooden hatchet; 1 leather hatchet.
Item: 1 wooden canopy; old Mahomet's head.
Item: 1 lion skin; 1 bear's skin; and Phaeton's limbs, and Phaeton chariot; and Argus' head.
Item: Neptune's fork and garland.
Item: 1 crozier's staff; Kent's wooden leg.
Item: Iris's head, and rainbow; 1 little altar.
Item: 8 vizards; Tamburlaine's bridle; 1 wooden mattock.
Item: Cupid's bow, and quiver; the cloth of the sun and moon.
Item: 1 boar's head and Cerberus's 3 heads.
Item: 1 caduceus; 2 moss banks, and 1 snake.
Item: 2 fans of feathers; Belin Dun's stable; 1 tree of golden apples; Tantalus's tree; 9 iron targets.
Item: 1 copper target, and 17 foils.
Item: 4 wooden targets; 1 greave armour.
Item: 1 sign for Mother Redcap; 1 buckler.
Item: Mercury's wings; Tasso's picture; 1 helmet with a dragon; 1 shield with 3 lions; 1 elm bowl.
Item: 1 chain of dragons; 1 gilt spear.
Item: 2 coffins; 1 bull's head; and 1 vulture.
Item: 3 tumbrils, 1 dragon in *Faustus*.
Item: 1 lion; 2 lion heads; 1 great horse with his legs; 1 sack-butt.
Item: 1 wheel and frame in the *Siege of London*.
Item: 1 pair of wrought gloves.
Item: 1 pope's mitre.
Item: 3 Imperial crowns; 1 plain crown.
Item: 1 ghost's crown; 1 crown with a sun.
Item: 1 frame for the heading in *Black John*.
Item: 1 black dog.
Item: 1 cauldron for the Jew.

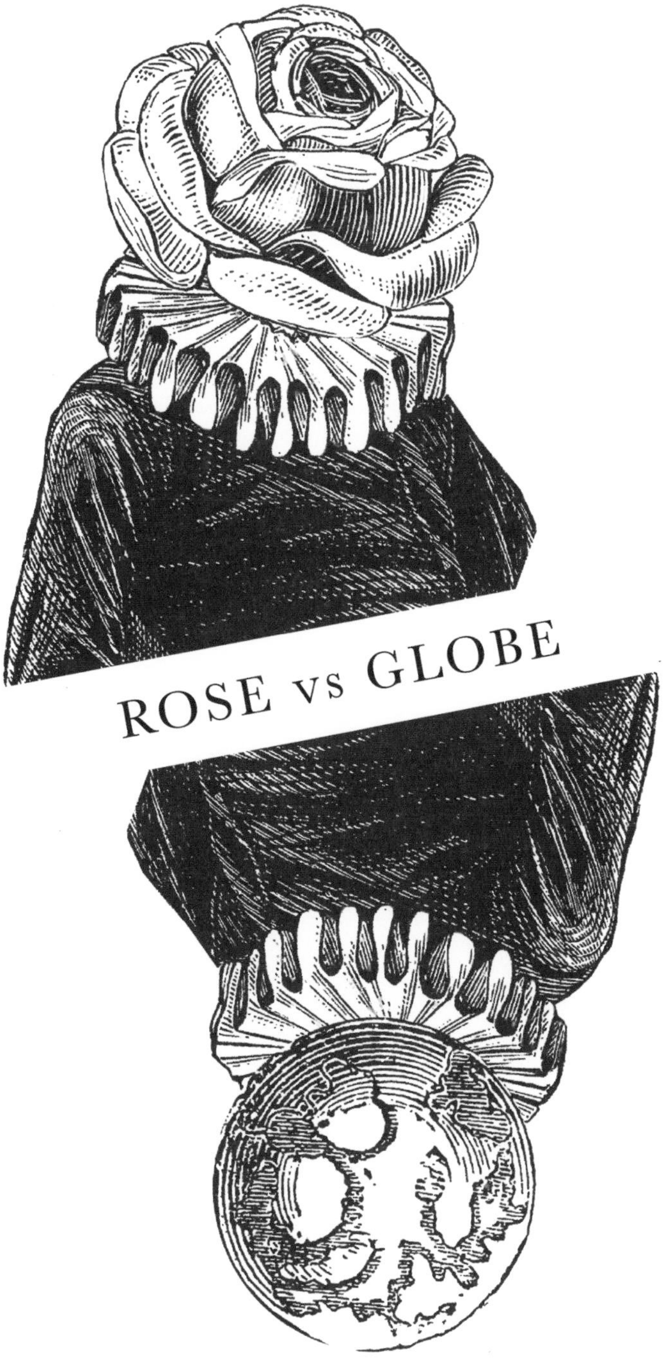
ROSE vs GLOBE

MIDWESTERNISMS

DAVID FOSTER WALLACE
1997

In April 2011, almost three years after his suicide at the age of forty-six, David Foster Wallace's unfinished novel, *The Pale King*—a sprawling, brilliant, and often difficult work largely set in offices of the Internal Revenue Service in the Midwestern United States—was published. Research for the novel had begun long before, in 1997, the year after publication of his magnum opus, *Infinite Jest*, at which point it had a working title of *Sir John Feelgood* ("SJF"). Wallace had himself been brought up in the Midwest and one of his first tasks in preparation for SJF had been to write, in his spiral notebook, this list of "Midwesternisms."

- Pronouncing 'theater' like it had a y in it — theayter theyater
- Pronouncing 'vehicle' with a h — pronouncing the h in 'vehicle'
- Solicism: 'Itty-tiny.' 'An itty-tiny little man
- 'Because you know why?'
- Preceding a question with 'Question': 'Question. Why aren't office supplies a revenue expenditure instead of an operating expense.'

Malaprops
- 'The office encouraged them that whoever had a problem should. . .'
- 'This stuff's all been mulling around in my head.'
- 'The more I keep [?], I realize how little I know.'
- 'That irks my feelings.'
- 'He would have made short work of me in a hurry.'
- 'The thing is that I'm serious.'
- 'It just got all scrabbled up in my head.'
- 'Involved' for 'evolved.' 'And it involved into a bad situation.'
- 'I had a circumstance happen.'
- 'Whatnot.' 'and whatnot.'
- 'Set' for 'sit.' 'Set down. Go on and set yourself down here.'
- Academic stutter (not a true stutter; the stutter of compression and density, the plosive a bottleneck – 'The the the the radical discontent of business under the New Deal.'
- 'Just let them get it under their belt and chew on it a while.'

[illegible] [illegible]

~97

'He'd like for you to call him.'

MidWesternisms (2)

- Prounceing 'theater' like it hade y in it – theayter (theyater)
- Pronouncing 'vehicle' with an h – pronouncing the h in 'vehicle'–
- Soleeism: 'Itty-tiny.' 'An itty-tiny little man
- 'Because you know why?'
- Preceding a question with 'Question.' : 'Question. Why aren't office supplies a revenue expenditure instead of an operating expense.'

Malaprops

- 'The office encouraged them that whoever had a problem should...'
- 'This stuff's all been mulling around in my head.'
- 'The more I keep coming, I realize how little I know'
- 'That irks my feelings.'
- 'He would have made short work of me in a hurry.'
- 'The thing is that I'm serious.'
- 'It just got all scrabbled up in my head.'
- 'Involved' for 'evolved.' 'And it involved into a bad situation.'
- 'I had a circumstance happen.'
- 'Whatnot.' 'and whatnot.'
- 'Set' for 'sit.' '~~Sit~~ Set down. go on and set yourself down here.
- Academic stutter (not a true stutter; the stutter of
- ~~[illegible]~~ compression and density, the plosive a bottleneck – 'The the the the radical discontent of ~~taxpayers~~ business under the New Deal.'
- 'Just let them get it under their belt and chew on it a while.'

NAMING THE PHONOGRAPH

THOMAS EDISON
November 1877

In November 1877, prolific American inventor Thomas Edison debuted his latest project, the "phonograph," a groundbreaking device that was capable of not just recording sound on its cylinders, but also replaying it, and which directly inspired the development of Emile Berliner's cheaper, and ultimately more successful, record-playing gramophone some years later. The earliest instance of the name "phonograph" can be found in a page of Edison's notebook dated August 1877. Shortly before its launch, however, he and his colleagues came up with dozens of alternative monikers for the device—most bearing prefixes of Greek or Latin origin—and collated them in this list. None was used.

T. A. Edison.

Auto-Electrograph = Electric Pen
Tel-autograph
Tel-autophone
Polyphone = Manifold Sounder
Autophone = Self sounder
Kosmophone = Universal Sounder
Acoustophone = Sound hearer = Audible speaker
Octophone = Ear-sounder = speaker
Anitphone = Back-talker
Liguphone = Clear speaker
Minuttophone = Minute-sounder
Meistophone = Smallest sounder
Anchiphone = Near sounder or speaker
Palmatophone = Vibration sounder
Chronophone = Time-announcer = Speaking clock
Didaskophone = Teaching speaker = Portable teacher
Glottophone = Language sounder or speaker
Climatophone = Weather announcer
Atmophone = Fog sounder or Vapor-speaker
Palmophone = Pendulum sounder or Sounding pendulum
Pinakophone = Speaking Register
Hemerologophone = Speaking almanac
Kalendophone = Speaking Calendar
Sphygmophone = Pulse speaker
Halmophone = Heart-beat-sounder
Seismophone = Earthquake sounder
Electrophone = Electric speaker
Brontophone = Thunder sounder
Klangophone = Bird-cry sounder
Surigmophone = Whistling sounder
Bremophone = Wind sounder
Bittako-phone = Parrot speaker
Krogmophone = Croaking or Cawing sounder
Hulagmophone = Barking sounder
Trematophone = Sound borer
Telephemist telephemy telepheme
Electrophemist electrophemy electropheme
Phemegraph = speech writer
Omphegraph-gram = voice writer or recorder
Melodograph Melograph Melpograph-gram = song writer
Epograph = speech writer, lecture or sermon
Rhetograph = speech writer
Kinemograph = motion writer
Atmophone = vapor or steam sound
Aerophone = air-sound
Symphraxometer = pressure measurer
Synothemeter = pressure measurer
Orcheograph = vibration record
Orcheometer

T. A. EDISON.

Menlo Park, N. J., ... 187

Auto-Electrograph = Electric Pen
Tel-autograph
Tel-autophone-
Polyphone = Manifold sounder
Autophone = Self sounder
Kosmophone = Universal sounder
Acoustophone = Sound hearer. = Audible speaker
Otophone = Ear-sounder = speaker.
Antiphone = Back-talker
Liguphone = Clear speaker
Minuttophone = minute-sounder
Meistophone = smallest sounder
Anchiphone = Near sounder or speaker
Palmatophone = Vibration sounder
Chronophone = Time-announcer = Speaking Clock
Didaskophone = Teaching speaker = Portable teacher
Glottophone = Language sounder or speaker
Climatophone = Weather announcer.
Atmophone = Fog sounder. or Vapor-speaker.

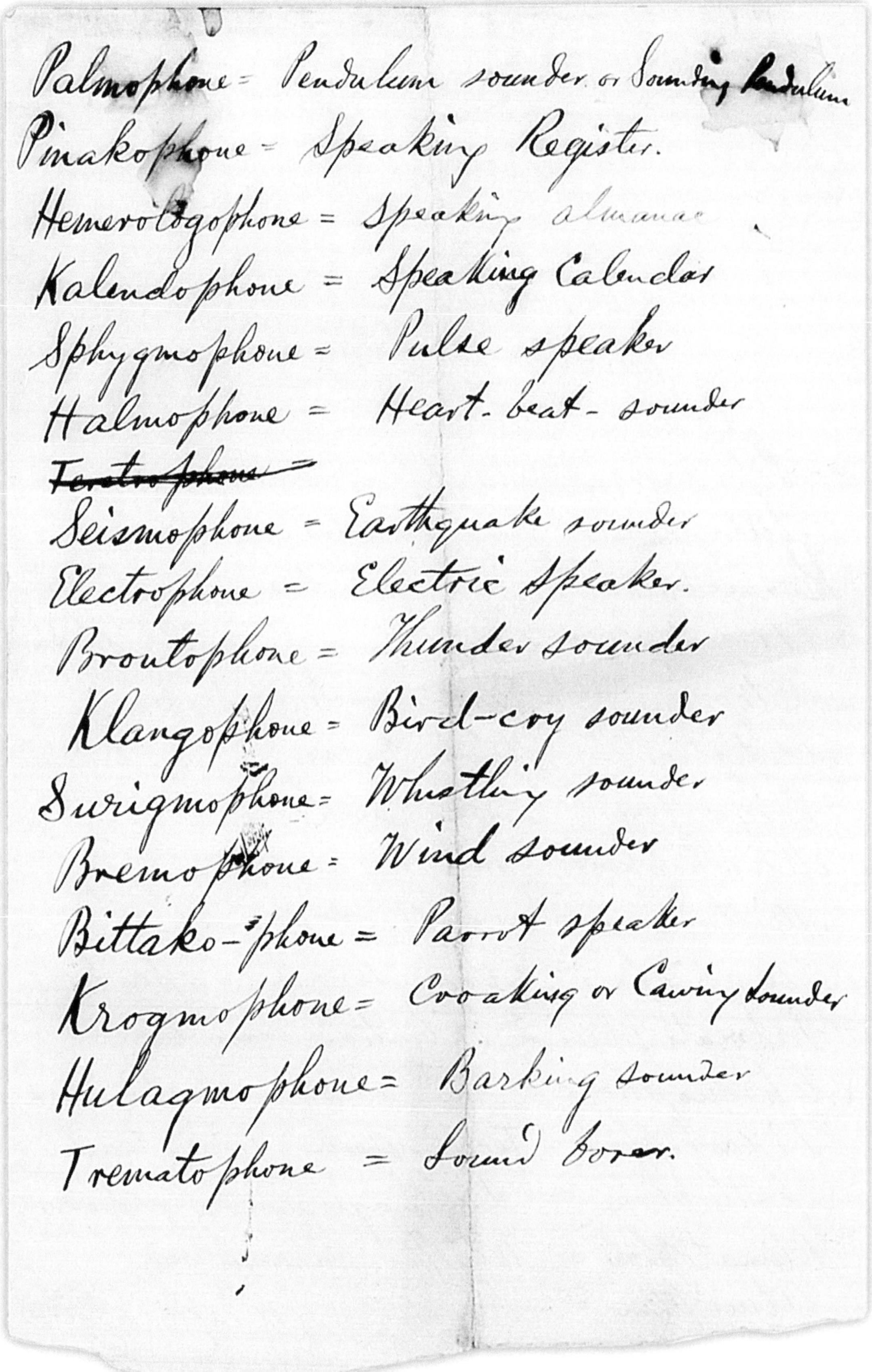
Palmophone = Pendulum sounder or Sounding Pendulum
Pinakophone = Speaking Register.
Hemerologophone = Speaking almanac
Kalendophone = Speaking Calendar
Sphygmophone = Pulse speaker
Halmophone = Heart-beat-sounder
~~Teratophone =~~
Seismophone = Earthquake sounder
Electrophone = Electric Speaker.
Brontophone = Thunder sounder
Klangophone = Bird-coy sounder
Surigmophone = Whistling sounder
Bremophone = Wind sounder
Bittako-phone = Parrot speaker
Krogmophone = Croaking or Cawing sounder
Hulagmophone = Barking sounder
Trematophone = Sound borer.

(PHONOGRAPH)
(1877?)

Telephemist. telephemy. telepheme.
Electrophemist. electrophemy electropheme.

Phemegraph. - speech writer.
Omphegraph. gram. - voice writer or recorder.

Melodograph. Melograph. Melpograph. - gram. song writer.

Epograph. - speech writer lecture or sermon
Rhetograph - " ".

Kinemograph = motion writer.

Atmophone ~~aerophone~~ = vapor or steam sound.
aerophone = air-sound.

Symphrazometer = pressure measurer.
Synothemeter - = pressure measurer.
Orcheograph = vibration record
Orcheometer

List No. 112

THINGS TO WORRY ABOUT

F. SCOTT FITZGERALD
1933

Scottie was just eleven years old and at camp many miles away from her family when, in August 1933, she received a heartening letter of advice from home. It was written by her father, F. Scott Fitzgerald, a man responsible for penning some of the most acclaimed novels of the twentieth century—and some of the most spirited, idiosyncratic letters. This particular missive contained a charming and timeless list of things for his daughter to worry/not worry about.

Things to worry about:

Worry about courage
Worry about cleanliness
Worry about efficiency
Worry about horsemanship
Worry about . . .

Things not to worry about:

Don't worry about popular opinion
Don't worry about dolls
Don't worry about the past
Don't worry about the future
Don't worry about growing up
Don't worry about anybody getting ahead of you
Don't worry about triumph
Don't worry about failure unless it comes through your own fault
Don't worry about mosquitoes
Don't worry about flies
Don't worry about insects in general
Don't worry about parents
Don't worry about boys
Don't worry about disappointments
Don't worry about pleasures
Don't worry about satisfactions

Things to think about:

What am I really aiming at?
How good am I really in comparison to my contemporaries in regard to:
(A) Scholarship
(B) Do I really understand about people and am I able to get along with them?
(C) Am I trying to make my body a useful instrument or am I neglecting it?

With dearest love,
Daddy

List No. 113

MARILYN MONROE'S DREAM LOVERS

MARILYN MONROE
1951

In 1951, as they flicked through a copy of the *Academy Players Directory* and discussed the actors of the day, twenty-five-year-old rising starlet Marilyn Monroe turned to roommate and fellow actress Shelley Winters, and said, "Wouldn't it be nice to be like men and just get notches in your belt and sleep with the most attractive men and not get emotionally involved?" Before long, they were sitting with pen in hand writing lists of the actors they would like to bed in such circumstances. Monroe's wish list can be seen here.

Zero Mostel

Eli Wallach

Charles Boyer

Jean Renoir

Lee Strasberg

Nick Ray

John Huston

Elia Kazan

Harry Belafonte

Yves Montand

Charles Bickford

Ernest Hemingway

Charles Laughton

Clifford Odets

Dean Jagger

Arthur Miller

Albert Einstein

List No. 114

QUALITIES OF CIVILIZED PEOPLE

ANTON CHEKHOV
March 1886

In March 1886, at the age of twenty-six, acclaimed Russian author and physician Anton Chekhov wrote an honest letter of advice to his troubled older brother, Nikolai. A talented painter and writer, Nikolai, just twenty-eight himself, had for many years been plagued by alcoholism—to the point where he often slept on the streets, his days a blur, and his notable skills as an artist largely untapped. Anton Chekov's letter contained the list seen here—eight qualities exhibited by "civilized" people—and was essentially Chekov's attempt at knocking some sense into the sibling he was slowly losing.

His older brother would die three years later.

To my mind, well-bred people ought to satisfy the following conditions:

1. They respect the individual and are therefore always indulgent, gentle, polite and compliant. They do not throw a tantrum over a hammer or a lost eraser. When they move in with somebody, they do not act as if they were doing him a favor, and when they move out, they do not say, "How can anyone live with you!" They excuse noise and cold and overdone meat and witticisms and the presence of others in their homes.

2. Their compassion extends beyond beggars and cats. They are hurt even by things the naked eye can't see. If for instance, Pyotr knows that his father and mother are turning gray and losing sleep over seeing their Pyotr so rarely (and seeing him drunk when he does turn up), then he rushes home to them and sends his vodka to the devil. They do not sleep nights the better to help the Polevayevs, help pay their brothers' tuition, and keep their mother decently dressed.

3. They respect the property of others and therefore pay their debts.

4. They are candid and fear lies like the plague. They do not lie even about the most trivial matters. A lie insults the listener and debases him in the liar's eyes. They don't put on airs, they behave in the street as they do at home, and they do not try to dazzle their inferiors. They know how to keep their mouths shut and they do not force uninvited confidences on people. Out of respect for the ears of others they are more often silent than not.

5. They do not belittle themselves merely to arouse sympathy. They do not play on people's heartstrings to get them to sigh and fuss over them. They do not say, "No one understands me!" or "I've squandered my talent on trifles! I am . . ." because this smacks of a cheap effect and is vulgar, false and out-of-date.

6. They are not preoccupied with vain things. They are not taken in by such false jewels as friendships with celebrities, handshakes with drunken Plevako, ecstasy over the first person they happen to meet at the Salon de Variétés, popularity among the tavern crowd. They laugh when they hear, "I represent the press," a phrase befitting only Rodzeviches and Levenbergs. When they have done a penny's worth of work, they don't try to make a hundred rubles out of it, and they don't boast over being admitted to places closed to others. True talents always seek obscurity. They try to merge with the crowd and shun all ostentation. Krylov himself said that an empty barrel has more chance of being heard than a full one.

7. If they have talent, they respect it. They sacrifice comfort, women, wine and vanity to it. They are proud of their talent, and so they do not go out carousing with trade-school employees or Skvortsov's guests, realizing that their calling lies in exerting an uplifting influence on them, not in living with them. What is more, they are fastidious.

8. They cultivate their aesthetic sensibilities. They cannot stand to fall asleep fully dressed, see a slit in the wall teeming with bedbugs, breathe rotten air, walk on a spittle-laden floor, or eat off a kerosene stove. They try their best to tame and ennoble their sexual instinct . . . to endure her logic and never stray from her. What's the point of it all? People with good breeding are not as coarse as that. What they look for in a woman is not a bed partner or horse sweat, . . . not the kind of intelligence that expresses itself in the ability to stage a fake pregnancy and tirelessly reel off lies. They—and especially the artists among them—require spontaneity, elegance, compassion, a woman who will be a mother, not a . . . They don't guzzle vodka on any old occasion, nor do they go around sniffing cupboards, for they know they are not swine. They drink only when they are free, if the opportunity happens to present itself. For they require a mens sana in corpore sano.

And so on. That's how well-bred people act. If you want to be well-bred and not fall below the level of the milieu you belong to, it is not enough to read *The Pickwick Papers* and memorize a soliloquy from *Faust*. It is not enough to hail a cab and drive off to Yakimanka Street if all you're going to do is bolt out again a week later.

You must work at it constantly, day and night. You must never stop reading, studying in depth, exercising your will. Every hour is precious.

PRESIDENT ROOSEVELT'S LIST OF BIRDS

THEODORE ROOSEVELT

1908

In 1908, as she worked on a new edition of her book, *Birds of Washington and Vicinity*, American historian Lucy Maynard asked then US president Theodore Roosevelt whether she could include mention of some of the birds he had seen near the White House. Roosevelt, an avid birdwatcher, replied, "I'll do better for you than that, I'll make you a list of all the birds I can remember having seen since I have been here." And here is that list: ninety-three birds seen in Washington, DC, by Roosevelt during his seven and a half years in power.

(*Denotes a species seen on White House grounds)

Night Heron. Five spent winter of 1907 in swampy country about one-half mile west of Washington Monument.

Mourning Dove.

Quail.

Ruffed Grouse. One seen on Rock Creek.

Sharp-shinned Hawk.

Red-shouldered Hawk.

*Sparrow Hawk. A pair spent the last two winters on and around the White House grounds, feeding on the Sparrows—largely, thank Heaven, on the English Sparrows.

*Screech Owl. Steady resident on White House grounds.

*Saw-whet Owl. A pair spent several weeks by the south portico of the White House, 1905.

Kingfisher.

*Yellow-billed Cuckoo.

Hairy Woodpecker.

*Downy Woodpecker.

*Sapsucker.

*Red-headed Woodpecker. Nests (one pair) on White House grounds.

*Flicker. Nests (several pairs) on White House grounds.

Whip-poor-will.

Nighthawk.

*Chimney Swift.

*Hummingbird.

Kingbird.

Great Crested Flycatcher.

Phœbe.

Wood Pewee.

Horned Lark.

*Crow.

*Fish Crow.

*Orchard Oriole. One pair nested in White House grounds.

Bobolink.

Red-winged Blackbird.

*Baltimore Oriole.

Meadowlark.

*Purple Grackle. Nests on White House grounds. Very abundant in early spring.

*Purple Finch.

*Thistle Bird (Goldfinch).

Vesper Sparrow.

*White-throated Sparrow. Sings; this year sang now and then all through the winter.

*Tree Sparrow.

*Chippie (Chipping Sparrow). Nests.

Bush Sparrow (Field Sparrow).

*Snow Bird (Junco).

*Song Sparrow. Nests.

*Fox Sparrow.

*Cardinal.

Towhee.

*Indigo-bird. Nests.

Tanager.

Purple Martin.

*Barn Swallow.

Tree Swallow.

Bank Swallow.

*Cedar Bird.

Logger-head Shrike.

*Red-eyed Vireo. Nests.

*Warbling Vireo. Nests.

*Black and White Warbler. Nests.

*Blue Yellow-backed Warbler (Parula Warbler).

*Cape May Warbler.

*Summer Yellowbird. Nests.

*Black-throated Blue Warbler.

*Black-throated Green Warbler.

*Myrtle Warbler.

*Magnolia Warbler.

*Chestnut-sided Warbler.

*Bay-breasted Warbler.

*Blackpoll Warbler.

*Blackburnian Warbler.

Prairie Warbler.

Oven-bird.

Water Thrush.

Kentucky Warbler.

*Yellowthroat.

Chat.

*Blue-winged Warbler.

*Canadian Warbler.

*Redstart. Nests on White House grounds.

Pipit.

Mockingbird.

*Catbird. Nests on White House grounds.

Thrasher.

House Wren.

*Carolina Wren.

Marsh Wren.

*Brown Creeper.

*White-breasted Nuthatch.

*Tufted Tit. Nest on White House grounds.

*Chickadee.

*Golden-crowned Kinglet.

*Ruby-crowned Kinglet.

Gnatcatcher.

*Wood Thrush. Nests on White House grounds.

*Bluebird.

*Robin. Nests on White House grounds.

PRESIDENT ROOSEVELT'S LIST OF BIRDS

SEEN IN THE WHITE HOUSE GROUNDS AND ABOUT WASHINGTON DURING HIS ADMINISTRATION

(*Denotes a species seen on Whité House grounds)

NIGHT HERON. Five spent winter of 1907 in swampy country about one-half mile west of Washington Monument.
MOURNING DOVE.
QUAIL.
RUFFED GROUSE. One seen on Rock Creek.
SHARP-SHINNED HAWK.
RED-SHOULDERED HAWK.
*SPARROW HAWK. A pair spent the last two winters on and around the White House grounds, feeding on the sparrows—largely, thank Heaven, on English sparrows.
*SCREECH OWL. Steady resident on White House grounds.
*SAW-WHET OWL. A pair spent several weeks by the south portico of the White House in June, 1905.
KINGFISHER.
*YELLOW-BILLED CUCKOO.
HAIRY WOODPECKER.
*DOWNY WOODPECKER.
*SAPSUCKER.
*RED-HEADED WOODPECKER. Nests (one pair) on White House grounds.
*FLICKER. Nests (several pair) on White House grounds.
WHIP-POOR-WILL.
NIGHTHAWK.
*CHIMNEY SWIFT.
*HUMMINGBIRD.
KINGBIRD.

List No. 116

FELLOWSHIP ASSETS

FRANK LLOYD WRIGHT
1943

In 1932, one of history's greatest architects Frank Lloyd Wright (1867–1959) founded the Taliesin Fellowship at his estate in Spring Green, Wisconsin, and welcomed twenty-three apprentices into his world. For the next twenty-seven years until his death, Wright taught and lived between Wisconsin and Taliesin West in Scottsdale, Arizona, with numerous sets of students, some of whom went on to work for his firm after graduating. Having evolved into the Frank Lloyd Wright School of Architecture, Taliesin still enrolls students. In his 1943 memoir, *Frank Lloyd Wright: An Autobiography*, Wright listed a Taliesin fellow's ideal qualities.

FELLOWSHIP ASSETS

I. AN HONEST EGO IN A HEALTHY BODY—GOOD CORRELATION

II. LOVE OF TRUTH AND NATURE

III. SINCERITY AND COURAGE

IV. ABILITY FOR ACTION

V. THE ESTHETIC SENSE

VI. APPRECIATION OF WORK AS IDEA AND IDEA AS WORK

VII. FERTILITY OF IMAGINATION

VIII. CAPACITY FOR FAITH AND REBELLION

IX. DISREGARD FOR COMMONPLACE (INORGANIC) ELEGANCE

X. INSTINCTIVE COOPERATION

List No. 117

THE BOOKSHOP

ITALO CALVINO
1979

Italo Calvino's 1979 *If on a Winter's Night a Traveler* is an enchanting novel that envisions you, the reader, attempting to buy and read Italo Calvino's novel *If on a Winter's Night a Traveler*. In the story's first chapter, the following types of reading material are listed as you navigate a crowded bookshop, eager to locate Calvino's book.

Books You Haven't Read;

the Books You Needn't Read;

the Books Made For Purposes Other Than Reading;

Books Read Even Before You Open Them Since They Belong To The Category Of Books Read Before Being Written;

the Books That If You Had More Than One Life You Would Certainly Also Read But Unfortunately Your Days Are Numbered;

the Books You Mean To Read But There Are Others You Must Read First;

the Books Too Expensive Now And You'll Wait Till They're Remaindered;

the Books ditto When They Come Out In Paperback;

Books You Can Borrow From Somebody;

Books That Everybody's Read So It's As If You Had Read Them, Too;

the Books You've Been Planning to Read for Ages;

the Books You've Been Hunting for Years Without Success;

the Books Dealing With Something You're Working On At The Moment;

the Books You Want to Own So They'll Be Handy Just in Case;

the Books You Could Put Aside Maybe To Read This Summer;

the Books You Need To Go With Other Books On Your Shelves;

the Books That Fill You With Sudden, Inexplicable Curiosity, Not Easily Justified;

the Books Read Long Ago Which It's Now Time To Reread;

the Books You've Always Pretended To Have Read And Now It's Time To Sit Down And Really Read Them;

the New Books Whose Author Or Subject Appeals To You;

the New Books By Authors Or On Subjects Not New (for you or in general);

New Books By Authors Or On Subjects Completely Unknown (at least to you)

BOOK SALE......
ANIL BOOK CORNER
PLAZA BLDG.
N. DELHI-
PH 3713223
BUYER & SELLER

List No. 118

VERB LIST COMPILATION: ACTIONS TO RELATE TO ONESELF

RICHARD SERRA

1967–1968

In the late 1960s, American sculptor Richard Serra wrote *Verb List Compilation: Actions to Relate to Oneself*. Written in pencil on two sheets of paper, Serra's four columns are composed mostly of verbs in their infinitive form–all of which describe actions that can be carried out on materials during the artistic process–as well as contexts for those actions. He then used the list as a blueprint for his later work.

to roll
to crease
to fold
to store
to bend
to shorten
to twist
to dapple
to crumple
to shave
to tear
to chip
to split
to cut
to sever
to drop
to remove
to simplify
to differ
to disarrange
to open
to mix
to splash
to knot
to spill
to droop
to flow

to curve
to lift
to inlay
to impress
to fire
to flood
to smear
to rotate
to swirl
to support
to hook
to suspend
to spread
to hang
to collect
of tension
of gravity
of entropy
of nature
of grouping
of layering
of felting
to grasp
to tighten
to bundle
to heap
to gather

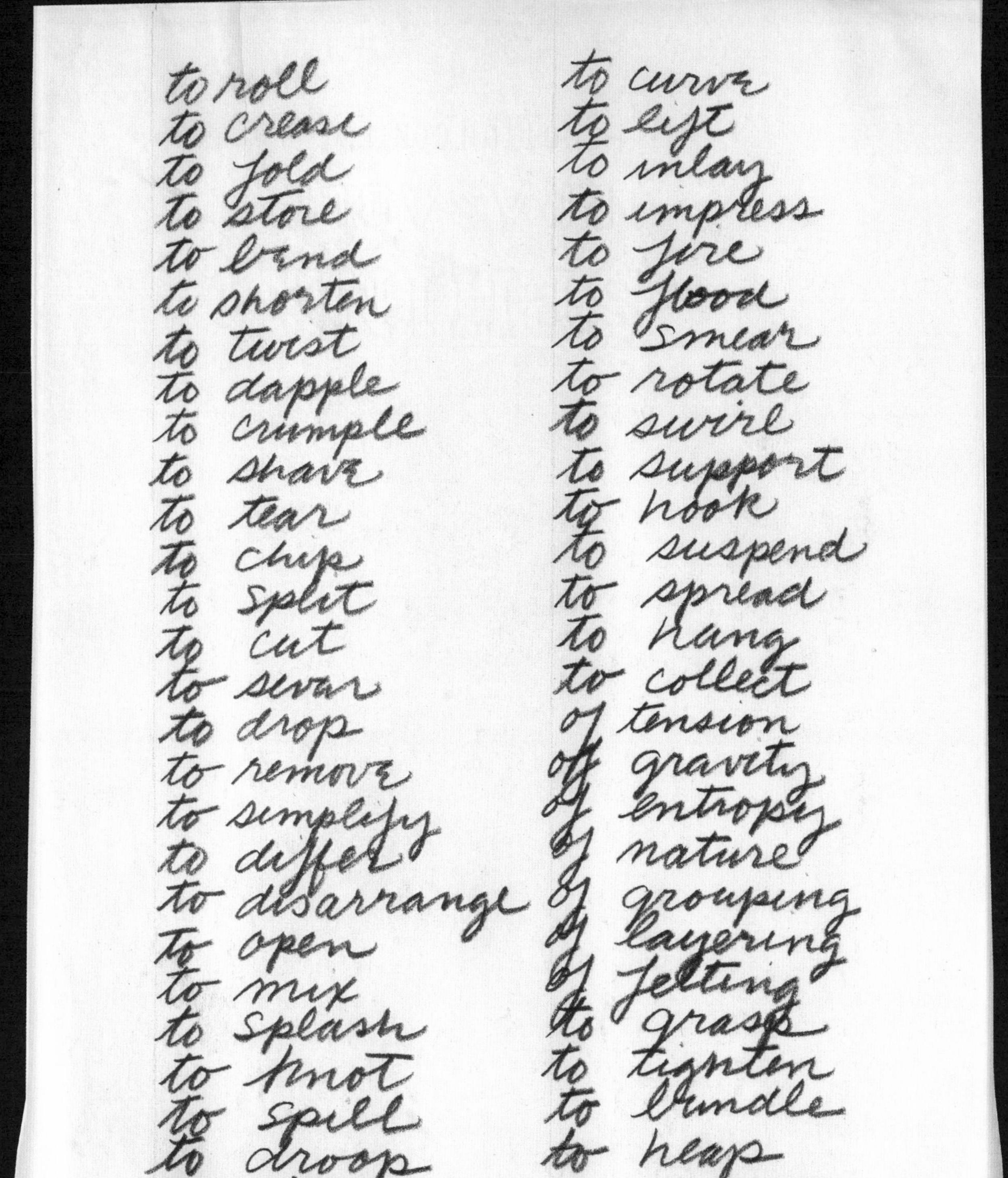
to roll
to crease
to fold
to store
to bend
to shorten
to twist
to dapple
to crumple
to shave
to tear
to chip
to split
to cut
to sever
to drop
to remove
to simplify
to differ
to disarrange
to open
to mix
to splash
to knot
to spill
to droop
to flow

to curve
to lift
to inlay
to impress
to fire
to flood
to smear
to rotate
to swirl
to support
to hook
to suspend
to spread
to hang
to collect
of tension
of gravity
of entropy
of nature
of grouping
of layering
of felting
to grasp
to tighten
to bundle
to heap
to gather

to scatter
to arrange
to repair
to discard
to pair
to distribute
to surfeit
to compliment
to enclose
to surround
to encircle
to hide
to cover
to wrap
to dig
to tie
to bind
to weave
to join
to match
to laminate
to bond
to hinge
to mark
to expand
to dilute
to light
to modulate
to distill
of waves
of electromagnetic
of inertia
of ionization
of polarization
of refraction
of simultaneity
of tides
of reflection
of equilibrium
of symmetry
of friction
to stretch
to bounce
to erase
to spray
to systematize
to refer
to force
of mapping
of location
of context
of time
of carbonization
to continue

to scatter
to arrange
to repair
to discard
to pair
to distribute
to surfeit
to complement
to enclose
to surround
to encircle
to hide
to cover
to wrap
to dig
to tie
to bind
to weave
to join
to match
to laminate
to bond
to hinge
to mark
to expand
to dilute
to light

to modulate
to distill
of waves
of electromagnetic
of inertia
of ionization
of polarization
of refraction
of simultaneity
of tides
of reflection
of equilibrium
of symmetry
of friction
to stretch
to bounce
to erase
to spray
to systematize
to refer
to force
of mapping
of location
of context
of time
of carbonization
to continue

UTOPIAN TURTLE-TOP

MARIANNE MOORE
1955

While attempting to find a name for their hugely anticipated new car, Ford Motor Company decided in 1955 to approach the most unlikely of people to assist in the matter: Pulitzer Prize-winning poet Marianne Moore. Moore, who was known by the wife of one Robert Young, an employee in the car manufacturer's marketing research department, was soon contacted by letter. She agreed to help and proceeded to supply Ford with numerous lists of delightful names, all of which are compiled here, ordered chronologically. Her final suggestion, sent to Young on December 8, was the amazing "Utopian Turtle-top."

The Ford Motor Company chose to ignore all of Moore's ideas and instead named their new car, which was ultimately released in 1957, after Henry Ford's son. The Edsel famously flopped.

The Ford Silver Sword
Hirundo
Aerundo
Hurricane Hirundo (swallow)
Hurricane Aquila (eagle)
Hurricane Accipter (hawk)
The Impeccable
Symmechromatic
Thunderblender
The Resilient Bullet
Intelligent Bullet
Bullet Cloisonné
Bullet Lavolta
The Intelligent Whale
The Ford Fabergé
The Arc-en-Ciel (the rainbow)
Arcenciel
Mongoose Civique
Anticipator
Regna Racer (couronne à couronne) sovereign to sovereign
Aeroterre
Fée Rapide (Aérofee, Aéro Faire, Fée Aiglette, Magi-faire) Comme Il Faire
Tonnere Alifère (winged thunder)
Aliforme Alifère (wing-slender, a-wing)
Turbotorc (used as an adjective by Plymouth)
Thunderbird Allié (Cousin Thunderbird)
Thunder Crester
Dearborn Diamante
Magigravure
Pastelogram
Regina-Rex
Taper Racer
Taper Acer
Varsity Stroke
Angelastro
Astranaut
Chaparral
Tir à l'arc (bull's eye)
Cresta Lark
Triskelion (three legs running)
Pluma Piluma (hairfine, feather-foot)
Adante con Moto (description of a good motor?)
Turcotinga (turqoise cotinga—the cotinga being a South-American finch or sparrow) solid indigo
Utopian Turtle-top

List No. 120

BILLY WILDER'S TIPS FOR SCREENWRITERS

BILLY WILDER
Late 1990s

Legendary filmmaker Billy Wilder (1906–2002) was responsible for writing and/or directing some of Hollywood's most iconic movies: *The Apartment*, *Some Like It Hot*, and *Double Indemnity*, to name just three. As a result, he remains one of the most nominated directors in the history of the Academy Awards. Spanning fifty-plus prolific years and the Golden Age of Hollywood, Wilder's was a voice worth listening to. A three-time Oscar® winner for his writing—on *Lost Weekend*, *Sunset Boulevard*, and *The Apartment*—in the late 1990s, he imparted his wisdom to fellow filmmaker Cameron Crowe in the form of this list of tips for screenwriters.

1. The audience is fickle.
2. Grab 'em by the throat and never let 'em go.
3. Develop a clean line of action for your leading character.
4. Know where you're going.
5. The more subtle and elegant you are in hiding your plot points, the better you are as a writer.
6. If you have a problem with the third act, the real problem is in the first act.
7. A tip from Lubitsch: Let the audience add up two plus two. They'll love you forever.
8. In doing voice-overs, be careful not to describe what the audience already sees. Add to what they're seeing.
9. The event that occurs at the second act curtain triggers the end of the movie.
10. The third act must build, build, build in tempo and action until the last event, and then—that's it. Don't hang around.

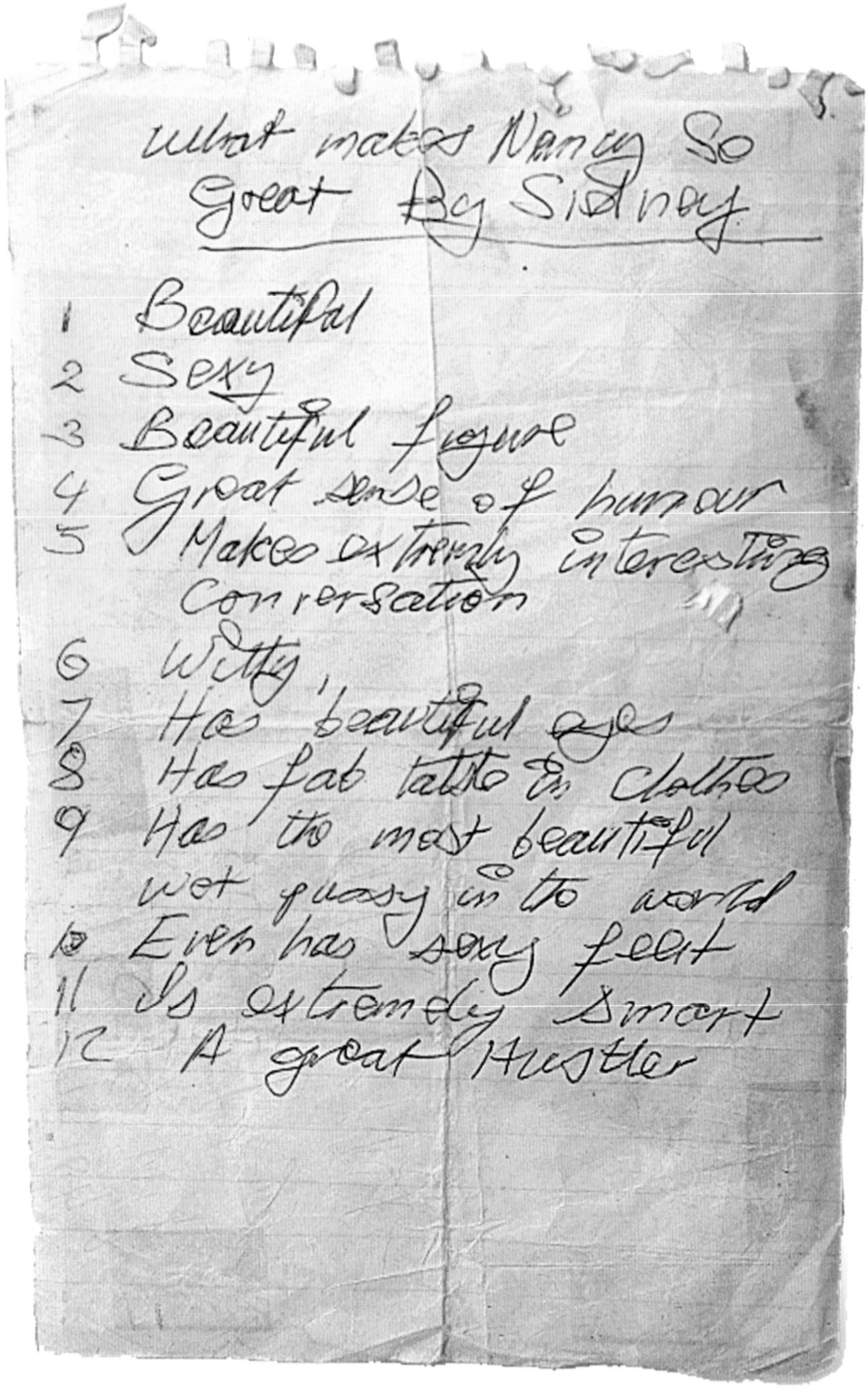

What makes Nancy So Great By Sidney

1 Beautiful
2 Sexy
3 Beautiful figure
4 Great sense of humour
5 Makes extremly interesting conversation
6 Witty,
7 Has beautiful eyes
8 Has fab taste in clothes
9 Has the most beautiful wet pussy in the world
10 Even has sexy feet
11 Is extremly smart
12 A great Hustler

WHAT MAKES NANCY SO GREAT

SID VICIOUS
1978

In 1978, punk icon and deeply troubled Sex Pistols bassist Sid Vicious handwrote a list of things that made his girlfriend of two years, Nancy Spungen, "so great." In October of that year, Nancy was found dead in their shared Manhattan hotel room with a stab wound to the abdomen. Four months later, on February 2, 1979, just before he was due to stand trial for her suspected murder, Sid fatally overdosed on heroin.

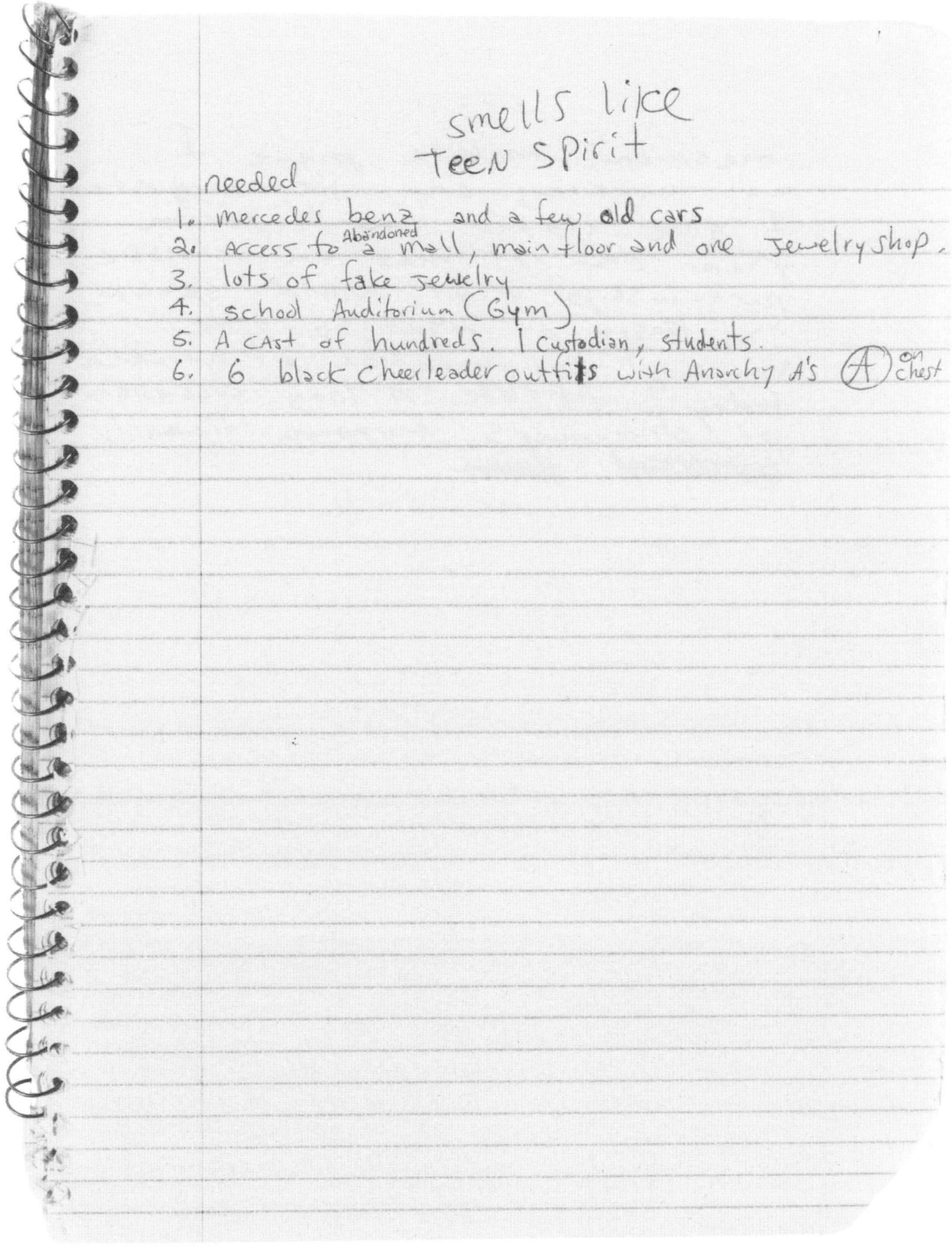
smells like
Teen Spirit

needed
1. mercedes benz and a few old cars
2. Access to a Abandoned mall, main floor and one Jewelry shop.
3. lots of fake Jewelry
4. school Auditorium (Gym)
5. A cast of hundreds. 1 custodian, students.
6. 6 black cheerleader outfits with Anarchy A's (A) on chest

"SMELLS LIKE TEEN SPIRIT"

KURT COBAIN

1991

Kurt Cobain was twenty-four years old and on the verge of mainstream stardom when he wrote this—a list of things needed in order to produce a music video for "Smells Like Teen Spirit," the lead single from his band's second album, *Nevermind*. Little could he or his bandmates have known how hugely popular their new album and the award-winning "Smells Like Teen Spirit" single and video would become—or that Nirvana would become one of the most influential bands of its generation.

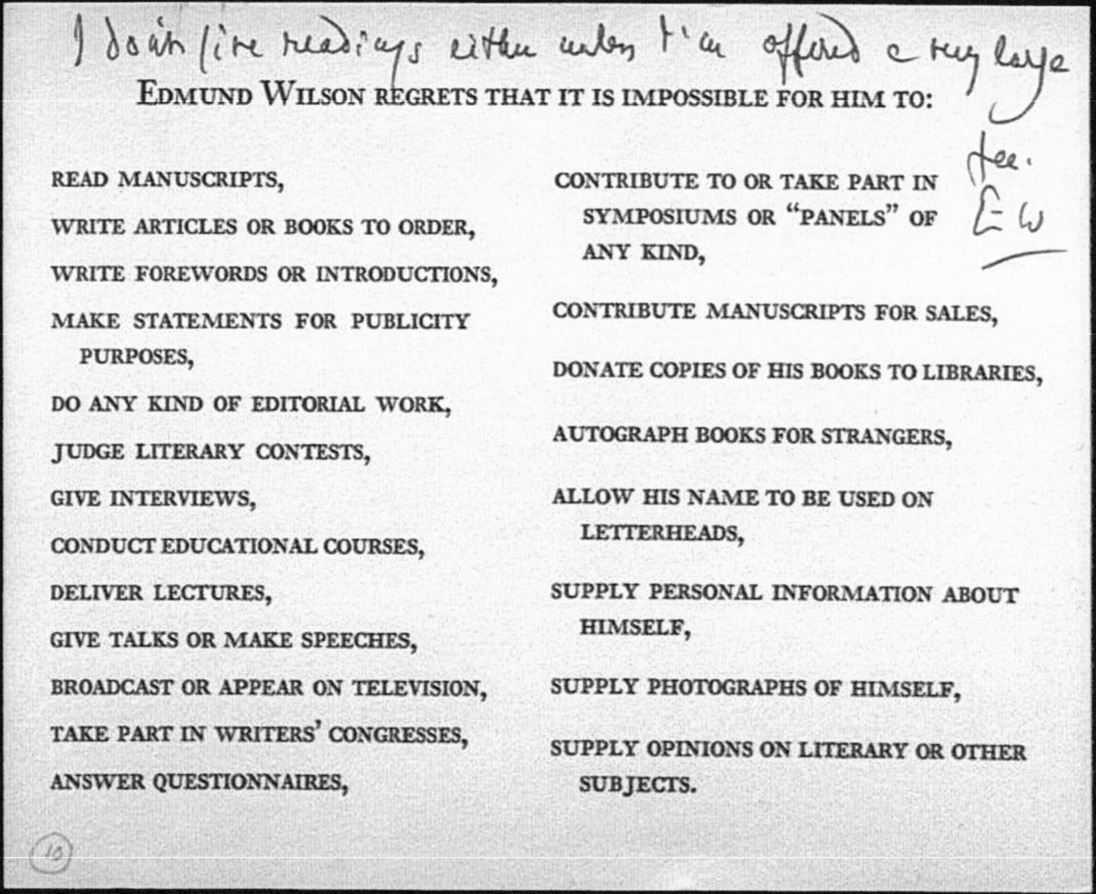
I don't give readings either unless I'm offered a very large fee. E.W.

EDMUND WILSON REGRETS THAT IT IS IMPOSSIBLE FOR HIM TO:

READ MANUSCRIPTS,
WRITE ARTICLES OR BOOKS TO ORDER,
WRITE FOREWORDS OR INTRODUCTIONS,
MAKE STATEMENTS FOR PUBLICITY PURPOSES,
DO ANY KIND OF EDITORIAL WORK,
JUDGE LITERARY CONTESTS,
GIVE INTERVIEWS,
CONDUCT EDUCATIONAL COURSES,
DELIVER LECTURES,
GIVE TALKS OR MAKE SPEECHES,
BROADCAST OR APPEAR ON TELEVISION,
TAKE PART IN WRITERS' CONGRESSES,
ANSWER QUESTIONNAIRES,
CONTRIBUTE TO OR TAKE PART IN SYMPOSIUMS OR "PANELS" OF ANY KIND,
CONTRIBUTE MANUSCRIPTS FOR SALES,
DONATE COPIES OF HIS BOOKS TO LIBRARIES,
AUTOGRAPH BOOKS FOR STRANGERS,
ALLOW HIS NAME TO BE USED ON LETTERHEADS,
SUPPLY PERSONAL INFORMATION ABOUT HIMSELF,
SUPPLY PHOTOGRAPHS OF HIMSELF,
SUPPLY OPINIONS ON LITERARY OR OTHER SUBJECTS.

10

EDMUND WILSON REGRETS

EDMUND WILSON
Date Unknown

As his popularity grew, the late literary critic Edmund Wilson (1895–1972) found himself forever responding to mail, to the point where he wasn't able to focus on his work. His eventual solution was to send this, a preprinted list of things it was regretfully impossible for him to do, to all who contacted him with a request he couldn't fulfill. Unluckily for Wilson, news of his unique rejection quickly circulated, and he was soon inundated with requests for the list itself.

SATCHEL'S RULES FOR THE GOOD LIFE

1. Avoid fried foods cause they angers up the blood.
2. If your stomach disputes you, lay down and pacify it with cool thoughts.
3. Keep the juices flowin' by janglin' 'round gently as you move.
4. Go very light on vices such as carryin' on in society. The social ramble just ain't restful.
5. Avoid runnin' at all times.
6. Don't ever look back. Somethin' might be gainin'.

SATCHEL'S RULES FOR THE GOOD LIFE

SATCHEL PAIGE
Date Unknown

Satchel Paige (1906–1982) was one of the most accomplished and recognized pitchers of his day. He joined the Chattanooga Black Lookouts in the Negro Southern League in 1926, at twenty years of age. He debuted in the Major leagues for the Cleveland Indians twenty-two years later, becoming the oldest person ever to do so. In 1971, he was inducted into the Baseball Hall of Fame, the first-ever to be elected for his play in the Negro leagues. Throughout his career, Satchel Paige dispensed his wisdom by handing out business cards with this list of advice printed on the reverse.

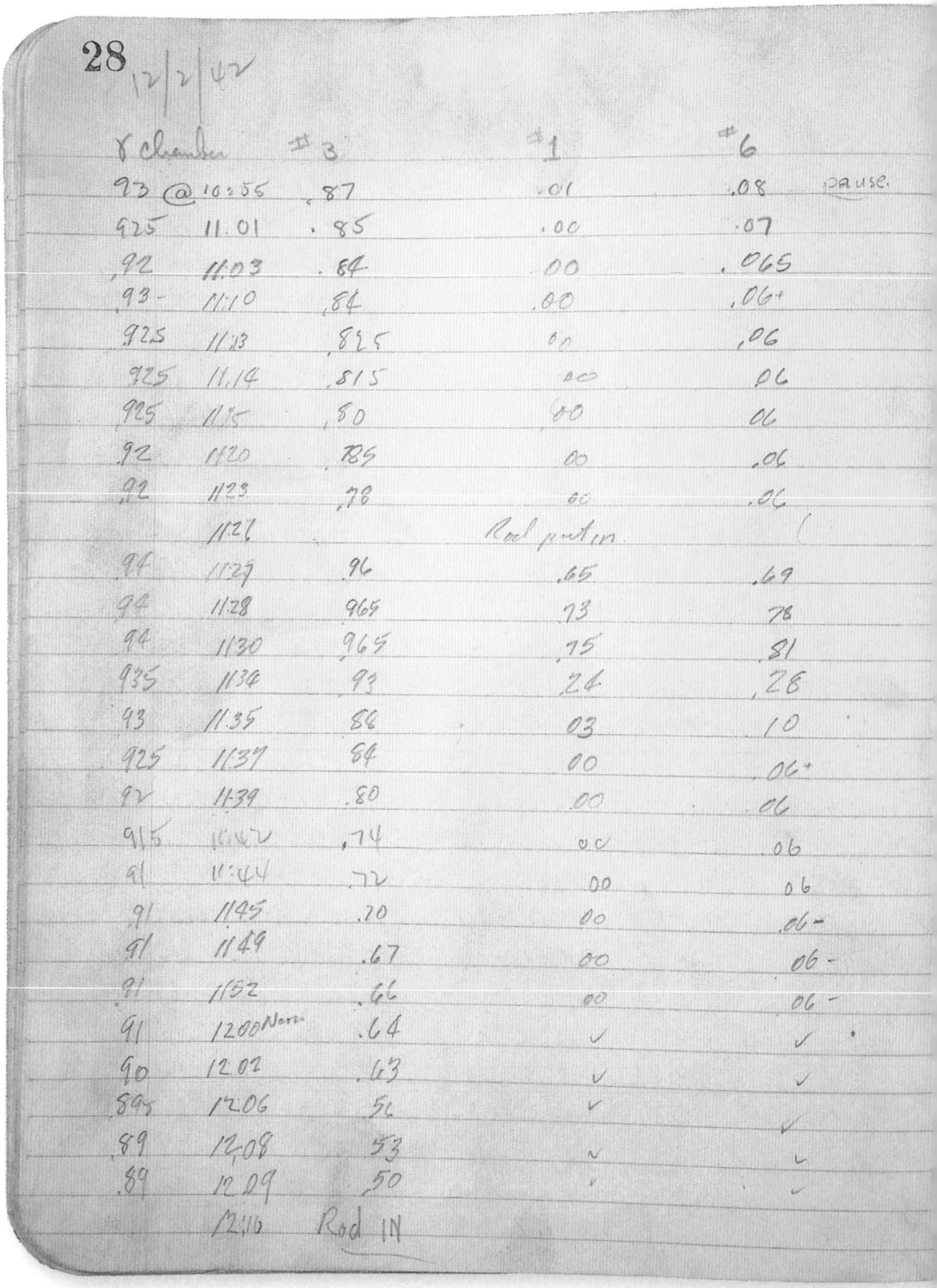
28 12/2/42

γ chamber		#3	#1	#6	
93	@ 10:55	.87	.01	.08	pause.
925	11.01	.85	.00	.07	
92	11:03	.84	.00	.065	
93-	11:10	.84	.00	.06+	
925	11:13	.825	00	.06	
925	11.14	.815	.00	.06	
925	11:15	.80	.00	.06	
92	11:20	.785	00	.06	
92	11:23	.78	.00	.06	
	11:27		Rod put in		
94	11:29	.96	.65	.69	
94	11:28	.965	.73	.78	
94	11:30	.965	.75	.81	
935	11:34	.93	.24	.28	
93	11:35	.86	.03	.10	
925	11:37	.84	.00	.06+	
92	11:39	.80	.00	.06	
915	11:42	.74	.00	.06	
91	11:44	.72	.00	.06	
91	11:45	.70	.00	.06-	
91	11:49	.67	.00	.06-	
91	11:52	.66	.00	.06-	
91	12:00 Noon	.64	✓	✓	
90	12:02	.63	✓	✓	
895	12:06	.56	✓	✓	
89	12:08	.53	✓	✓	
89	12:09	.50	✓	✓	
	12:10	Rod IN			

WE'RE COOKIN!

RICHARD WATTS

December 2, 1942

From 1939 until 1945, fearful that the Germans would beat them to it, an enormous team of scientists led by the United States spent billions of dollars in a race to build the first atomic bomb, in a program named the Manhattan Project. A major development came in 1942, when physicists successfully orchestrated the first controlled, self-sustaining nuclear chain reaction—an experiment during which Richard Watts listed the ongoing results in his notebook. The second page seen here shows the very moment when fission occured, labeled "We're Cookin!"

The race was won three years after these lists were written, when two atomic bombs were dropped on Japan. Over 200,000 people perished.

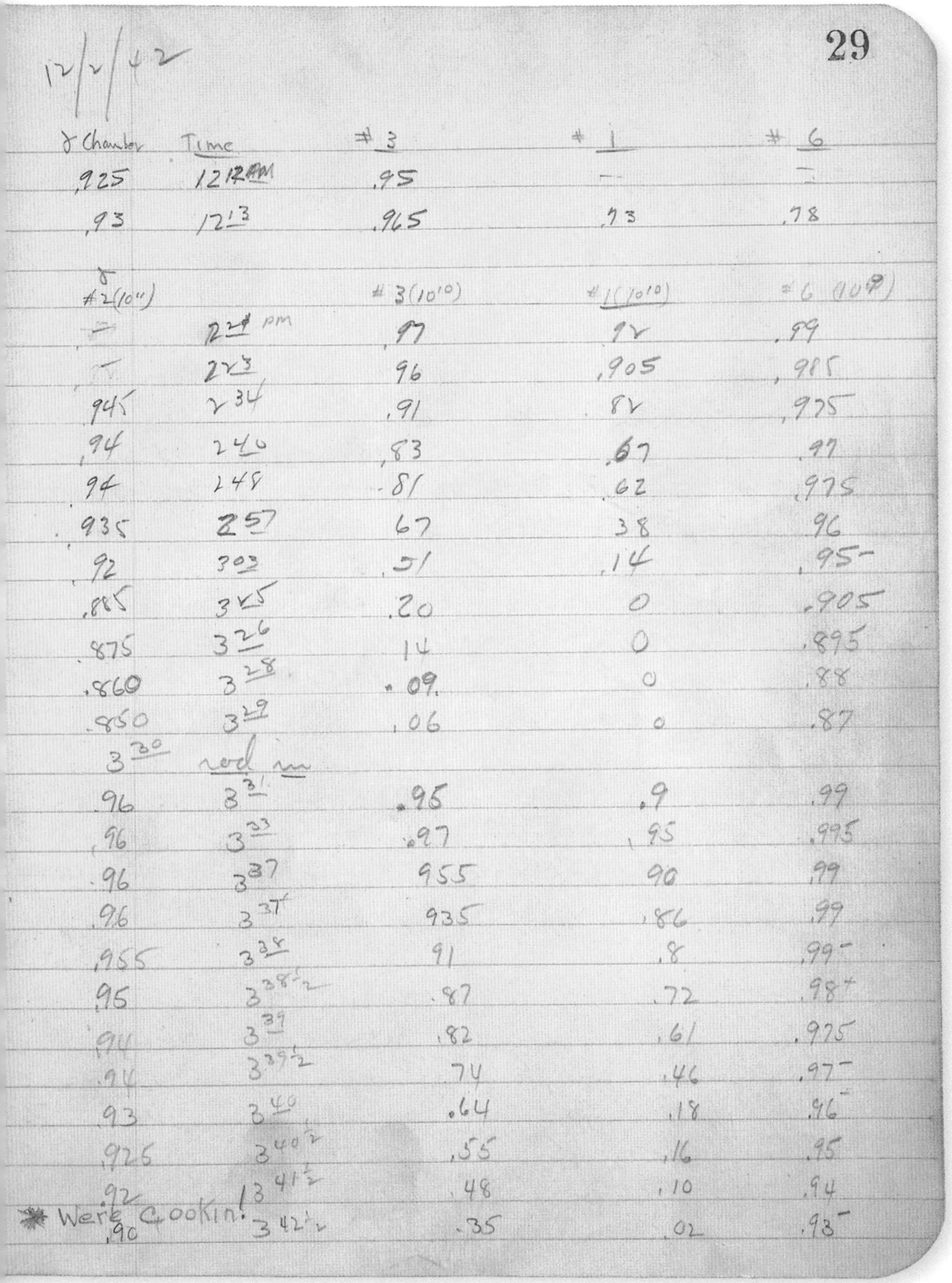

29

12/2/42

γ Chamber	Time	#3	#1	#6
,925	12^{12} AM	,95	—	—
,93	12^{13}	,965	,73	,78

γ #2(10'')		#3(10'0)	#1(10'0)	#6 (10'0)
—	2^{24} pm	,97	92	,99
—	2^{23}	96	,905	,985
945	2^{34}	,91	82	,975
,94	2^{40}	,83	,67	,97
94	2^{48}	,81	,62	,975
,935	2^{57}	67	38	,96
,92	3^{03}	,51	,14	,95–
,885	3^{25}	,20	0	,905
,875	3^{26}	14	0	,895
,860	3^{28}	,09	0	,88
,850	3^{29}	,06	0	,87
3^{30}	rod in			
,96	3^{31}	,95	,9	,99
,96	3^{33}	,97	,95	,995
,96	3^{37}	955	90	,99
,96	3^{37}	935	,86	,99
,955	3^{38}	91	,8	,99–
,95	$3^{38\frac{1}{2}}$	,87	,72	,98+
,94	3^{39}	,82	,61	,975
,94	$3^{39\frac{1}{2}}$	74	,46	,97–
,93	3^{40}	,64	,18	,96–
,925	$3^{40\frac{1}{2}}$	,55	,16	,95
,92	$3^{41\frac{1}{2}}$	,48	,10	,94
,90	$3^{42\frac{1}{2}}$	,35	,02	,93–

✱ We're Cookin!

ACKNOWLEDGMENTS

Creating a book like this is a mammoth task that requires assistance and guidance from a number of very important people, beginning with—and not just for her help during the often hellish, stress-inducing production of *Lists of Note*, but for her constant support in general—my wife, Karina, someone whose patience has been tested to its fullest since I began writing books but who has somehow managed to stay calm throughout. Special mention must also go to Cathy Hurren, my superhuman production manager, without whom this book literally would have taken a decade to reach the (wrong) printers, no doubt filled to the brim with factual errors, spelling mistakes, and no artwork. Untold thanks also go to the following wonderful people: permissions wizard Fred Courtright; John Mitchinson, Rachael Kerr, Dan Kieran, Isobel Frankish, Caitlin Harvey, Charlie Gleason, Emily Bryce-Perkins, Tim Mahar, Justin Pollard, Xander Cansell, and everyone else at the mighty Unbound; the incomparable Jamie Byng and his brilliant team at Canongate; everyone at Chronicle Books for their tireless work; the great Jeff Nolan; all at MailChimp; Natalie Bradbury, who designed this beautiful book, and everyone else at Here Design including Julie Martin and Caz Hildebrand; every single archivist I have had the pleasure of meeting, online and off, all of whom have been more patient than I thought humanly possible; the legend that is Rob "Scabbs" Gibbons; and, as always, my friends and family.

Finally, a massive, heartfelt thank you to two vitally important sets of people: first, all those who had a hand in writing the lists of note contained in this book; and second, each and every person who made this book a reality by pledging support via Unbound. I will be eternally grateful.

SUBSCRIBERS

This book was originally published in the United Kingdom thanks to the support of subscribers to Unbound, whose books are funded directly by readers. A very popular idea during the late eighteenth and early nineteenth centuries, it has now been revived for the internet age. It allows authors to write the books they really want to write—and readers to support the writing they would most like to see published. If you'd like to join them, visit: www.unbound.co.uk.

And so now to the most important list of all. The names listed below are of readers who have pledged their support and made this book happen. If you'd like to join them, visit: www.unbound.co.uk.

Chris Adams / Fiona Adams / Julie Adams / Phil Adams / Gail Affleck Ward / Ann-Maria Ahern / Marcus Ainley / Adrien Albert / Bruce Alcorn / Justine Alderman / Andy Aldridge / Alison Alexander / Robert Alexander-Sinclair / Romjan Ali / Moose Allain / Errol Allcock / Jamie Allen / Damian Amberg / Terje Ruud Andersen / Douglas Anderson / Nicola Anderson / Tom Anderson / Igor Andronov / Angel Of the North / Anonymous / Paul Anson / Sara Appleton / Izzy Appleyard-Yong / Cheryl Arany / Celia Armand Smith / Barbara Arnest / Penny Arrowood / Ara Lucia Ashburne / Sadif Ashraf / Amelia Ashton / Nesher Asner / James Austin / Amal Awad / Bryan Bailey / Susi Bailey / Abbie Baker / Jonathan Ball / Paul Ball / Connor Barclay / Clare Barker / Damon Barker / Leo Barker / Kevin Barrett / Duncan Barrigan / Chris Bartlett / Matt Barton / Isabella Sophia Barzanti Fernandez / Natasha Batsford / Juliet Bawden / Suzanne Bayon / Laura Bayzle / Clive Beautyman / Lynne Bebout / Pete Beck / Tom Beckett / Margaret Bell / Jo Bellamy / Martin Bellamy / Tracey Bellow / Catherine Benson / Howard I. Berrent / Jane Berry / Paula Best / William Bettridge-Radford / Matt, Terri and Joseph Betts / Kieran Binchy / Sally Bindari / Christopher Bishop / Stephen Blackwell / Christopher Blankenship / Robbert Bloem / Nicholas Bond / Nicky Bond / William Bonwitt / BookCunt / Gregory Boone / Ian Botterill / Caroline Bottomley / Wendy Boucek / Karl Bovenizer / Jamie Bowden / Lisa Bowen / Matthew Bowers / Kate Boydell / Geoff Boyle / Carrie Boysun / Geraldine Bradbury / Claire Bradley / Kirstin Bradshaw / Martin Brady / Janey Brant / John Brassey / Richard W H Bray / Leo Breebaart / Ryan Breedon / Sherry Brennan / Stephen Brennan / Sophie Bridge / Rebecca Broadbent / Matt Brockwell / Jane Brookes / Anne & Joe Brophy / Jade Broughton Adams / Claire L Brown / Steven Brown / Sue Brown / Neil Brown and Kristina Dietz / Kala Brownlee / Megan Bryan / Emily Bryce-Perkins / Philip Bryer / Gareth Buchaillard-Davies / Anthony Bunge / Debra Bures / Chris Burns ('Wee Chrissie B') / Kevin Butcher Marcus Butcher / Fiona Butler / Tom Byrne / Georgina Calder / David Callier / Andrew Campling / Andy & Joy Candler / Stefano Canducci / Alistair Canlin / Xander Cansell / Tony Cantafio / Wharton Caroline / Caroline-Isabelle Caron / Martin Carr / Amy Carroll / Paul Carroll / Melanie Carruthers / Chloe & Greg Carter / Laura Carus / Leslie Casse / Roger Cavanagh / Elizabeth Caygill / Michael Chang / Jeffrey Chase / Andrew Chern / Cheryl Cheryl / Helen Chesshire / James Chilton / Ana Victoria Chiu / Nick Chominski / Tina Chopee / Dr Nicholas Andrew Vance Clarke / Richard Clarke / Elliott Clarkson / Timm & Sam Cleasby / Nic Close / Thom Clutterbuck / Garrett Coakley / Alex Coats / Lorna Anne Coffey and Elizabeth Louise Franke / Helen Collard Was Marriott / Pamela Collett / Gavin Collins / Tara Condell / Philip Conner / Edward Cook / Caroline Cookson / Antony Coombs / Glenda Cooper / Tracey Cormack / Elaine Corrington / Alberto Corubolo / Mike Coulter / Robyn Cowan / Amanda Cowlrick / Elizabeth Cox / Joanna Cox / Adrian Crabtree & Debbie Blanchard / Alex Crawford / John Crawford / Victoria Croft / Andrew Croker / Shane Cullinane / Heather Culpin / Bethan Cunnane / Ann Cunningham / Brenda Curin / Cornelia Daheim / Andrew & Antonia Dalmahoy / Felix Dańczak / Alexander Dao / Anne-Marie Dao / Sophia Darlington / Heena Dave / Emma Davies / Harriet Fear Davies / Matt & Owen Davies / Ian Davison / Tom Dawkins / Nelius De Groot / Lindsey Dear / Marjan Debevere / Mary Decious / Benny Declerck / Rachel Deeson / Forrest DeMarcus / Jamie Dempster / Andrew Denton / John Dexter / Nikhil Dhumma / Guy Dickinson / Alistair Dinnie / Ritchie Djamhur / Shereen Docherty / Andrea Dolan / Jacky Dols / Kate Donachie / Julie Donovan / Cressida Downing / Linda Watt Doyle / Liz Drabble / Tracey Drost / Tim Durham / Julie Durkheimer / Dave Dyke / Thom Dyke / Cornelia Eberhardt / Hillary Edwards / Jennie Eggleston / Lisa

Elliott / Stefanie Epstein / Karsten Eriksen / Christopher Esposito / Peter Ettedgui / Cath Evans / Charles Evans / Dor Evans / Julie Evans / Jonathan Everall / Pete Faint / Peter Falconer / Jane Farey / Ewan Farry / John Fellows / Gregory Fenby Taylor / Ella Ferdenzi / Melissa Ferreira / Paul Fischer / Susan Foote / Debbie Ford / Doug Forrest / Marco Fossati-Bellani / Clare Fowler / Lynsey Fox / Stephanie Fox / Louise Foxcroft / Stephanie Frackowiak / Ann Frank / Isobel Frankish / Christopher Fretwell / G. Funk / Simon Gadd / Matthew Gallagher / Paul Garbett / Penny Gardiner / Richard Garnett / Annabel Gaskell / Patrick Gatenby / Carl Gaywood / Amro Gebreel / Saunders Gemma / Emma Giacon & Chris Helsen / Jack & Ellie Gibbons / Rob & Joanne Gibbons / Clare Gill / William Gill / Sealy Gilles / Simon Gillis / Matthew Giordano / Dominic Gittins / Tim Godby / Claire Goddard / Daniel Godfrey / Sunita Goli / Philip Goodman / Jim Goody / Bharadwaj Gopinath / Jess Gordon / Peter Gorrie / Jo Gostling / Michele Govier / David Graham / Ritchie Graham / Rebecca Granshaw / Fiona Green / James Green / Jonathan Green / Chris Greenway / Michelle Greenwood / Helen Gregory / Kate Gregory / Peter Griffiths / Frank Guerra / Adam Guest / Rich Gunn / Gwennyth Gwennyth / Sophie H / William Hackett-Jones / Katharine Halcrow / Alfie Hall / Catherine Hamilton / David and Katrina Hancock / John Handley / Lex Hands / Susan Hanlon / Emily Hanson-Coles / Lina Hardenburg / Ruth Ann Harnisch / Jordan Harper / Brian Harrison / A.F. Harrold / Caitlin Harvey / Kate Hawkings / Christina Hawley / Elspeth Head / In memory of my mother, Louise Hefter, who left me many beautiful lists. / Helen / Emma Helenius / Brian Henderson / Mark Henderson / Kevlin Henney / Frida Henriquez Kiely / Kirstie Hepburn / Jason Hesse / Robert Hicks / E O Higgins / Davida Highley / ElisabethHill Hill / Alexia Hill-Scott / David Hiltscher / Sigi Hirschbeck / Cheryl Hodgkinson / Joanna Holland / Karen Hollands / Roger Horberry / Bill Horton / Christine Houser / Jenny Howard / Catherine Howard-Dobson / Zoe Howe / Susannah Howell / Matt Huggins / Susan Hughes / Noortje Huisman / Lucy Hunt / Henri Hunter / Giselle, Dan & Maila Huron / Cathy Hurren / Lee Hurst / Mike Hutchinson / Neil Hutchinson / Sylvia Huynh / Malcolm Ingram / Bjarni Ingvarsson / Lori Irving / Alanna Evelyn Irwin / Erin Rachel Irwin / Kaushik Iyer / Madeleine Jackson / Pete Jackson / Michael Jagger / Natalie Jarian / Charlie Jarpvall / Karen Jaunzems / Laura Jellicoe / Nimet Johnson / Sandra Johnson / Alex Johnstone / Elspeth Johnstone / Helen Jones / Josie Jones / Karen Jones / Mark Jones / Martin Chad Jones / Meghan Jones / Michelle & Stuart Jordan-Smith / Peter Karpas / Michael Kauffman / Linda Kaye / Deborah Kee Higgins / Steven Kehoe / Andrew Kelly / David Kelly / Alex Kennedy / Mike Kennedy / John Kent / Jennifer Louise Kerr / Rebecca Kerr / Maria Kerschen / Mobeena Khan / Sahira Khwaja / Dan Kieran / Kevin Kieran / Meg Kingston / Katrina Kirkby / Steve Kirtley / Jon Kitto / James Knapman / Peter Knocke / Melanie Knott / Bill Kohn / Matthew Kotok / Gabe Krabbe / Sean Kretz / Stephan Kurz / Nikki Kuyt / Mark Lacey / Mark Lally / Jenny Landreth / Kat Larkin / Jean-Jacques Larrea / Kim Le Patourel / Michael Leader / Johnny Leathers / Anne Frances Leners / Ashley Lewis / Daniel Lewis / Elen Lewis / William Lewis / Lidbert / Claire Liddle / Caroline Lien / Adrian Lightly / Diane Lindquist / Margaret Lindsay / Joonas Linkola / Helen Lippell / Robert Lischke / Tim Litsch / Allen Loades / Eugenia Loh / cmczz London. / Nate Long / Kyle Lonsdale / Isabell Lorenz / Anita Loveland / Dave Loverink / Alison Lowe / Dianne Lowry / Adam Lucas / Magdeline Lum / Bonnie Ma / Sue McAlpine / John MacBrayne / Tara McCausland / Anne Macdonald / Bethany Macdonald / Rob McDonald / Neil Macehiter / Bridget McGing / Helen McGovern / Carole McIntosh / Pete MacIntyre / Gavin McKeown / Maureen Mckerrall / Jonathan Macklin / Elodie Macknay-Swanepoel / Claire McClean / Heather Macleod / Susan McClymont / Kevin McMahon / Debbie McNally / Bryan McNamara / Michelle McNish / Stephen McConnell / Calvin Mcphaul / Helen Macpherson / Gary L. Maddox / Mick Mahoney / Sharoz Makarechi / Lindsey Malcolm / Debra Malouf / Michelle Maltby / Hedy Manders / Rashida Mangera & Hady Bayoumi / Jane Manning / Fabien Marry / Rhodri Marsden / Jane Marshall / Louise Marston / Andrew Martin / Toby Martin / Abigail O. Martone / Alexander Mason / Patrick Mason / Richard Mason / Emma Mathews / Walter Mayes / Sarah Mayfield / Natasha Mayo and David Mayo / Juan Miguel Mazoy / Brian Meacham / Chris Mead / James Medd / Ross Medley / Judith Mellor / Lynne Mendoza / Ann Menke / Doug Merrett / Sarah Merrett / Roger Miles / Tracy Miller and Paul Arnest / Fran Miller-Pezo / Adam Mills / Ruth Mitchell / John Mitchinson / Ronald Mitchinson / James Moakes / Stuart Moffatt / Cameron Moll / Simon Monk / Jim Mooney / Ellen Moore & Paul Arnott / Rose Morley / Helen Morris / Milo F. S. Morris / Nancy Morris / Lucy Moss / Leigh Mower / Niall Muckian / Christopher Mudiappahpillai / Ben Mueller / Nigel Muir / Wesley Mullen / Jane Murison / Brendan Murphy / David Murphy / Ewen Murray / Susie Murray / Nalini Arti Narayan / Stu Nathan / Andrew Neve / Linda Newbown / Andy Nichol / Vic Nicholas / Michelle Nicholson / Chris Niehoff / Stewart Nolan / Greg Norman / B.J. Novak / Peter Nowell / Ethna Nugent / Jim-Robin Nymoen / Neil Oatley / Angela O'Connor / Georgia Odd / Sue Odd / Aude Odeh / Anita Ogilvie / Jenny O'Gorman / Mary O'Malley / Nelleita Omar / Anna O'Neill / Kate Onyett / Susan O'Reilly /

Max Orgeldinger / Monica Ormonde / David Overend / Valerie Louise Pace / Asa Packer / Sarah Paley / Shahan Panth / Carol Parker / Luke Parker / Rachel Parker / Richard Parker / Sally Parker Mitchell / James Parsons / Laura Pashby James / S. Pasian / Diana Passy / Martha Patrick / Jonathan Pavey / Noah Payne-Frank / Rachel Peacock / Eric Pearce / Nicholas Pearce / Ben Pearson / Bella Pender / Ben Pert / Kate Pert / Vivien Pert / Mason Petrie / Rose Phillips / Kerry Philpott / Anna Pick / Debra Pickering / Gregory F. Pickersgill / Cynda Pierce / Sarah Pinborough / Marco Piva-Dittrich & Solveig Dittrich-Piva / Justin Pollard / Claire Poore / Elspeth Potts / Jenny Pourian / Jean Power / Richard Preston / Neil Pretty / Robert Print / David Pritchett / Emma Probst / Ruth Puttick / Linda Quattrin / Gavin Quinney / Harold Raitt / Rakhi Rajani / Lane Rasberry / Michele Howarth Rashman / Jonathan Ratcliff / Christopher J.R. Ratcliff OBE / Rauf Rawson / Billy, Harry & Wayne Rayner / William Read / Alan Redman / Amy Rees / Guy Reeves / Margaret Reeves / Phillip Reeves / David Reidy / Hugh Richards / Olly Richards / Ali Richardson / Kath Richardson / Terri Richardson / Simon Ricketts / Clare Riding / Phillippa Ritchie / Jeff Robbins / Emma Roberts / Jonny Roberts / Wyn Roberts / Iain Robertson / Andrew Robinson / Clive Robinson / Jayne Robinson / Rachael Robinson / Samantha Rogers / Alison Rogerson / Dr. Redentor Rojales / Steve Ronksley / Alison Rooney / Robyn Roscoe / Rebecca Rose / Andrew Rosenberg / Katharine Roseveare & Martin Raymond / Catherine Rossi / Laurie Roth / Katharine Rowan / Kirsty Rowan / Allan P Russell / Benjamin Russell / Grant Russell / Ruth & Nigel / Keith Ryan / Mary Saisselin / Adam Sales / Kay Salmon / Christoph Sander / Val Santiago and Marie Chan / Shrikant R Sawant / Neil Sayer / Kim Schilling / Cecilia Schoenbaum / John Schoenbaum / Carl Schwab / Gary Scott / Jillian Scott / Lina Scroggins / James Seabright / Matthew Searle / Will Sefton / Fabio Sensi / Beth Serota / Denise Shanks / Neil Sharma / Dinesh Shenoy / Gary Shewan / Rachael Simmons / Julian Simpson / Bette Sinclair / Mike Singleton / Jan Skakle / Roger Smethurst & Paula Forbes / Christopher Smith / Scott Smith / Simon J Smith / Barbara Snow / Matthew Soar / Todd Solomon / Stuart Southall / James Spackman / Kerri J Spangaro / Joe Sparano / Matthew Spicer / Kylee St George / Kelly Stanford / Pam Stanier / David Stelling / Jim Sterne / Kelly Stevens / LeAnne Stevens / David Stevenson / Lindsay Stewart / Alan Stoll / Julia Stone / Nina Stossinger / Katie Stowell / Michael Strawson / Simon Street / Jessica Stroup / Bob Stuart / Yonga Sun / Ross Sussman / Laura Sykes / Soulla Tantouri Eriksen / Beverley Tarquini / Alison Tarry / Ezra Tassone / Amanda Taylor / Maisie Taylor / Mike Teasdale / Ryan Teel / Melissa Terras / Andrea Thoene / Glenn Thomas / Jayne Thomas / Lynda Thomas / Wayne Thomas / Andrea Thompson / Simon Thompson / Ian Thompson-Corr / Joe Thorley / Amanda Thurman / Denise Tierney / Alice Tjiu / James Tobin / Andy Tootell / John Townley / Catrin Treadwell / Sarah Tregear / Alex Trew / Ma. Angela Tripon / Tjarda Tromp / Shelley Tule / Neil Turton / John and Lindsay Usher / Karen Usher / Ellen Van Gelder / Filip Vandueren / Nikki Vane / Phil Vaughan / Heleen Veerman / David Verey / Linda Verstraten & Pyter Wagenaar / Sarrah Vesselov / Prashanthy Vigneswaran / Thomas Vincent-Townend / Janne von Busse / Jo W / Greg Waddell / Jason Wainwright / Claire Walker / Joel Walker / Sam Walker / Stephen Walker / Steve Walker / Matt Wallace / David Wallman-Durrant / Chelsea Walsh / Rob & Liz Walsh / Josie Ward / Lynne Waters / Richard M. Watt / Catherine Watts / Simon Watts / Tanya Weaver / Rosie Weeks / Andreas Weinberger / Daniel Weir / Annie West / Paul Whelan / Levin Wheller / Rosemary White / Rosemary White / Simon White / Stephen White / Jacob Whitlow / Brenton Whittle / Hayley Wickens / James Wickham / Ali Wiff / Patrick Wilcox / Cary Wilkins / David Wilkinson / Rosie Willescroft / David Williams / Julian Williams / Reshma Williams / Jim Willis / Alexa Wilson / Iain Wilson / Kellie Wilson / Kirsten Wilson / Julie Woodgate / George Woodhouse / Stacey Woods / Ryan Woodward / Ashley Woolf / Anne Wright / Steve Wright / Debbie Wythe / Nicholas Yates / Riana Yeates / Stephen Alan Yorke / Carol Young / Rebecca Young / Simon Young / Jane Zara / Michelle Zitzmann

PERMISSION CREDITS

p. 1 Photo copyright © Julien's Auctions; p. 1 Reprinted by permission of Lou Robin for the John R. Cash Irrevocable Trust; pp. 2–3 Reproduced by kind permission of Cambridge University Library; pp. 4–7 Georges Perec, "An Attempt at an Inventory of the Liquid and the Solid Foodstuffs Ingurgitated by Me in the Course of the Year Nineteen Hundred and Seventy-Four" from *Species of Spaces and Other Pieces*. Copyright © 1974 by Éditions Galilée. Translation copyright © 1997, 1999 by John Sturrock. Reprinted by permission of Penguin Group (UK) Ltd; pp. 8–9 Photograph copyright © Alexander Autographs; p. 10 © Succession Picasso/DACS, London 2014; p. 11 A list written by Pablo Picasso of European artists to be included in the 1913 Armory Show, 1912. Walt Kuhn, Kuhn family papers, and Armory Show records, Archives of American Art, Smithsonian Institution; pp. 15–16 Image copyright © The Royal Society; pp. 17–18 Translation courtesy of Prods Oktor Skjaervo, Harvard University; p. 19 Courtesy of The International Dunhuang Project, The British Library; p. 20 Octavio Corp; p. 28 Edmund Wilson, "The Lexicon of Prohibition" from *American Earthquake: A Documentary of the Twenties and Thirties*. Copyright © 1958 by Edmund Wilson. Used by permission of Doubleday, a division of Random House, LLC; p. 29 © Bettmann/Corbis; p. 31 Wellcome Library, London; p. 33 Image courtesy of the George Washington Papers, Series 4, General Correspondence, Library of Congress, Washington, D. C.; p. 34 ©Bettmann/Corbis; p. 35 Copyright © Autry Qualified Interest Trust; p. 36 Chrissie Hynde, "Advice to Chick Rockers or 'How I Did It'" from *Mouth2Mouth* (1995). Copyright © 1995. Reprinted with permission; p. 37 Fin Costello/Redferns/Getty Images; pp. 38–39 Courtesy of The Karpeles Library; p. 40 Reprinted by permission; pp. 43–45 © The Trustees of the British Museum; pp. 46–47 Arts Center Melbourne, Performing Arts Collection; pp. 46–47 Reproduced by permission of Nick Cave; p. 48 The Walt Disney Company; p. 49 Hulton Archive/Stringer/Archive Photos/Getty Images; p. 52 George Rose/ Hulton Archive/Getty Images; p. 53 Susan Sontag, "Rules of Parenting" (September 1959) from *Reborn: Journals & Notebooks 1947–1963*. Copyright © 2008 by Susan Sontag. Reprinted by permission of Farrar, Straus & Giroux, LLC Hamish Hamilton/Penguin Group (UK) Ltd; p. 54 Harry Ransom Center, The University of Texas at Austin; p. 54 Courtesy of Daniel Selznick; p. 60 By permission of the Estate of Geoffrey Handley-Taylor; p. 61 Culture Club/Hulton Archive/Getty Images; p. 62 © Bettmann/Corbis; p. 64 Reprinted by permission of Ed Gombert; p. 65 Courtesy of Morgan Wright; p. 65 © Harry Gibson; p. 68 Harry Ransom Center, The University of Texas at Austin; p. 68 Used by permission of the Julia Child Foundation; pp.70–71 Clara Barton, "Register of Missing Men of the Army, No. 2 Miss Clara Barton" (1865). Clara Barton National Historic Site, CLBA 4. National Park Service, Museum Management Program, Carol M. Highsmith, photographer; p. 73 Boston Public Library Department of Rare Books and Manuscripts; p. 74 Louis Monier/Gamma-Rapho/ Getty Images; p. 75 Roland Barthes, "J'aime, je n'aime pas" from *A Roland Barthes Reader*. Copyright © 1977. Reprinted by permission of Hill & Wang, a division of Farrar, Straus & Giroux LLC and Random House (UK) Ltd; pp.76–80 © The Trustees of the British Museum; p. 81 Photo copyright © The King Center, Flip Schulke, Benedict Fernandez; p. 81 © The Estate of Martin Luther King, Jr.; p. 83 © Bettmann/Corbis; pp.84–85 Roald Dahl, "The BFG's Vocabulary List" Copyright © RDNL. Reprinted with the permission of David Higham Associates, Ltd., on behalf of The Roald Dahl Museum and Story Center; The Roald Dahl Museum and Story Center; pp.86–87 Royal Collection Trust / © Her Majesty Queen Elizabeth II 2014; pp. 89, 93, 95, 97, 99, 101 Courtesy of Folger Shakespeare Library; p. 105 Reproduced by kind permission of Cambridge University Library; p. 106–107 "New Year's Rulin's" by Woody Guthrie. January 1, 1943. New York City, New York. © Woody Guthrie Publications, Inc.; pp. 106–07 Woody Guthrie, "New Year's Rulin's" (1941) from Woody Guthrie Foundation; p. 108 Marilyn Monroe, "Marilyn Monroe's To-Do List" (1955) from *Fragments: Poems, Intimate Notes, Letters*, edited by Stanley Buchthal and Bernard Comment. Copyright © 2010 by LSAS International, Inc. Reprinted by permission of Farrar, Straus & Giroux, LLC; p. 109 Michael Ochs Archives/Stringer/Getty Images; p. 110 Noel Coward, "Rules of Palship between Esmé Wynne and Noël Coward" (August 11, 1915) from *The Letters of Noël Coward*, edited by Barry Day. Copyright © 2007 by N. C. Aventales AG. Used by permission of Alfred A. Knopf, an imprint of the Knopf Doubleday Publishing Group, a division of Random House, LLC. All rights reserved; p. 111 © Pictorial Press Ltd/Alamy; p. 115–16 Richard S. Westfall Short-Writing and the State of Newton's Conscience, 1662 (1), 1963; Used by permission of the Royal Society; p. 117 Photo copyright © The Fitzwilliam Museum, Cambridge UK; p. 118 Sei Sho-nagon, excerpts from *The Pillow Book*, translated by Meredith McKinney. Copyright © 2006 by Meredith McKinney. Reprinted by permission of Penguin Group (UK) Ltd; pp. 121, 123 Courtesy of the Library of Congress; p. 126 Norman Mailer, "Ten Favorite American Novels" from a letter to Helen Morris (January 16, 1988) in "Norman Mailer: Letters to Jack Abbott" from *The New York Review of Books* (March 12, 2009). Copyright © 1988 by Norman Mailer. Reprinted by permission of The Wylie Agency, LLC; p. 127 Lange Jacques/Paris Match Archive/ Getty Images; p. 128 Courtesy of Pook & Pook, Inc.; p. 129 Courtesy of Dartmouth College Library; p.129 Courtesy of The Robert L. May Co.; pp. 130–31 Royal Collection Trust / © Her Majesty Queen Elizabeth II 2014; p. 132 Library of Congress, Prints & Photographs Division, Exit Art's "Reactions" Exhibition Collection, LC-DIG-ppmsca-01671; pp. 134–35 Farrell Grehan/National Geographic/Getty Images; p. 136 Jack Kerouac, list of "Belief & Technique for Modern Prose" excerpt from a letter to Donald Allen (1958) from *Heaven and Other Poems*. Copyright © 1959, 1960, 1977 by the Estate of Jack Kerouac. Reprinted by permission of Sterling Lord Literistic LLC; p.137 © Allen Ginsberg/Corbis; p. 138 © Bettmann/Corbis; p. 139 Sylvia Plath, two lists from December 1952 ["I will not overwhelm him . . ." and "Back to School Commandments"] from *The Unabridged Journals of Sylvia Plath: 1950–1962*, edited by Karen V. Kukil. Copyright © 2000 The Estate of Sylvia Plath. Used by permission of Anchor Books, a division of Random House, LLC and Faber and Faber, Ltd; p. 141 © Victoria and Albert Museum, London; p. 142 Courtesy of the Trustees of the Boston Public Library/Rare Books; pp. 143–45 Permisson granted by the Trans-Allegheny Lunatic Asylum; pp. 150–151 © Thelonious Monk; p. 153 Courtesy of Biblioteca Nazionale Centrale di Firenze; p. 154 Sister Corita Kent, "Immaculate Heart College Art Department Rules" from Jan Steward and Corita Kent, *Learning by Heart: Teachings to Free the Creative Spirit*. Copyright © 2008 by Jan Steward and Corita Kent. Reprinted with the permission of Skyhorse Publishing, Inc.; p. 155 Reproduction permission of the Corita Art Center, Immaculate Heart Community, Los Angeles; pp. 156–59 Harry S. Truman Presidential Library and Museum; p. 160 © Bettmann/ Corbis; p. 161 David Ogilvy, "How to Write" from *The Unpublished David Ogilvy* Copyright © 1986, 2012 by The Ogilvy Group. Used by permission of Crown Publishers, a division of Random House LLC; pp. 162–63 David Markson, list of 54 rejections of Wittgenstein's Mistress. Reprinted by permission of the David Markson Estate; pp. 164, 166–72 © H.P. Lovecraft; p. 165 © Pictorial Press Ltd/Alamy; pp. 173, 175 William Safire, "Fumblerules of Grammar" from *Fumblerules: A Lighthearted Guide to Grammar and Good Usage*. Copyright © 1979, 1990 by William Safire. Reprinted with the permission of Janklow & Nesbitt Associates; p. 174 Diana Walker/ The LIFE Images Collection/Time & Life Pictures/Getty Images; p. 176 Christopher Hitchens, excerpt from "The New Commandments" from *Vanity Fair* (April 2010). Copyright © 2010. Reprinted with permission of the Estate of Christopher Hitchens; p. 177 John Donegan/ Getty Images Entertainment/Getty Images; p. 179 Courtesy of The British Library; p.180, 182–83 Edna Woolman Chase and Ilka Chase, excerpt from *Always in Vogue*. Copyright 1954 by Edna Woolman Chase and Ilka Chase. Used by permission of Doubleday, a division of Random House LLC; p. 181 George Karger/The LIFE Images Collection/Time & Life Pictures/Getty Images; pp. 184–85 James Agee, "Contempt or hatred for" list (December 26, 1937) from *Unclassified: A Walker Evans Anthology* (Scalo, 2000). Reprinted with the permission of the James Agee Trust c/o The Wylie Agency, LLC; p. 186 The Metropolitan Museum of Art, New York. Walker Evans Archive, 1994. 1994.250.4.21; p. 187 © Charles Green Shaw; pp. 188, 190 Lucas Amory, "Ten Composers I Like Best" from Anthony Tommasini, "Ten Composers: A Young Reader Responds" from *The New York Times* (February 15, 2011). Reprinted with the permission of the author; p. 192 Bob Landry/The LIFE Picture Collection/Time & Life Pictures/Getty Images; p. 193 "What's So Funny?" from *Thurber Country* by James Thurber, Copyright © 1953 by Rosemary A. Thurber. Reprinted by arrangement with Rosemary A. Thurber and The Barbara Hogenson Agency, Inc. All rights reserved. To read more about James Thurber, go to www.ThurberHouse.org and to hear the HarperCollins James Thurber Audio Collection Performed by Keith Olbermann visit: http://www.harpercollins.com/books/ James-Thurber-Audio-Collection-Unabridged/; p. 194 Reprinted by permission; p. 195 © Steve Schapiro/Corbis; p. 197 Steven L. Raymer/National Geographic/Getty Images; p. 201 © Hulton-Deutsch Collection/Corbis; pp. 204–05 A list of Aline Bernstein's "good qualities," written by Eero Saarinen around the time of their marriage, 1954. Aline and Eero Saarinen papers, Archives of American Art, Smithsonian Institution; p. 206 F. Scott Fitzgerald, excerpt from "To cocktail" from a letter to Blanche W. Knopf (January 1928), from *A Life in Letters*, edited by Matthew J. Bruccoli. Copyright © 1994 by the Trustees Under Agreement Dated July 3, 1975, Created by Frances Scott Fitzgerald Smith. Reprinted with the permission of Scribner Publishing Group; p. 207 Harry Ransom Center, The University of Texas at Austin; p. 208 Jean-Regis Rouston/Roger Viollet/Getty Images; p. 209 Henry Miller, list of "Commandments" from Henry Miller on Writing. Copyright 1944, © 1957, 1964 by Henry Miller. Copyright 1939, 1941, © 1957 by New Directions Publishing Corp. Reprinted by permission of New Directions Publishing Corp.; pp. 216, 218 Motion Picture Association of America; p. 217 Vintage Images/Archive Photos/Getty Images; pp. 220–21 Reproduced with the permission of the Syndics of Cambridge University

Library and William Huxley Darwin; pp. 222–23 Kurt Vonnegut, "Vonnegut's Commitments" (January 26, 1947) from *Kurt Vonnegut: Letters*, edited by Dan Wakefield. Copyright © 2012 by The Kurt Vonnegut, Jr., Trust. Used by permission of Delacorte Press, an imprint of The Random House Publishing Group, a division of Random House, LLC. Any third party use of this material, outside of this publication, is prohibited. Interested parties must apply directly to Random House, Inc. for permission; p. 226 REX/Alan Messer; p. 227 © Estate of Don Van Vliet; pp. 228–35 The Thomas Edison Papers at Rutgers University; p. 238 Bob Landry/The LIFE Picture Collection/Time & Life Pictures/Getty Images; pp. 239 Preston Sturges, list of "11 Rules for Box-Office Appeal" (1941). Reprinted by permission of the Preston Sturges Estate c/o Tom Sturges; p. 242 Reprinted with the permission of the Hitchcock Estate and the cooperation of the Margaret Herrick Library of the Academy of Motion Picture Arts and Sciences; p. 243 © AF archive/Alamy; p. 244 Dinodia Photos/Hulton Archive/Getty Images; pp.245–46 Tina Fey, excerpt from *Bossypants*. Copyright © 2011 by Tina Fey. Reprinted by permission of Little, Brown and Company; p. 249 Bridgeman Art Library International; p. 252 Raymond Chandler, list of similes. Reprinted by kind permission of the Estate of Raymond Chandler; p. 253 © Bettmann/Corbis; pp.252, 254 F. Scott Fitzgerald, "Turkey Remains and How to Inter Them with Numerous Scarce Recipes" from *The Crack-Up*, edited by Edmund Wilson. Copyright 1945 by New Directions Publishing Corp. Reprinted by permission of New Directions Publishing Corp.; p. 255 Copyright © 2014 Bonhams & Butterfields Auctioneers Corp. All Rights Reserved; p. 255 Reproduced by permission of the Estate of John Lennon; p. 256 Ernest Hemingway, list of his favorite books from "Remembering Shooting-Flying: A Key West Letter"from *Esquire Magazine* (February 1935). Reprinted in *By-Line: Ernest Hemingway: Selected Articles and Dispatches of Four Decades*, edited by William White. Copyright © 1967 by Mary Hemingway. Reprinted with the permission of Scribner's, a division of Simon & Schuster, Inc.; p. 257 Kurt Hutton/Stringer/Picture Post/Getty Images; pp.258–59 Photo copyright © Sotheby's; p. 260 NewspaperArchive.com; p. 263 Alinari Archives/Alinari/Getty Images; p. 264 © Bettmann/Corbis; p. 267 Rex/CSU Archives/Everett Collection; p. 268 Jorge Luis Borges; p. 269 © Horacio Villalobos/Corbis; p. 272 Bertrand Russell, "A Liberal Decalogue" from *The Autobiography of Bertrand Russell*. Originally from *The New York Times Magazine* (December 5, 1951). Reprinted with the permission of The Bertrand Russell Peace Foundation and Taylor & Francis; p. 273 © Bettmann/Corbis; p. 274 Used by permission of the David Foster Wallace Literary Trust; p. 275 Harry Ransom Center, The University of Texas at Austin; pp.277–79 The Thomas Edison Papers at Rutgers University; p. 280 F. Scott Fitzgerald, letter to his daughter Scottie (August 8, 1933) from *A Life in Letters*, edited by Matthew J. Bruccoli. Copyright © 1994 by the Trustees Under Agreement Dated July 3, 1975, Created by Frances Scott Fitzgerald Smith. Reprinted with the permission of Scribner Publishing Group; p. 281 Hulton Archive/Stringer/Archive Photos/Getty Images; p.282 © Marilyn Monroe; p. 283 Michael Ochs Archives/Stringer/Getty Images; pp. 284, 286 Anton Chekhov, letter to his brother Nikolai (March 1886) from *Anton Chekhov's Life and Thought: Selected Letters and Commentaries*, translated by Michael Henry Heim. Copyright © 1997 by Michael Henry Heim. Reprinted with the permission of Northwestern University Press; p. 285 Mondadori/Getty Images; p. 289 Courtesy of Swann Auction Galleries; p. 290 Alfred Eisenstaedt/The LIFE Picture Collection/Time Life Pictures/Getty Images; p. 291 © ARS, NY and DACS, London 2014; p. 292 Italo Calvino, excerpt from *If On a Winter's Night a Traveler*. Copyright © 1981 by Harcourt Brace. Reprinted by permission of The Wylie Agency, LLC and the Houghton Mifflin Harcourt Publishing Company. All rights reserved; p. 293 © Nick Rains/Corbis; pp. 294, 296 © ARS, NY and DACS, London 2014; pp. 295, 297 The Museum of Modern Art, New York, NY, USA. Digital Image © The Museum of Modern Art/Licensed by SCALA/Art Resource; p.298 Marianne Moore, "Marianne Moore's Car Names" from *Marianne Moore and David Wallace, Letters from and to the Ford Motor Company* (New York: Pierpont Morgan Library, 1958). Reprinted by permission of the Literary Estate of Marianne C. Moore, David . Moore, Esq., Administrator. All rights reserved; p. 299 © Everett Collection Historical/Alamy; p. 300 Billy Wilder, list of tips for screenwriters from Cameron Crowe, Conversations with Wilder. Copyright © 1999 by Cameron Crowe. Used by permission of The Robbins Office and Alfred A. Knopf, an imprint of Knopf Doubleday Publishing Group, a division of Random House LLC. All rights reserved; p. 301 © Raul Vega/Corbis; p. 302 Courtesy of Hard Rock International; p. 302 Reproduced with permission of the Estate of Sid Vicious; p. 303 Kurt Cobain, list of items needed for "Smells Like Teen Spirit" music video (1991) from Journals. Copyright © 2002 by The End of Music, LLC. Used by permission of Riverhead Books, an imprint of Penguin Group (USA) LLC and Penguin Group (UK) Ltd; p. 304 Edmund Wilson, "Edmund Wilson Regrets. . ." Reprinted with the permission of the Estate of Edmund Wilson; p. 305 Satchel Paige™ licensed by Satchel Paige Enterprises c/o Luminary Group LLC, www.SatchelPaige.com; pp. 306–307 Records of the Atomic Energy Commission, National Archives.

TYPEFACES AND EDITORIAL NOTE

The introductions to the lists are set in DIN, a sans serif font defined in 1931 by the Deutsches Institut für Normung (the German Institute for Standardization). It is the typeface used on German road signs and on all kinds of technical documents. For a long time it was regarded as the classic example of a corporate typeface (the German Green party rejected its use on a proposed new logo in 2006), but it was clearly influenced by the geometric typeface experiments of the Bauhaus school, and research by the Dutch designer, Albert-Jan Pool, suggests that it wasn't just the work of a committee. He identifies the designer as Siemens engineer Ludwig Goller (1884–1964), who was chairman of the DIN committee for design. Pool himself went on to design a full family of DIN fonts in the mid-1990s. Its clarity and legibility mean it remains one of the most popular sans serif fonts. Type historian Evert Bloemsma attributes its success to the following formula: 80% hi-tech, 10% imperfection (which equates with charm), and 10% static.

The transcripts of the letters are set in Ehrhardt, a typeface developed in 1937 by Stanley Morison while at the Monotype Corporation. Morison was responsible for making modern versions of many antique faces, including Bembo and Baskerville, and designed the now ubiquitous Times New Roman. The creator of the original Ehrhardt typeface is unknown but it is named after the late- seventeenth-century Ehrhardt foundry in Leipzig and is similar to some Dutch typefaces of that period produced by the Amsterdam printer Anton Janson. The typographical historian Robin Nicholas believes Ehrhardt was Morison's take on Janson, "made a little heavier and narrower to give improved legibility and economy."

Unless followed by my initials or otherwise noted in the introduction to a list, comments in brackets within the lists are copied from the source documents.

INDEX